CUT THE STEMS AND PLUNGE WITHOUT DELAY INTO FRESH WATER. (THE STEMS RESEAL VERY QUICKLY)

THE FLOWERS

DR LISA COOPER

**FOR MY FATHER
GARY COOPER
THE BUTCHER.**

(1950–1988)

THE FLOWERS

DR LISA COOPER
PHOTOGRAPHED BY HAROLD DAVID

MURDOCH BOOKS

FOREWORD

THE RED ROSE FROM ST THÉRÈSE — PRESSED AND TRAVELLED HOME IN BOB'S CHANEL TIE BOX.

To begin, you have to imagine an old port town two hours or so northwest of Paris. Located in Normandy on the banks of the estuary of the River Seine is Honfleur, a popular tourist destination from which travellers can explore the region: the D-Day beaches are nearby, and Monet's famous garden at Giverny is just an hour away by car. And it's not surprising that those travelling to nearby Lisieux to pay homage at the Basilica of Saint Thérèse would also choose to stay in the historic seaside town rather than join the million other tourists at France's second most popular pilgrimage site after Lourdes.

On the outskirts of Honfleur is its famous hotel, La Ferme Saint Siméon. A cluster of restored seventeenth-century timbered and shingled farmhouse buildings, many adorned with fragrant window boxes, the hotel was once the haunt of Impressionist painters. The likes of Gustave Courbet, Claude Monet and the locally-born Eugène Boudin were drawn not just to the surrounding gardens, but to the coast, enchanted by the light and the mackerel skies … the many moods whipped up by the turbulent waters of the Channel.

A few years ago, a young artist and her friend on a research trip to France decided to book into La Ferme Saint Siméon. While its illustrious artistic history was an obvious attraction, the real reason was a growing fascination with the life and work of Saint Thérèse of Lisieux.[†]

‡

Now imagine this: early morning and coffee has been ordered. A gentle knock and a tray is delivered: two cups and saucers, a pot of steaming coffee and a jug of warm milk. La Ferme Saint Siméon, two weary but excited travellers, the start of day one …

The young artist and her friend have booked into the hotel for four nights. They are on a pilgrimage, bound for Lisieux and, overlooking it, the Basilica of Saint Thérèse, the focus of their journey. On their way to Lisieux later that morning, roses are bought – an offering for St Thérèse. The nuns, they have heard, say that when Thérèse hears your prayers a rose will be received in return.

In the chapel for silent prayer, the young artist asks St Thérèse for inner peace … an enduring calmness to end difficult and unsettling years. Laying down her gift of roses, it's time, she thinks, to garner strength and put the past to rest … or, rather, to find ways of using it to energise the artworks she imagines she will be making. The enigmatic saintly figure has been a glowing presence since childhood: now Thérèse of Lisieux emerges as catalyst, surrounded by roses and radiating light, perhaps she will suggest a way forward … a path to follow.

Day two at La Ferme Saint Siméon begins as the first – the knock at the door and morning coffee. The tray is set as before, but today a single red rose lies beside the cups.

A sign? A rose in return? The friends decide it is a gift to be pressed between paper sheets, flattened and preserved ... a bloom to be kept and treasured.

There's more exploring to be done in St Thérèse's domain before leaving France: another two days to discover more about this woman and the miracles she performed. Two more breakfasts to be delivered, each knock and tray eagerly anticipated.

But there would be no more roses. That single, mysterious rose the day after the offering to St Thérèse was it ... it had to be a sign. As the nuns had said, St Thérèse had heard her prayer.

For the young artist, the gesture was an affirmation, a beginning. The opening verses of 'My Joy' – one of 54 poems included in an authorised edition of St Thérèse's writings (published by ICS Publications in 1995, translated by Donald Kinney) – provided solace and inspiration:

There are some souls on earth
Who search in vain for happiness,
But for me, it's just the opposite.
Joy is in my heart.
This joy is not ephemeral.
I possess it forever.
Like the springtime rose,
It smiles at me every day.
Truly I'm so happy.
I always have my way ...
How could I not be joyful
And not show my cheerfulness?
My joy is to love suffering.
I smile while shedding tears.
I accept with gratitude
The thorns mingled with the flowers.

As it turns out, that rose on the breakfast tray (hastily pressed but a preservation failure, hidden in a tie box and smuggled back home) grew to become an enduring obsession. For the artist it has come to symbolise the gift of giving. And a way forward has been found in the love of working small miracles with flowers.

‡

THE FLOWERS, a photographic project tracing the journey of plants and flowers from their growers to the Sydney Flower Market, to a studio and into the hands of an artist, represents the blooming of that young artist.

In many ways the book is a natural progression from postgraduate studies, a doctoral thesis and a voyage of self-discovery that culminated in a trip to France to trace the life of one of her heroes, St Thérèse of Lisieux. But the seeds for the floral compositions reproduced to accompany the stories and anecdotes that make up this book were sown much earlier in 'The Crucible Project' (2008) – an installation of six video works completed as the artistic manifestation of the ideas explored in the doctoral thesis, *METAXU: A Metaphysics of the Annihilation of Self in Video-Portraiture. (Imaging Mediations Between the Human and Divine)*, 2009. Presented in a wharf-side, refurbished industrial space, 'The Crucible Project' was my introduction to the work of Lisa Cooper, 'The Butcher's Daughter' ... soon to be Dr ...

The projections – video portraits with compelling titles: 'Self portrait with onions'; 'Silence has teeth'; 'Still waiting for Weil'; 'Self portrait waiting in marionette F1 crash on Judgment Day for Jesus to call with a safe place'; 'Actor failing to describe the space between God and Man'; and 'A lament' – blurred boundaries between the technology of production, notions of representation, and the self. The work encapsulated the artist's fascination with 'the space between' – metaxu.

Still the Doctor works between. The floral compositions merge an art practice that once focused on solid, permanent materials with an idiosyncratic creative process that now involves the ephemeral, the temporal and the fragile bursts of nature. THE FLOWERS – while a celebration of everything that is vibrant and dynamic – reminds us all that our passions are tempered by circumstance, and that our strengths are masks for vulnerabilities. Life – as Doctor Cooper has discovered in her love of roses – is about accepting the thorns amidst the flowers.

Ewen McDonald

† Marie Françoise-Thérèse Martin, born 1873, became a Carmelite nun in her teenage years. Sister Thérèse of the Child Jesus of the Holy Face devoted her life to saving souls. Two years after her death in 1897, her grave became a site for those seeking the miraculous – especially French soldiers during the First World War. By 1923 beatification had begun: her remains were removed to the Cemetery of the Carmelite Convent and in 1925 she was canonised. It was decided that a large basilica dedicated to her would be built in the place where she lived and worked. The foundation stone was laid in 1929 and a crypt decorated with mosaic representations of the spiritual life of Saint Thérèse was finished in 1944. It was here that locals and the Carmelites took refuge during the fighting of the summer of 1944. The basilica was finally completed in 1954. In 2000, adjoining the crypt, a chapel was built, devoted to silent prayer.

CONTENTS

✢

PAGE 10
INTRODUCTION

PAGE 18
THE STUDIO

PAGE 36
THE GROWERS

PAGE 110
THE FLOWERS

PAGE 248
THE FOLK

MY MATERNAL GRANDMOTHER'S SILK SCARF.

INTRODUCTION

THE LITTLE FLOWER.

As far back as I can remember, a wooden oval-framed picture of a beautiful woman holding a bunch of roses and a crucifix has hung above my bed – and it hangs there still. I think it was my paternal grandmother who must have put her there; my grandmother, an artist, was for my childhood self, 'Minister Concerned with the Decorative'.

Through the years the woman in the frame was just 'the woman in the frame'. I was quite indifferent to the image ... with the exception of a mention here and there from my father who, I recall, would suggest that 'we' might ask her to help us with this or that problem.

We knew very little of her except for what the picture revealed – that she was connected to God, a God with whom both of my grandmothers were au fait (and who according to my father was everywhere in nature).

When I was older I was 'confirmed' into the Catholic Church and, as is customary, I had to choose a name from the community of saints in order to honour and demonstrate a special devotion. I chose Thérèse ... but only because my elder sister had already taken Mary, the female heroine.

Early in my formal education, everything became the basis for relentless artistic research, fodder for symbolic and conceptual meaning ... and it was all co-opted into my artistic practice. It was during my undergraduate years that I learnt about Thérèse – the saint whom I had chosen to honour and serve with demonstrable devotion. She was Saint Thérèse of Lisieux and, unbeknown to me, it was her image in the oval frame; she had been watching over me all my life.

Saint Thérèse became an obsession, and I have spent a great deal of time researching her life – recently culminating in a visit to her Basilica in Lisieux, a tour of her childhood home, and travel to the places where she had lived and worked.

For the purpose of this book, though, it is enough for the reader to know that she is the Patron Saint both of Florists and of Lost Parents. Her attribute is the rose and she is known to those who love her as 'The Little Flower'. I have been 'guided' by her all my life and have her – and my paternal grandmother – to thank that I have found my calling.

I'll not have anyone tell me otherwise.

‡

As very small children my sister and I were each bought a dress intended for special occasions such as weddings, christenings and funerals. My dress was very striking, a deep royal blue velvet, edged with satin ribbon and a few bows; my sister's dress was cream coloured, a setting for countless pink roses so thick that the background fabric almost disappeared under the crush of them. The roses were so massed and rambling, they seemed narrative to me – heavy in symbolism, this dress, to my mind, was far superior in both beauty and interest to the blank, textural depth of my velvet one. I found my own way to rise above this disappointment: because the dress was my sister's, I was better able to behold it. At least that's what I kept telling myself.

‡

I began to work professionally with flowers when I incorporated them into my artwork. The flowers formed both the pictorial and conceptual element in numerous pieces. As my practice developed, I came to appreciate flowers as powerful signifiers – their potency meant that they became as crucial in my artwork as paint, gold, plaster, video technology, installation and projection.

During my years of study I worked at a distinguished flower shop under a renowned master, where I picked up the trade of floristry. I have a deep affection and respect for the trades and their system of training, whereby practical and theoretical knowledge is passed from master to apprentice, who becomes journeyman before becoming the master themselves. (I see these as my journeyman years.) It is worth mentioning that in the eyes of the 'establishment' I am 'untrained' (and gratefully so: I have personal ambitions for revolutionising the training 'standards' in professional floristry – the system as it stands is impenetrable).

‡

For as long as I can remember I have been possessed of a philosophical disposition, an inclination to extract meaning from the physical and experiential world. In early childhood my father – a butcher – was diagnosed with an aggressive cancer, which had the effect of greatly exaggerating his own deeply philosophical nature. This had a profound and permanent effect on me.

The trade of butchery was to my father's reckoning aligned with that of the artistic practice of sculpting … perhaps it was the influence of his mother, who was a painter. He spent his working life with a carcass over his shoulder, with the blood of another animal under his nails, and he often bled with them – a consequence of his tools of trade. As butchers do he became a master at 'breaking down' the beast and feeding the reductions to a locale that adored him; he did so with great respect and gratitude for the extinguished life before him, and a unique understanding of his role in the nature of things as well as his role in his community.

The experience of having been the butcher's daughter is deeply linked to my training, my studies, my art practice and my work with the flowers.

As a child I intuited that my father spent his days – therefore, his working life – at the intersection of man and nature. His daily toil was geared toward feeding people, while the arc of his trade permitted him to become tangibly skilled in his work; I believe that my witness of this bore my own comparable ambitions.

While my work is fundamentally concerned with building up the elemental through composition, the method of my father's work was to compositionally break down the whole beast to component (and edible) pieces. Despite these formal differences, many of the blessings of his work have been passed to me in mine and I am very grateful for that.

When I was aged around eleven, some five years into my father's illness, and a few years before he passed away (and the flowers would come, bunches and bunches and bunches of them), he went on a pilgrimage to Melbourne. During the course of my childhood, 'travel' was non-geographical; a father with a serious illness meant that for reasons economical our 'travel' was communicative and theoretical. If the world were made up of the vistas of human emotion, feeling and thought we saw the world over and again many times; however, in the mid 1980s my father travelled to Melbourne, in a gold Holden Gemini, to meet a man who had 'Conquered Cancer', and I was well intrigued.

The Conqueror could not in the end alter my father's destiny nor my own, but he represented for my father 'hope' and for me the notion of faraway lands and different modalities of thought ... this in a childhood that transpired within the perimeter of a few blocks. Five minutes to the shops, a ten-minute walk to school – broken up with 'day trips' to our grandparents and notable trips to Canberra and Aunty Fenella and Uncle Jim's farm in Tamworth.

Melbourne had become the place where the rest of the world began, a setting where the authoritative Conqueror went to be heard. For the time that my father was in Melbourne I imagined deeply about his experiences: what he would eat there, who he would talk to, how he would be changed.

Upon his return my sister and I were each gifted a ring. On a stainless steel retractable 'one size fits all' band was glued a white oval-shaped disc with a coloured print of a blue iris flower in my case and in my sister's ... I believe it was a rose. All the world was contained in that ring.

For some the blue iris symbolises Faith and Hope, but that ring, a tangible and material gift, came to embody all things intangible and unobservable. As well as Faith and Hope, it epitomised Love. This was the first time I realised the power of giving and how a simple object could encapsulate more than the world ... the universe.

‡

The distinction of my work is the gravity I afford the flowers. To my mind they are neither quaint nor twee, though of course they have great charm and whimsy; rather, the flowers are singularly effective symbols for the lived experience. That ring was more than its material components and the flowers are more than their quantifiable structure. Children are more than offspring, water is more than its chemical composition and a kiss is more than flesh meeting flesh.

The flowers are transient, metaphorical and evocative; they are at once of heaven and earth in that while they come from the soil, they are also entirely inexplicable and enigmatic. The primary concern of my art and flower practices is the attempt to make visible ineffable human experience – to make abstract human emotion visible. Perhaps the most compelling and elusive of these emotions is Love, and the flowers are for me the pinnacle material for such an ambition.

I have grandfathers on both sides of my family to thank for the influences that impact upon the work that I do today. My Australian paternal grandfather, Frank Cooper, grew roses on all sides of his three-bedroom A. V. Jennings home that was sanctuary to the undulations of my childhood. His favourite roses were 'Candy Stripe' and the 'Blue Moon'; as grandfathers are wont to do, he would cut a few stems and wrap them in aluminium foil as a gift for my school teacher.

But as is usually the case, flowers were peripheral to the gesture. In the landscape of neon, puffy paint and illness that was my 1980s, the growing, cutting and repetitive gifting of my grandfather's roses became like learning lines, numbers and figures, formulae and concepts through endless reiteration. I garnered a little of the modesty, dignity and kindness that a lifetime of experiences in a world that preceded my own had afforded him – the Depression, the War, the milk he delivered. The losses and the gains of his life seemed crowned by this gesture of roses wrapped in foil.

My maternal grandfather, Luigi Scalese, left the poverty of rural Italy for Australia in the 1960s. Like so many at this time, he left a great deal behind so that he could make a better life for his family. During the years of my childhood – before I had a passport – Italy was a three-bedroom suburban concrete home in Brookvale, Sydney, a place built by my grandparents' hands with love and determination.

Walking through the front door the air was thick with passata, olives and plenty. From the back step to the back fence, plant life flourished. With my grandfather as guide my sister and I would tour the garden; the eggplants, the tomatoes, the beans, the chickens, the eggs, and so it went on. If the season were right we'd be ushered into the garage where the smell of the best salami of your life would hit your nose and heart before you could raise your eyes up to the ceiling to take in the awesome sight. Hundreds of sausages hanging, drying, waiting for their moment to become the prize of a dining table that exceeded its potential by holding many times more souls for dinner than the six or eight it was built to accommodate.

There was a language barrier between my grandfather and me. Not so much so that we couldn't communicate the most important things to each other, but such that we were unable to have the type of conversation that truly meanders. However, before the passage of time put my grandparents in the ground and the house in Brookvale in the past, we would sit and he would hold my hand. As we listened to the women talk (though it sounded like yelling, my mother would assure me it was impassioned light conversation), he could distinguish only youthfulness and play in my hands ... I could sense his pride that they had not yet known toil or hunger or great fear. His years of hard work had remedied that.

I knew all I needed to know about him by the coarseness of his skin and the permanent dirt that seemed to stain his hands. In silence we would travel time and space together; he'd transport me by the texture of his hands back home to Italy, to all the gardens he had grown and the people he had nurtured. In return, I offered something of the future. Despite my naivety, I was potential: I became 'one of his', who would graduate with a PhD, who would decide to become an artist and businesswoman. And now THE FLOWERS. I would remember his garden and write about him ... his love of the earth, the seasons, the harvest and toil and be moved to write about THE GROWERS.

‡

Once my father said something to me that pierced me to the core. We were in the Blue Mountains, about an hour-and-a-half inland from Sydney. Standing at Echo Point, the place to look out across the awesome Jamison Valley, we were silenced by the breathtaking grandeur and the optically distorted panorama. Spread out before us were thousands upon thousands of enormous, ancient trees and billions of green leaves – leaves so dense that you felt you could jump off the rocky outcrop into that vast soft blanket of green. After some time, my father turned to me and said ... 'Every leaf on every tree you see out there represents the opportunities you will have in this life.'

Some words are like seeds.

THE FLOWERS ARE TRANSIENT, METAPHORICAL AND EVOCATIVE; THEY ARE AT ONCE OF HEAVEN AND EARTH IN THAT WHILE THEY COME FROM THE SOIL, THEY ARE ALSO ENTIRELY INEXPLICABLE AND ENIGMATIC. THE PRIMARY CONCERN OF MY ART AND FLOWER PRACTICES IS THE ATTEMPT TO MAKE VISIBLE INEFFABLE HUMAN EXPERIENCE — TO MAKE ABSTRACT HUMAN EMOTION VISIBLE. PERHAPS THE MOST COMPELLING AND ELUSIVE OF THESE EMOTIONS IS LOVE, AND THE FLOWERS ARE FOR ME THE PINNACLE MATERIAL FOR SUCH AN AMBITION.

MY FANCY 'GOLD' SECATEURS.

THE STUDIO

MY DAY BEGINS, BEFORE DAY.

A few hours before dawn the alarm begins its menacing, and no sooner have I thought, 'What the devil?' than the 'tradie' in me rises to make tea. I am really awake only minutes before I walk out the door and leave my domestic life behind for many hours, often too many hours. It is not yet morning and I am already at work.

The drive to the flower market is all contemplation … my mind is rested and there is little distraction offered by the world sleeping beyond my van. It is a unique time. I am able to reflect and strategise, particularly concerning the flowers I am determined to acquire. The market is for 'the quick and the dead': out there on that massive concrete block, under fluorescent lights, as the day breaks, everyone is there to get the 'bloody' good flowers. Competing at the market is a skill of which I am yet to be a master … nevertheless I do hold my own. The game itself is multi-levelled, but suffice to say, it is all about strategy, timing, tenacity and resolve. The flower market is not for the faint-hearted.

When the roller doors go up in unison at the strike of 5 am, a world that has been awake for many hours is revealed. As the growers show their blooms, there is a stampede to become involved in the melee, a rush to see and obtain the best of the day. It is still dark at this hour but by the time we – the buyers – all emerge with our produce, the sun has risen. There seems to be a kind of homeopathy at play: it's as if Dr Bach's concept of Flower Therapy has been confirmed by the rush of positive feelings induced by being in the midst of so many flowers and their fragrances. The actions of observing, handling and smelling the blooms culminate on each market day with a sense of proper elation.

‡

I return to the studio, which is a rectangular workspace measuring 8 by 3 metres that accommodates two custom-built workbenches made by Mr Johnson. Together, Mr Johnson and I planned the ergonomic superiority of the benches by determining

MY BOOTS.

MY BRIEFCASE, FOR THE PAPERWORK.

their height, the measurement taken from the concrete floor to my waist. We measured the paper that I wrap the flowers in and, in the design, incorporated gliding drawers to hold the sheets. We also conceived of four smaller drawers in each bench that would become the domain of, respectively, ribbon, business cards, gift cards, sticky notes, secateurs, flower ties, scissors, pens, notebooks and various other bits that I deem retainable.

Conventionally the Studio or Atelier refers to a space where an artist or maker is committed to the continuing education of his or her discipline. Following on from my formal education in art and my training in floristry I decided to set up a space where I could practise and flourish – initially to develop my artwork and then for my work with flowers. Increasingly my employ of mediums other than the floral has all but fallen away – flowers are now my core ... my medium and obsession.

Research and practice-based development is central to my studio work and progress. Rather than having conversations with clients about specific flowers that will be used in an installation or in a gift bunch and how they will be arranged, discussions tend to focus on the theme and the motivation for the event or occasion.

The context of the flowers then becomes the starting point for what I consider to be a commission. In the same way that an artist might bend their practice to fit a commission based on the proclivities or circumstances of a patron, I too bend the concerns of my practice to best accommodate the needs of my client.

The premise, restraints and parameters of a large-scale installation become a springboard for personal development, often demanding new methods of making and alternative approaches to working with flowers. Likewise – although on a smaller scale (but to no lesser degree) – the impetus for sending a gift of wrapped flowers also drives my practice to new realms ... not just in the way I construct the bunch but also in the combination of flowers I choose to put together.

‡

The studio holds an arsenal of black buckets, a cache of glass vases, an army of silver bowls, a store of industrial garbage bags, wires, tape, pins, bolt cutters, wire cutters, a saw, a hammer, short and long rulers, cable ties, sand bags, knives – both butter and bread types – foam oases for bases, a sharpening stone and a measuring tape, as well as many other items critical and trivial.

I have a beautifully aged and tolerant wood and red leather chair that has been in every studio I've occupied since my undergraduate days – it came to me via a fellow student who was 'upgrading' ... the fool! I have made a convenience of that chair every day; it has been my companion in work for many, many years. It is curious how some objects ingratiate themselves to the level of an essential element. When my work life is over, that chair will see me through my later years, of that I am certain.

As a child, my grandfather Frank Cooper and I would spend hours in his workshop in the garage making things: cars ... houses ... animals. We were like Sunday painters who reflect in their output the tangible world around them. When construction was complete, we would take the item inside and consult with my grandmother about how it should best be embellished with paint. We'd choose colours that would make whatever object/replica/model we had been working on even more realistic.

The workbench was built of wood panels that started their life as the dray body of the horse and cart with which my grandfather and his brother had started their milk delivery business – a business that was, in contrast to their Depression-era childhood, a feat of monumental ambition. Both would go on to run their own businesses and be self-made men; in both instances the humble nature of their occupation belied the security and advantage its resources would bring their families.

The bench had a vice whose lever I tormented with relentless tightening and loosening, severely testing its mechanism, as children are wont to do with the few things they can reach.

MY PRUNING GLOVES.

MY WORK BAG.

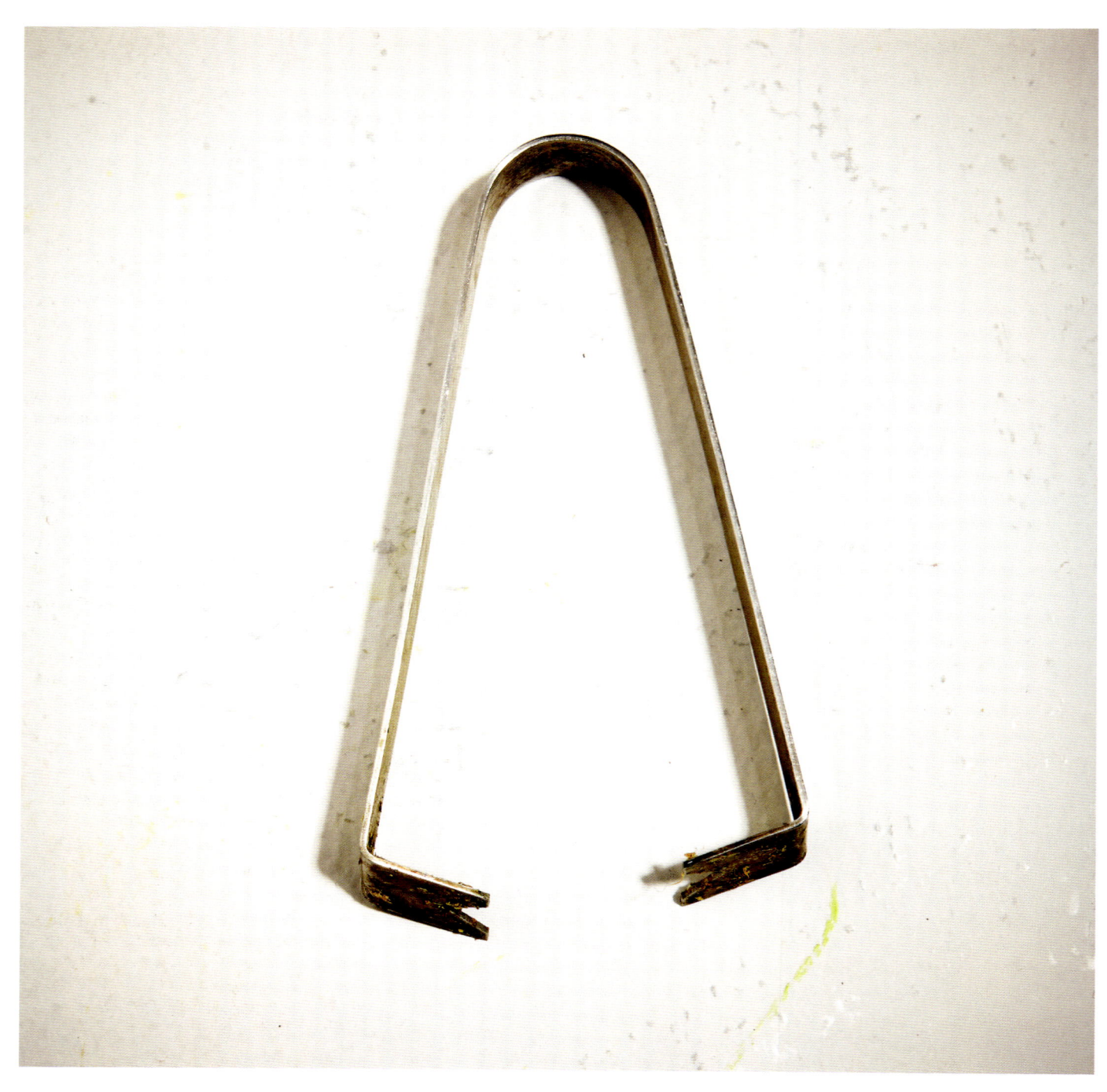

ROSE-STRIPPERS.

These words are being summoned in my studio with my grandfather's bench as support. Each workday I put my laptop on this structure, open it up and begin the tasks of my own small business. I deal with the immediate – the things that must be achieved this day. I also receive correspondence about the future – about jobs and opportunities that may take days, weeks or years to become reality. I plan, respond, print, begin and complete the many written aspects of my trade: it all starts on the workbench where, many years ago, I first learnt that one might have an idea and then with vision and effort make it into a thing to behold. I'm still turning and tormenting the vice ...

‡

On one of the two long white walls that make up the four walls of the studio, four calendar months are ruled up in lead pencil; they hover above seven clipboards that are labelled with the days of the week in gold letters. The ruled squares that map our days, by the month, are brimming with future projects and the clipboards are loaded with notes and information about pending work. Alongside the agenda is a large rectangular mirror with two odd circles cut from it (for what reason remains a constant source of bewilderment). Saved from the street, this mirror sees all. No flowers leave the studio before being reflected in the looking glass. In the reflected flower composition I am better able to see its form. The mirrored flowers seem more objectively viewed. Through their reflected image I am able to more fully comprehend the way that the viewer or recipient will perceive them and thus better able to manipulate and perfect their form.

Around 6.30 am each morning I turn the key in the lock and flick on the studio light ... a classic, caged mechanic's lamp, suspended in the centre of the space. These types of industrial lights have of course been plagiarised and popularised in contemporary interior design, but I chose it for its likeness to those cartoon images that use the lit bulb to symbolise the birth of an idea. Every day when the light comes on, I return momentarily to this motivating notion.

Then I open the laptop, attach it to the printer and the emails start to appear, often orders for gift bunches that have materialised overnight which now need to be added to the day's clipboard.

I delegate jobs: in my mind I rank them by urgency and divide the work to be done between my assistant and myself. Those tasks that I identify as Sophie's are both scribbled on a piece of paper and, as they crystallise, shouted out across the room; she acknowledges my list, her words singing out over the sound of running water, the filling or emptying of this or that, as she carries flowers from the van into the workspace. One of the many peculiarities of being 'the boss' is that although these tasks are assigned, until they are complete they remain my concern ... so for the rest of the day I am adding to the list and checking on the progress of the work at hand. As the jobs are resolved I delete them from the list in my mind. Meanwhile, the emails and telephone calls continue into the day and so the delegating, resolving and deleting intensifies.

There are handwritten cards to be attached to wrapped bunches and correspondence that needs responding to lest the correspondent decide that I am lacking in interest or professionalism. And there is usually something that needs to be collected or delivered outside business hours: so my flower courier 'G', which stands for both Gavin and Gangster – he was a rapper in a past life – will usually receive a pre-business text to which he responds with an affirmative 'X', meaning job done.

In the meantime, Sophie has been filling the benches with bundles of flowers that I have collected from the market. She doublechecks with me those bunches that need water most urgently, and which of the blooms need to be prepared promptly for inclusion in urgent arrangements. As these logistics are decided, we continue to unwrap the flowers and prepare them by removing as little or as much foliage as necessary, depending on a combination of my aesthetic proclivities as well as the condition and potential longevity of the leaves. Each stem is then cut and plunged directly into fresh, cold, tap water. I am obsessive about the placement of the blooms into buckets of water because, from my experience, I understand to what degree flowers will open and how much space they will require to unfurl without the risk of bruising or folding. I wonder sometimes if Sophie thinks I'm mad ... but then I chose her as my assistant because I perceived in her a little of my madness.

As we prepare the flowers an opera of sorts arises from our actions, the cacophony of stripping, cutting, ripping and sawing. The musicality of our ritual is supplemented by a commentary about the materials we are working with as we go back and forth, drawing each other's attention to the unique and idiosyncratic individuals we locate in the abundance of flowers before us. It is the start of our awareness of them as distinct elements – to my mind the ability to decipher the qualities and characteristics of a single bloom is the foundational philosophy for doing justice to the sublime beauty of the flowers. It is also at this time that we catch up with each other, what we had for dinner last night, who said what, plans for the week ahead. Then Sophie gets me a coffee and a nut-bar ... but not one of those weird nut-bars ...

While Sophie continues to organise, I begin to work on arranging the flowers: hand-held bunches to be wrapped and hand delivered as gifts, or arrangements in glass or silver vessels to be taken to locations where their purpose is to decorate and enthuse. Other flowers are grouped in readiness for tomorrow's orders. In this process I am deft and meditative. My instinctual choosing and combining of the flowers is the culmination or materialisation of a compulsion I may have had that morning at the flower market when I eyed off some incredible floral component, or the result of a concept that I may have formed many months prior when thinking about a future event.

‡

The studio is the site of my own attempts at a type of emotional purification through artistic renewal and restoration. Catharsis. The space is not open to the public ... it's not even a place to meet with clients. The studio

THE RIBBON-CUTTING SCISSORS.

THE SECATEURS CHOSEN FOR THEIR COLOUR.

is an embodiment, a private place in which to make work – which, for me, is a deeply personal act.

The butcher shop and the butcher's workroom are vastly different domains, and so too are the artist's atelier and the art gallery. Similarly, the florist's studio is distinct from the place where their work is presented. In each instance chaos is turned to order by the transformation and re-articulation of material.

In the butcher shop one sees a chop or a sausage, not the hacking, pulverising and shattering of bones. In the art gallery the viewer is subject to a work of art and not to the physical and expressive undulations that bore the work. And in a room of finely dressed guests one is able to view a beautiful arrangement of flowers wholly detached from the mysterious natural world that created it, the human toil that assisted it, and the florist who arranged the composition. I am not suggesting that in any of these examples the viewer is ignorant of or oblivious to this context: it is my belief that the passion, creativity, vigour and atmosphere that produces these things is contained within the work, an inherent quality that can be sensed by the patron.

I recall as a child witnessing different aspects of the character of my father, the butcher ... the act of butchering the animal alongside the act of charming his customers and trading his produce. The former embodied unwavering attention, force and skill, while the latter personified passion and charisma. Within the four walls of the studio I too become unyielding purpose, attention and skill. While my daily life is punctuated by myriad insecurities, in the studio I possess a resolute and determined belief in my ability to sense, distinguish and create beauty.

It is in the pursuit of beauty that I spend my days, perhaps in defiance of a kind of 'cruelty' I see in life. Nothing of course compared with the horrors that befall millions of poor souls with whom we share this world. But, rather, matters of personal gravity that because of my disposition I seem to be inordinately moved by. This disposition may be thought of as artistic sensitivity.

In the studio I am able to deal with emotional responses via the medium of flora. The nature of my practice both feeds my proclivity for composition, palette, texture and form and serves my disposition: each day the world intrudes but the fragility of human existence, and the vulnerabilities revealed, compel me toward expressions of beauty, the majesty of flowers in three-dimensional form.

In a room of fragrant blooms and my tools, I am a 'tradie' ... a person with whom toil agrees.

MY HAT.

WITHIN THE FOUR WALLS OF THE STUDIO
I TOO BECOME UNYIELDING PURPOSE,
ATTENTION AND SKILL. WHILE MY DAILY
LIFE IS PUNCTUATED BY MYRIAD INSECURITIES,
IN THE STUDIO I POSSESS A RESOLUTE AND
DETERMINED BELIEF IN MY ABILITY TO SENSE,
DISTINGUISH AND CREATE BEAUTY.

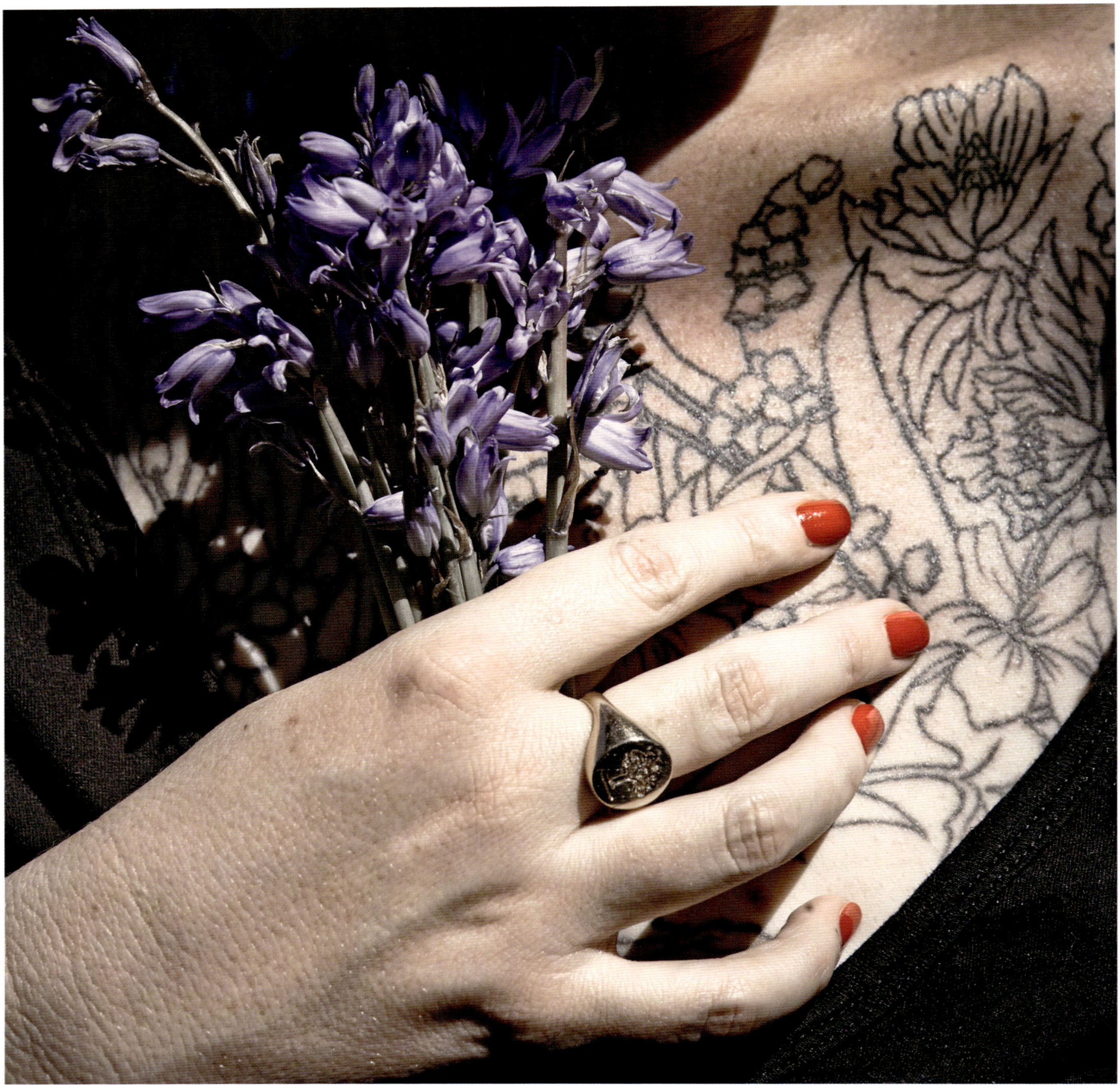

THE GROWERS

THE ACCOUNT OF AN ELEGANT EXCHANGE BETWEEN MAN AND NATURE.

My primary observation of growers is that they are neither aware of, nor concerned about, their poetical contribution to the lives of those who do not grow a thing. They will read this text and likely think me absurd. Yet they are distinguished by their impact on the daily lives of those of us who do little in the proliferation of that which feeds our physical hunger and nourishes our desire for beauty. While the course of my professional life has brought me into contact with people from many different disciplines and lines of work, none has fascinated me more than this group of growers. The proximity of their work to mine is a singular blessing.

The livelihood of the grower is, like all incomes, subject to economic and circumstantial influences, but theirs is also directly subject to the forces of nature: to weather, ecosystem and pestilence. Perhaps it is this daily relation to nature's forces that calls 'the salt of the earth' to the vocation of growing. Our personal character is, I believe, largely dictated by where we focus our attention. There is something essential and authentic about turning a seed and earth into a thing that feeds the stomach and eye. Those whose thought and toil are fixed on promoting and improving the growth of a plant by attention and labour are rare – and the reward for their effort is rarer still. It is astonishing to me that these individuals are humble despite having assisted nature in the creation of a miracle – a bearded iris for example. If I were to do such a thing on the scale that they do, I would not be able to disguise my terrible pride.

The observer's gaze is as much a feature in the domain of the grower as it is in the art world. The flower market – and to a lesser degree the flower farm – is a site for the exhibition and trade of the grower's produce. The marketplace represents the culmination of their effort, the place where they relinquish their yields to florists and flower buyers. In this exchange, the crop that they have tended passes into a phase where blooms become a medium to be arranged and presented ... the ultimate viewing. The passage from seed to sapling to matured bloom that will be cut, traded, composed and placed in myriad contexts is the account of an elegant exchange between man and nature.

Many are born to this work, while others have made vast departures from their lineage in order to follow a passion. For some, farming is intuitive, they seem to draw from their own bloodstream for their approach; for others, it is a science and an art. Likewise, their properties reflect these approaches – some are orderly and precise, while others are rambling. And there are many variants between. Common to all, however, is a love of what they do ... one would never work that hard without passion.

Any book titled THE FLOWERS must include a chapter such as this one. I intended this title to of course indicate the book's subject – flowers – but also to evoke the people: the growers and other individuals whose influence and guidance I speak of in this book.

For photographer Harold David and me, the experience of visiting the farms and growers – whose portraits are reproduced in the following pages – was inspirational. In each instance we found ourselves warmly welcomed, liberally fed and watered; in the midst of such natural beauty, the growers were incredibly generous with their time. In particular I will never forget our visit to Phil and Ray. After we had toured Phil's amazing property and Harold had got what he wanted in terms of his portrait of our subjects – a photograph depicting two generations of growers – we were joined by Ray's wife Rosa, 'Bob' and Karl. A very memorable barbecue followed ... full of laughs, mostly at my expense, teasing me about my proclivity to be so earnest and sentimental as I waxed lyrically about how precious was the work that they do.

It was one of the last times I would see Karl ... but it was the first and only time I really saw him. Before this visit Karl was the silent giant who worked with Phil on the stand at the flower market. It was Karl who would deliver the massive branches of crab apple and the like to the van and somehow concertina them without damage into a space way too small. Karl was Phil's boyhood friend – they had grown up together; later he would become Phil's right hand on the farm. From childhood he was family. That day as we took in the fields, the two of them were speaking about their approach to planting and Phil revealed to me Karl's remarkable horticultural knowledge. Karl, ever the silent one, just shrugged him off.

In my monologue at the lunch table I had brought myself to tears responding to Phil's enquiry about my choice to work in this area, given my academic background. I explained that the land moved my soul and its yield was the crux of my passion. I looked over at Phil's right-hand man and Ray's 'other' son and he, too, had water in his eyes. After lunch Karl took us to view the wallpaper of 'nudes' in the shed across the way, assuring us that many were rare images taken from impossible to find 1970s/80s *Penthouse* and *Playboy* magazines. I looked over at Karl and noticed that the tears in his eyes had been replaced by a twinkle.

PAULA'S FARM

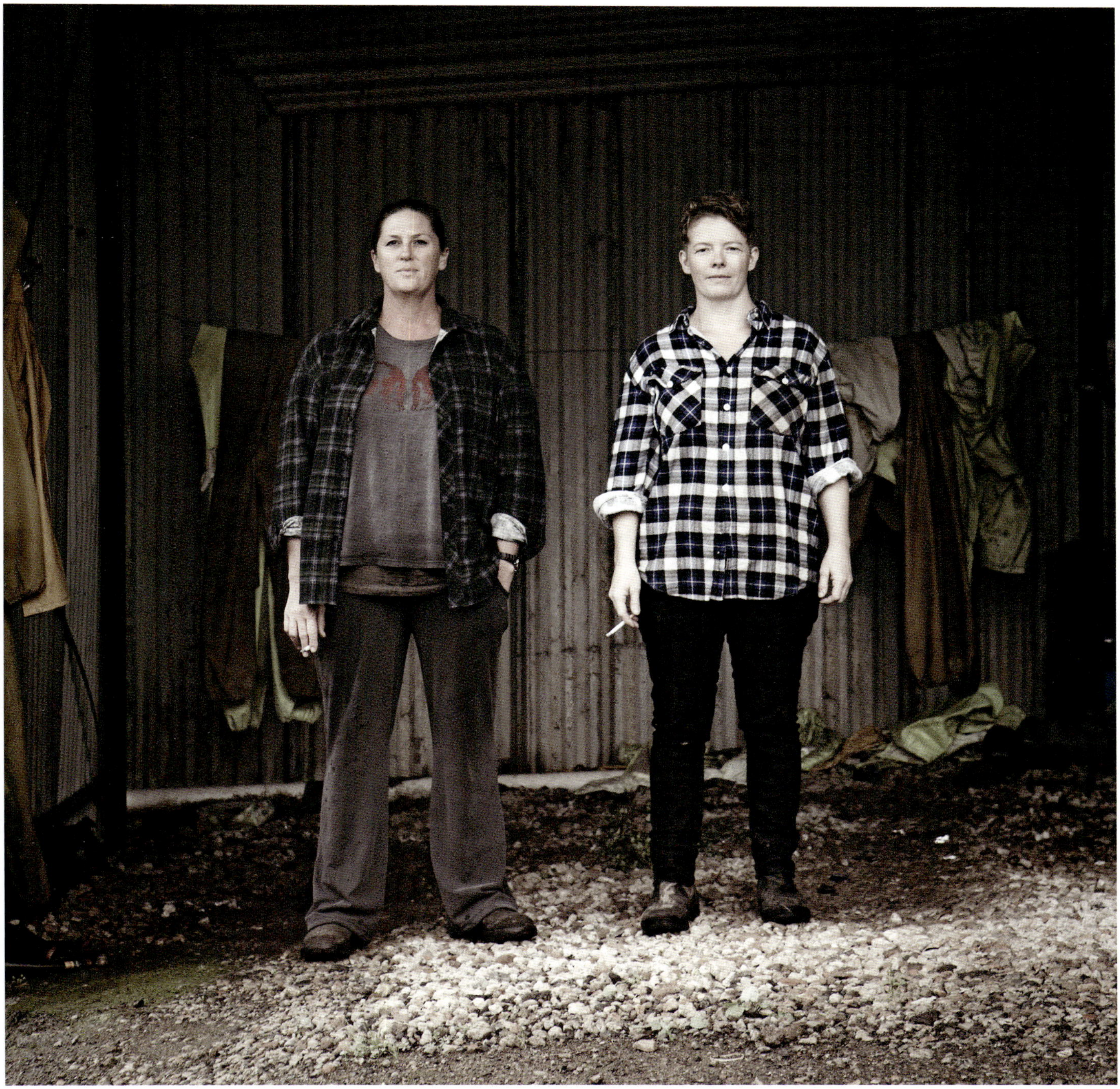

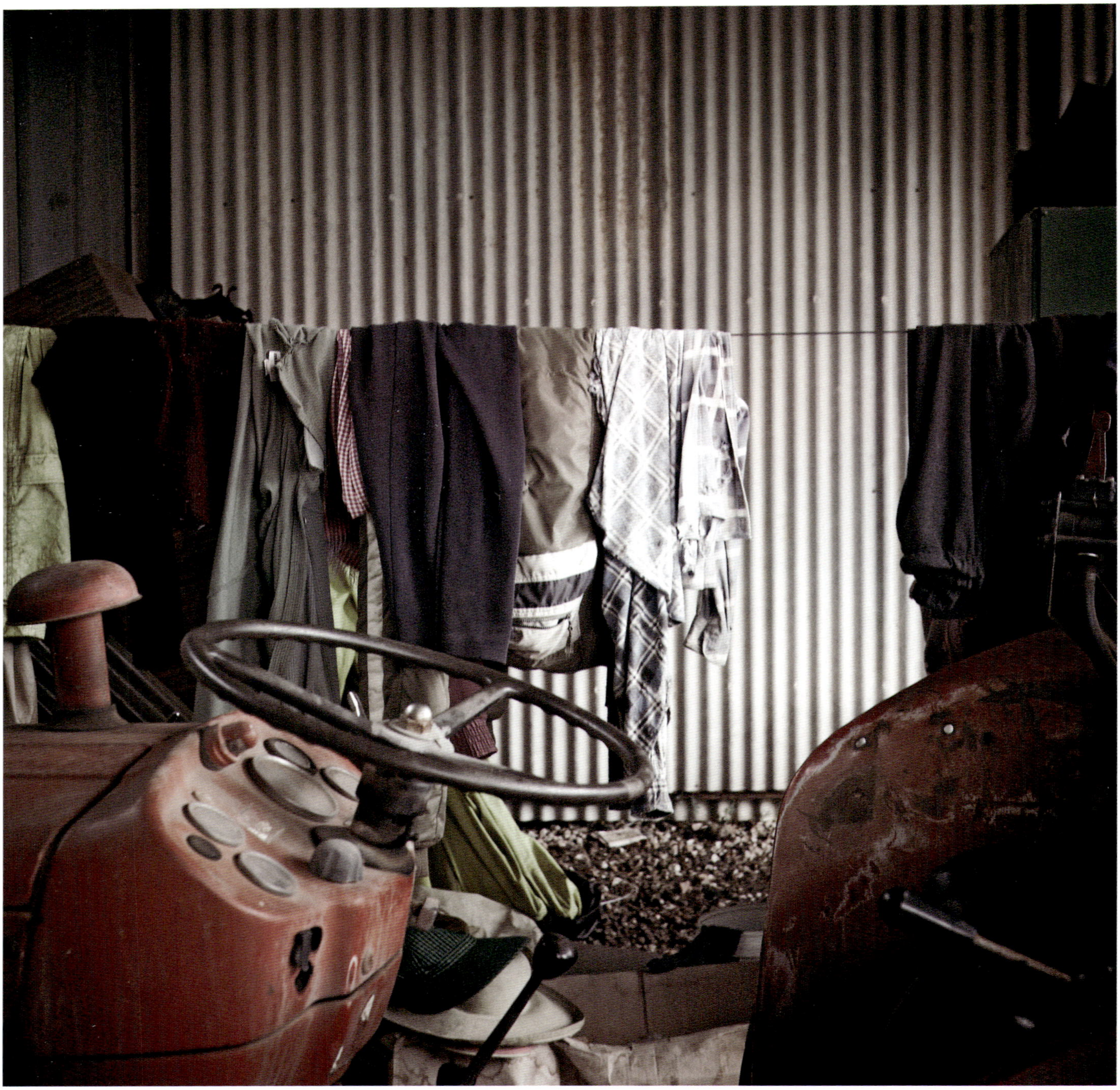

**THE FRAGRANCE ALWAYS REMAINS ON THE HAND THAT GIVES THE ROSE.
— MAHATMA GANDHI**

When I first came across Bob (Paula) and Bob (Tam) I was terrified of them. Paula is formidable: she appears fearless and resilient. Tam presents as tough, firm and composed. Their stand at the flower market is easily one of the most prolific and astonishingly beautiful. To my fantasist mind the contrast of these two 'fixed' characters surrounded by such ethereal beauty was – and remains – magnetic.

Paula's female parrot is called 'Bob', due to some early confusion. She and Tam call each other 'Bob' … and they call me 'Bob' too. Those who spend some time on the farm are eventually christened 'Bob'. It is another word for 'Mate'.

Paula grows roses and she grows the 'living daylights' out of them. They are the type of roses that one might associate with the Romantic Period, with art, literature and song. The kind of roses that would have incited the work of Honoré de Balzac and Gustave Courbet. They are rambling, garden-grown and assuredly fragrant because Paula is one of the brave – she grows them for their fragrance above all else. Her method of cultivation is such that the roses are allowed to develop spontaneously … They see the sun, the rain; they feel the wind and grow in their own time, allowing them to develop character and deep, impossible fragrances.

‡

In 1951 at the age of twenty-one, Paula's father Vito travelled to Australia from his home in Alberto, northern Italy: he was a pioneer in his family and paved the way for his father and brothers to follow. Upon arrival he made his way to Beecroft, a suburb of northern Sydney, and found employment at the brickworks and accommodation at a boarding house run by a family from his own home town. The marriage of their daughter Eliza to Vito was to be an enduring one, despite the family's disapproval.

In the early years of their union Eliza worked as a dressmaker for a highly respected fashion house and Vito continued to labour at the brickworks; their toil enabled them to purchase their first plot of land, 9 acres, off a dirt track in a semi-rural suburb of Sydney's Hills District. For many years they continued in their respective employment and began farming their land, growing vegetables and eventually settling on carrots and tomatoes. As Paula tells it: 'Lots and lots and lots of carrots and tomatoes.' Eventually farming became the young family's primary income and Vito's obsession ... he would become a 'giant' at Sydney's produce market in Haymarket (which pre-dates the produce market that is now found in the Sydney suburb of Flemington).

The farm produced prolific amounts of the highest quality tomatoes and carrots, and Vito became a greatly respected grower and marketer. Meanwhile, the couple were raising their own farm hands in the form of their two eldest daughters, Leonie and Paula (two younger sisters, Vicky and Vanessa, would come later, but I'm told they 'got off easy').

I get the feeling that if Paula were to write a memoir the early chapters would be titled 'Tomatoes and Carrots'. She and sister Leonie would hurry home from school each day, get changed and start work ... and it was no different on the weekends. At dusk one of the daughters would help with cooking the evening meal while the other would continue working until dinnertime. Paula was the one to stay in the field. She loved it. Her father said to her often, 'If you grow good stuff you can sell it', a simple wisdom that she has held her whole life. When I ask Paula what her dad was like, she responds with a list of her own character traits – a chip off the old, hard, block.

In time Paula met Marco, who was the son of local rose growers, and they married. Her father offered them some of his land to grow something in order to give them a start. The arrangement was that the newly wed couple and Paula's parents would all 'go in together' and farm carnations: they planted fifty thousand. After the first year there was an agreeable separation of interests, and for the next decade Paula and her father farmed their own separate crops of carnations on the same land, competing with each other for whose were the best. Over time the market became flooded with carnations, they declined in popularity ... and the young couple parted ways.

Paula and Marco had in this period also planted a small field of mini-roses. When the time came to reassess the carnation crop she thought, 'If I can grow them I can grow other roses too'. Further influencing her decision was the fact that growing carnations was too similar to the farming of carrots – both are annuals that require constant, staggered re-planting. Roses are perennials – and with proper cutting and pruning they will flower for many years. Paula planted ten thousand fragrant field-roses, what she calls 'going in hard'.

‡

'Philia' is one of four ancient Greek words for love; it translates into what the Ancients thought of as the most symmetrical and precious form of love and the crown of life – friendship. This farm that grows love's archetypal symbol is truly embedded in my heart.

Bob (Tam) came to work with Paula after more than twenty years in floristry. She had owned shops in Adelaide, and later the renowned 'Rococo' with partner Deborah Klinger in Sydney's inner-city Darlinghurst. I came to know my now 'Dear Bob' when she had already been working for some years as Paula's right-hand man. My perception of her impenetrable facade and reserve was a challenge, and I thought her to be like Dolly Parton's notional 'Joshua' up there on the farm. Bob is a person of few words but I coax stories out of her now and then. Early in our friendship she told me about the time in kindergarten when her teacher had sat the class in a circle and one by one had them answer the question, 'What would you like to be when you grow up?'. When her turn came, the class responded with rapturous laughter ... her answer: 'a bird'. When I pressed for her thinking she said the question had been qualified by the teacher – 'If you could be anything you wanted to be'.

Knowing the Bobs as I do now I can assure you, 'The fragrance always remains on the hand that gives the rose'.

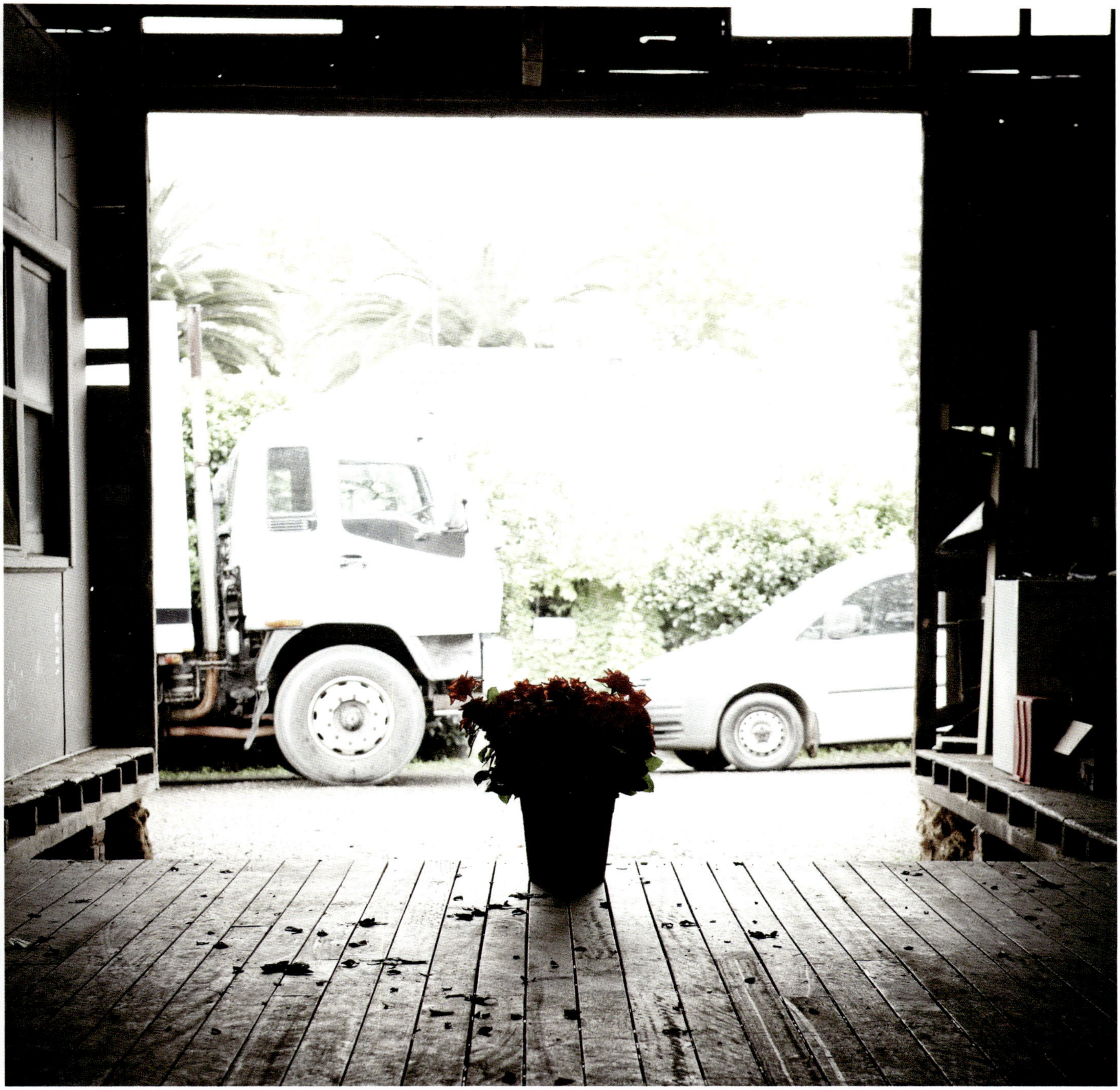

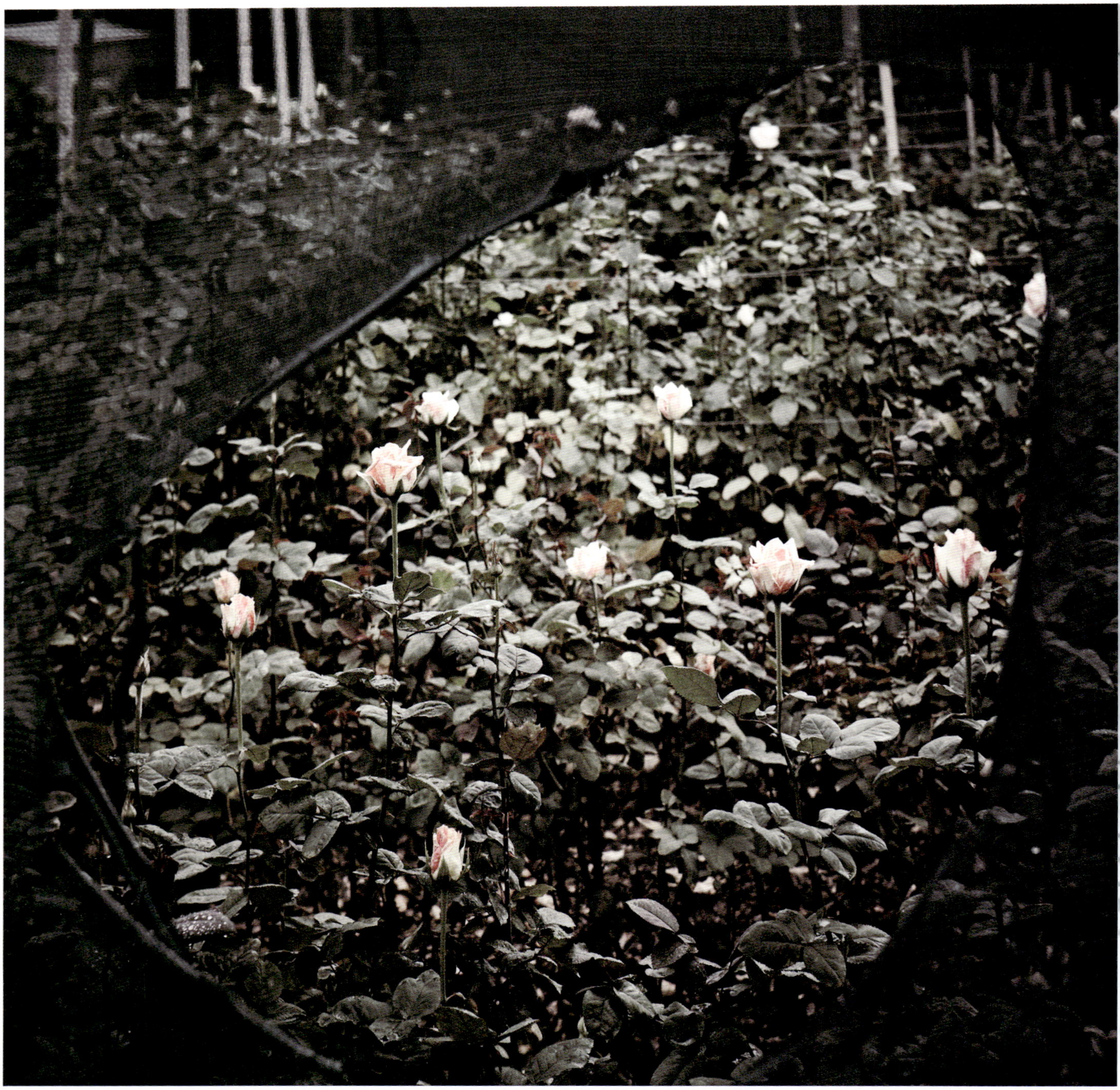

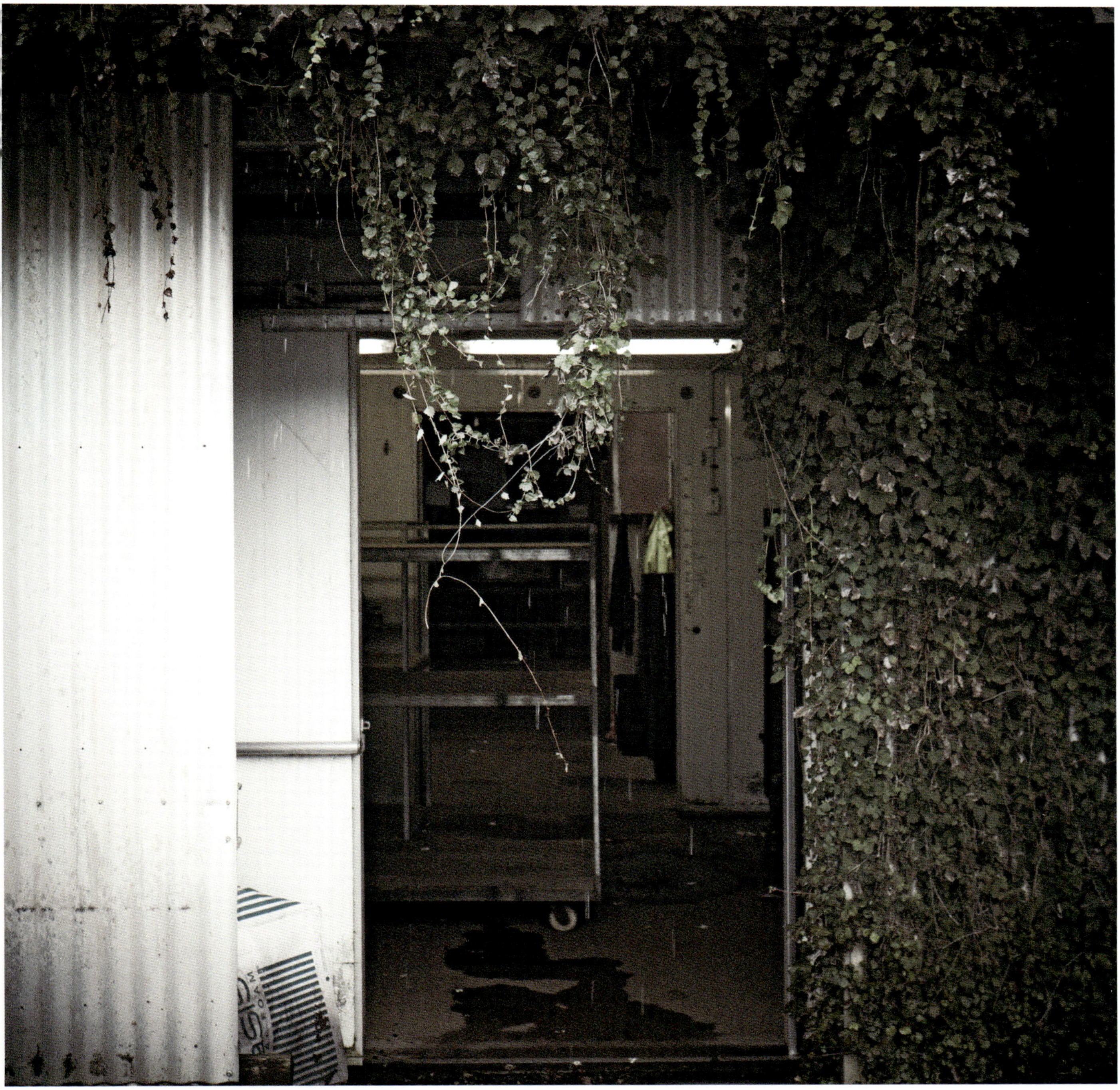

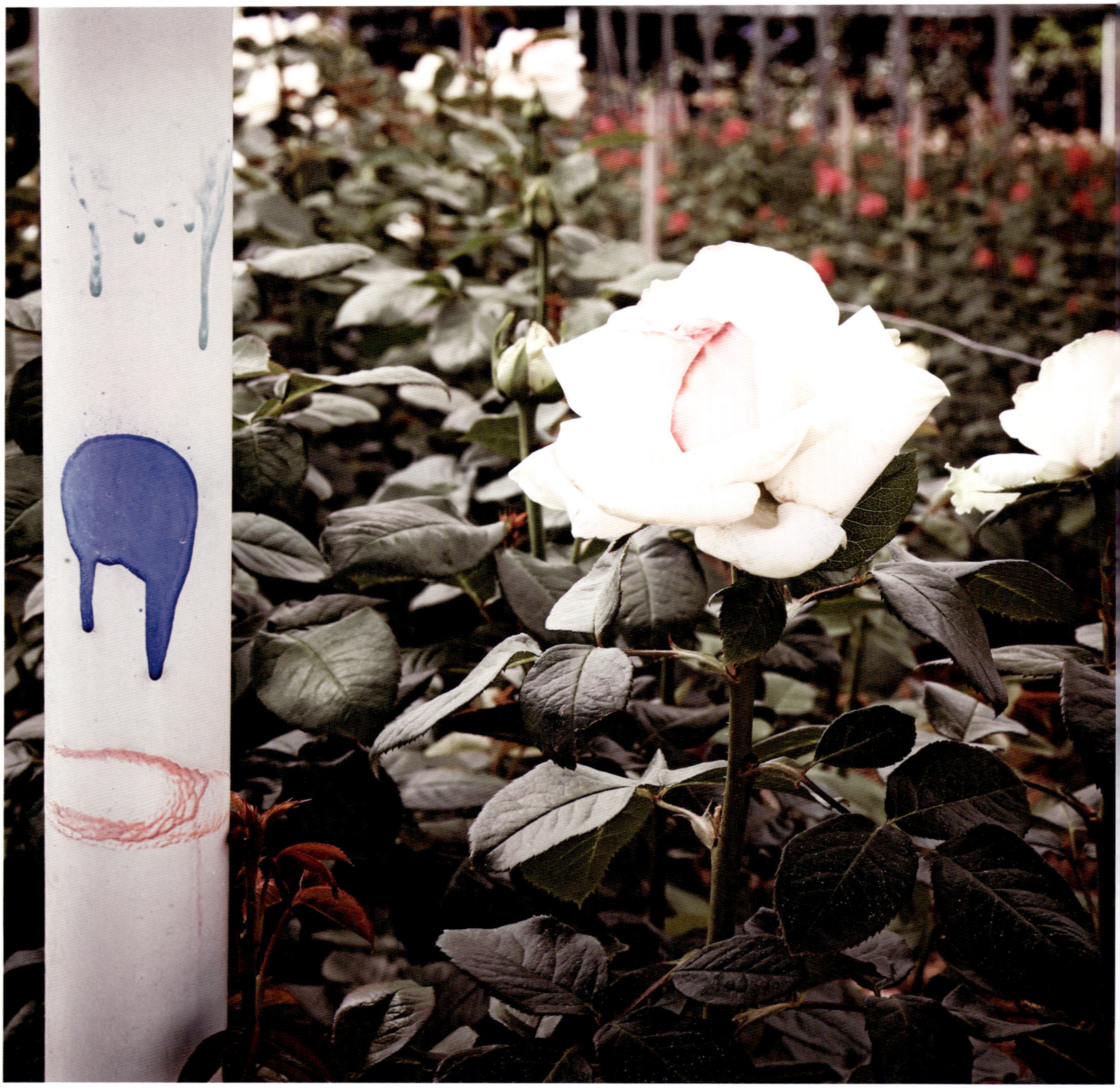

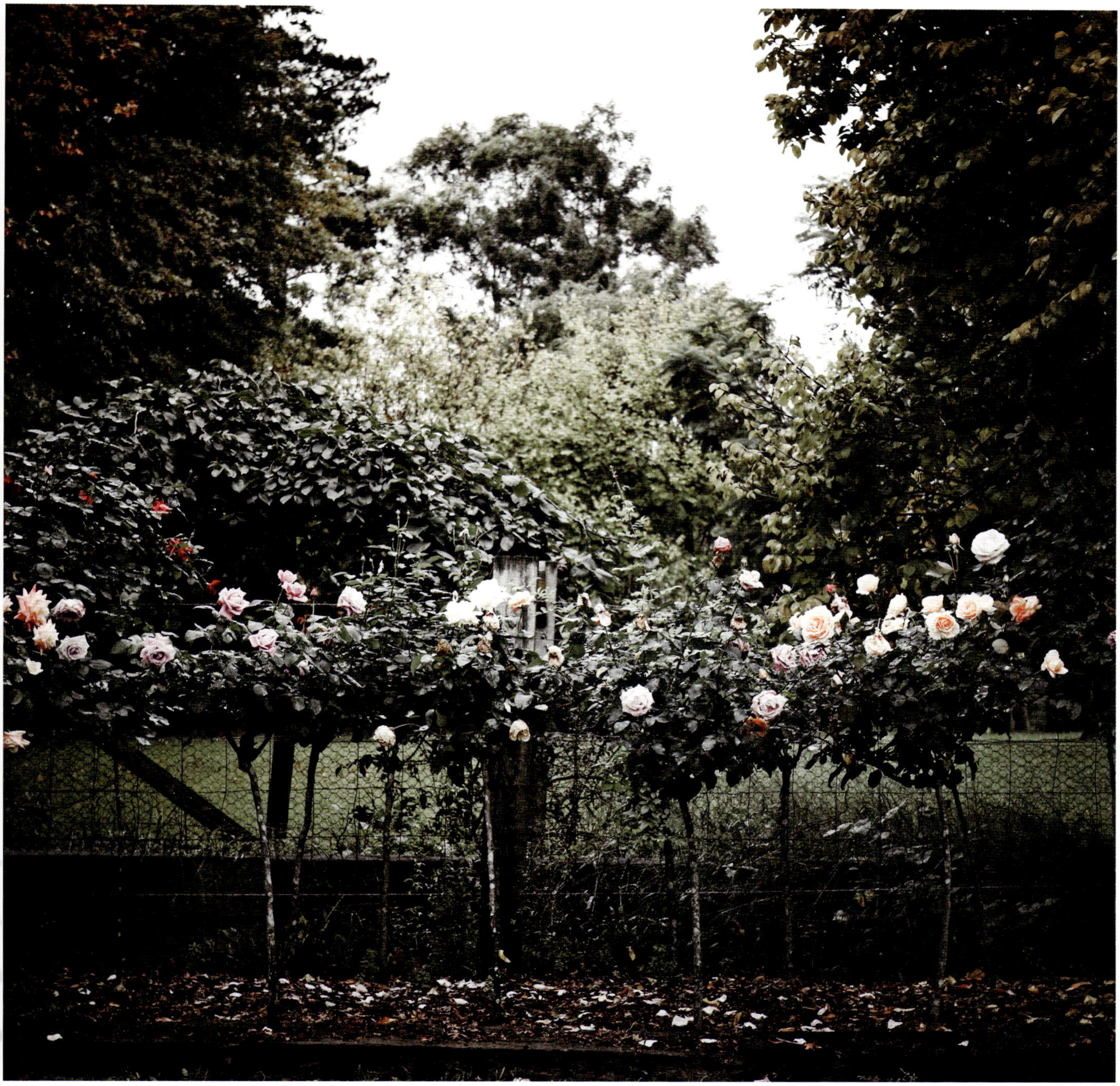

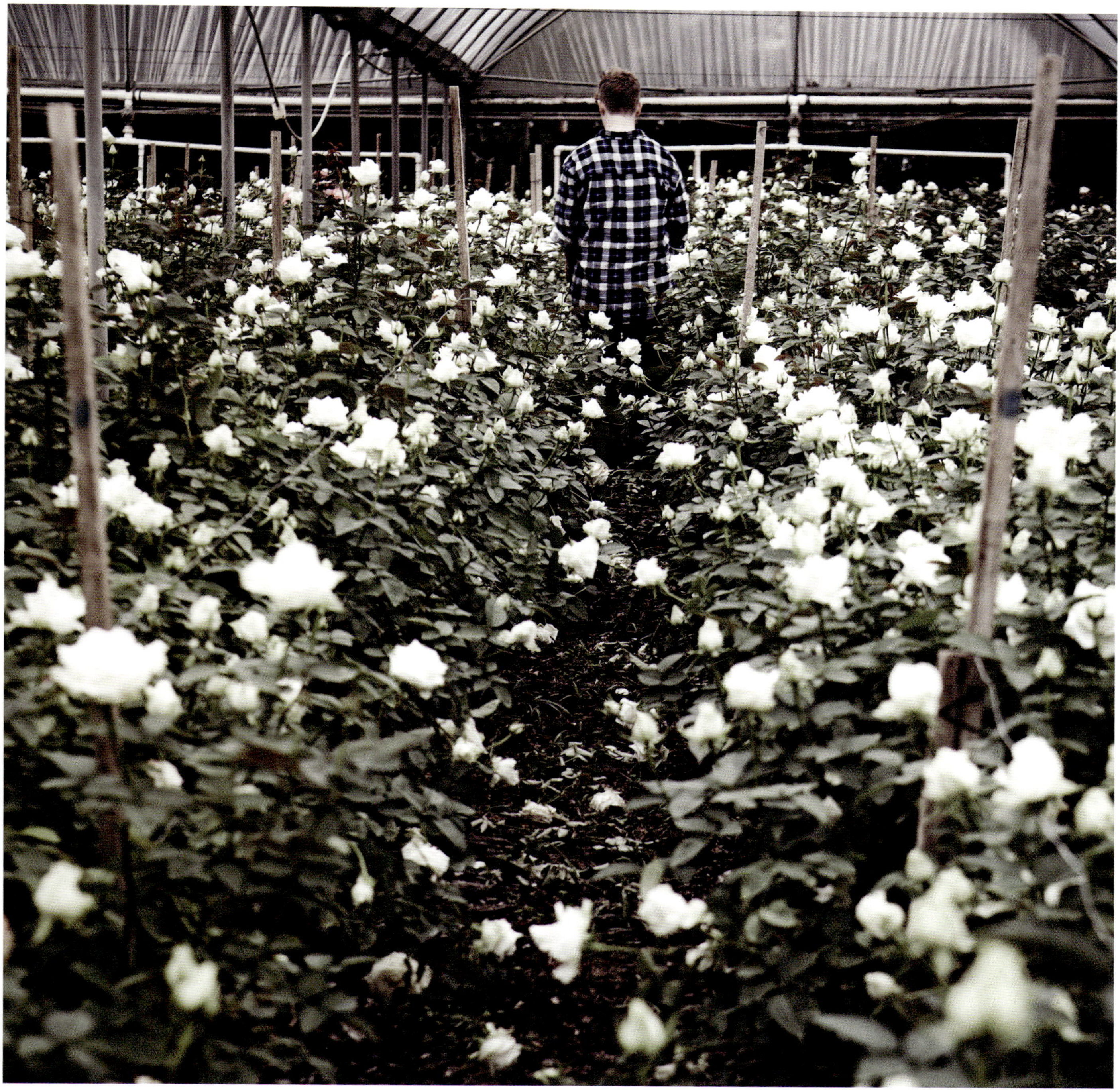

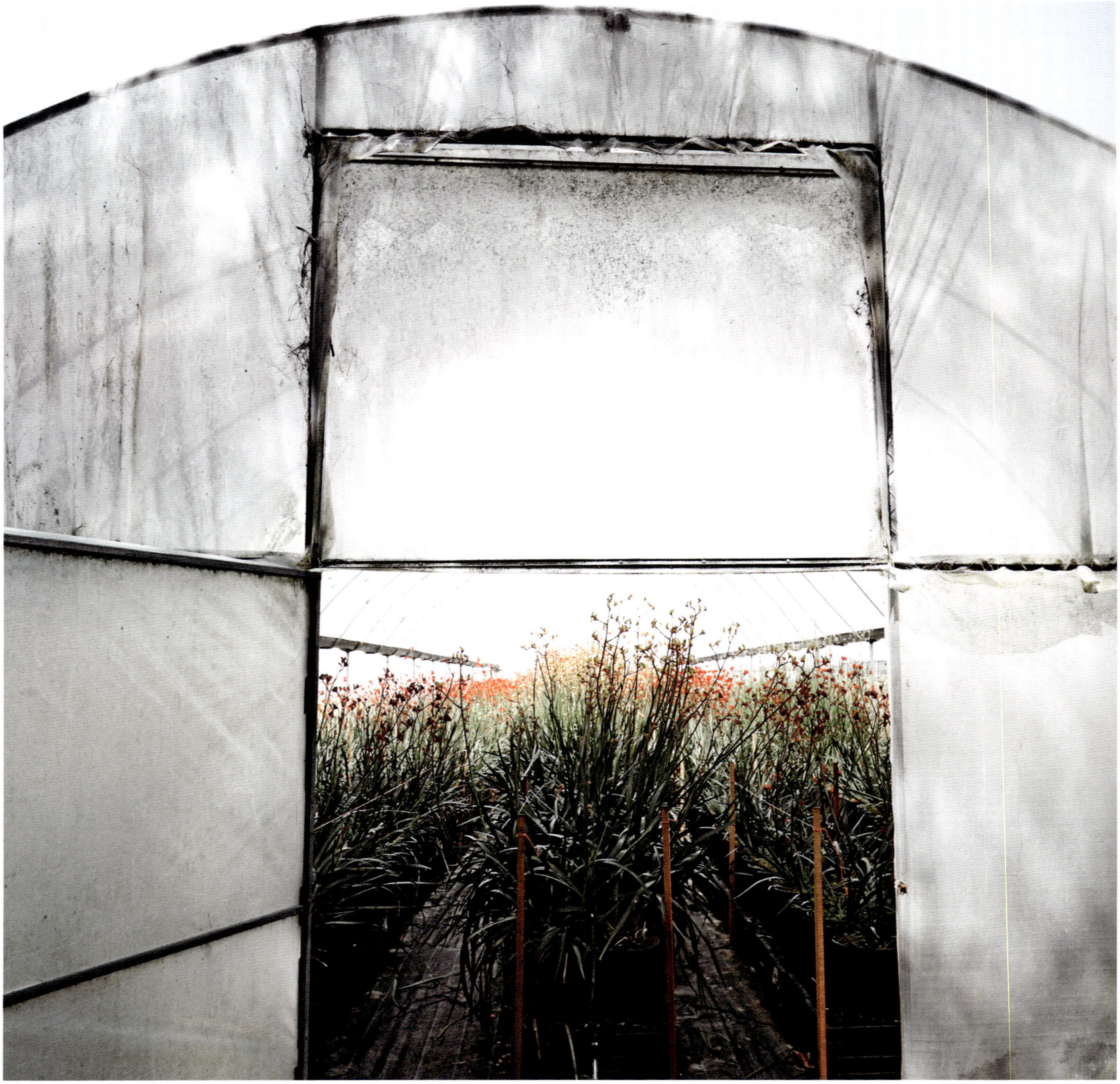

THE BLOOD FLOWER, LOSS AND BEAUTY.

For some growers, working with flowers is an inter-generational business, passed down through the family. For Craig it began with his great-grandfather, then his grandparents and later his parents ... a long thread linking wildflowers, cut flowers and the Sydney Flower Market.

Craig's great-grandfather, William, or 'Robbo', was a skilled forager of some infamy. In the early 1900s he sold Australian wildflowers from an ingenious position at Sutherland Railway Station, located on a major passenger route through bushland near a national park in Sydney's south. In that era, similar to today, 'pickers' were issued a licence by the National Parks Association, which allowed them to pick and sell whatever was in season: boronia, Christmas bells, waratah, eucalyptus, Christmas bush and the like. His grandfather's work was Craig's father Colin's introduction to the cut flower trade. In the ensuing years, it was Colin's parents Veronica and Roy who would take over Robbo's wildflower business. Colin would be raised in the foraging way – as a schoolboy picking natives at sixpence a bunch for his pocket money.

Veronica – Craig's grandmother – also ran Scott's Florist in Sutherland, which she had taken over from her father, who had opened the doors in 1918. She also owned the fish and chip shop next door. Veronica had the entrepreneurial spirit. There is a great deal of this spirit in Craig's bloodline. His father Colin had a flower shop inside Sydney's Rookwood Cemetery from 1959 to 1969 – Rookwood happens to be the largest cemetery in the Southern Hemisphere, and Colin's shop was a raging success. Open just three days a week, it did a roaring trade selling wrapped bunches of Australian wildflowers that appealed for their longevity and their nationalistic beauty. Some of the flowers sold were foraged, while others were farmed. Both Colin and his father Roy grew, among other things, asters, roses, gladioli, jonquils and daffodils – supplying the Rookwood outlet and Veronica's shop, as well as selling their produce at a stand in Sydney's flower market, then located in Haymarket in the city. At that time before the influx of interstate and overseas imports, Colin remembers the market routinely selling out of flowers.

Just as his father had worked as a forager for his grandparents, as a boy Craig would help out at Colin's flower market stall before school and work on his parents' farm after school. And on his way to school, he acted as courier – travelling on the bus with armfuls of this or that flower bound for delivery to Scott's Florist. He assures me it was deeply uncool for a young lad to be seen carrying flowers on the school bus.

In 1968 Colin was able to buy a 50-acre property at Mangrove Mountain, a rural suburb on the Central Coast of New South Wales, where he grew Gymea lilies, waratah, bloodwood gumnuts and Christmas bush. He became one of Sydney's only native-species cultivators for the cut-flower market. This lag in the market would change in the 1980s, when encouragement came from the NSW Department of Agriculture and the Technical and Further Education Department to expand the native flower industry – possibly due to the burgeoning interest and investment in the export of Australian native flora, particularly to Japan.

Craig and his wife Angela now farm this land in Mangrove Mountain, where they have raised their daughters and toiled toward the dream home they would one day build on a nearby property. With farming in his blood and a Certificate in Horticulture under his belt, Craig put down the tools of his training as an auto mechanic and planted his first crops. In their first year on the farm the couple planted nine thousand dahlias, ten thousand asters, three thousand delphiniums and countless native species. While his work is focused on flowers, he has on many occasions picked up his auto-mechanic's tools to complete tasks on the farm.

On the farm, fields of flowers that I might pass over at the market intoxicate me. There is something about seeing them grow in such volume, height and bulk. Each manicured and tended crop is something of a revelation, in contrast to the native 'arrangements' that one might see at the service station. Here, out in the open, rows of densely planted flannel flowers seem to dance – light as the breeze, exceedingly tall and elegant. This mass of white is like an apparition – the whole flower, stem included, creating a field of brightness that is truly ethereal.

Kangaroo paw, likewise, are commanding in stature and palette: massed as they grow in the wild, their colours and powdery texture seem otherworldly … especially fascinating is the way that the bud forms at the end of a vast, slender stem.

Wandering the farm we take in the enormous ancient eucalyptus trees that flank the fields and see flowering gum so incredibly beautiful it seems impossible that one might prefer a peony to this phenomenal work of nature.

The thick, richly pigmented tones of the many-layered waratah flower, along with the bolt-upright determination of its stem, attest to the Indigenous culture's ancient Dreamtime accounts. In these spoken stories that reason aspects of the natural world, the stem of the waratah has been likened to the spear carried by a warrior killed in battle. While the flower head is the red of the cockatoo-feather cloak worn by the warrior's lover, who died of grief upon learning of his death.

But it is Sturt's desert pea, known to the Indigenous Euahlayi people of South Australia as the blood flower, that has captured me. The blood flower is a low ground-covering plant that has thick powdery grey-green leaves arranged spirally on its main axis. Its flowers are a vivid red, pea-like form, each with a bulging black centre or 'boss', which grow in clusters of around half-a-dozen or so on thick vertical stalks protruding from the prostrate stem. In my obsession with this flower, I have spent much energy and summoned all of my charm over the past eighteen months trying to convince Craig that I should be given all that he has of them. My proclivity for 'the pea' has been insatiable: they are rare and difficult to propagate, regardless of how prolifically they cover the ground in the arid regions of Central, South and Western Australia.

There is another reason for this obsession. Over these same eighteen months I have suffered a period of personal grief, and on a visit to a healer was asked what flower I am most drawn to. When I answered 'the blood flower', she told me that the essence of this flower has the power to release and heal hurt, pain and grief … This notion follows from the Dreamtime stories about the ancient bloom, whereby a flower emerges from the blood-soaked earth as a consequence of death and bereavement. The blood flower is the embodiment of the transformation of an event of great loss into a moment of sublime beauty.

About its intoxicating powers, I'll not be told otherwise.

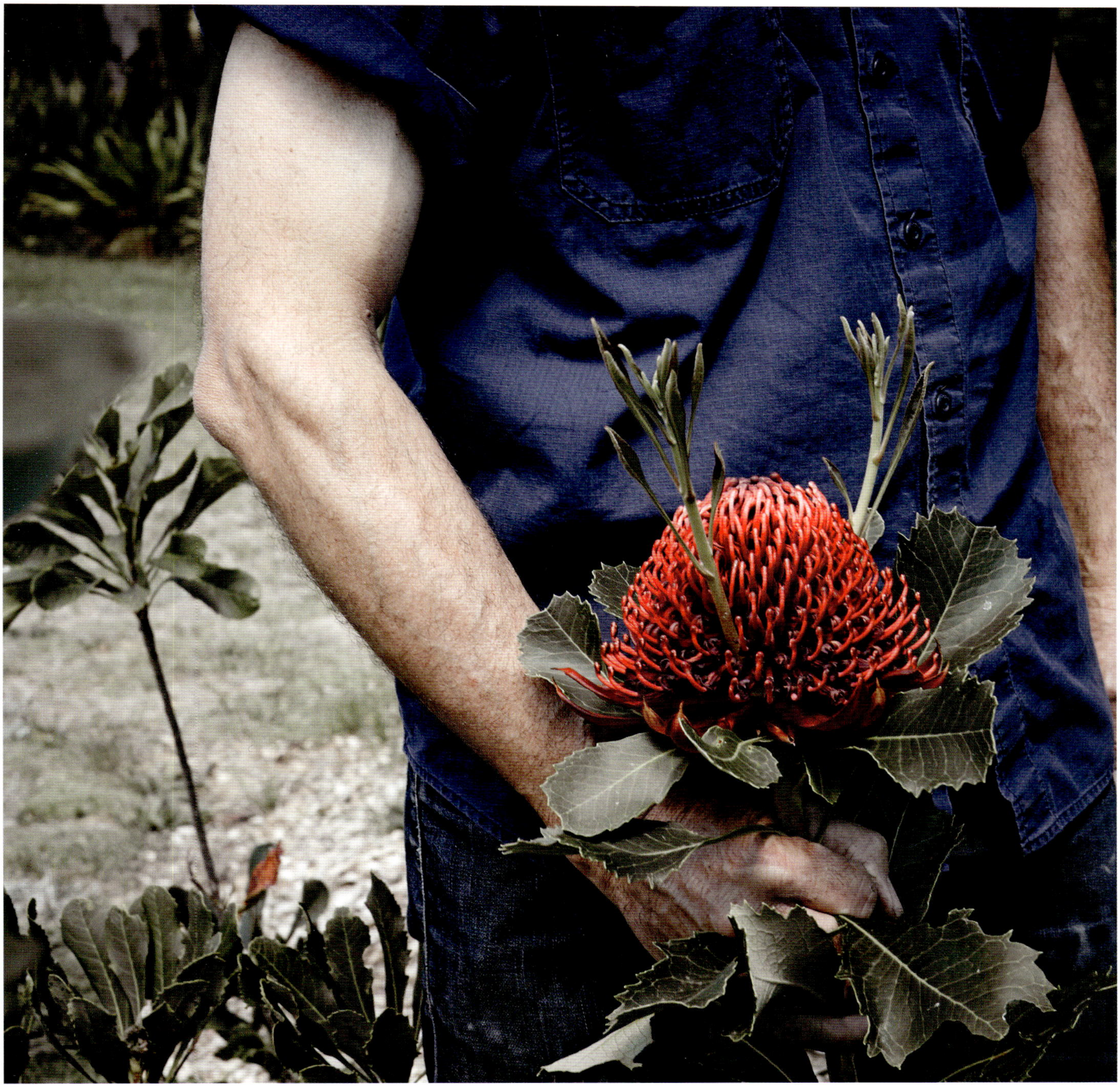

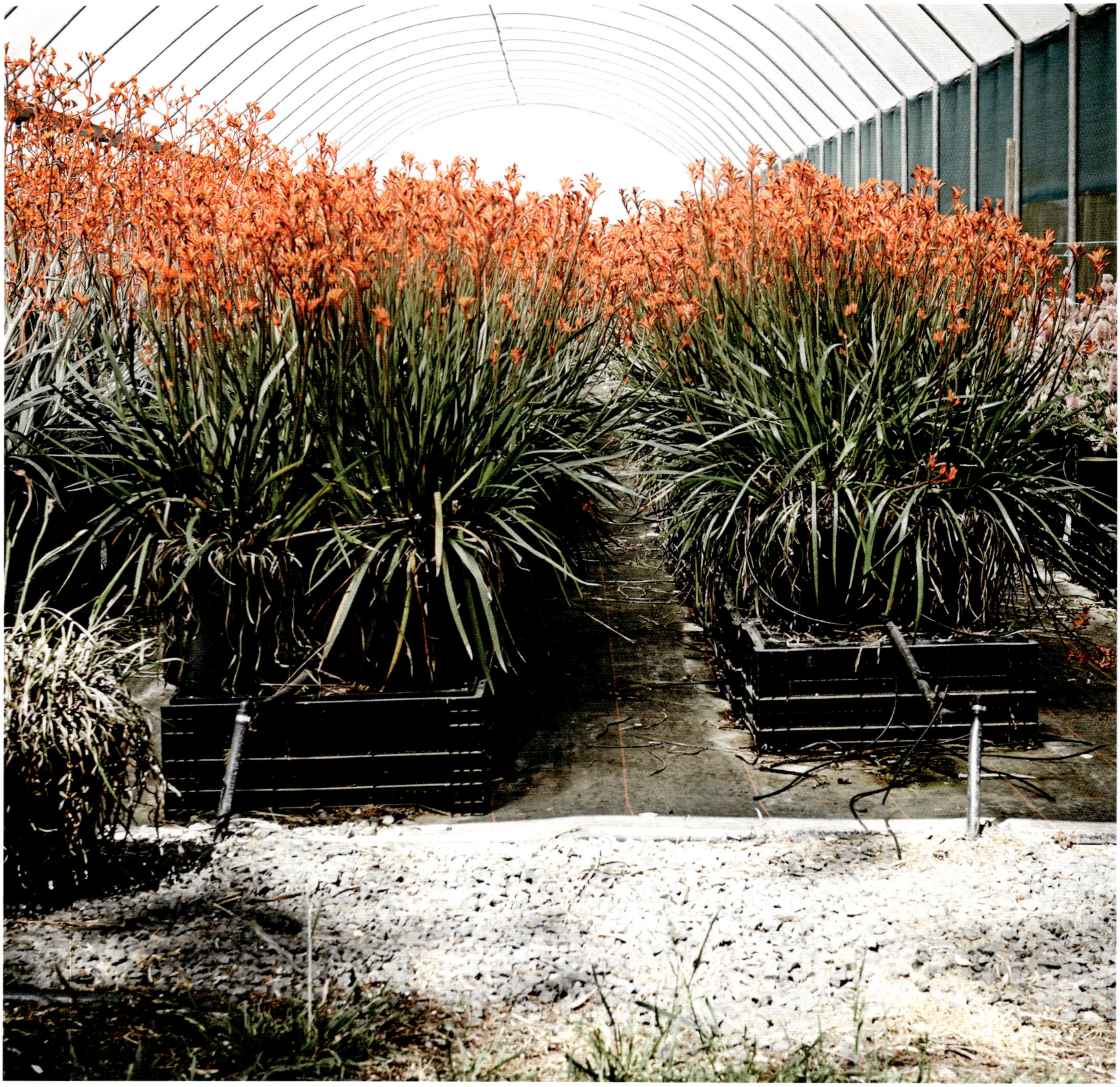

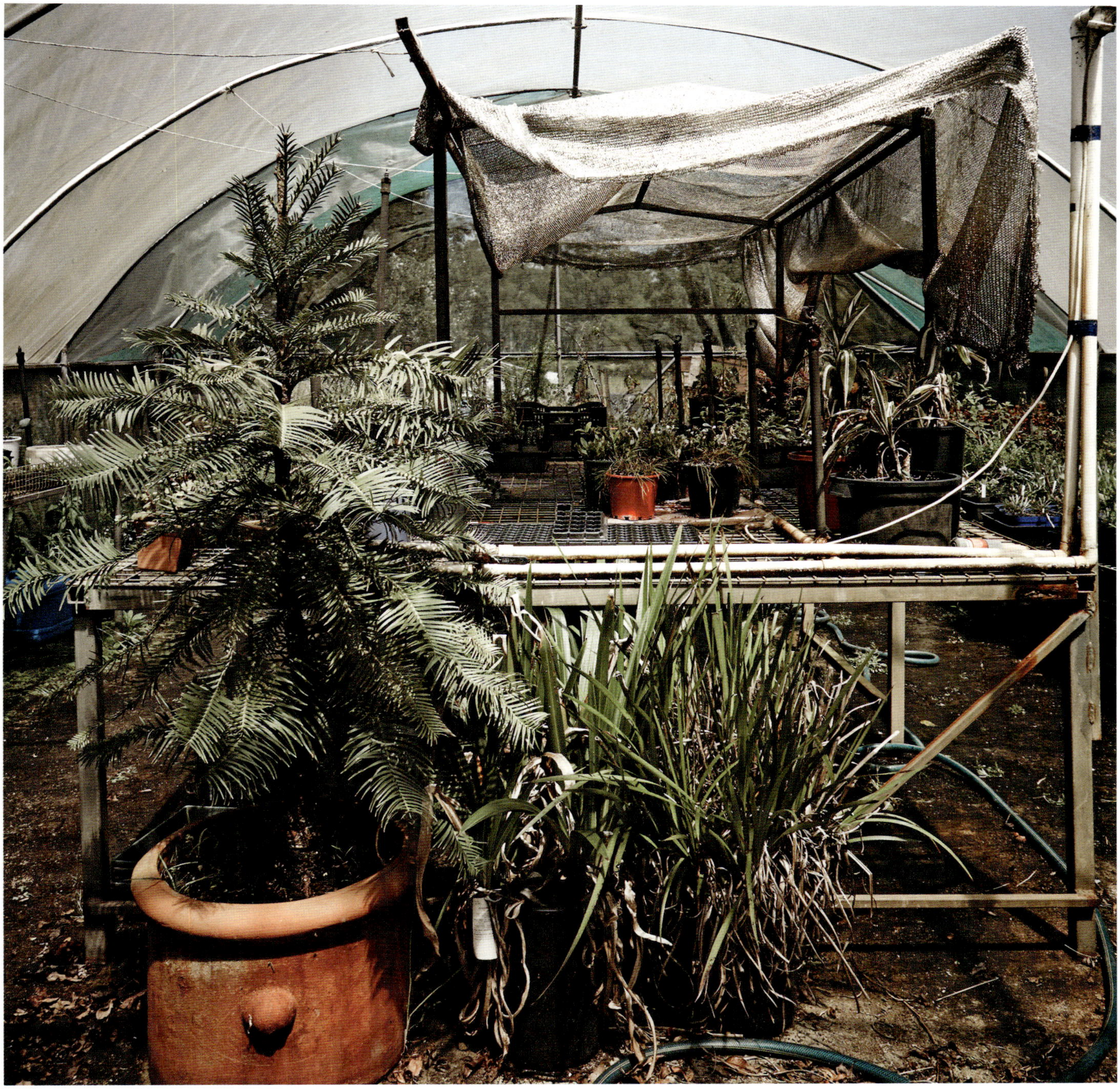

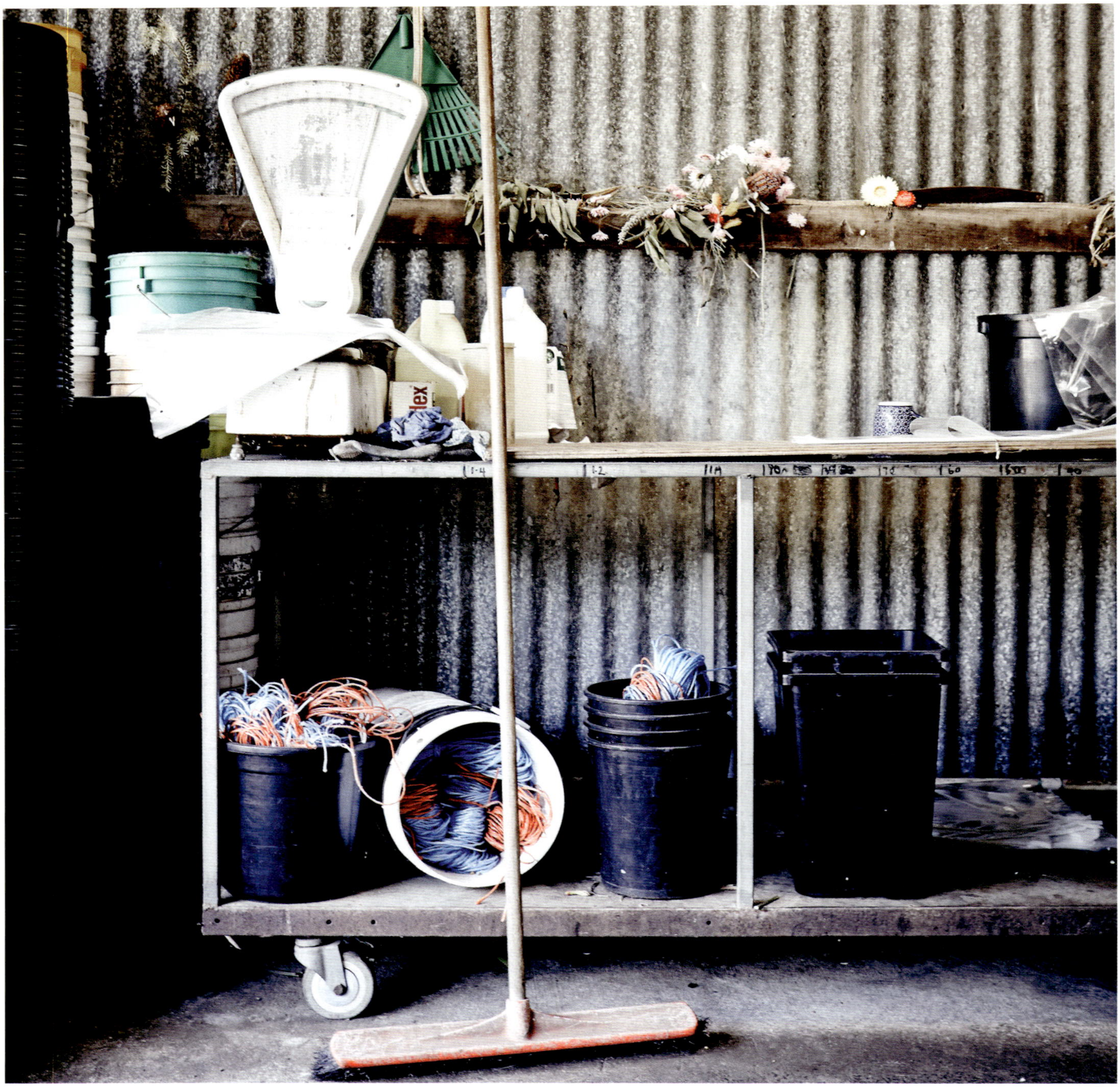

61

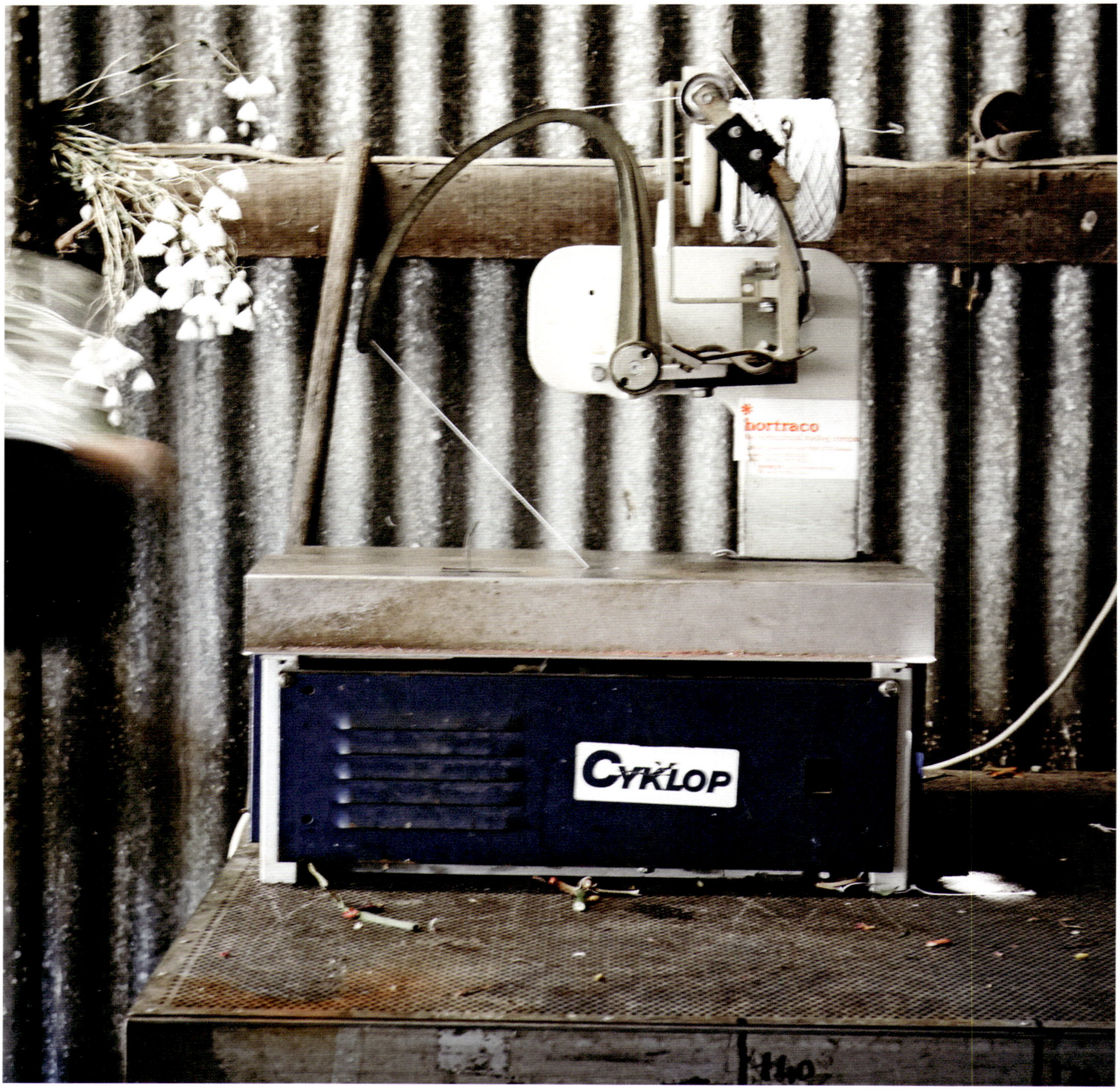
bortraco
CYKLOP

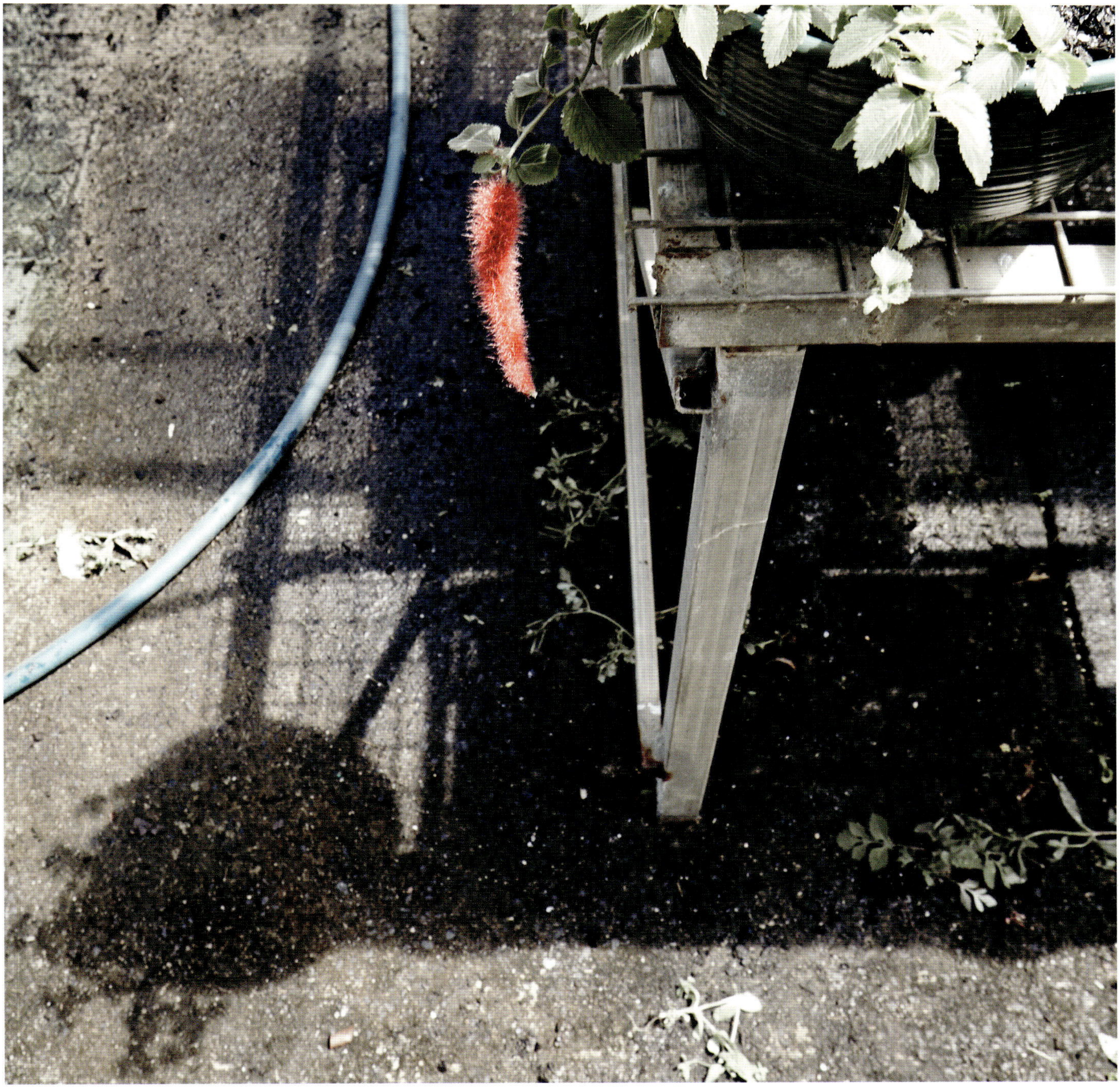

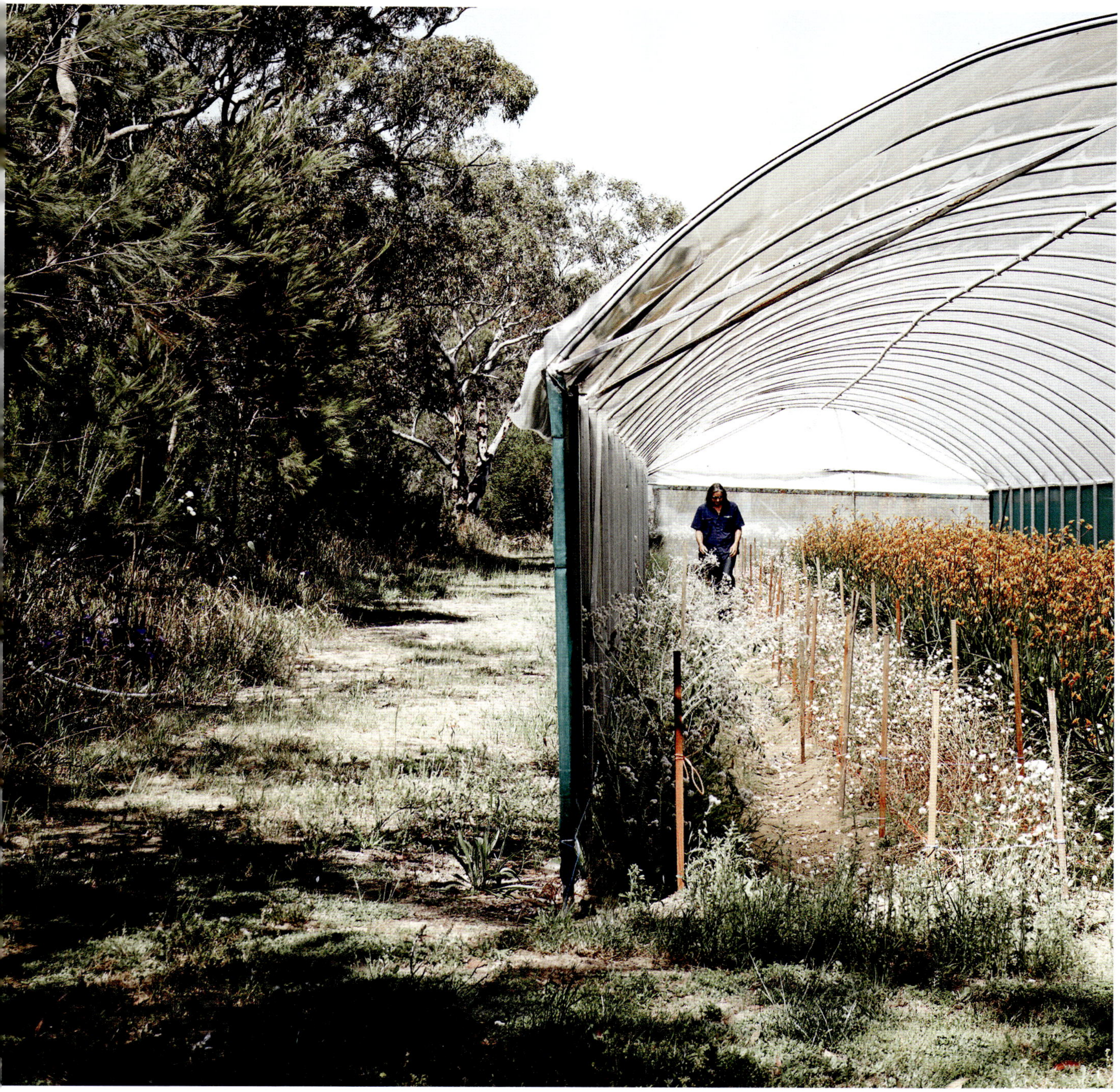

ANDREW'S FARM

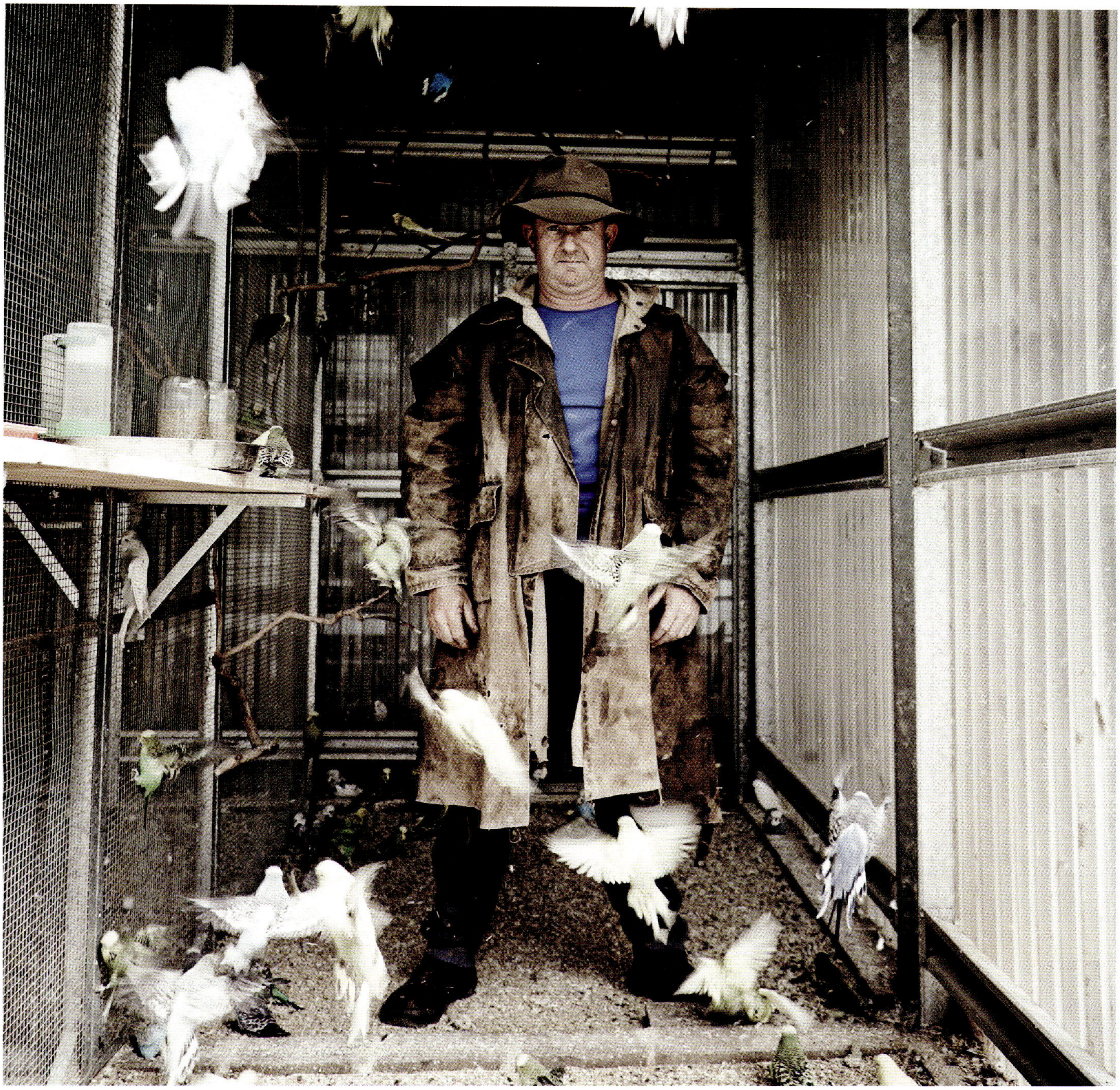

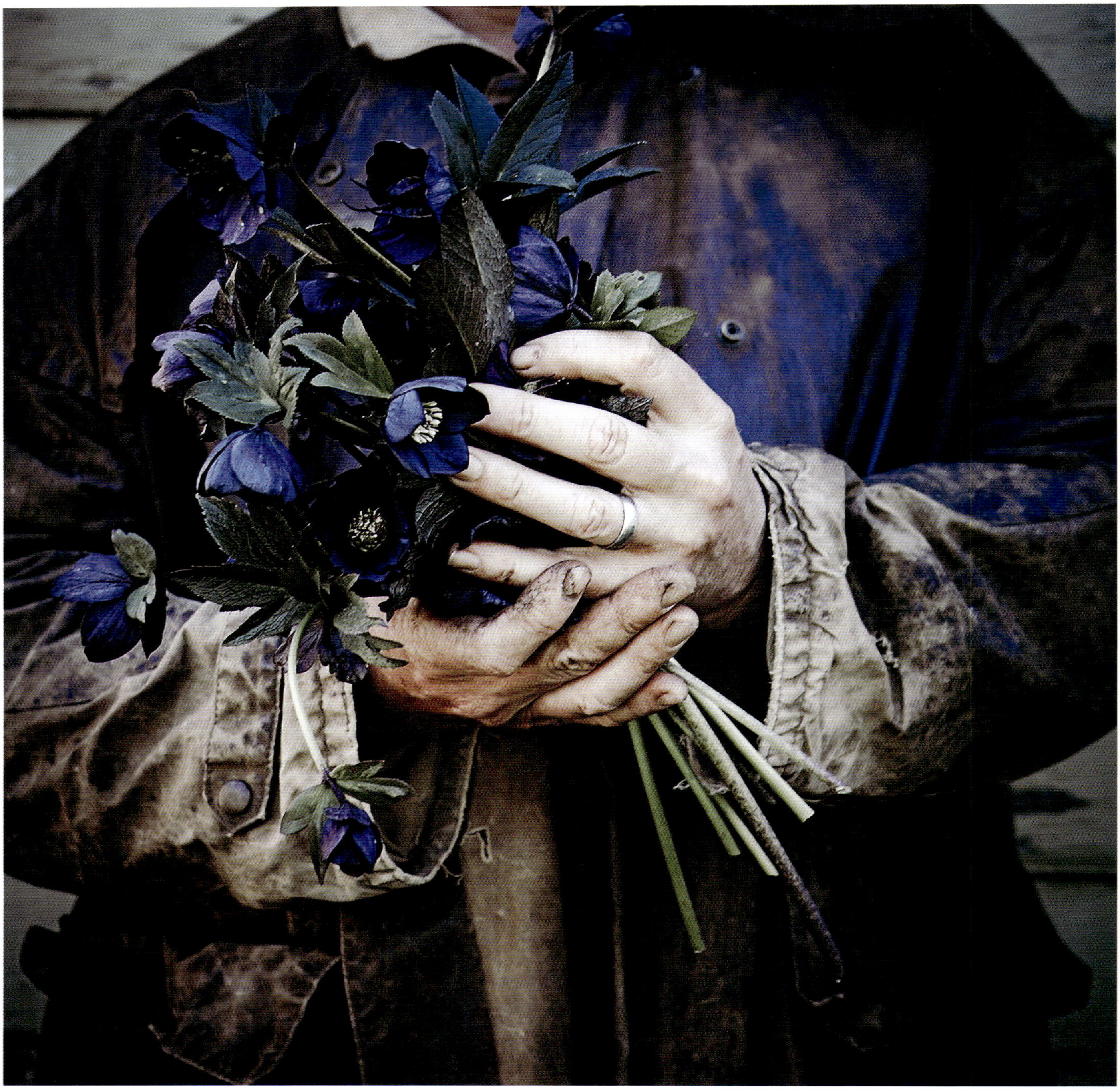

WHILE I LIVE I'LL GROW.

Andrew's 60-acre property in Oakdale, a semi-rural suburb in Sydney's southwest, is fixed in my heart. The moment I set foot on the farm I felt a deep affinity with the land. Perhaps the morning tea of fresh scones engendered this feeling; maybe it was the homemade jam and fresh hand-whipped cream that Andrew's wife Freda had effortlessly summoned to the generous veranda that flanks the farmhouse. I have, since my first bewitching visit, had the pleasure of Freda's baking on numerous occasions. Her food seems to travel from gullet to stomach and straight to one's very soul.

My first memory of the farm is the first time I saw 'my tree' – a massive oak that stands in the field across from the house, wholly unobstructed in the landscape. In fact, it seems framed in perfect equilibrium to its surrounds. Full and balanced, it is the kind of tree that might comfortably house a family if one happened to be a carpenter. It stands about 20 metres tall, its branches reaching out about 18 metres from the trunk – its core.

Andrew tells me that the oak standing majestically before me grew from an acorn. It was planted in the spot some fifty years prior. Anthony Hordern & Sons, who from the turn of the twentieth century had the largest department store in Sydney, gave acorns as endowments to their customers – each in a little bag printed with their trademark image, an oak tree, and their motto, 'While I live I'll grow'.

The company gave away thousands of acorns and the trees that they became are said to grow all across Sydney – these trees are Hordern's legacy. Sydney's famous Hordern Pavilion is in turn the legacy of Anthony's brother, Sir Samuel Hordern, who was the president of the Royal Agricultural Society from 1915 to 1941 and played a large part in transforming the city's Royal Easter Show into one of the world's largest agricultural events.

While the motto, 'While I live I'll grow', and the image of the oak were adopted by the ambitious Horderns to symbolise growth in commerce, for me both the tree on Andrew's farm and the proverb have a profound personal resonance. On that initial visit I was brought to tears by the sovereignty and wisdom of that great oak ... I was so moved that I had a likeness of the tree embedded in a gold wax-seal signet ring, reminding me daily that 'While I live I'll grow'.

Andrew's grandmother, Clair, saw Halley's Comet appear on two occasions – a testament to her durability and persistence, as it is only possible to see the comet twice in a human lifetime. She was no slouch – and neither are her progeny. Like all farmers, Andrew works very hard: he is accomplished, knowledgeable and he has 'guns' – that is, extremely developed biceps. He reminds me of The Man from Snowy River. His father, John, was schooled at Knox Grammar, a privileged education on Sydney's North Shore. Upon completing his own schooling Andrew followed his father into the family business – C. H. McFarland Pty Ltd – who were, by far, Australia's biggest importers and restorers of grand pianos. At the height of the business, he employed sixty full-time staff including French polishers, carpenters and tuners: the company name remains etched upon thousands of pianos around Australia.

Andrew's mother, Barbara, was born in Scotland and came to Australia as a child – she was an ardent horse rider, and rode in the discipline of dressage at many regional shows, including Sir Samuel Hordern's Royal Easter Show. In 1972, when Andrew was twelve years old, his mother convinced his father to buy the 60-acre property that Andrew farms today. It was a time when Andrew's school reports testified that he was often caught 'looking out the window as though he wanted to escape'. His escape, as it turned out, was the property 'Eugalo' in Oakdale. He tells me that he caught his first fish in the property's dam in the first hour he was there; and he laid the foundations for his life in trade in the first year that his family owned 'Eugalo' – catching red-bellied black snakes and selling them on the 'black market' to reptile handlers and the like. By the time he had that first fish on the line he knew he was home, and that the land was where he would make his life.

Barbara was determined to make the farm self-sufficient, so Andrew helped her with all of the tasks: milking cows, growing vegetables, rearing and slaughtering ducks and chickens and trading their produce for the lamb and pork that they didn't raise. His father continued to run the family business, and planted 25 acres of turf on the farm.

Barbara's enthusiasm for horses was passed on to Andrew; the property held their own six horses as well as up to 30 agisted racehorses, giving rise to her son's proficiency in dressage, roping and camp-drafting – The Man from Snowy River. In the ensuing years he finished his schooling and under the wing of Mr Hore, a renowned and maverick station manager, he learnt 'bush crafts' such as bailing hay, erecting stock fences and mustering sheep and cattle.

Andrew initially enrolled in Agriculture at Hawkesbury Agricultural College, but immediately transferred to Horticulture, where he studied plant science and learnt Latin plant name identification. While undertaking this study he established his first nursery at 'Eugalo', specialising in grafting and budding fruit trees. Before he had completed his course he was already in business with his head lecturer, with whom he was farming over 150 acres of land over three properties. At the conclusion of his study he was offered the opportunity to be involved in the development of the Fruit Production Breeding Program at Florida University. But to teach is not to grow things.

Andrew's stand at the Sydney Flower Market is testament that one day shortly thereafter he turned his attention to flowers – millions and millions of expertly cultivated flowers. On another day the farmer's attention turned to the breeding and exhibition of budgerigar. For Andrew, attention quickly turned to obsession, and in the following days an elaborate aviary was built that now houses 800 perfectly bred birds and their offspring ... next door 250 plump ISA Brown chickens chat away oblivious to their award-winning neighbours. While the land that flanks the coop produces 'manna from heaven', across the seasons.

'While he lives he'll grow.'

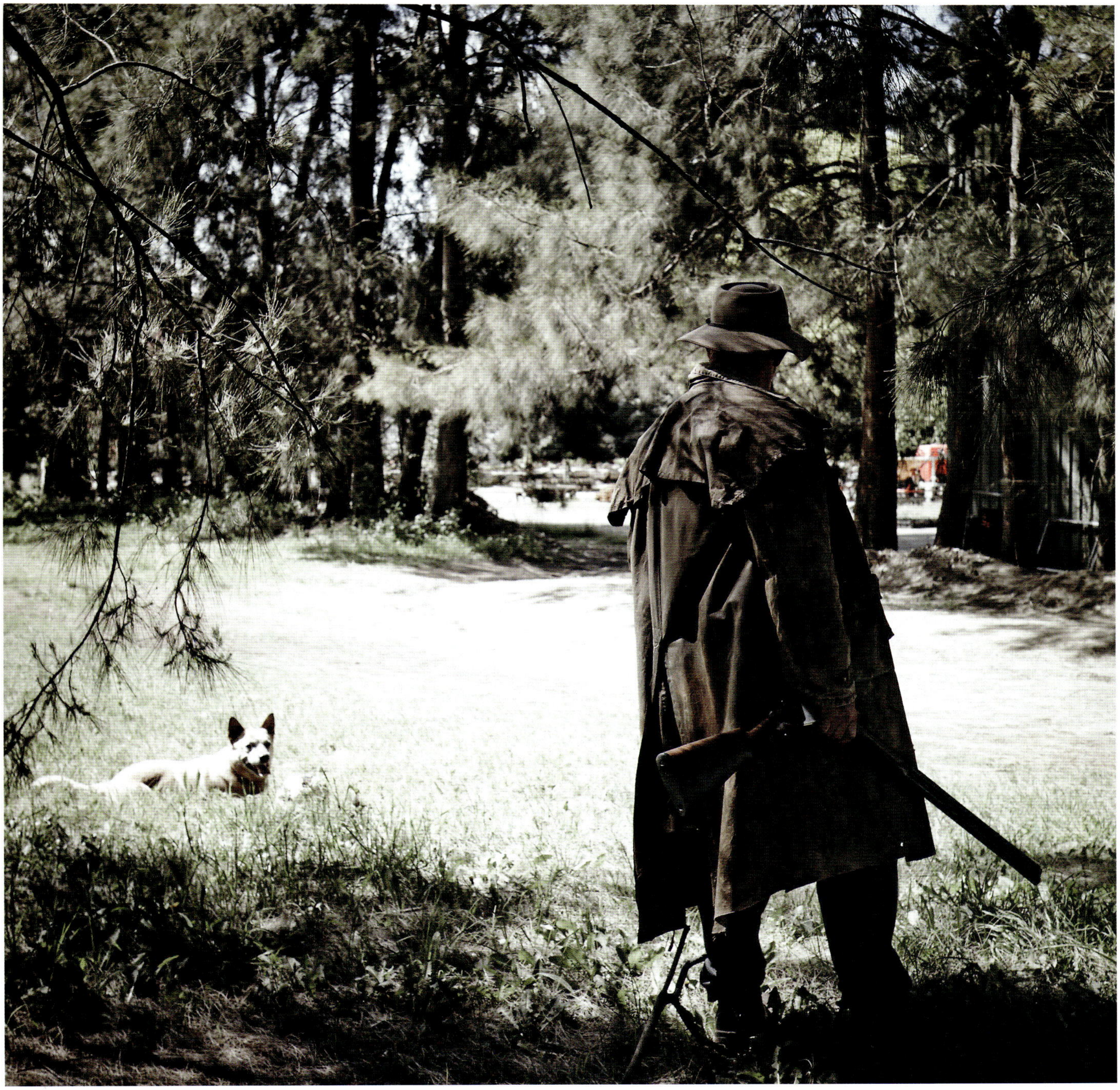

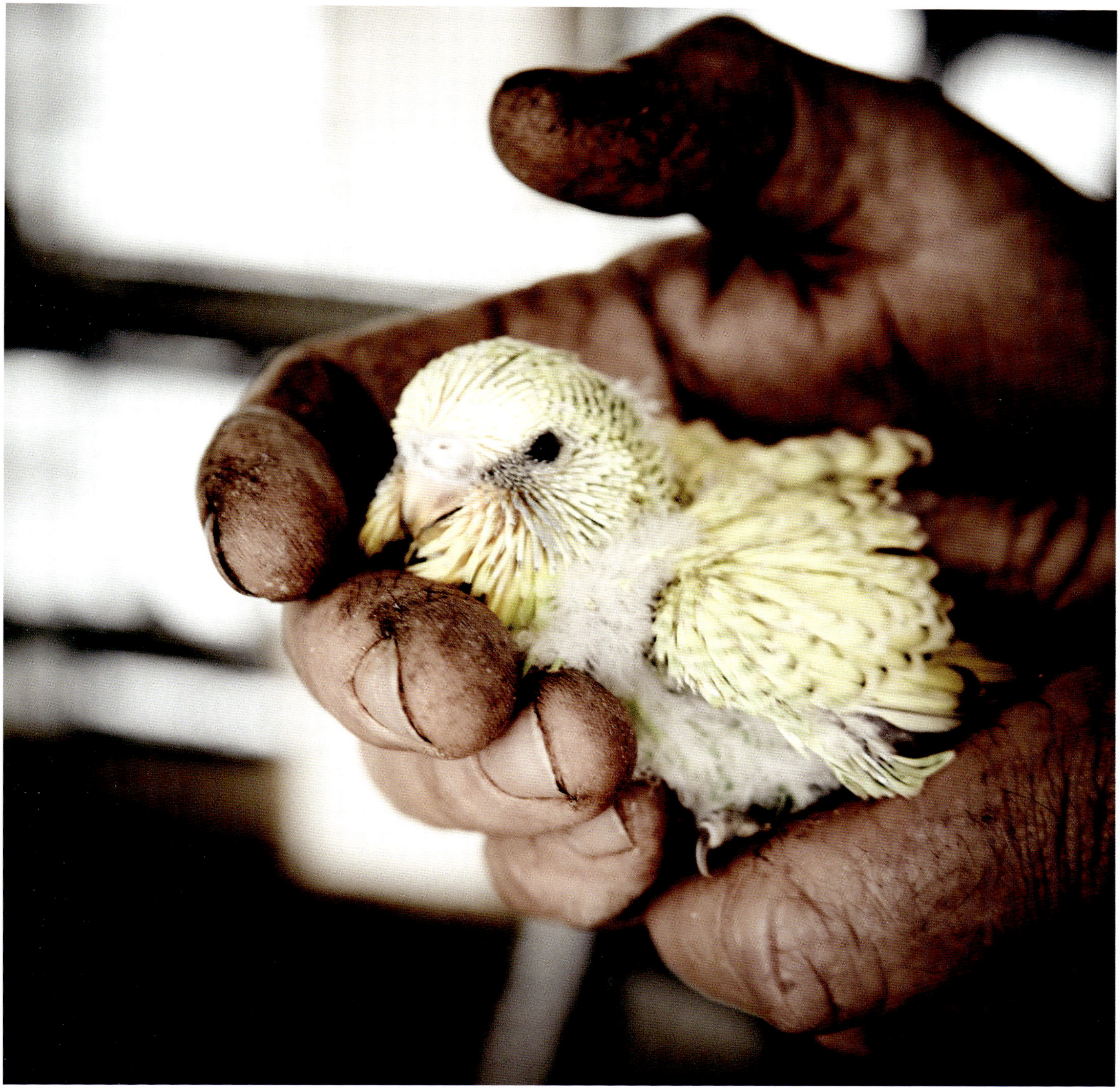

WAYNE'S FARM

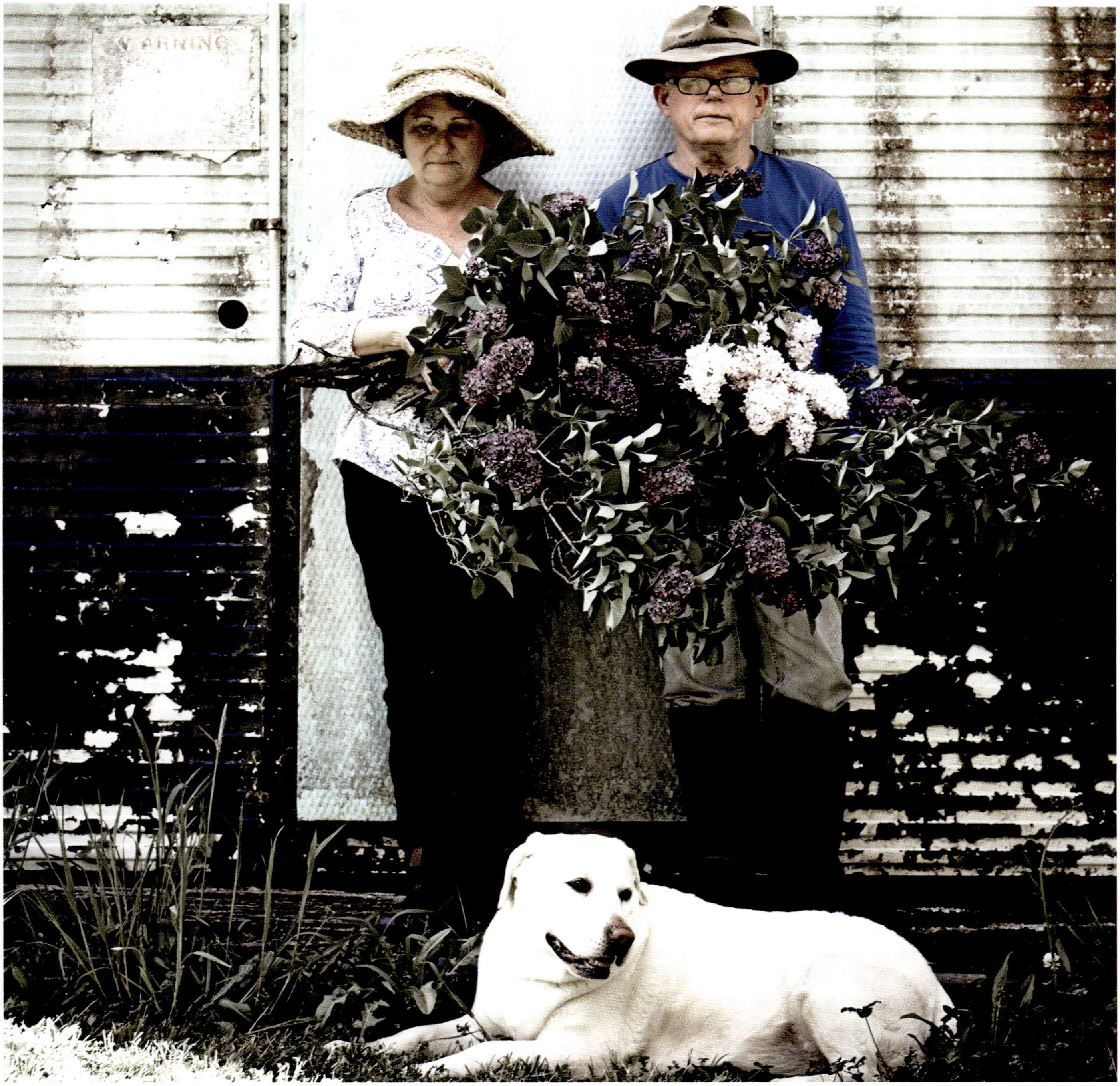

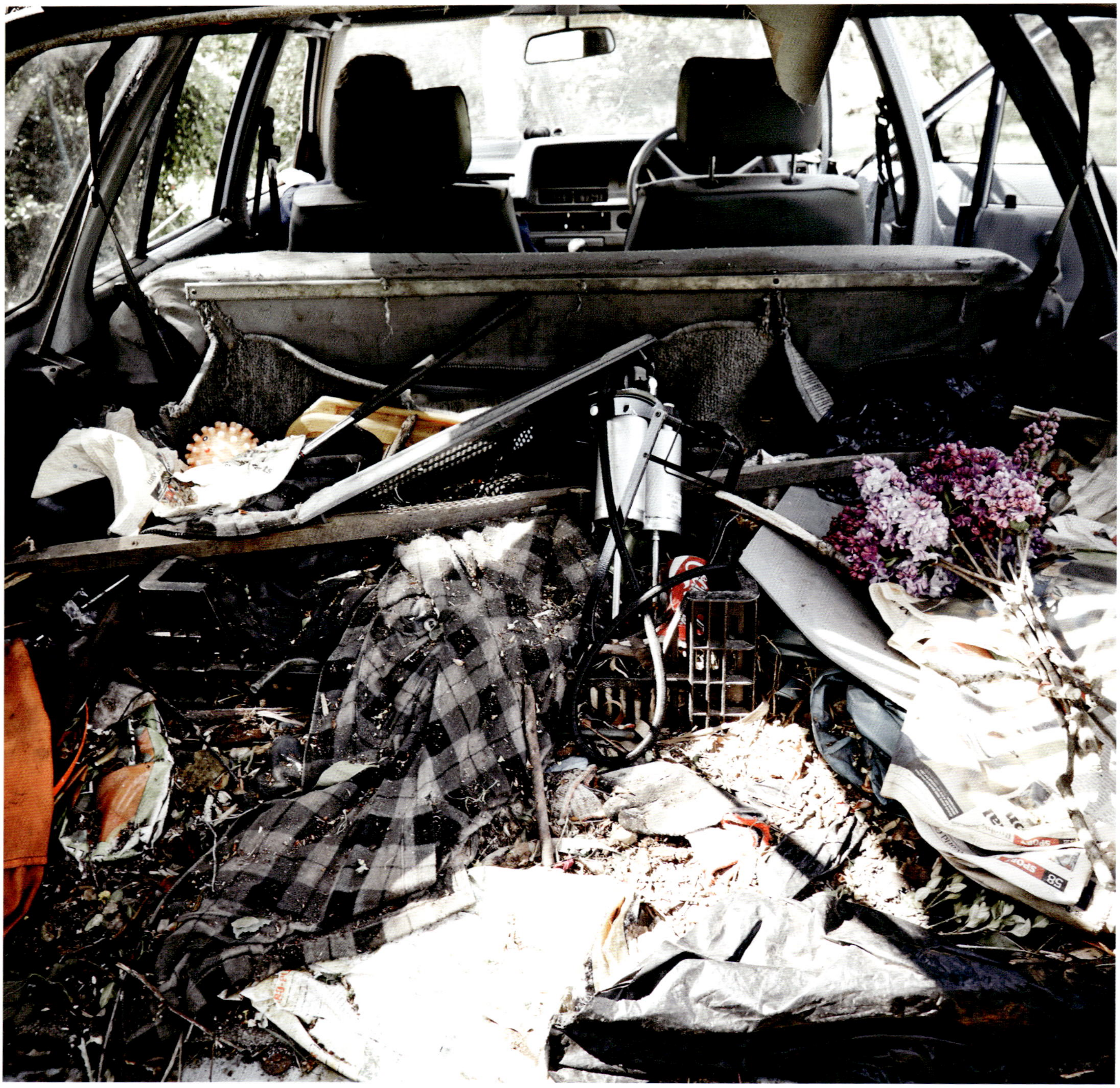

THE VERY FIRST FARM.

Wayne and his wife Alison consider themselves the 'caretakers' of their 10-acre property in a small town on the historic Bells Line of Road, an arterial road west of Sydney. Both left their demanding jobs in finance in Corporate Sydney in order to 'grow' their family in a way that allowed for school pick-ups, supervised homework and more time spent together. And they are reaping what they have sown, with one of their sons recently qualifying as a doctor of Medicine and the other a practitioner and tutor in Exercise Physiology.

It was one of Wayne's final appointments in finance that became the catalyst for what would become his life in flowers. He had been employed to undertake a forensic reconstruction of a wholesale flower business, and through the course of his investigations found himself at the Sydney Flower Market at the 'crack of dawn' in an atmosphere of 'exhilaration', he says. For Wayne the frenetic and direct approach of the marketers epitomised grassroots commerce and exemplified the origins of trade.

He became so intoxicated by the market environment that he left the corporate financial world to become a grower and wholesaler working in partnership on a large-scale flower business for over a decade. In this time he and his then business partner grew tulips, planting 480,000 bulbs in their first crop in the Southern Highlands of New South Wales.

At the conclusion of the partnership Wayne and Alison felt compelled toward a more direct approach to flower trading, and eleven years ago they found the property that reflected this new focus. Ten acres in one of the world's top ten microclimates: a unique ecosystem that sees prolific rainfall, making it ideal for agriculture; and a place of great beauty where they could grow and then sell their own produce. For over a decade now they have been contentedly working in the most ancient form of trade, whereby the individual assists nature through toil, producing a yield to be traded to the market.

‡

A few short years ago I got my driver's licence, many years too late and after an embarrassing number of attempts, and I bought a very small red car. Through my work with notable Sydney theatre designer Alice Babidge and theatre director Benedict Andrews, I came to the attention of Tiffany Moulton. Tiffany was a beautiful former Australian Ballet dancer who worked for the Sydney Theatre Company in the capacity of philanthropy executive. Despite the perverse size of my car (particularly for a florist) and my lack of proven flower work, she bizarrely saw fit to offer me the job of doing the flowers for an event at the Theatre Company. It was my big break in flowers and the catalyst for my first farm visit. Through her work Tiff gave wings to many artists, but, tragically, her life was cut short. In February 2014, as I arranged hundreds and hundreds of fragrant white garden roses upon her casket on the main stage of the Sydney Theatre Company, I thought about how our first meeting was imbued with great privilege and our last with unmitigated honour.

‡

In order to realise my grand ambitions for that first Theatre Company job I spoke with many of the growers at the flower market – where I am now known to most as 'doc' (at the time I was 'who's that one with the tattoo?', at best). I tried with very little in the way of inducement to get them to part with their best blooms and to share with me the unique and exceptional elements that I sensed they were withholding.

Across the board my attempts were met with ambivalence … as is to be expected, I must have appeared something of an 'upstart'. I have since learnt that there is an honour code between the growers and the florists, which is based on loyalty, consistency and admiration – and I had not yet paid my dues. Perhaps it was that he recognised my passion and ambition, more probably it was generosity, but Wayne invited me to THE FARM! I scrambled to lock in the date and time, lest he change his mind! And a few days later I visited my first flower farm in pursuit of blooms for my first big job. I will never forget this kindness nor the absolute beauty of Wayne and Alison's rambling, captivating property.

‡

The couple had known the previous owners socially, and in the time between entertaining the notion of buying and actually buying the farm they had occasion to spend the night on the property. The following day the majestic quality of the morning light and the thick mist that seemed to blanket the land brought them to their decision and they bought the lot – the farm, the house, the tractor, the truck and the stand at the flower market. The former owners, accomplished flower growers themselves, had passed on to Wayne and Alison a property that was both abundant and diverse, vowing upon their departure that all the land had been planted to grow elements that could be sold and grown again.

In their first year on the property the new owners were continuously astounded by the variety and beauty of the erupting seasons. In their turn *Hydrangea paniculata*, mock orange, daphne, lilac, dogwood, pieris and cherry blossom would flower. At other times hellebore, camellia, lily-of-the-valley, stachyurus, tulip tree, and plum, apricot and peach trees would bloom. Innumerable varieties of foliage and vast amounts of viburnum offered shade for the more delicate flowers. Over the years the keepers of this botanical standard have added fig trees, guelder rose, and more dogwood, laurel, camellia and hydrangea … and this does not constitute an exhaustive list. Their land is uniquely undulant and rambling, it is truly breathtaking for its bulk of mysterious and precious flowers and foliage.

It is a treasured picture: the very first farm that I visited in my capacity as a proper florist, on a proper job in an improper car.

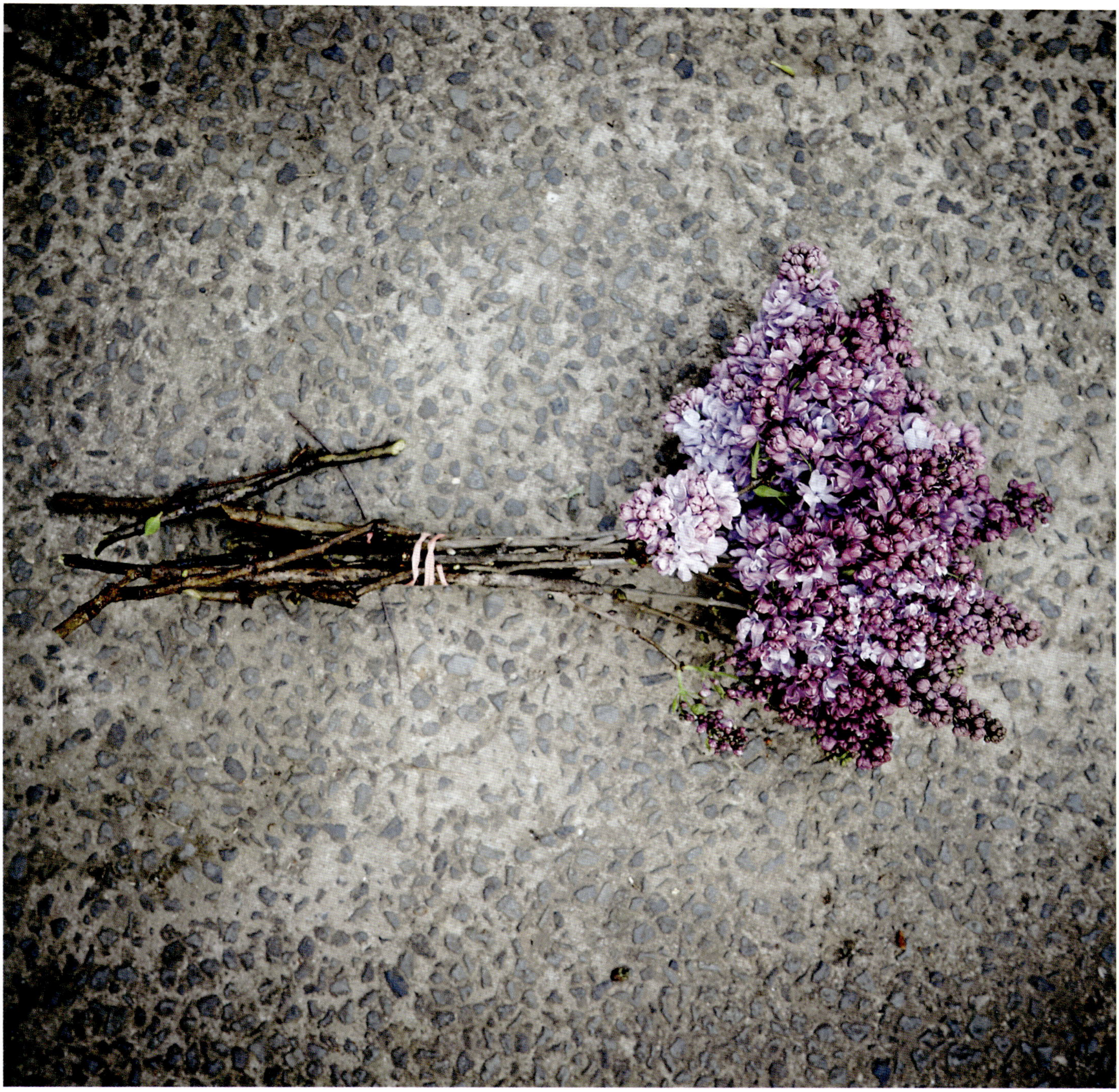

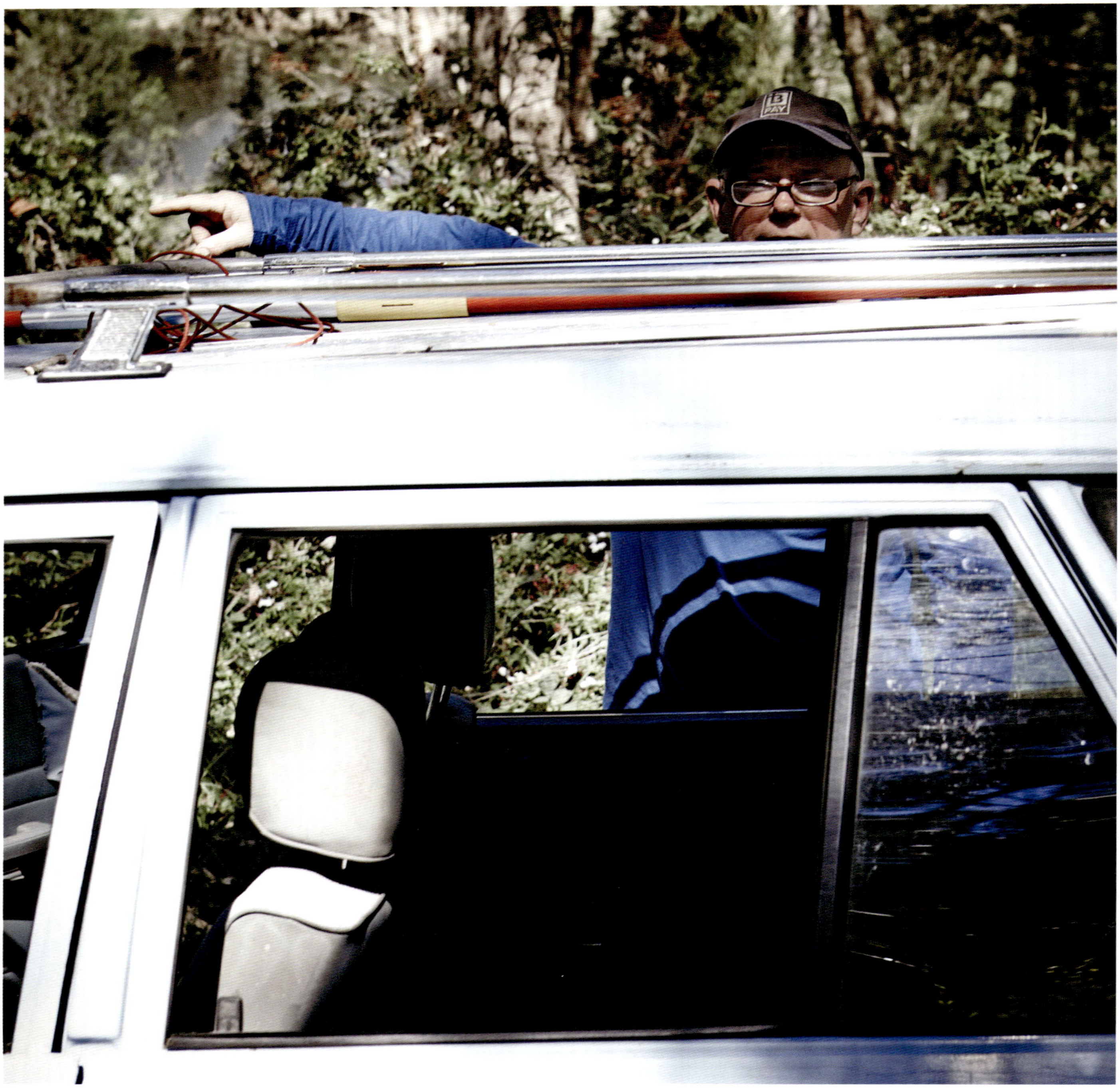
B PAY

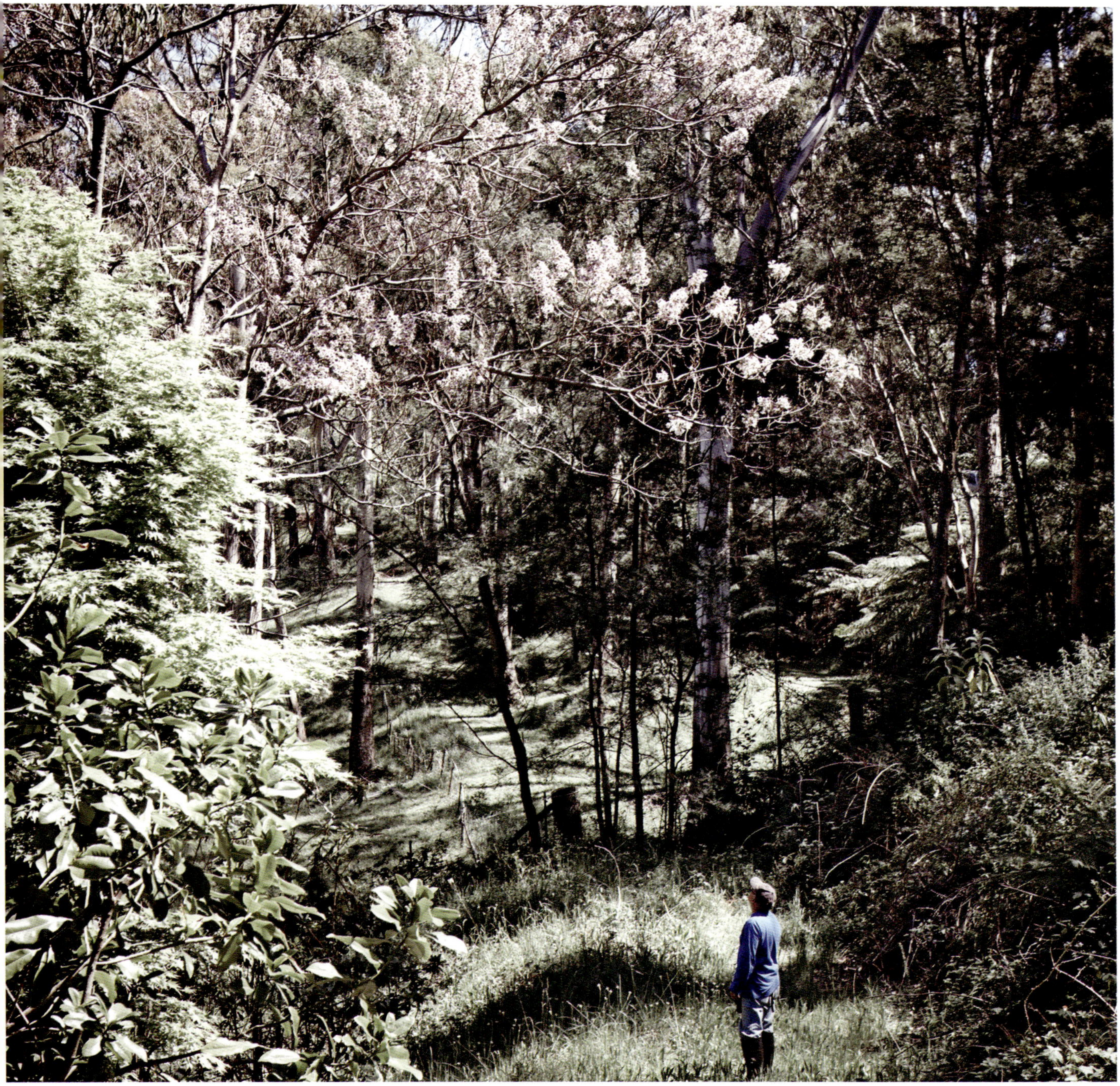

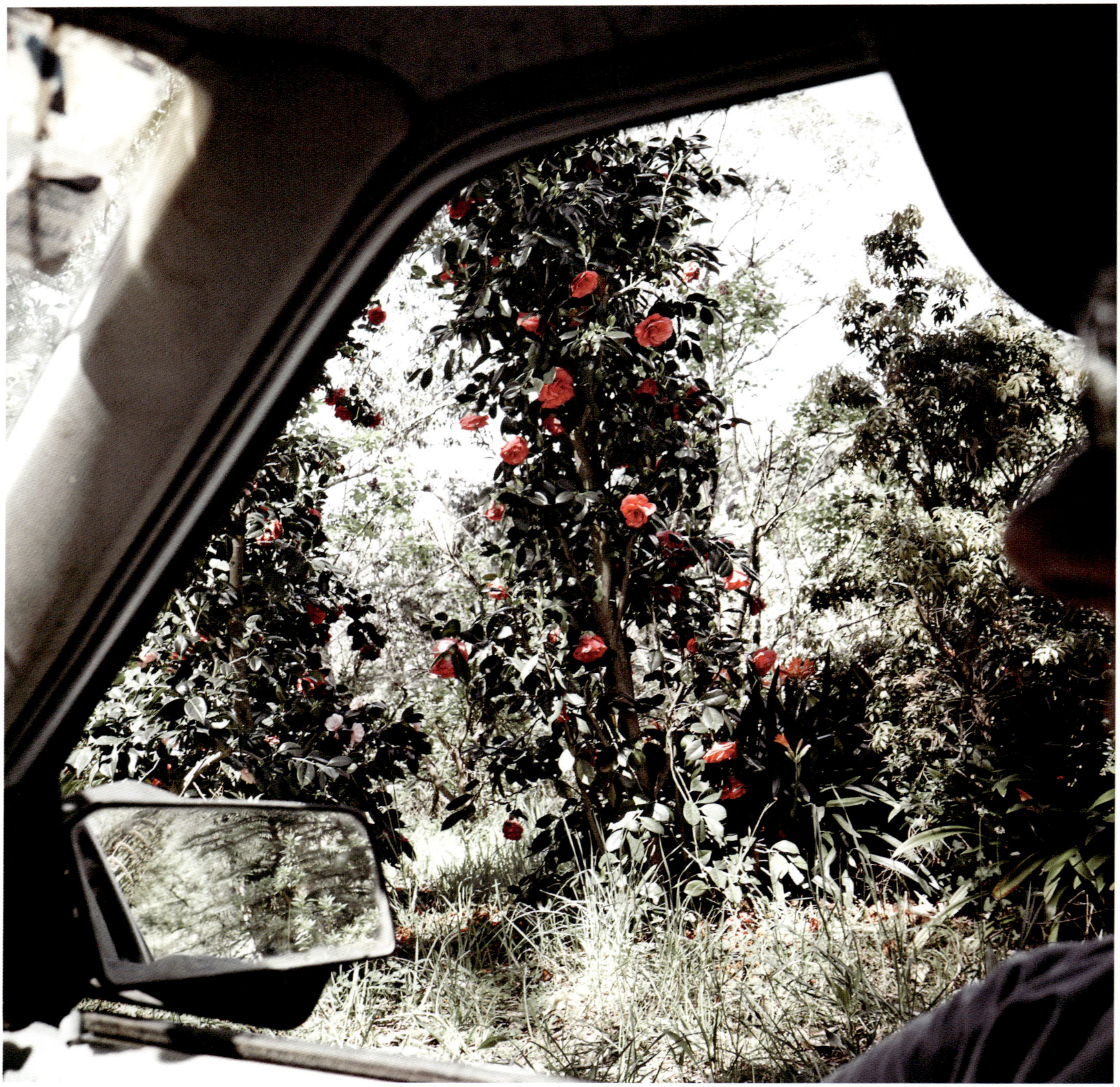

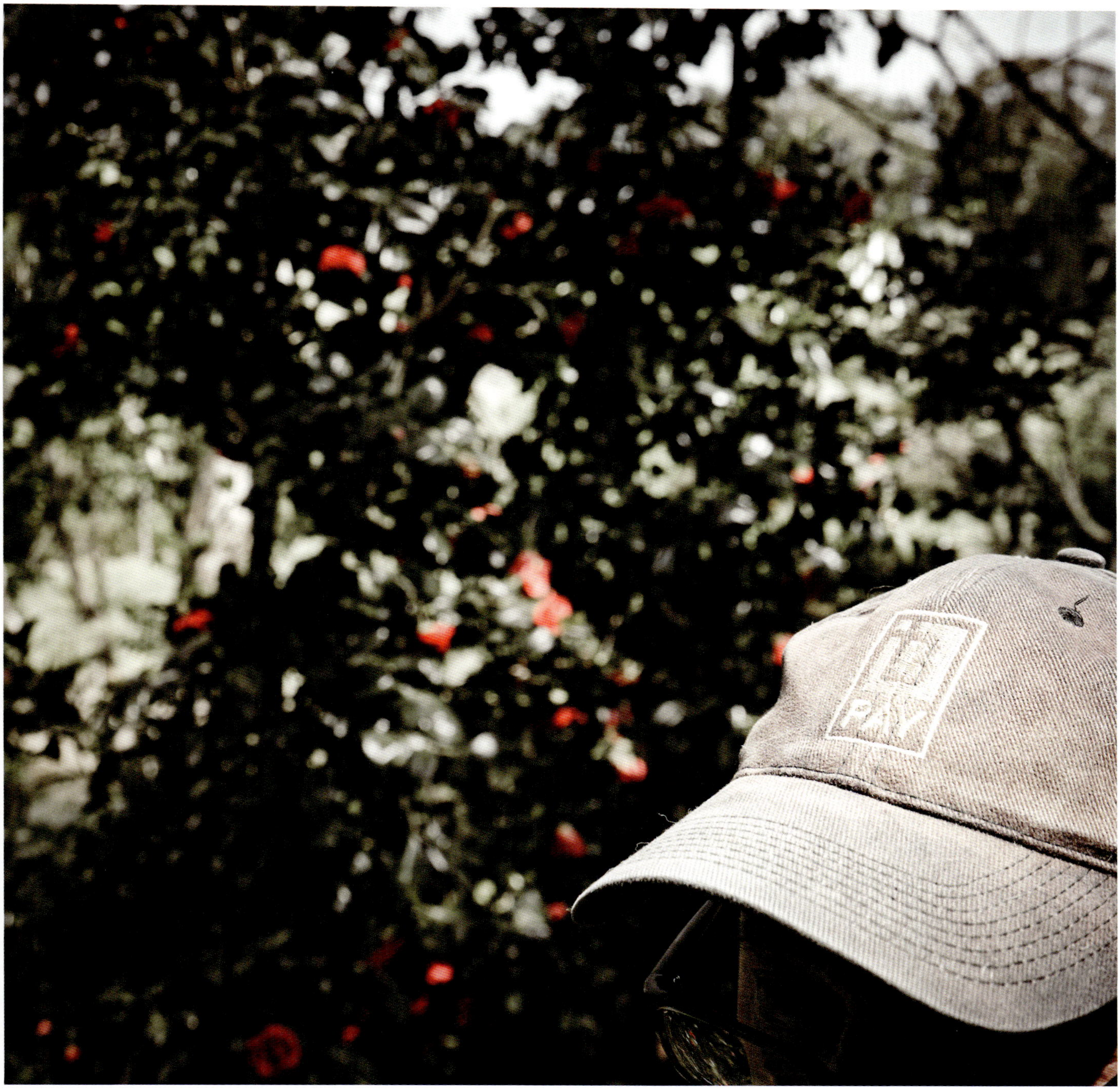
RAY

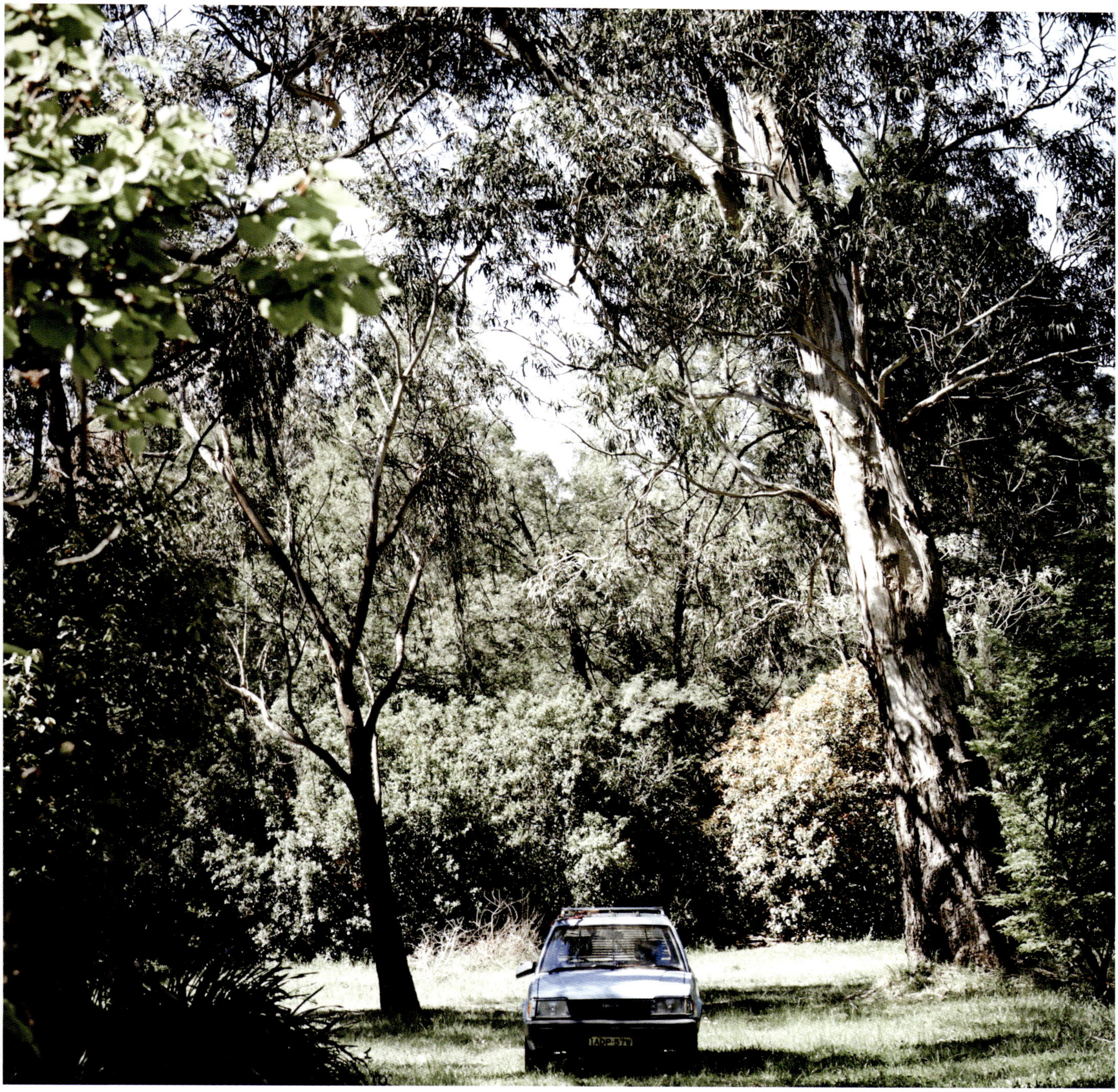

PHIL'S FARM

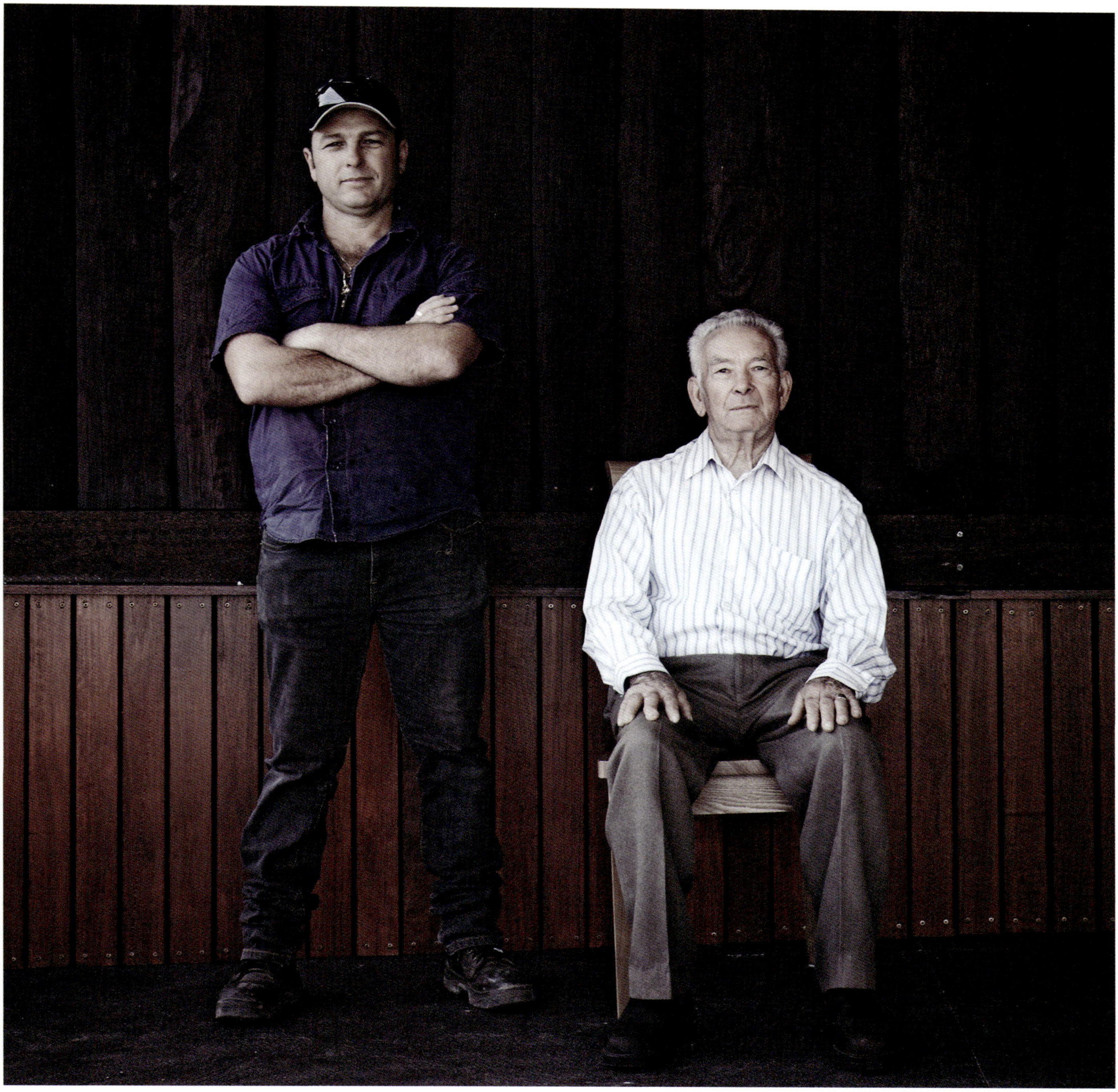

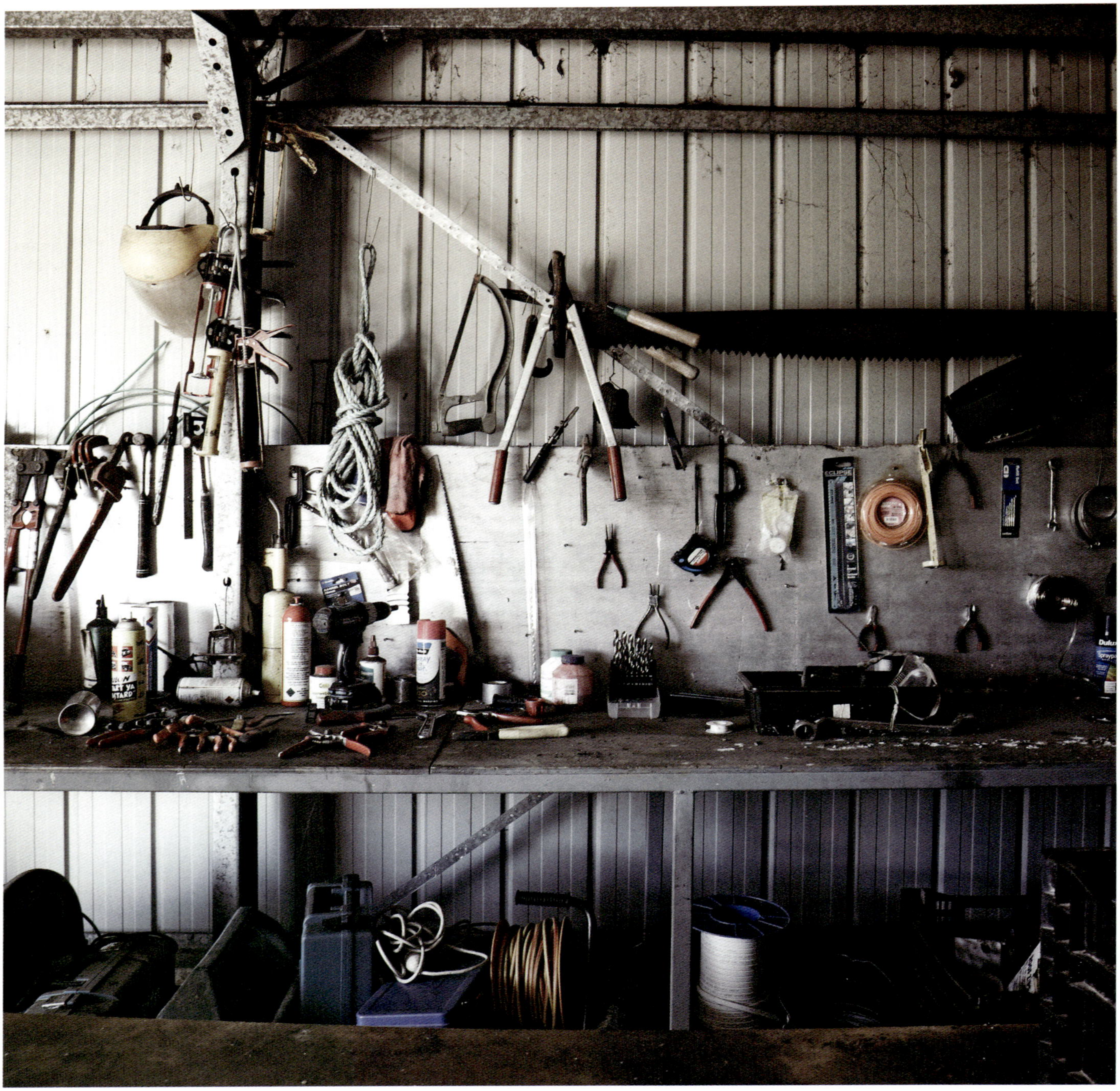

ON THIS LAND, AMONG THE LILIES.

Phil's flower stand is situated at the outermost position of an arterial lane in the flower market. His father, Raphaeli, in defiance of his age, is a constant at the mouth of the stand, each morning welcoming and bidding farewell to the stream of regulars whose orders have been filled, bundled and labelled. 'Ray' has been a market grower for more than five decades and I doubt he has ever missed a market day. The way Ray pronounces my name is identical to the way my Italian grandfather did: between his accent and the figs, I am transported. Flowers and manners take me back – generations back.

It is pre-dawn and it's cold, the kind of cold unique to flower markets in the winter the world over; an enormous 'shed' on a concrete block brimming with water and buckets and all manner of flora. I start at Phil, setting the tone of our tri-weekly interactions: What's around? What looks incredible? What's coming on? Can you cut that taller? Can I get that wider?

'Why don't you come up to the farm,' he asks, 'and have a look for yourself?'

With this offer the atmosphere of the morning develops a gilt diffusion and in my fancy I am proper inner circle – I've been called – I am a woman of the flowers. Anyone can get into the markets (a sore point, as the Sydney Flower Market is one of the few in the world that permits the public entry without at least the concession of allowing the professional buyers priority) but not everyone is invited to The Farm. Or at least I don't think so ... Only the serious ones? I've never checked the vetting process. However, the invitation has the effect of an appointment on me, it gives me a sense of being 'seen'.

It is my proclivity to want what is difficult to attain and it is passion and generosity that has Phil showing me, in a winding logic, the elements that I might choose from: tall beams of hydrangea foliage, figs with architectural limbs, impeccably upright kale, camellia lunging under the weight of its flowers. Hellebores await their moment while seedlings and saplings lie in neat and manicured rows for their season.

I'm always asking Bob to tell me stories about the flower market before my time ... about who was there and how today's florists and growers figure in her knowledge of the ancestral thread. Through her recollections I create images in my mind of the way it all used to work. According to Bob there has been a great deal of passing the baton.

Phil's father Ray arrived in Sydney by boat from his birthplace in Italy in 1961. As Phil tells it, his father got off the boat and travelled to Ryde, a suburb to the northwest of the city centre, to work with an uncle growing the 'old-fashioned' flowers: asters, daisies and poppies. Eventually his labour on his uncle's farm would afford Ray both the finances and experience to buy and farm his own land in a rural suburb a little further afield, but again to the northwest of the centre of Sydney. Here Ray and his wife, Rosa, grew their family, vegetables, roses, carnations, November lilies, sweet William, chrysanthemums and countless other blooms.

It was on this land, among the lilies, that Ray's gold signet ring with a 'beautiful' nude woman etched into its plate would be forever lost in the frenzy of harvest. The loss of the ring, a gift from Rosa, was deeply felt and so she had another made to replace it. The result is the handsome jewel piece that can be seen on Ray's hand in pictorial reproduction in these pages. He explains to me that while the craftsmanship and make of the replacement ring are of a high quality, the 'woman' (the sketch of the female form) has nothing on the one he lost.

‡

The familial mandarin tree that flanks their home is, Phil explains, the one that the kids eat from between laps of the property – the one thing I can't have: his wife would 'kill him'. Heaving with fruit and shaped like the 'first tree' that we all drew in our childhoods, I can picture just one of its many boughs spread the length of my wooden dining table. I can imagine my dinner guests furnished with little pots of smooth vanilla bean panna cotta enveloped by the considerable scent of the mandarin rind and the ambience of plucking the fruit from the branch; peeling its bright skin and taking segments between spoonfuls of the sweet cream. I am told no.

But in the end he concedes.

‡

The idea of including a crude, organic element in the creation of a meal is not new, it follows in the tradition of grapes or figs with cheese – why not elaborate upon this convention? Why not a whole branch of pears with an oversized wheel of d'affinois? From wherever you are reading this, your options for acquiring such a branch will be idiosyncratic or particular to your location. Some will have the option to wander down the yard and choose a branch at leisure, while others may call upon the gardens of in-laws or grandparents and twist arms. Some will have the option to travel to farming towns where a visit will be met with handmade signs and honesty boxes – proof that visitors play a vital role in the local economy. Where one finds boxes of this and that fruit, flowers and vegetables, one might also find growers and branches!
    Alternatively, in most towns and cities across the planet where there's a proliferation of regional growers' markets, there may be no need to drive into the country. I recommend sidling up to the person standing behind the boxes of mandarins at your local growers' market and as the friendship burgeons, lay it on them. Like I did with Phil.

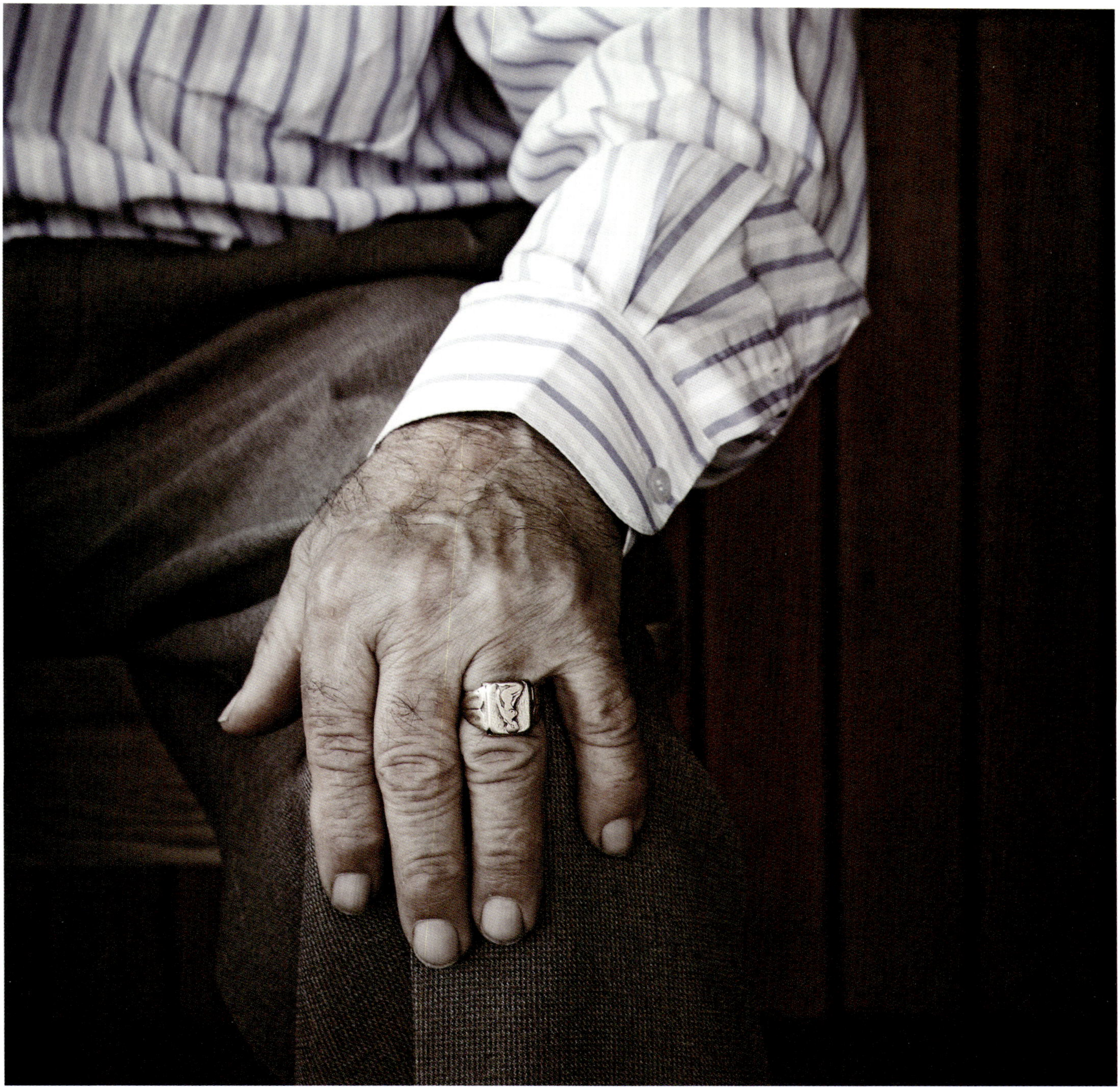

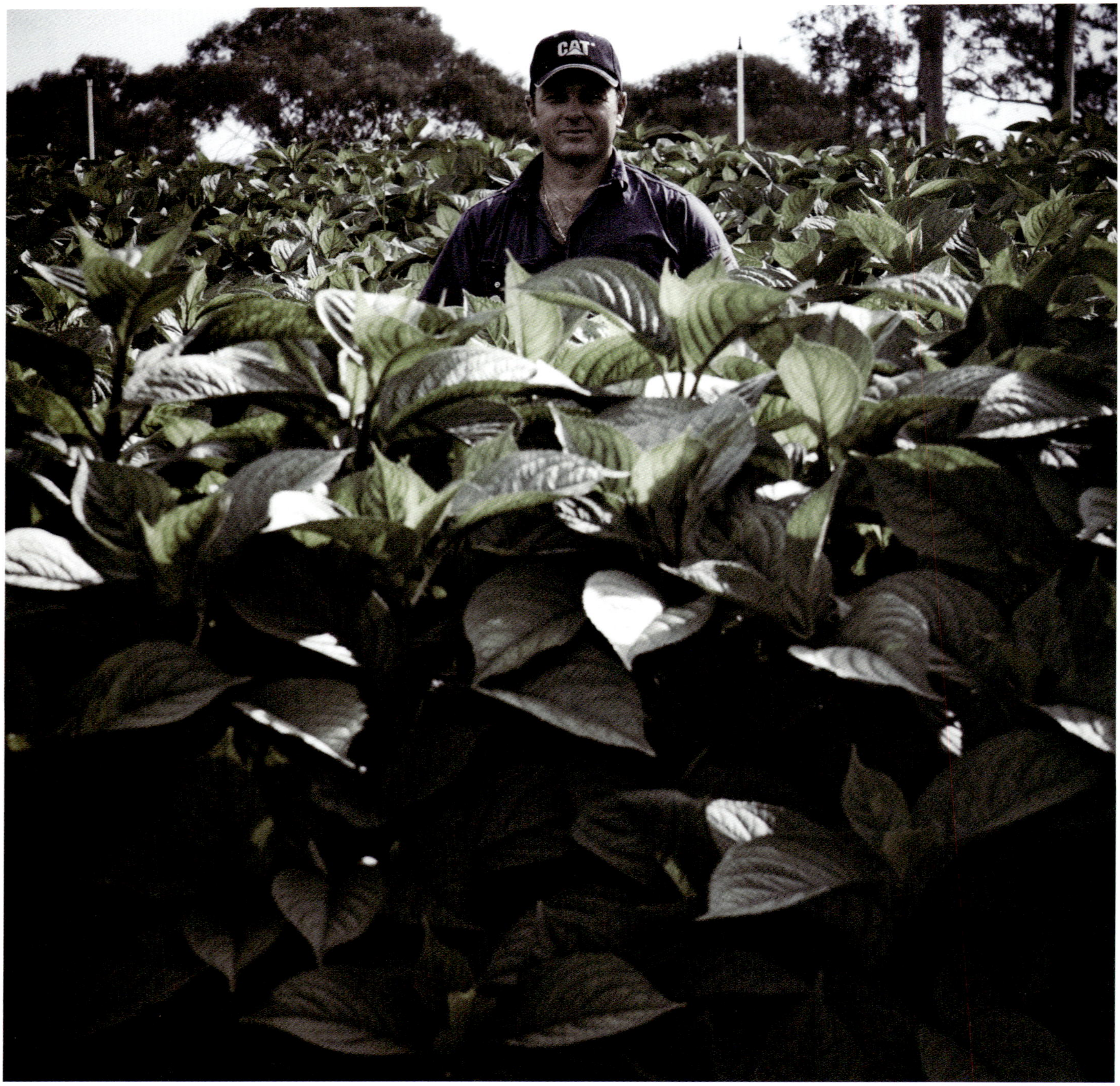
CAT

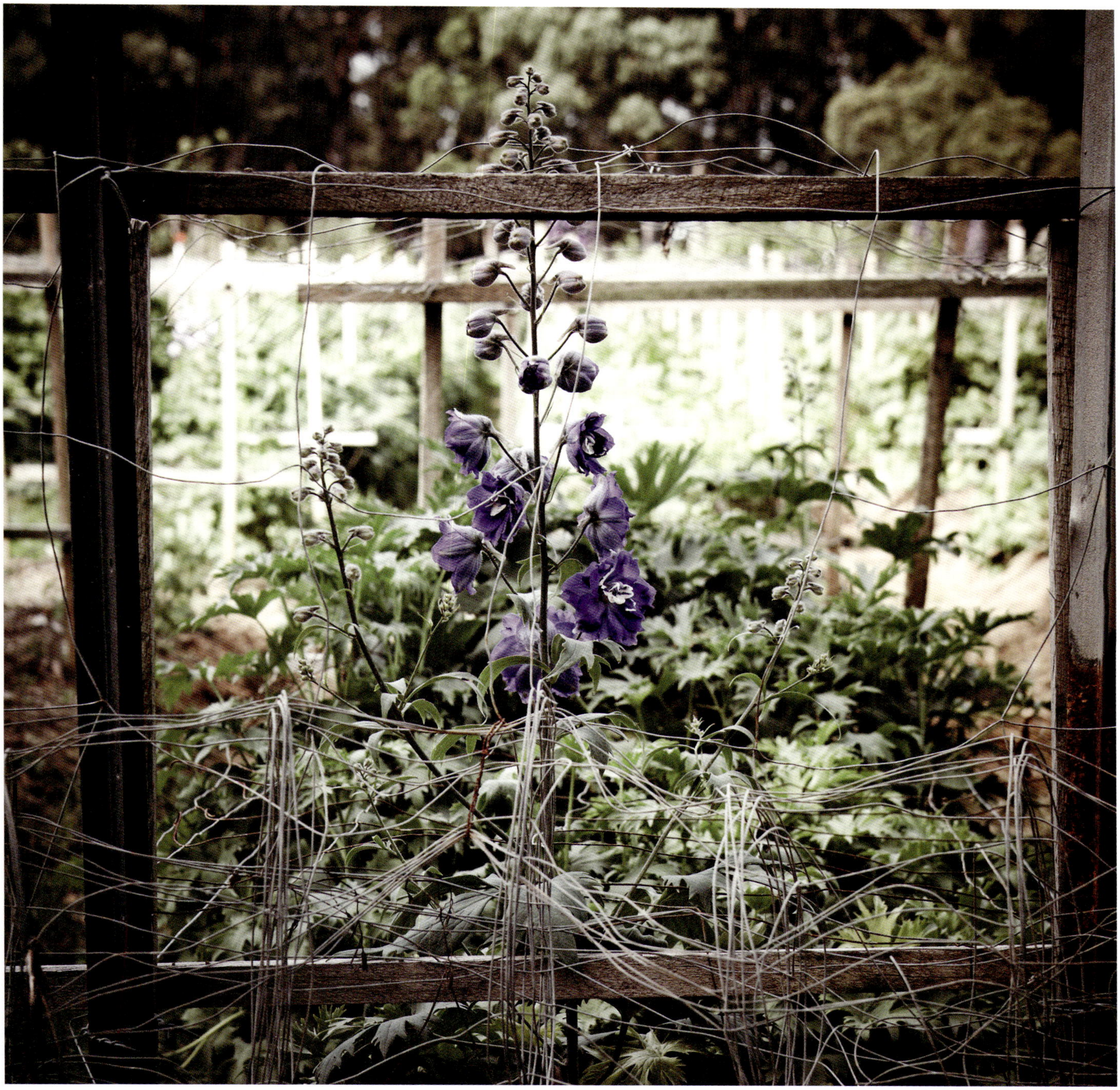

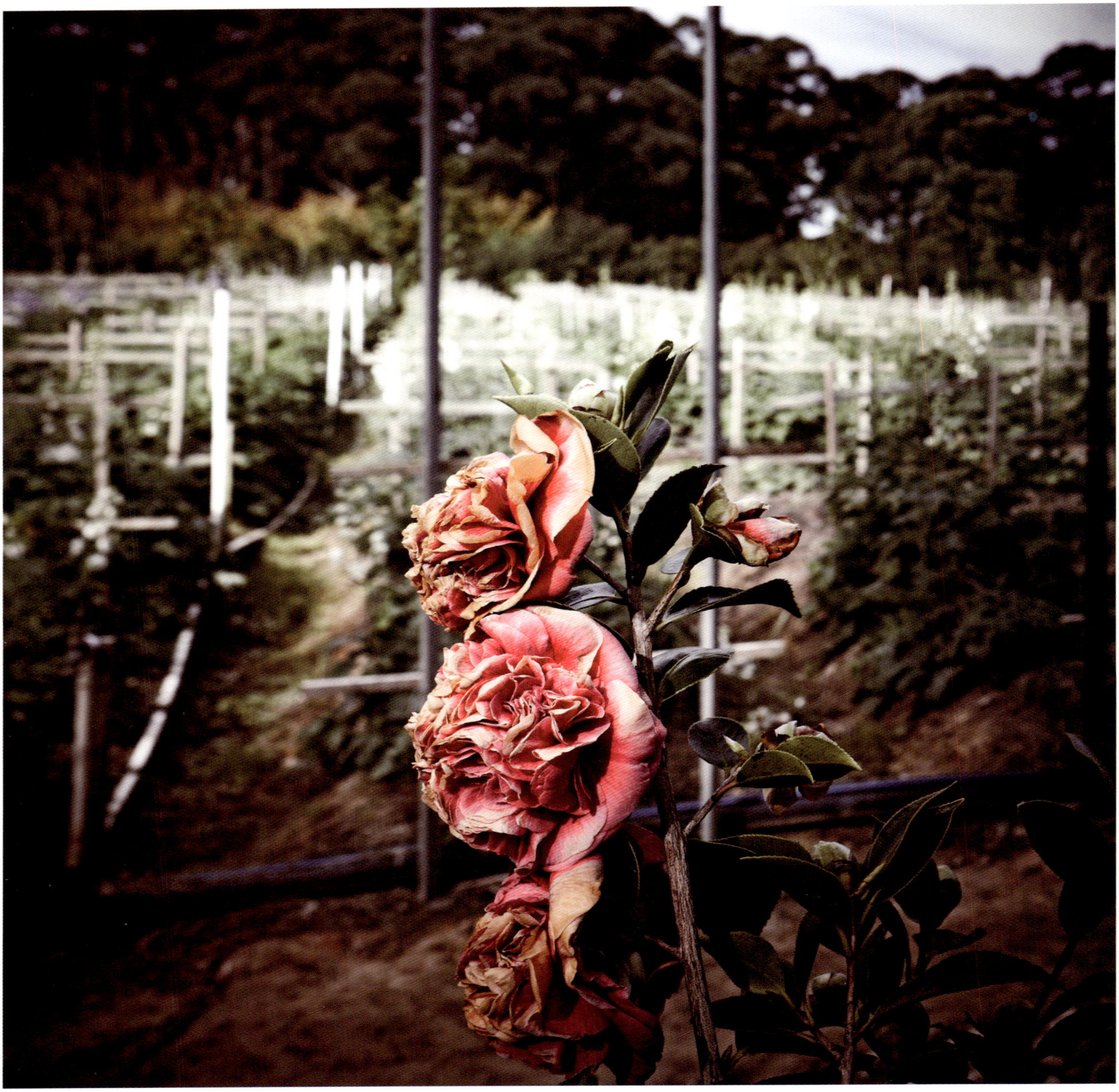

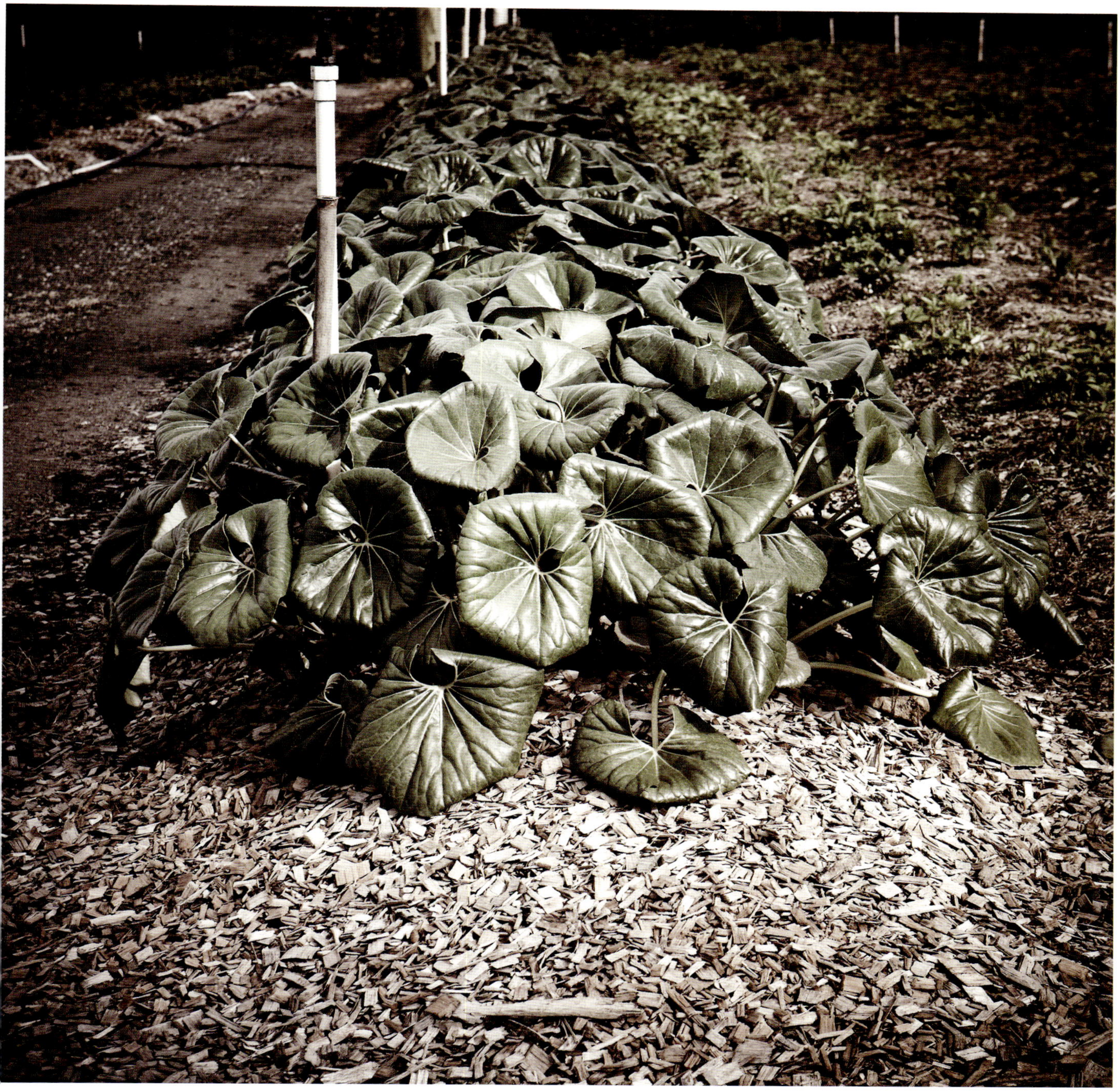

SARINA'S FARM

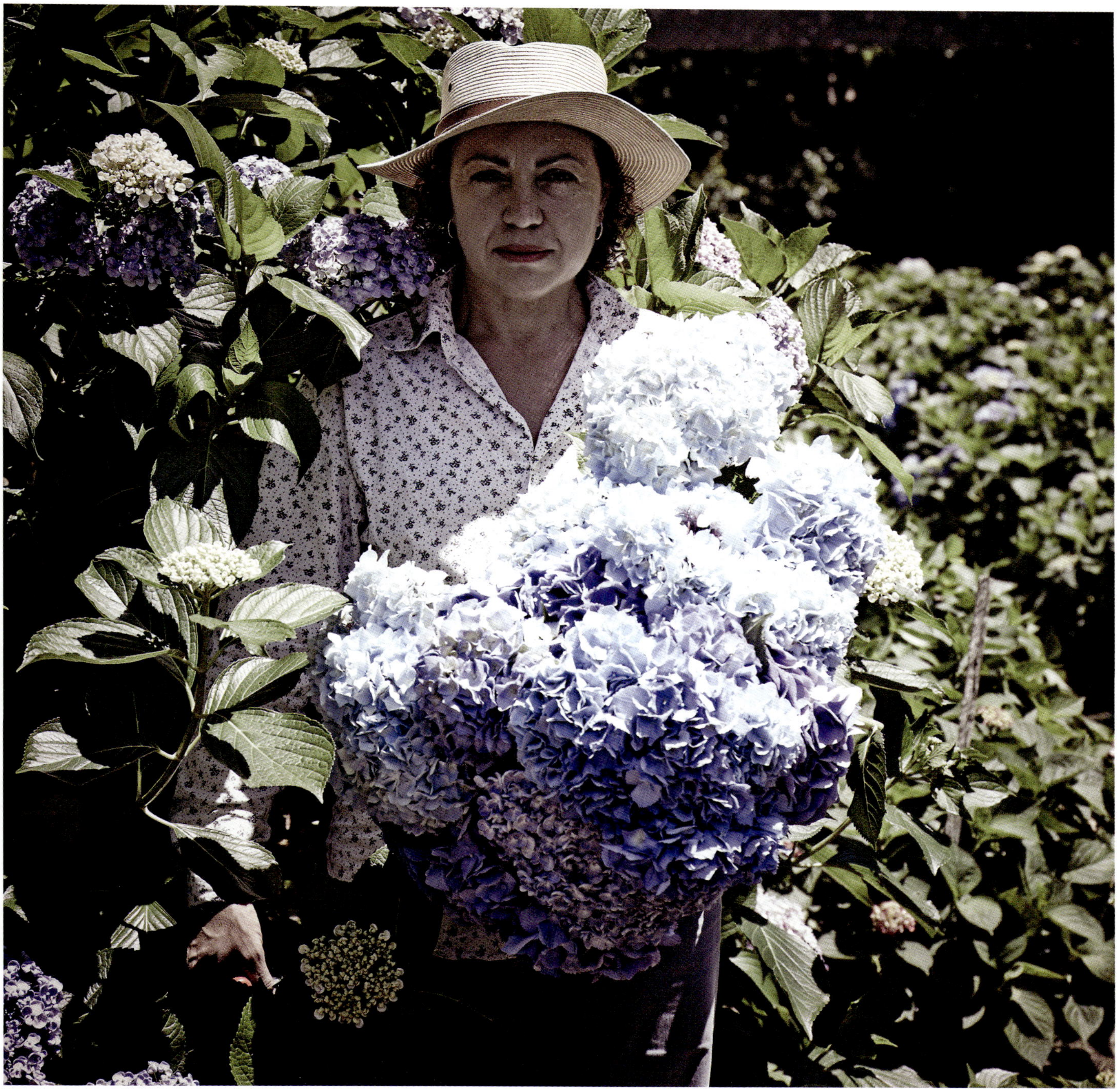

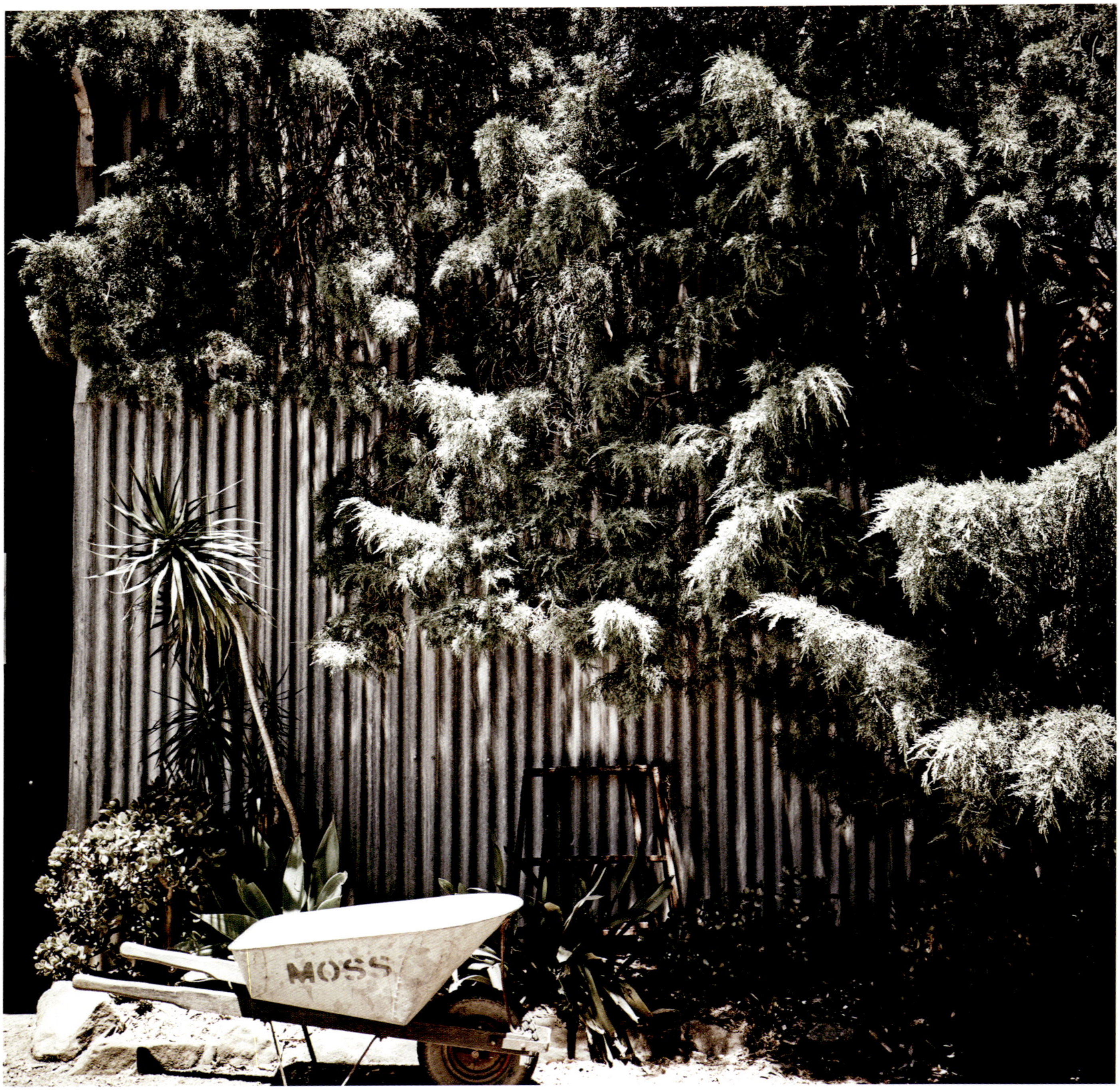
MOSS

WHAT? SHOULD I PUT MYSELF IN A GLASS CABINET?

Sarina's mother, Domenica, and her father, Francesco, eloped: Domenica was just fifteen years and nine months and Francesco was a youth of twenty years. They were in love …

When Domenica's father, Giuseppe, found out about the marriage, he immersed himself in a period of mourning – wearing only black for more than a year. When others recognised his grief and enquired who had died, he would answer, 'my daughter'.

Giuseppe had travelled to Australia from Italy in the early 1950s and became a share-farmer of citrus in Kenthurst, a suburb northwest of Sydney. After a number of years of hard work, Giuseppe was able to raise the passage for his wife and three daughters to join him and start their new life as a family. At the family's reunion on Sydney's foreshore, Giuseppe discovered that Domenica was pregnant … his loathing of Francesco intensified.

By 1958 Giuseppe had raised enough money to buy 21 acres of land in Glenorie – a twenty-minute drive from the citrus farm in Kenthurst. For a number of years the family lived and worked in the property's only dwelling, a packing shed 3 metres square, until the couple were able to build a simple home on their land. The previous owners of the property had grown passionfruit and peaches, and Giuseppe continued to farm these varieties while adding vegetables across all of the seasons.

Around this time Domenica's husband Francesco arrived in Australia, and he and his young family moved to Wangaratta, in northeast Victoria – a good seven to eight hours drive from her father and the farm in Glenorie.

‡

In Wangaratta the young couple – now with two infant daughters in tow – began share-farming tobacco. After two years of hard work on the farm, a copper boiler in the laundry of their humble lodgings caught fire and their home and all of their belongings burnt to the ground. With no other choice, the couple returned to Domenica's family in Glenorie, working hard again until they could put a deposit on a 10-acre property in Kenthurst. Again, in that property's only dwelling – a packing shed – they both lived and worked, but this time the rock-burdened bushland and the packing shed were their own.

In order to make the land workable, Francesco had to dynamite boulders and move countless stones – Sarina and her sister Maria were in constant demand by their father as 'stone couriers'. In place of the stones he planted tomatoes, cauliflower, cabbage and capsicum, among other vegetables. In those early years on the farm Francesco would cultivate the rocky earth with a horse and plough.

Of the sisters Sarina was the 'tomboy' … a wild, energetic and robust child. She worked with her father, lugging this and that, while also attending the local primary school. Both of Sarina's parents worked extremely hard on the farm raising their two daughters who, in time, were joined by two younger siblings, Angela and Rose. When Sarina recalled for me her father asking her to accompany him in the early hours to the Sydney Markets in the laden truck – so that she might talk or sing to him to keep him awake – we both became emotional. She described how, often, he would be up all night packing vegetables and loading them on the truck after a long day working on the farm.

But his hard work was about to bear fruit in the form of carnations.

‡

One day, possibly in a stupor of exhaustion, Francesco was struck by a determination to grow carnations. He prepared the land and planted sixty thousand of them. They sold like mad and he was able to acquire another 15 acres nearby and plant a hundred thousand more … again the carnations sold like mad. And then another 11 acres in the next suburb, where he continued to cultivate carnations by the thousands, and they too sold like mad. It went on like this for many years: the family worked hard and grew prolific amounts of beautiful, fragrant carnations – the flowers became their fortune. In the mid 1980s, however, the popularity of carnations waned greatly, and so Francesco decided to grow eucalyptus and various other types of foliage, which were becoming fashionable in cut-flower arranging at the time.

‡

A decade later, on a family holiday to Sicily in 1978, Sarina met and fell in love with an Italian police officer, Gaetano. After a two-year engagement of penned and telephonic courting, the young couple married in Sydney and returned to Tèrmini Vigghiaturi, a municipality of the province of Messina in Sicily. Soon they had two children – a daughter, Marlena, and a son, Domenico – and the family lived happily in Sicily for thirteen years. As the children were growing, the couple foresaw better opportunities for their education and future employment in Australia: this foresight – along with concerns about Francesco's increasing back problems (a result of many years of hard toil) – led to the family returning to Australia.

For the first few years Gaetano and Sarina worked with Francesco on the properties growing at least five types of eucalyptus, as well as other foliage. But as with the carnations, again the market changed: there was an oversupply of leaves. The family decided that, while retaining some flowering eucalyptus, they would also begin to grow magnolia. A few years later, the young couple and Sarina's parents pooled their resources and purchased 11 acres in a neighbouring suburb, Arcadia, where they planted ten thousand magnolia trees. On other properties they began to grow viburnum and sunflowers, also in great quantities.

About fifteen years ago, Sarina and her father were researching something that would grow well under the dappled light of the enormous gum trees that loomed in every corner of their property in Arcadia – something that would contrast with magnolia's winter season. The answer came in the form of a powerful memory. Sarina remembered that when she was a child, her grandparents had a 20-metre-long, deep, profuse and high crop of hydrangeas that grew down one side of their house. In the winter her grandfather would prune 'the living daylights' out of them, leaving nothing but scrawny sticks poking out of the earth. But each spring was a revelation for Sarina ... the sticks would become stems reaching upward, often 5 metres or more, each loaded with large, shiny, thick leaves. Come summer, there would be enormous flower heads of stunning blue.

If I walked into Sarina's kitchen and saw her, her father, and her Herculean-statured son and farm manager 'Dom' taking espresso and biscotti with Mother Nature herself, it would not be enough to reason the breathtaking hydrangeas they produce yearly. Sarina tells me she will 'take it a bit easier' as she gets older, unlike her father. She, apparently, would never say, as her eighty-year-old father does: 'What? Should I put myself in a glass cabinet?'

Sarina ... Never.

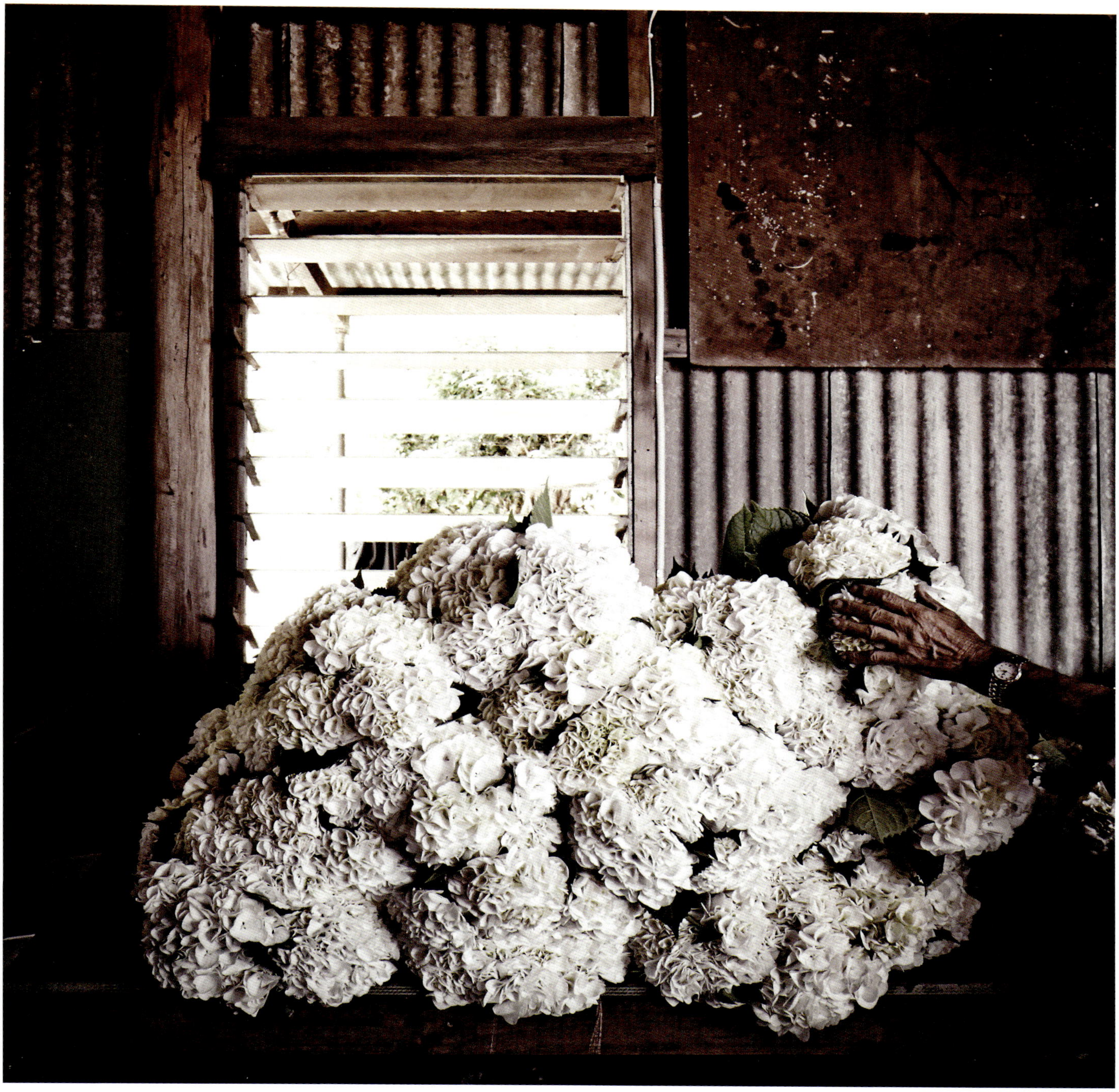

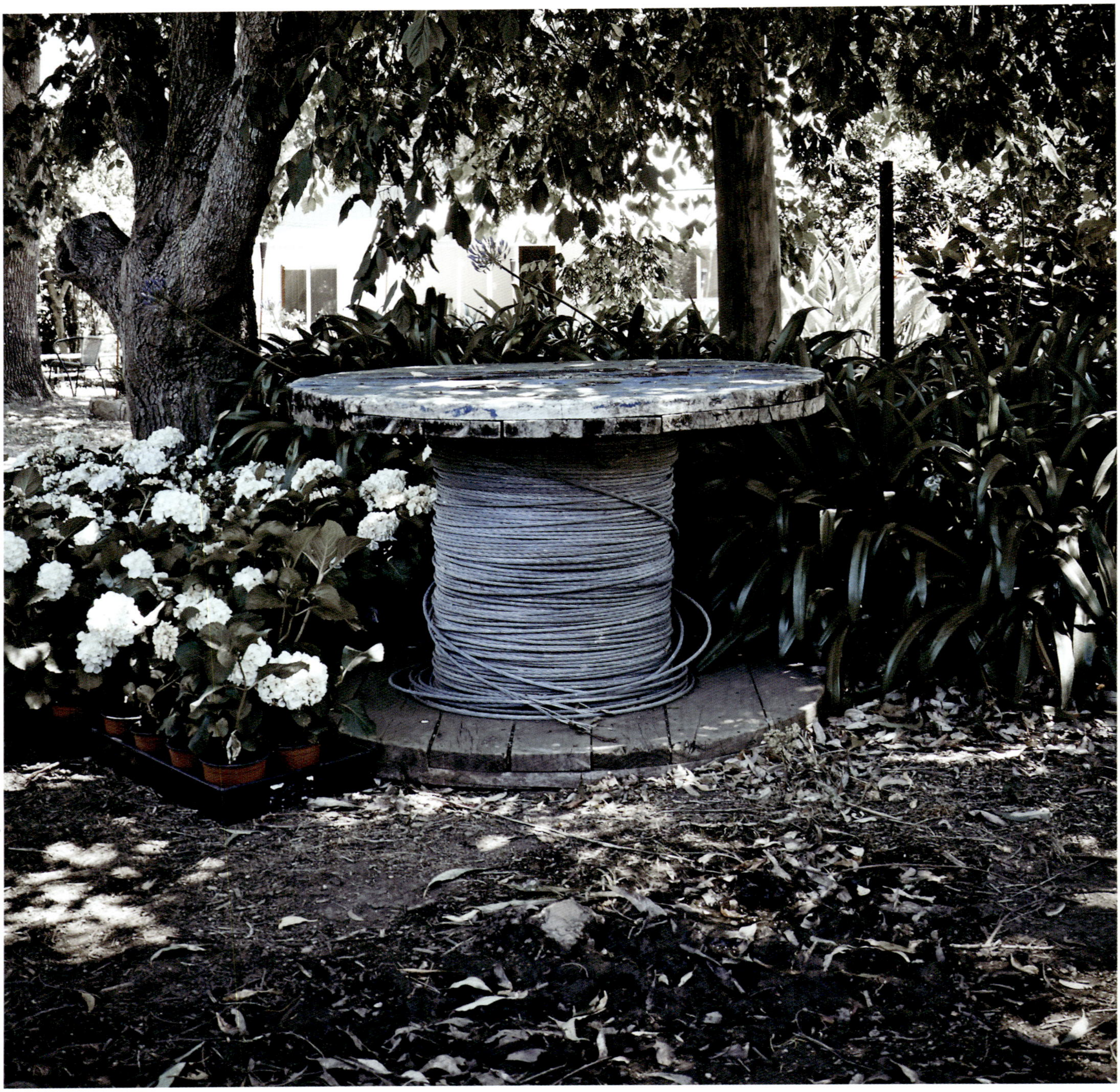

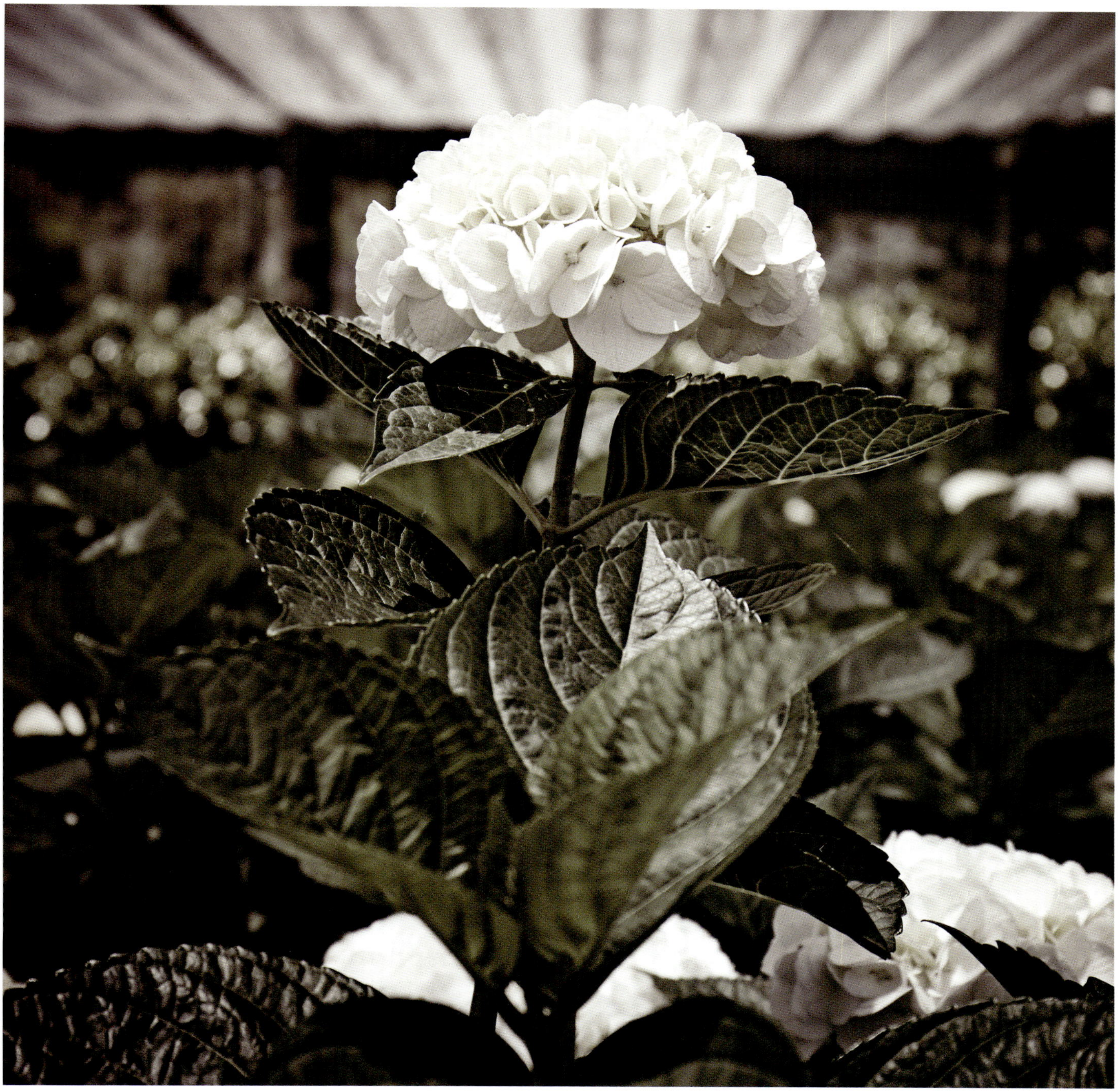

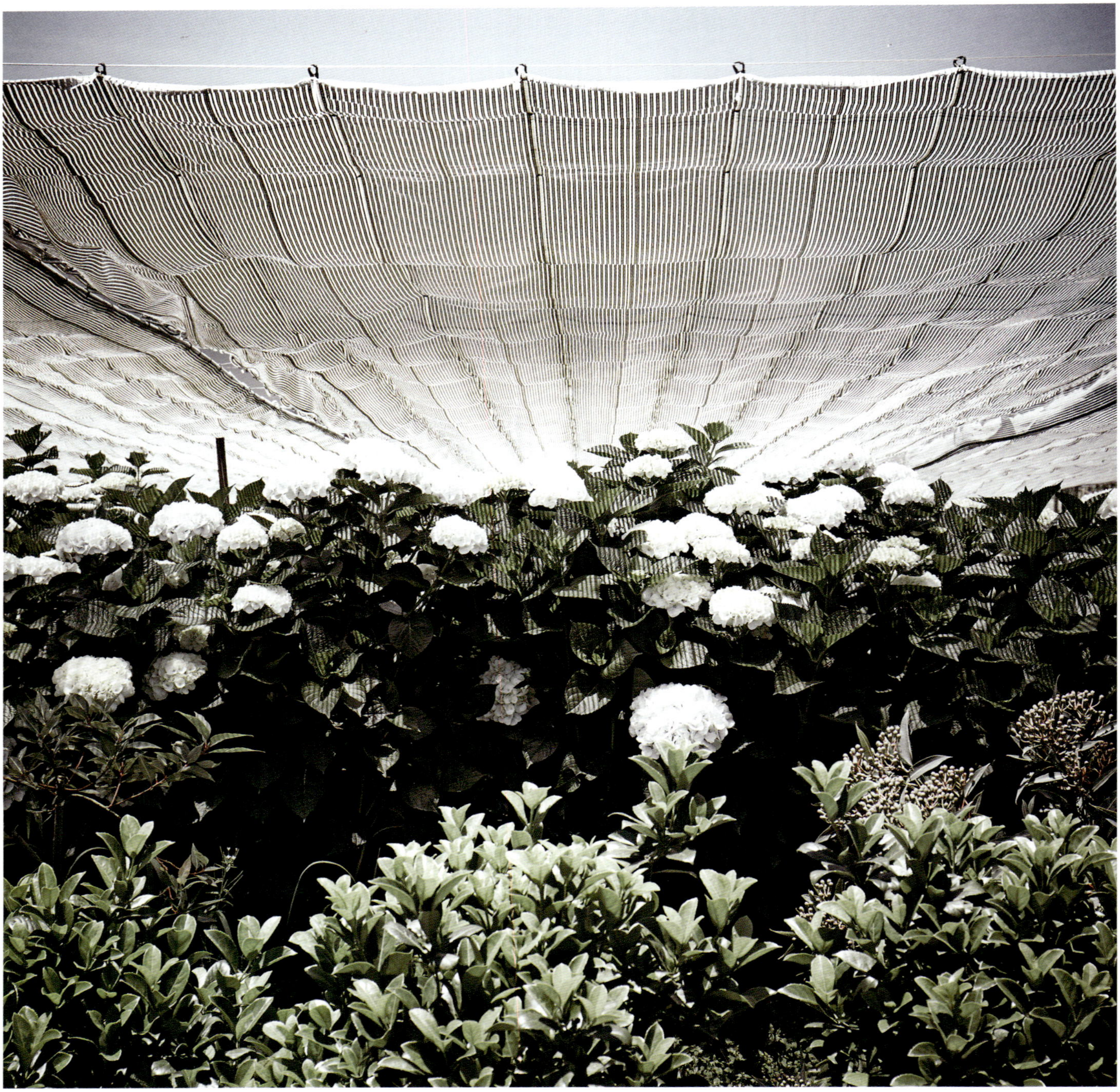

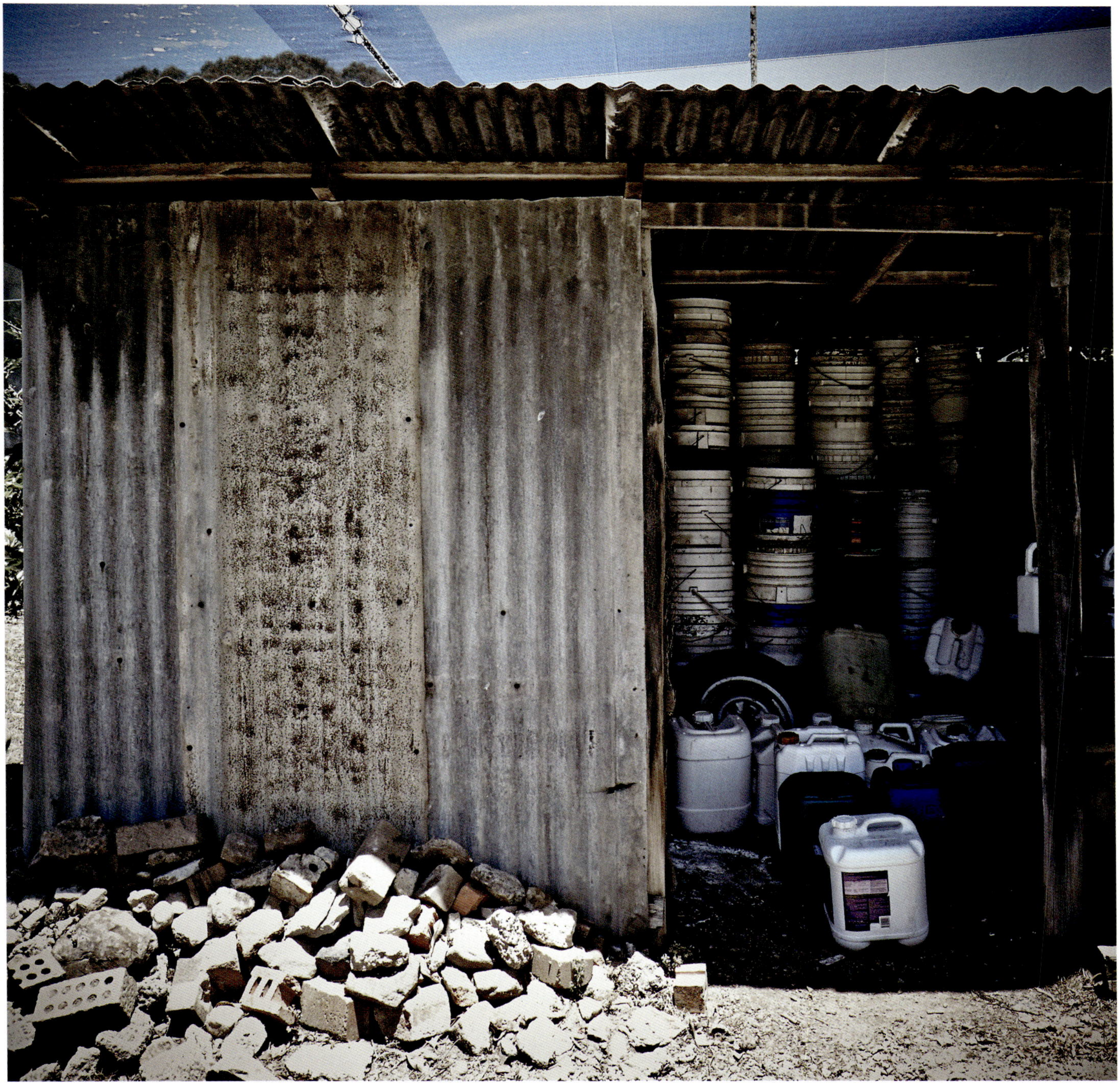

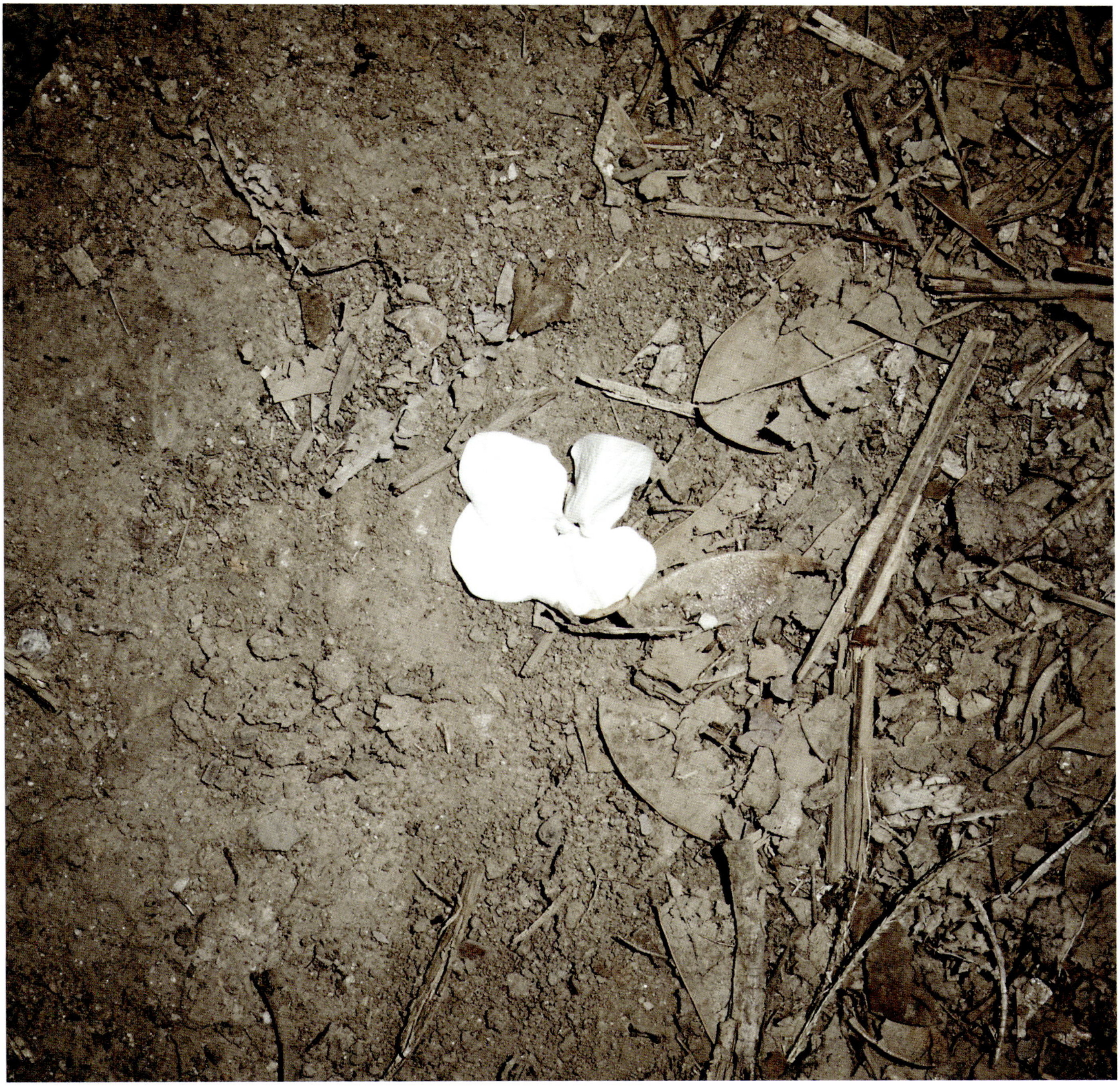

THERE IS SOMETHING ESSENTIAL AND AUTHENTIC ABOUT TURNING A SEED AND EARTH INTO A THING THAT FEEDS THE STOMACH AND EYE. THOSE WHOSE THOUGHT AND TOIL ARE FIXED ON PROMOTING AND IMPROVING THE GROWTH OF A PLANT BY ATTENTION AND LABOUR ARE RARE — AND THE REWARD FOR THEIR EFFORT IS RARER STILL.

THE FLOWERS

THROUGH THE LOOKING GLASS, THE SEQUEL TO ALICE'S ADVENTURES IN WONDERLAND, WAS MY FAVOURITE BOOK AS A CHILD. THE FOLLOWING IS MY GARDEN OF LIVE FLOWERS.

ALICE WAS SO ASTONISHED THAT
SHE COULD NOT SPEAK FOR A MINUTE:
IT QUITE SEEMED TO TAKE HER BREATH AWAY.
AT LENGTH, AS THE TIGER-LILY ONLY WENT
ON WAVING ABOUT, SHE SPOKE AGAIN,
IN A TIMID VOICE — ALMOST IN A WHISPER.
'AND CAN ALL THE FLOWERS TALK?'
'AS WELL AS YOU CAN,' SAID THE TIGER-LILY.
'AND A GREAT DEAL LOUDER.'

LEWIS CARROLL, THROUGH THE LOOKING GLASS (1871), CHAPTER 2,
'THE GARDEN OF LIVE FLOWERS'

THE PICTORIAL GARDEN ROSE 'MOUNTAIN' AND INGRID'S HELLEBORES

—

LOOK AT THE FLOWERS. THE INDIVIDUAL ELEMENTS HAVE MUCH TO COMMUNICATE ABOUT THEIR PLACEMENT.

The 'mountain' of garden roses pictured here illustrates the universal importance of intention when arranging flowers. A quantity of one type of flower arranged with purpose can be every bit as beautiful and interesting as more complex multi-flower compositions. This notion of massing is connected to the way that flowers grow in fields, on farms and on mountains – even on the side of the road, often in great quantities. It is for this reason that much of my recreational time is spent looking at flowers wherever they grow. In my own work I approach arranging with a recollection of the flowers and the many ways they grow and flourish. My recollection of Ingrid's hellebores is so vivid that I will speak of them here, but illustrate my thoughts with garden roses. The emphasis being on massing all and any type of flower.

‡

As I write this, it is August in the Southern Hemisphere. It seems a weak shade of winter ... more like early spring. I'm thinking of a bloom to illustrate the 'mass-of-one-type' arrangement but I cannot get past the hellebore. It is one of the most enchanting plants for me: the heavy, single petal flower hangs from a fine stem that flows from a more substantial stalk. On one cut stem, for instance, perhaps five or six flowers in different stages of maturity will be found – one or two may be in 'cup' form (a nod to their familial link to the buttercup), another may be mid bloom, while some will be in full flush. One such stem seemingly encapsulates a botanical study, as if explaining the developmental evolution of the flower.

Ingrid would be a dab hand at arranging a mass of hellebores. She has been growing them for years, looking at them for years ... she knows their every undulation and idiosyncratic twist. Ingrid is no longer in full flight as a grower – she's now of the semi-retired variety. She doesn't travel to the markets, she doesn't peddle her wares: but on her patch of the world, Ingrid grows hellebores because she can't help but be a grower. The commerce of it all seems to be

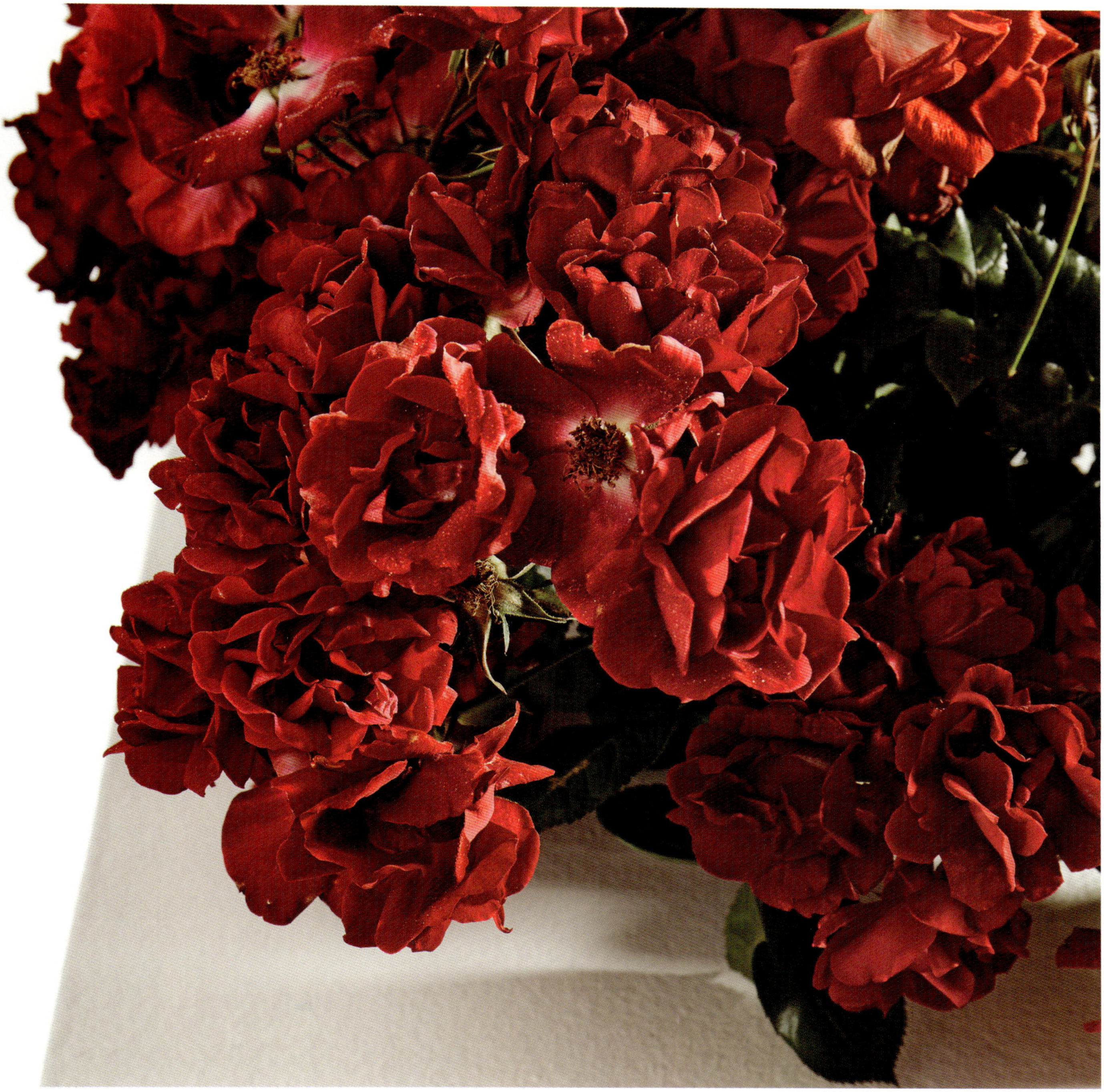

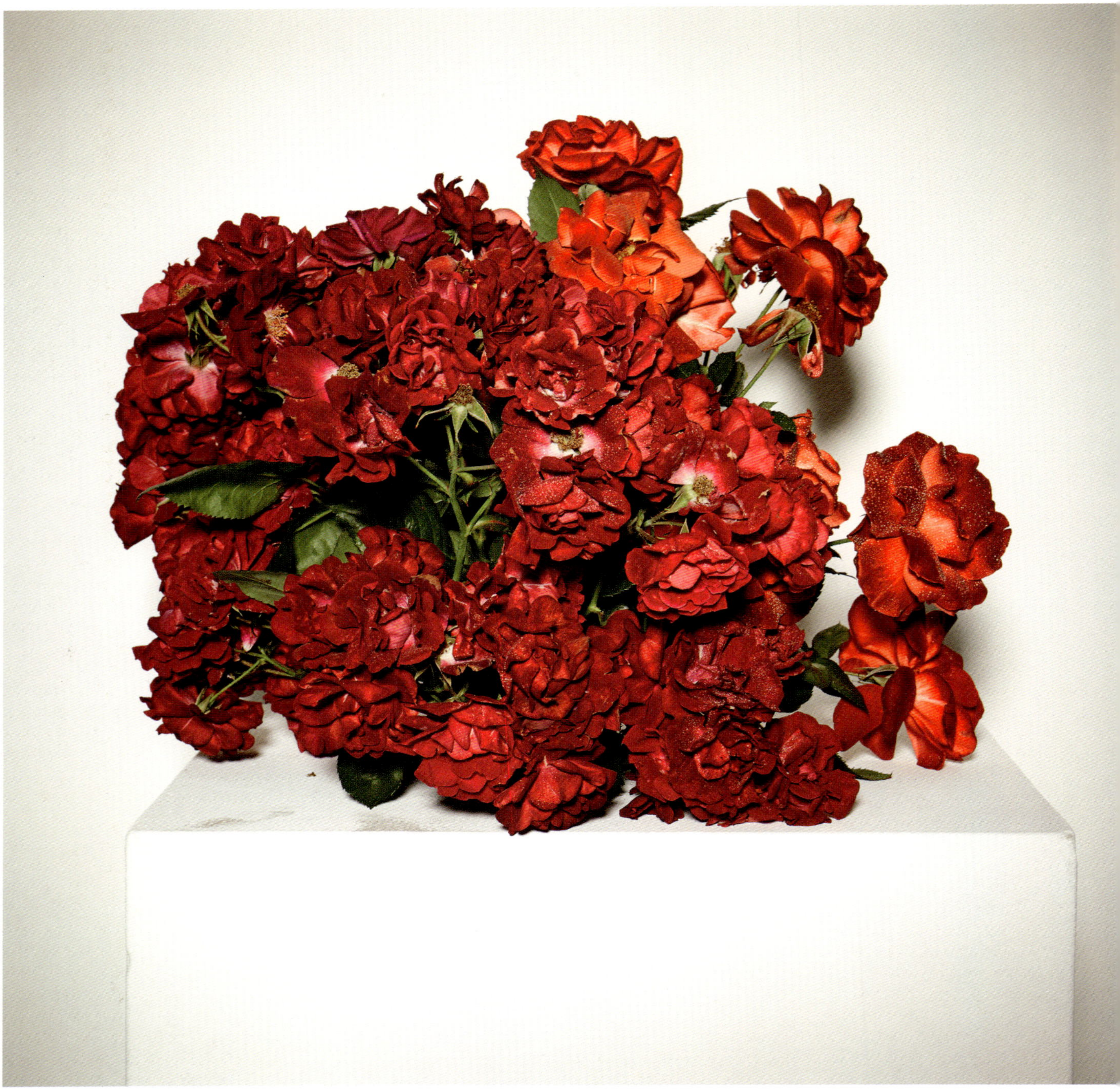

of very little interest to her – she is a grower in the sense that life is the pursuit of life and she is one that helps flowers to grow.

‡

In the pursuit of proficiency and skill in arranging flowers, it is essential to begin with an intimate knowledge of the medium. A study of any subject begins this way; study is another word for attention. Compositional forms that manifest in the natural world are a study of the most sophisticated and complex relationships – whether it is the way combinations of different species of roses grow closely together, seeming to marry and merge in indescribable harmony, or in the mad wonder of gnarly forms to be found in the branches of an old fig tree.

A bunch of hellebore from your local florist will have half-a-dozen or so stems and many, many flowers. Three bunches would be a generous number to play with and will create an impressive arrangement. In terms of expense they are middle-of-the-road – they are not 'investment' flowers that last for weeks on end in a vase, but for however long they do last, hellebores will speak of life and its seasons. There are many schools of thought about getting the best out of cut hellebore: some will say burn the stalk for five seconds over a gas flame, others suggest immersing them in the hottest tap water, others prick up the stem with a pin. I subscribe to the school of lots of fresh cold water, cutting the stems with very sharp secateurs and plunging them immediately into water while the stem is 'open'. One must change the water and re-cut the stems daily.

Engaging in observing each of the blooms that you will use in this arrangement is both the essence of the project and what I see as the distinction between those who are skilful with flowers and those who are not. Accomplished florists have as their distinction the conscious and considered placement of each element – choice of vessel, and positioning of the final bouquet. The choice of vase or vessel for the flowers will depend on the scale of the flowers; choose a vase with correlative proportions, in which the head of the bloom will sit well above the lip of the container. Consider also the positioning of the arrangement: will it be viewed only from the front, on a mantel? Or will it be visible from all sides? Now, as a painter begins by studying the masters – with nature as master – take an example of composition from nature as your guide. You could either choose one you know and can see clearly in your mind, or put up a photograph or a postcard of an image such as a tree or even a mountainscape on the wall in front of the bench where you will work. Looking at the image, isolate the overriding shape and draw an imaginary line undulating across the image to create a silhouette. Now you have intention for the placement of your flowers.

With your vase around three-quarters filled with water, your flowers and secateurs in front of you, pick up each stem and inspect it for imperfections … brown or dead leaves, weak and broken petals … and manicure them. Then lay the flowers in a 'good' pile. This process shouldn't take very long and will get easier and quicker with experience.

Now, beginning with the extremities of the arrangement, cut each stem to an appropriate length and start to build your design. Position each stem in the vase with its most beautiful aspect to advantage, creating height, density and dimension to reflect the silhouette of your 'muse' image. As you begin to build the shape and form of your arrangement, bear in mind the placement of the vase and choose stems whose organically occurring shape lends to their position in the composition.

Repeat. With garden roses et al.

‡

When I am working at my bench, not only am I inspired by the shapes and forms of the flowers before me, I am also inspired by the day-to-day lives of the growers. Laying out the stems of flowers, I think of Ingrid and her patch of earth and how, with work and love, her hellebores thrive, and I think I might make a 'mountain' in her honour.

Look at the flowers. The individual elements have much to communicate about their placement.

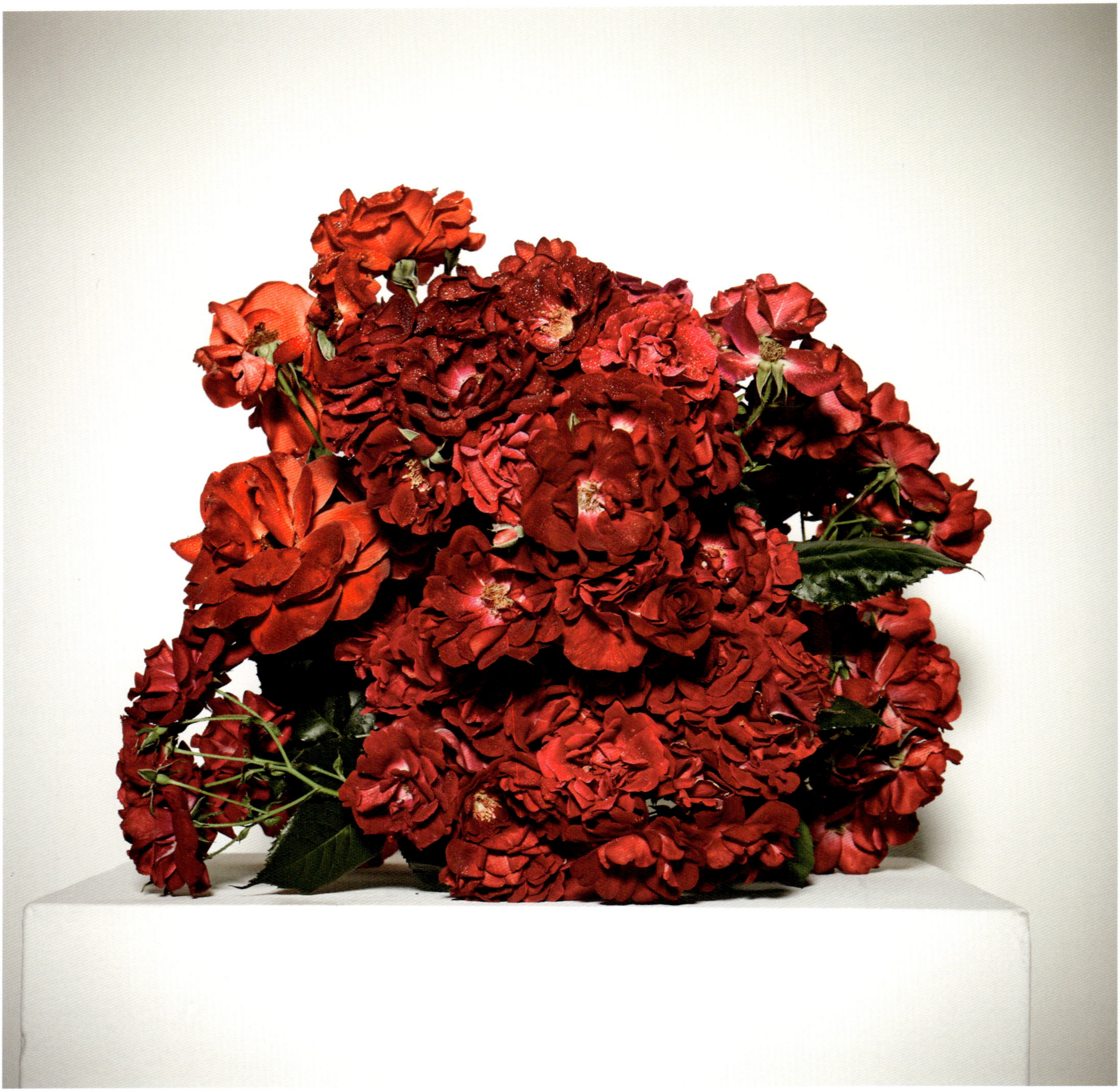

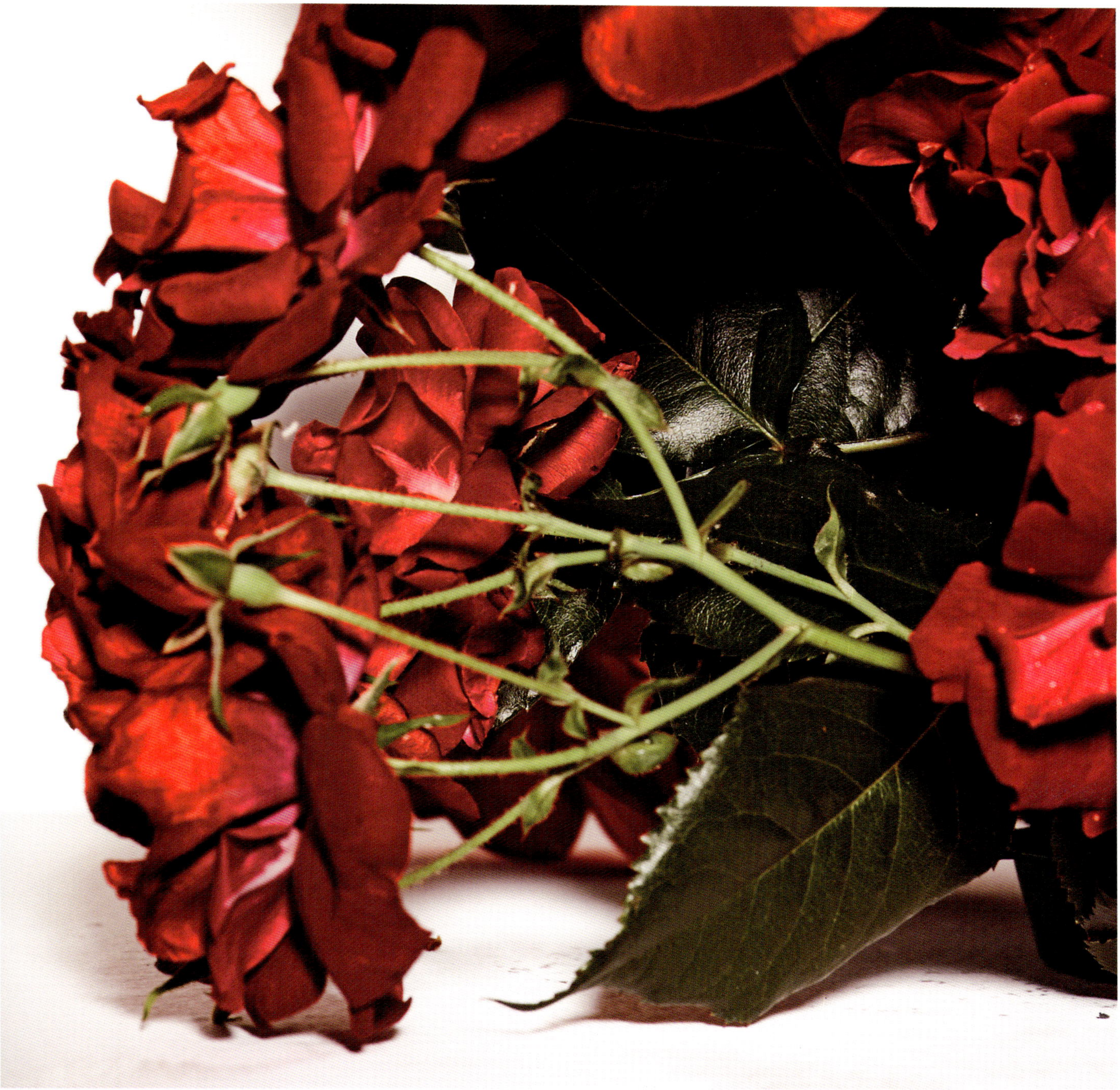

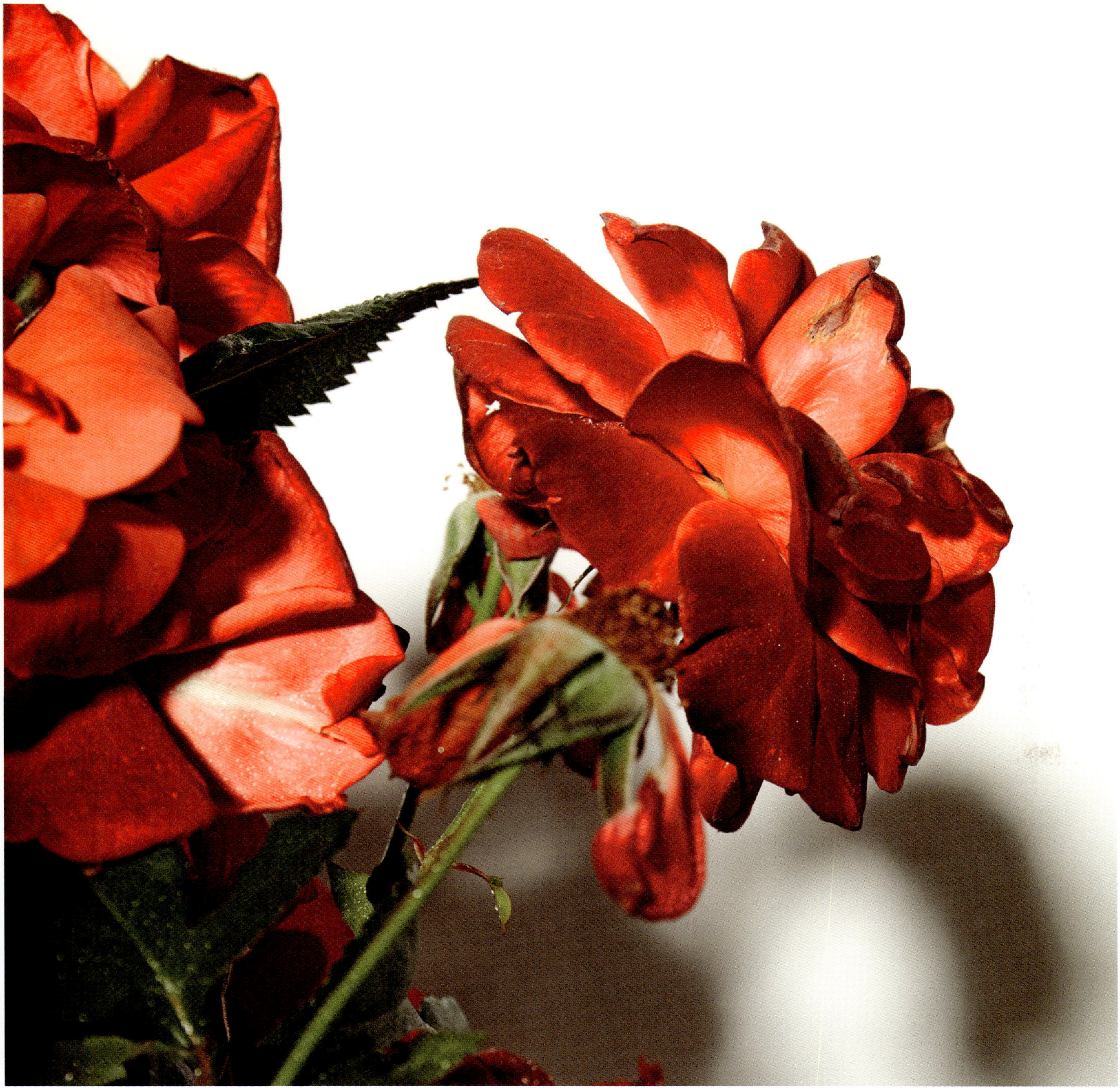

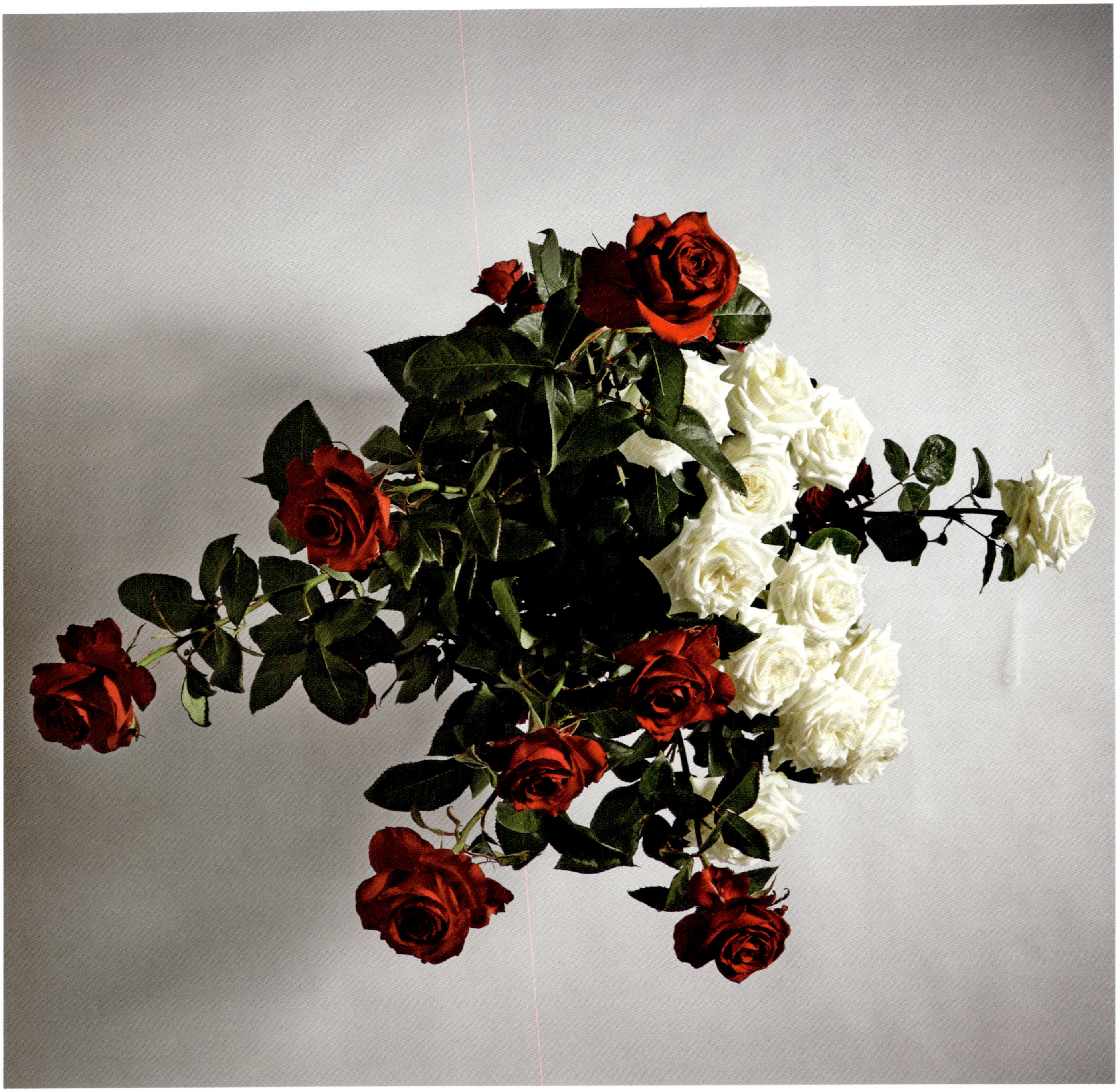

MY MOTHER, THE ROSES

—

AS A CHILD IN ITALY MY MOTHER HAD A CAT SHE NAMED ROSA.

My mother was like a rose. She was petite and slender and had thick glossy black hair and fair skin. Her feet were delicate and small and her hands were elegant and fine. I thought she was the most beautiful woman in the world and, for my world, she was. As a child I expected that I would grow to be like her ... but my father was 6'4" and because I was 'grafted' to his 'variety', I grew bigger, a great deal bigger than my mother, which was a source of bitter disappointment to me. Bitter, because in my reckoning beauty was diminutive – and beauty was my mother. As will have become evident in this book, despite the insecurities that punctuate the rest of my life, I have, ever since a child, been absolutely sure of my perception of beauty. My discernment of beauty is the one area in which I have never doubted myself. In the manner of a consolation, I have a freckle in the centre of my bottom lip – like my mother – and my hands appear like they were cast from the mould of her hands.

‡

My mother was like a rose. Roses grow on plants which produce stems that can climb and trail; the entire plant in most varieties is armed with sharp prickles or thorns. In the course of my work – and due to my proclivity for roses – my awareness of this attribute of the rose is intimately known and often experienced. As a result, I have developed methods for the removal of thorns from my hands, ranging from drawing ointments to more primitive methods of extraction, such as digging into the surface layer of the flesh with a sharp implement, which to me is the more satisfying option. With the varieties of roses I encounter in my work, I have met with thorns of varying size, strength and density. Some species of rose have stems with only a few small, almost soft thorns that pose a very minimal threat to the one who beholds its flower. These types of thorns are easily removed by dragging a tea towel down the stem. Others (often the most fragrant roses) have enormous, gnarly, poisonous thorns that cover every inch of the stem – at their most vicious, these types require individual cutting with secateurs because the trade tools developed for the purpose of their removal always fail. Of course, there are innumerable types in between these two extremes that florist-trade 'rose-strippers' remove as per their design. However, no matter the number and characteristics of the thorns on a rose stem, anyone who trades in roses has to do battle with them.

‡

Through my friendship with 'Bob' (as mentioned previously in The Growers, Paula's Farm), I have been afforded the unique satisfaction of witnessing the roses growing across the seasons and in great numbers. In the floristry trade, one works with the rose as a cut flower dissociated from the woody shrub that bore it. In the ferocious 'cutting-back' of the bushes in winter, I have seen the poetic, verdant, heaving masses that were fields of colour in the spring and summer, replaced by the smallest remnant of colourless wood left emerging from the soil. On these winter days it is impossible to imagine that this stub rooted to the earth, devoid of all growth, relieved of its dead wood, might ever again become the masterwork of nature that only months before stood in its place. As winter again turns to spring, the process of renewal that occurs for the rose is as tangible as the change of the season – vivid green stems begin to emerge from the woody remnant and with it leaves that grow in an alternate pattern up the stem. By mid spring the buds are 'cracking', and through until late autumn the rose will bloom over and again many times ... these surges of blooming are called 'flushes'.

In my training years I worked with a master florist and a number of others at differing stages of experience around a big wooden rectangular table – a workbench so immense in the space that it seemed plausible that the room had been built around it. We laboured around this enormous bench and talked ... coming to know each other like school children do by virtue of our converging paths and the hours we spent together. As one does in these kinds of scenarios, I reaped wisdom, friendship and proficiency in the course of these years. But, as the child does in the schoolyard, I also learnt discernment in this environment – extracting pearls from the 'wisdom' encircling me.

At a stage in my early practice as a florist I recall creating an arrangement that was predominantly constructed of red and white roses. I was enthralled by the combination of flowers and was floating, as I worked, in and out of a recollection of Lewis Carroll's 'playing card' men – the loyal servants and guards for the Queen of Hearts in *Alice's Adventures in Wonderland* whom Alice first meets in the Queen's castle garden, where they are 'painting the roses red'. I remember being shocked from my absorption of the combination of roses when one of my more seasoned counterparts screamed in the manner of the Queen of Hearts herself: 'blood and bone', 'blood and bandages'.

For many thousands of years cultures have assigned symbolic meaning to plants and flowers – though the practice seemed to peak in Victorian England during the nineteenth century, when blooms, plants and specific floral arrangements were employed as a way of sending coded messages to recipients, allowing the sender to express feelings that could not be spoken aloud in polite Victorian society.

In the Victorian era my arrangement of red and white roses would have symbolised 'Unity'. I still work with this combination because for me the juxtaposition of white and red flowers has a dynamic visual effect that I am unable to abandon, the fair-skinned petals of one contrasting with the luscious blood-red fleshiness of the other. A unity of opposites ... a precarious balance ... the fragility of beauty.

While my discernment of beauty is the one area in which I have never doubted myself, there are always recollections to remind me where this ability to discern came from, and they emerge unexpectedly when working with flowers. The red and white roses bring to my mind the contrast between the mass of blooming colour and the severely pruned plants riding out the winter chill on Paula's farm; the company of florists around the workbench engrossed in flowers but immersed in talking about life and experiences; then suddenly I think of the things we do with plants and flowers to bring happiness to others – even if it means painting white roses red to please the thorny Queen of Hearts.

And then there's my mother and the cat she called Rosa. My mother, who made me resilient by the quality of her 'thorns' ... I have her hands and I inherited that freckle in the centre of my bottom lip. Often in the presence of the flowers I think of her and am reminded that the first thing I learnt to recognise was beauty.

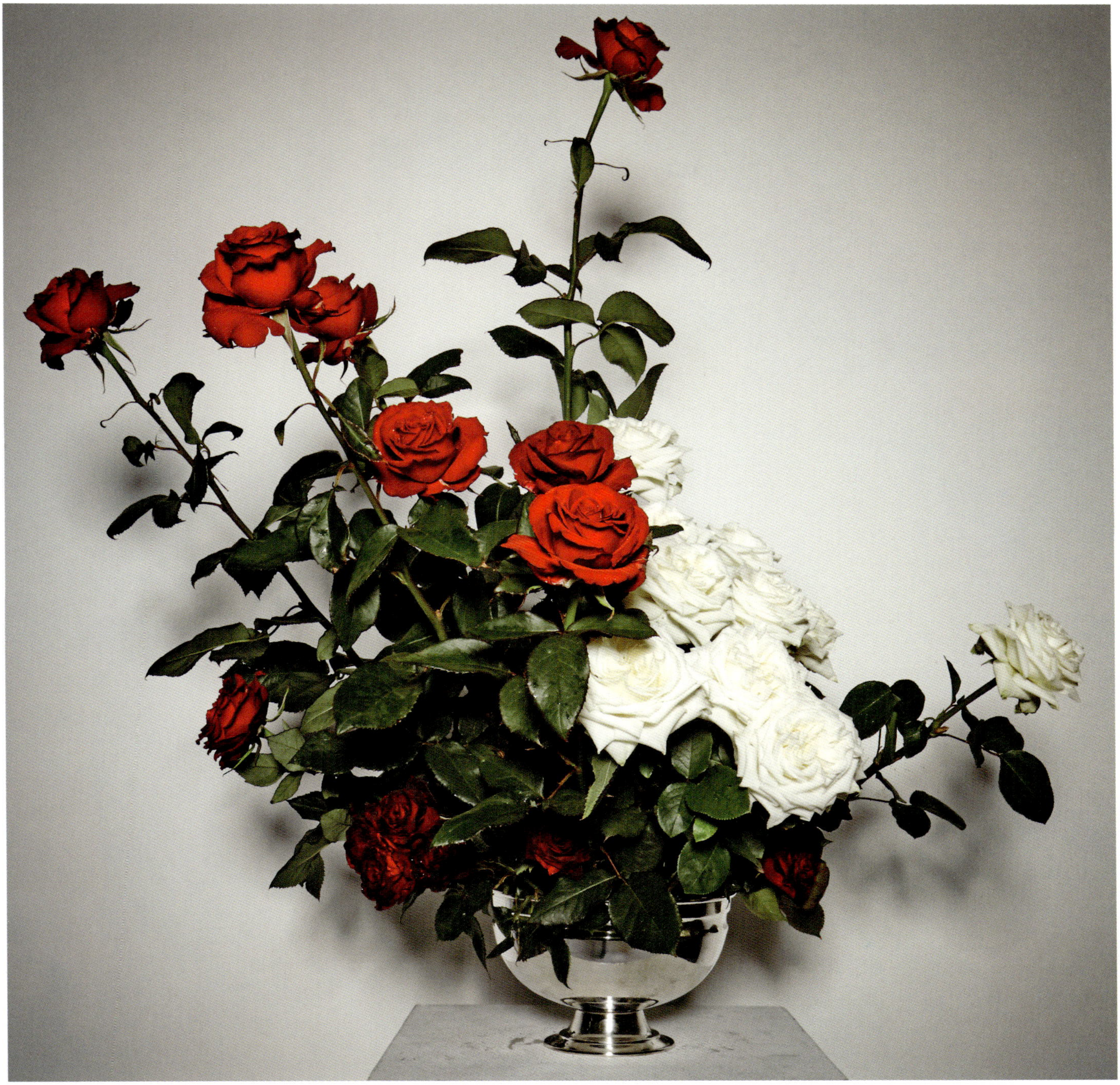

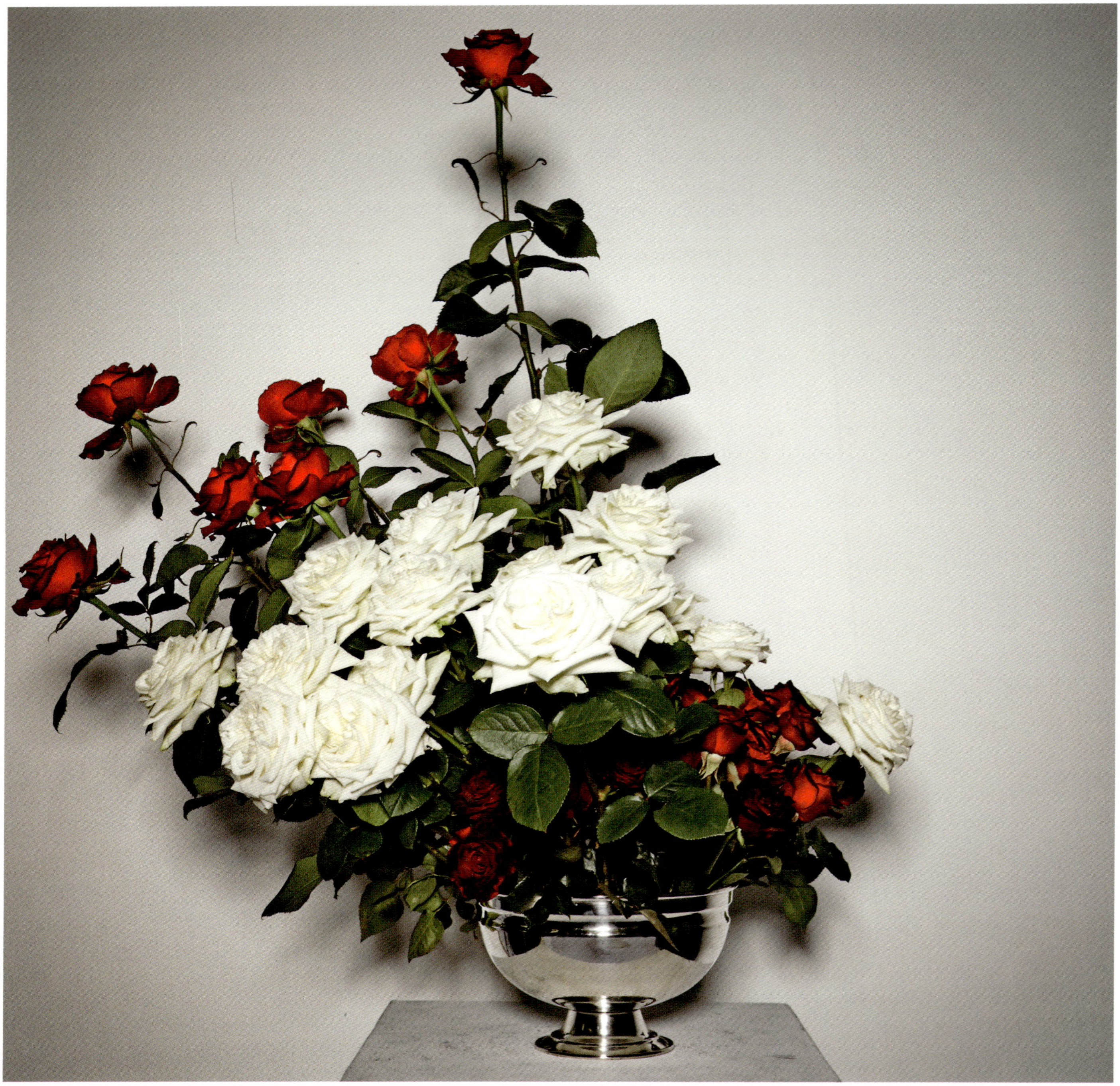

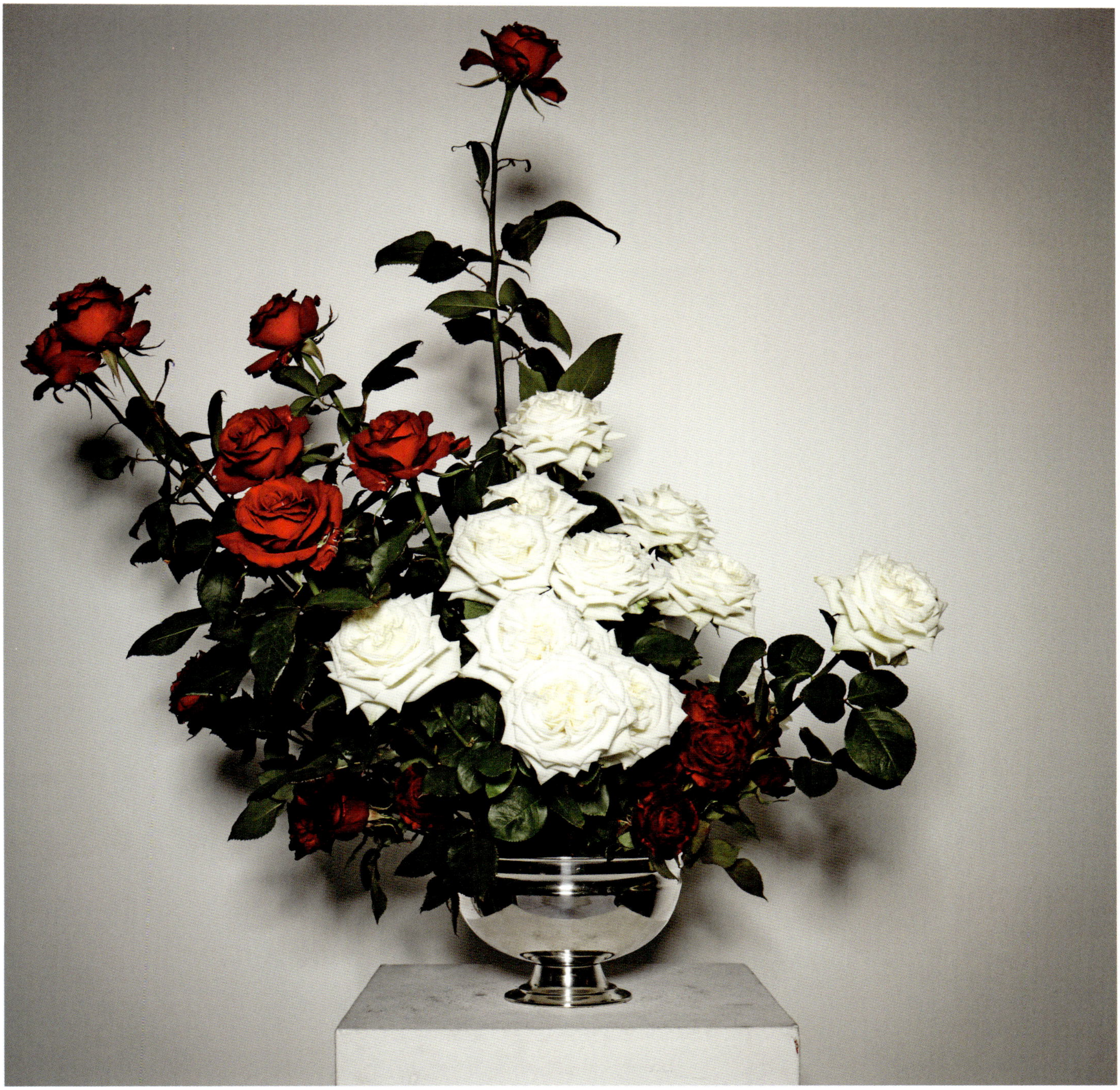

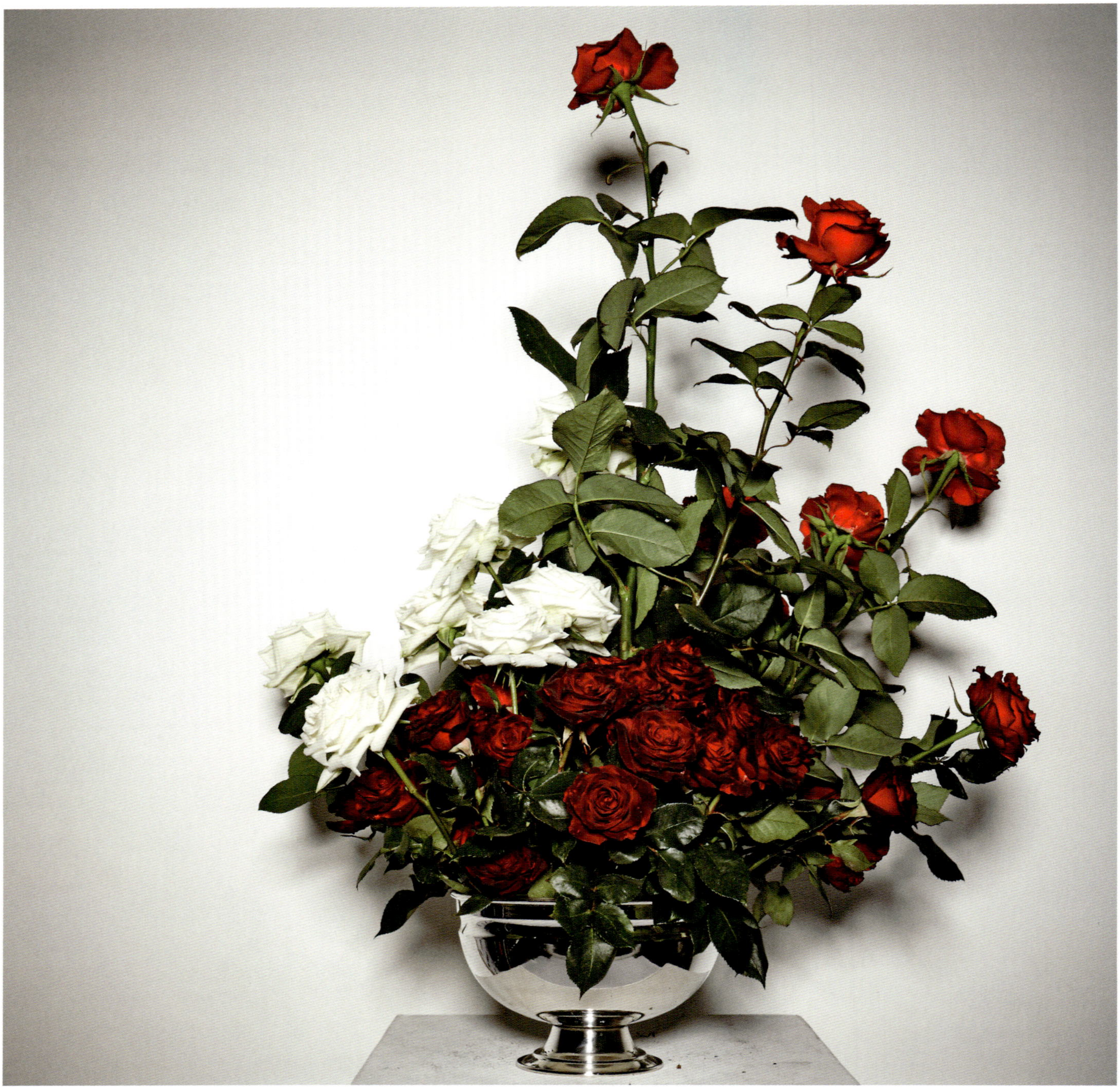

AWE AND THE MUSTARD ROSES
—

IT IS POSSIBLE I HAVE SPENT MY LIFE IN PURSUIT OF AWE.

A three or so hours' drive south of Sydney is the National Gallery of Australia. Located in Parkes, an inner southern suburb of Canberra, within the Australian Capital Territory, it is one of the largest art museums in the country. The Brutalist-style building opened in 1982 and holds approximately 166,000 works of art: the collection comprises items from every conceivable period of human history, from across the planet, and also includes a Sculpture Garden abundant with Australian native flora.

Over the Gallery's distinguished history it has mounted numerous major exhibitions and important retrospectives, showing the work of countless significant local and international artists. From December 2014 to June 2015 the Gallery purpose-built the spectacular installations of American-born artist James Turrell (b. 1943): in specially constructed spaces a comprehensive exhibition of his holograms, drawings, prints and photographs was assembled. *James Turrell: A retrospective* explored fifty years of the artist's practice that since the early 1960s has focused on light and space. As I write this, I have just completed a flower commission from the Gallery's events team to embellish their impressive Gandel Hall for a gala dinner in celebration of the Turrell exhibition.

In December 2014 I travelled to Canberra to meet the organisers and view the exhibition, in order to begin to conceptualise a response in flowers. It was agreed that I would create flower arrangements for two long tables that would run the length of the enormous room and, as well, create a flower sculpture to dominate the end wall of the hall opposite the stage.

I met with my contact Corinna, who had booked us in to Turrell's *Bindu shards, 2010* – an immersive installation that is a light cycle designed to be experienced by one person at a time. The viewer signs a waiver to do with epilepsy, removes their shoes and hangs a 'panic button' around their neck, before lying down on a mechanised 'bed' and putting on a pair of head phones.

The experience begins when a mechanism causes the sliding 'bed' to retract into a white metal sphere, locking the viewer into 'space' – an endless, bodiless field of light bereft of walls, corners or edges.

Incredibly, the experience of having viewed the scale of the sphere from the outside, standing in the centre of the gallery only seconds earlier, does nothing to contradict the feeling of limitless space within the installation. And it begins. An expanse of blue light is shattered by high-speed flashing colours that kaleidoscopically pulsate from one colour to the next. The viewer is rendered bodiless, such is the intensity of 'seeing' ... it seems like everything else – the world – just falls away.

I was completely in awe.

‡

I like to be awed a great deal. Awe is the overwhelming feeling of reverence, an emotion comparable to wonder – but wonder is more joyous, while awe is sober. It is possible that I have spent my life in pursuit of awe. I am certain that it is a sense of awe that has led me to my work with the flowers ...

In considering my approach to the 'Flowers for Turrell', the palette of coloured light in *Bindu shards, 2010* was uppermost in my mind. I decided early on to make flower arrangements in block colours faithful to those fields of light within the many artworks in the exhibition, and to place them in the manner of a chromatic spectrum. I used each distinct colour in groupings of between three and seven arrangements, so that when placed down the length of the white cloth-draped table each colour was heightened and visually effective – one block of colour flowing into the next. As is often the case with flowers, the palette of the concept dictated the types of flowers appropriate to the project. Gladly, roses and carnations would work within the palette and offer the density of colour required ... and god knows, I love a rose.

The sculpture for the facing wall had to possess a relationship to Turrell's work: its

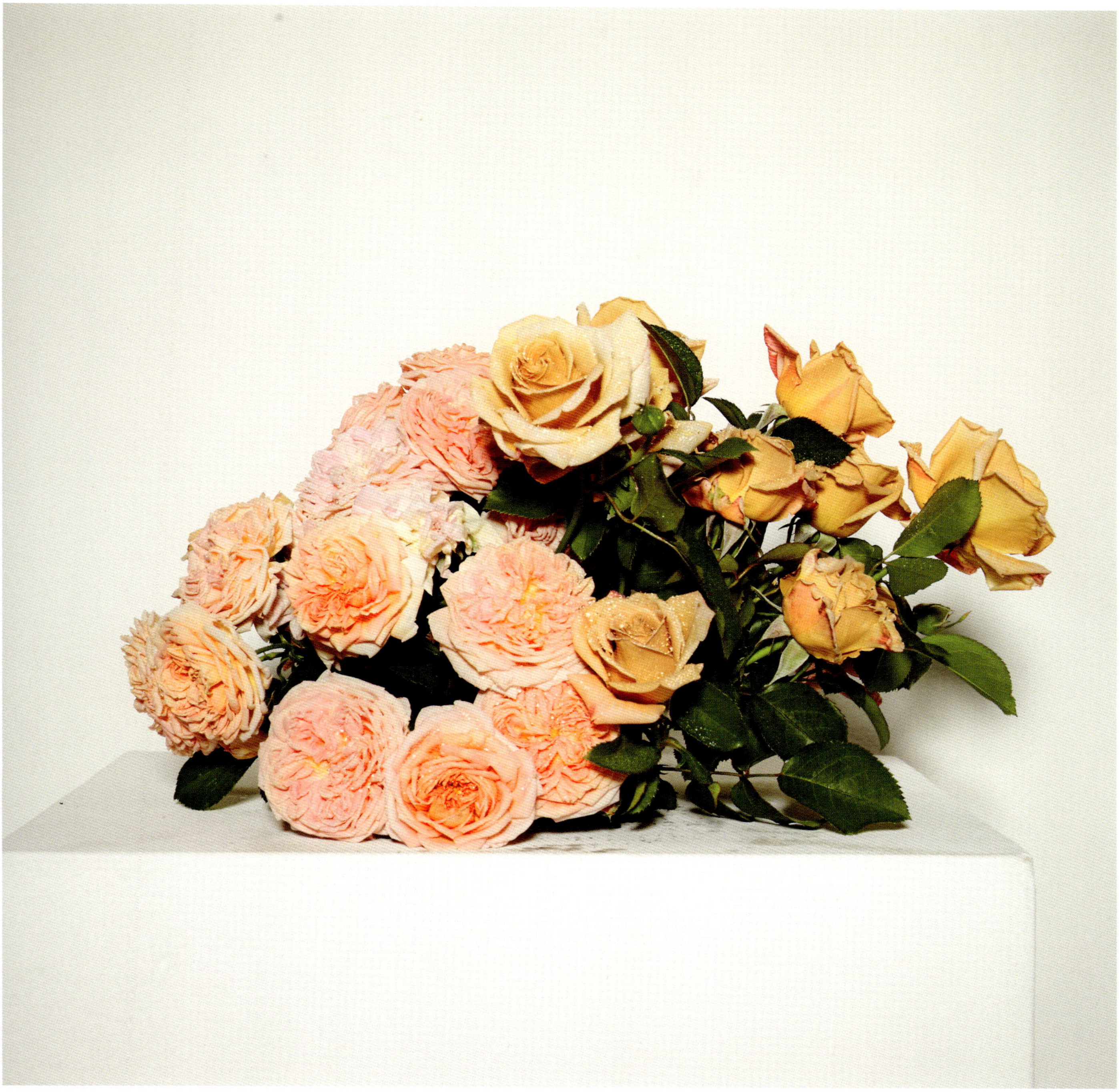

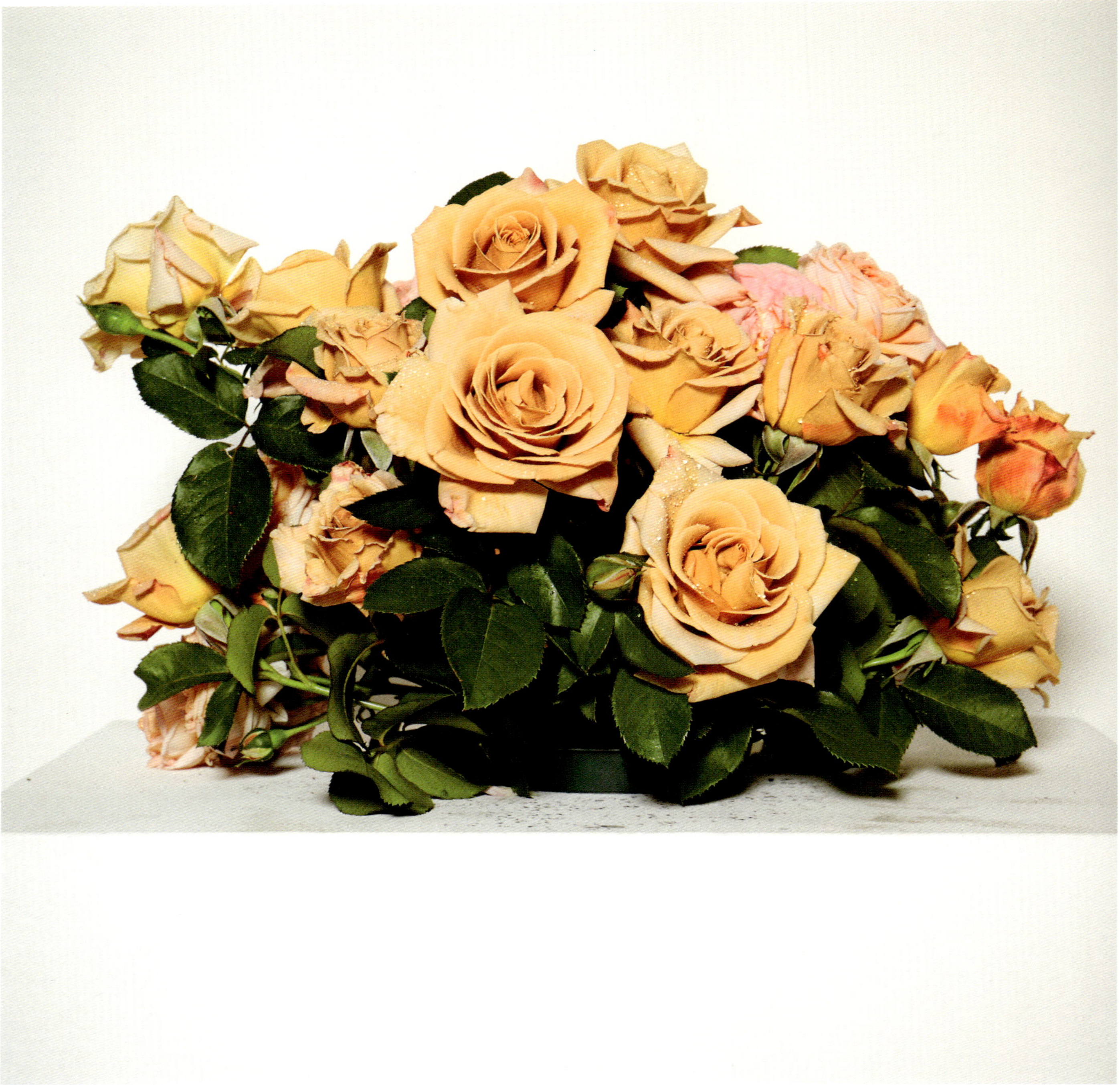

structure (like Turrell's) had to inspire awe and, in relation to the human body, possess a spatial dominance. The final construction was a disc – 3 metres in diameter – that seemed to hover in the space, while the element of awe was effortlessly provided by the countless blooms that covered the structure on all sides. On the outer face of the structure I used amaranthus (because it looks like paint), 'Turrell orange' roses and the 'mustard' rose that is arranged with David Austin's 'Evelyn' rose in the image I have selected to accompany this text.

The mustard rose is very dominant in my day-to-day flower work. If I were to have a 'signature' flower it would be hotly contested between this rose and the ruby-red. My feeling of awe at its beauty is always as intense as the very first time I saw it. I often have it at home so that I can watch the flower fully bloom and then fade to the most delicate, inexpressible, soft deerskin colour. I have so often seen the same response from my clients and recipients of my flowers ... one dear, kindred woman called me in tears when she saw this change in colour. And my team and I witnessed the same reaction again and again during the two days we worked in the great Gandel Hall. Many times over, staff, and curious and brave visitors to the Gallery who had stumbled upon an open door, would come to have a look at the thousands of blooms being prepared and worked into arrangements – and of all of the magnificence they would gasp at the sight of the 'mustard'.

The mustard rose pictured in the accompanying pages, along with a significant spray of the many-layered David Austin 'Evelyn' rose, might offer the flower enthusiast the impetus to combine two varied colours and varieties of rose. I think it is one of the simplest ways to create an interesting composition. In combining the two roses, the texture, tone and colour of each seems to be somehow amplified, while the blending of their fragrances will surely inspire awe.

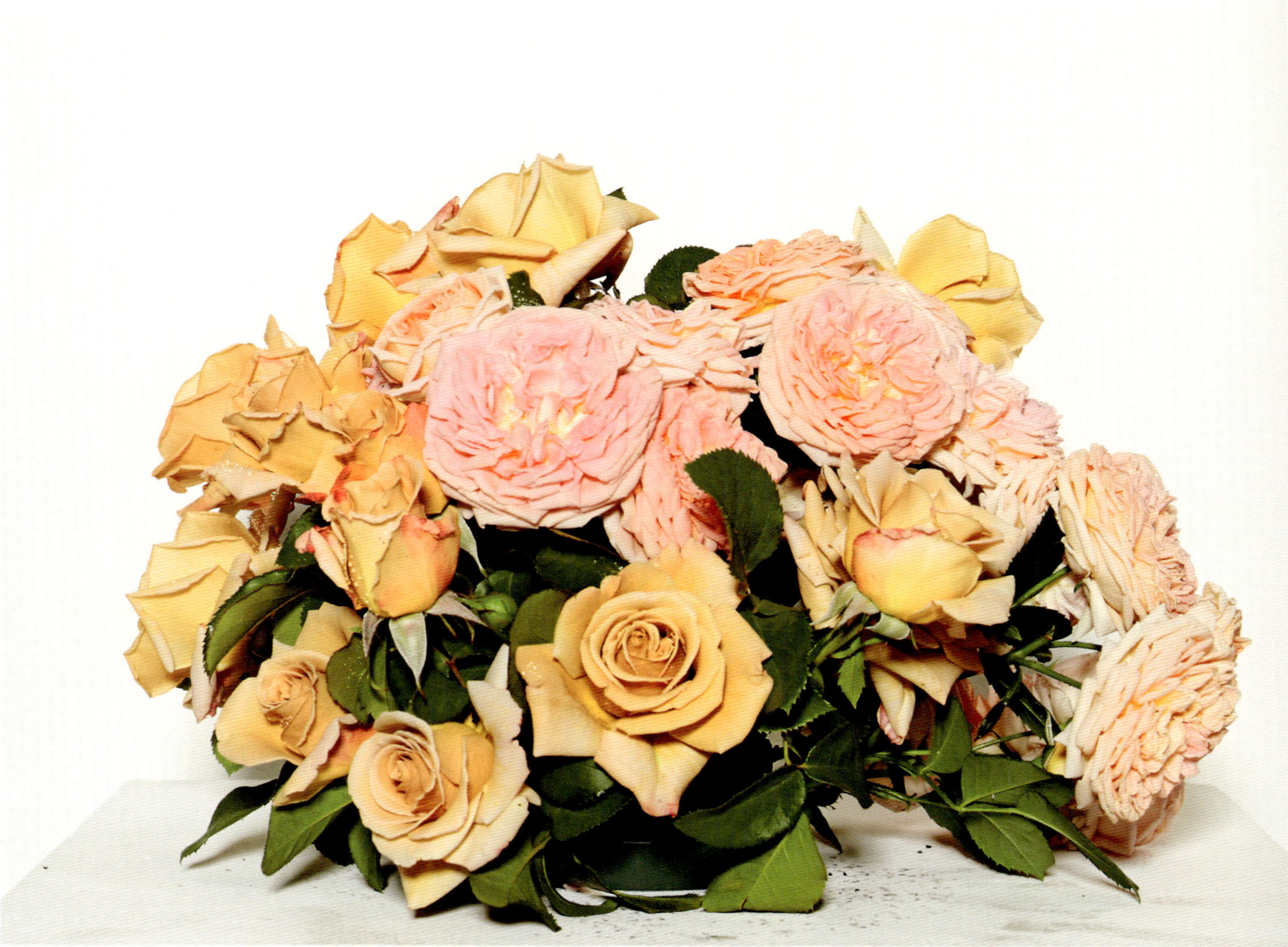

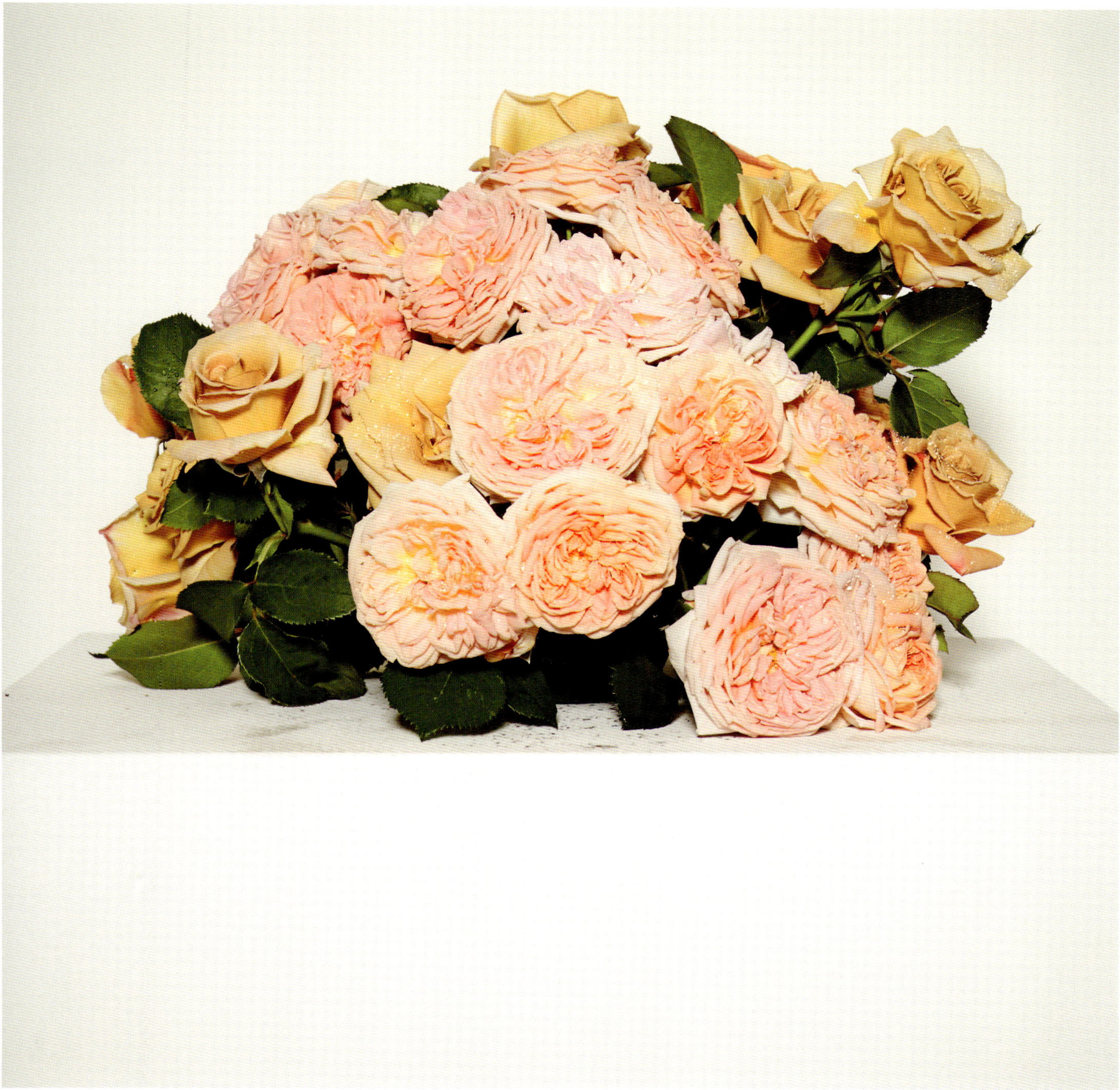

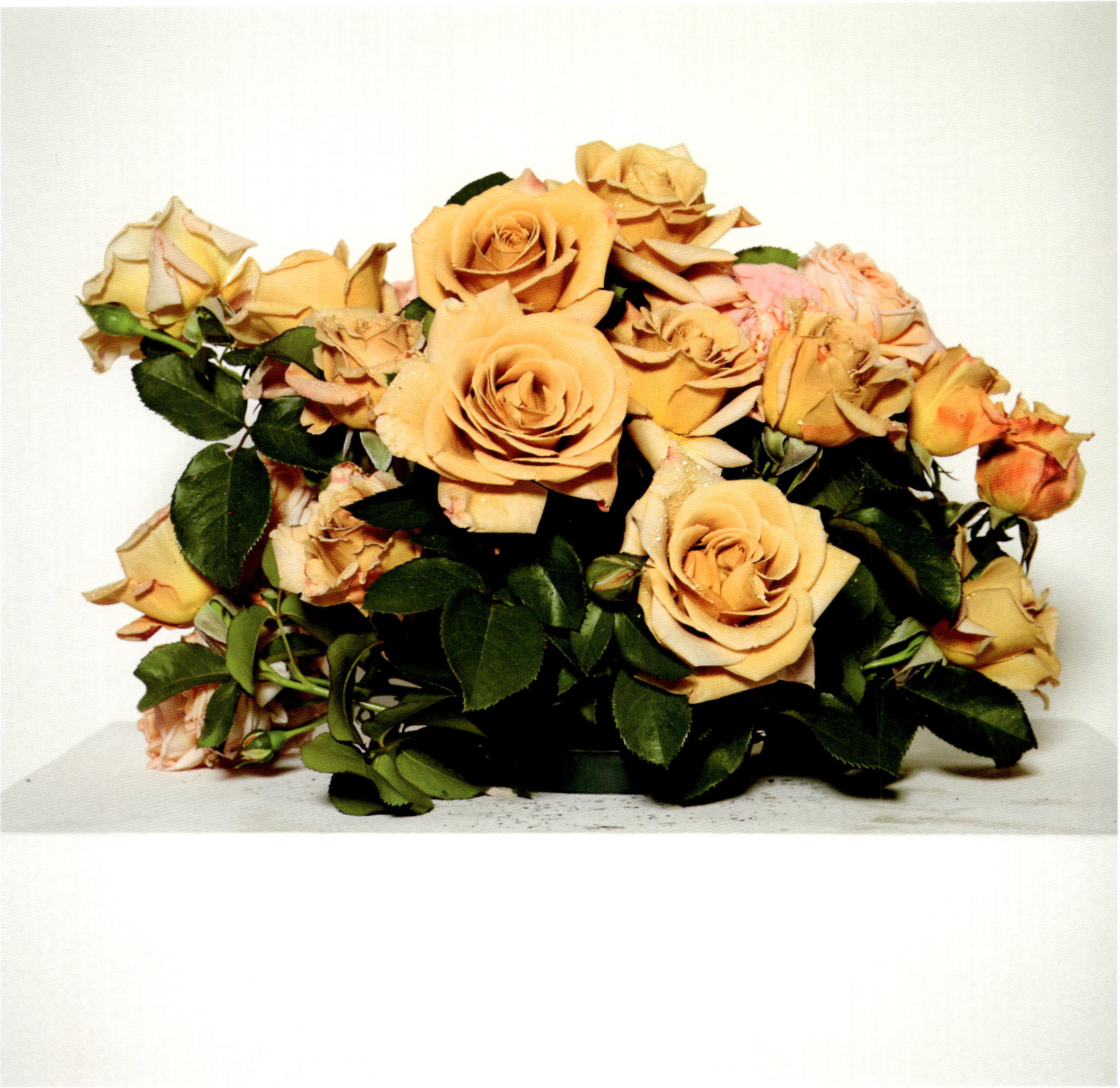

THE PINK HYDRANGEA

—

LOOK AT HOW BEAUTIFUL THE BLOOM IS, TURN IT IN YOUR HAND.

On a recent visit to a hydrangea farm at the peak of the season, I found myself quite overwhelmed by the majesty of this most impressive and popular flower. One row of the many hundreds on the farm had not yet been picked and the branches were absolutely heaving with enormous, pink flowers. The bushes themselves were easily 4 to 5 metres in height – the stems thick, strong, laden with handsome, shiny, deep-green foliage. The scale and splendour of the towering trees leaning in from both sides of the narrow track where I stood had the quality of a cathedral. In the same way that the architectural grandeur and vast embellishment of the ancient basilicas provoke solemnity and awe, so did the extent and beauty of the scene affect me.

‡

I don't very much like to have my picture taken, but as a result of the intoxicating hydrangea, I am in possession of a portrait of myself that shows me happily disregarding the camera: it captures me one autumn day in London looking straight down the lens. At the time I was staying with friends in Shoreditch in London's East End; I had decided to walk to the Columbia Road Flower Market one Sunday morning to reward my hosts' generosity with a few arrangements of flowers. Each Sunday, traders set up their stands full to the brim with myriad seasonal plants, shrubs, bulbs and cut fresh flowers. Most of the traders are the second and third generation in their families to sell at the market, and there is definitely something in their repeated appeals that seems to reinforce the notion of generational trading, 'the ol tray faw a sixa' or 'phree for a tena' and 'at's bewtiful innit'.

By the time I had walked the length of Columbia Road, high on the market atmosphere and the eccentricities of the traders, my arms were full of the most incredible, enormous hydrangeas. The kind of load one might balance on one's shoulder to try and distribute the weight. I often buy too many flowers … if there is such a thing as too many flowers.

‡

Near my home in an inner-city suburb of Sydney there is a harbourside bay where I walk in the mornings – that is, when the flower trade permits it. My habit is to take the same route from my apartment to the foreshore and join the other locals taking their 'morning constitutional' around an established pathway. To the left as one enters the park that hedges the shore, there is a fenced portion of land rising upward to an apartment building above. It is a decent-sized mass of land – around 20 by 30 metres: its mere existence in this densely populated area begs the question of how it can be that nothing has been built in the spot. Still, every square inch is embedded with hydrangea, and in the summer and well into autumn it is such a scene. There are hundreds of plants that grow – as hydrangeas do – to differing heights, but some are monumental, reaching 4 or 5 metres in stature. They undulate and link, growing near and through each other, and they bloom in every conceivable colour, all mixed together by haphazard planting. I have never seen anyone garden this patch nor anyone pick flowers there – though I have often imagined myself in the role of harvester. There is much in Sydney that foretells the warmer weather, but for those local to this area, the buds that emerge in the spring in this hallowed place are their surest sign.

‡

Hydrangeas, being what they are – a dense mass of smaller flowers that make up the whole near-spherical flower head – lend themselves to 'massing'. The act of arranging flowers is always undertaken with the intention of exploiting the natural beauty of the specimen. The voluminous flower head of the hydrangea and its rich green, deeply lined and serrated leaf, seem to beg for their own company; the naturally occurring variance in tonality, shape and palette means that the hydrangea doesn't need contrast with other floral elements for it to be texturally and compositionally interesting. Rather, massing the flowers seems to amplify

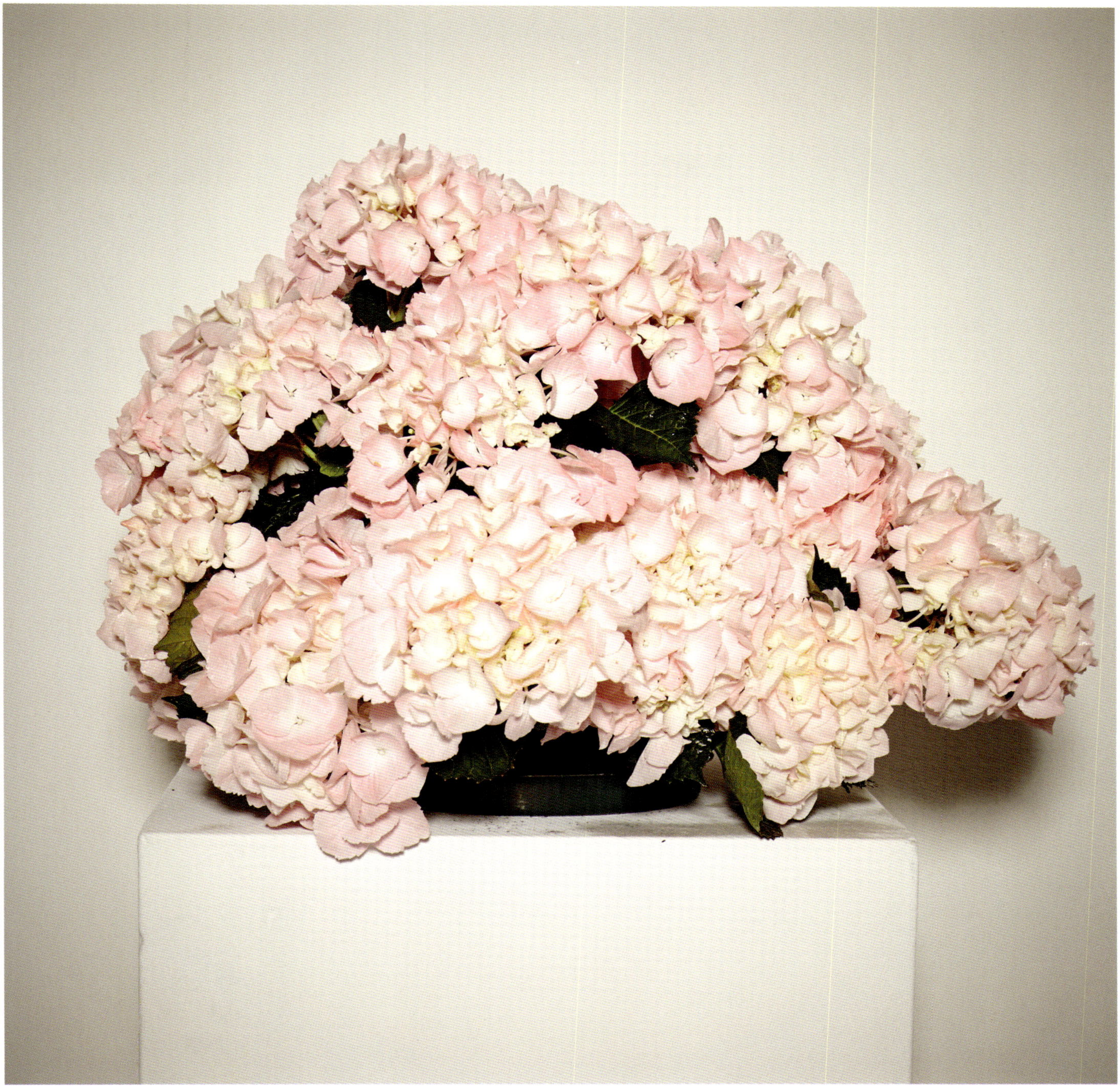

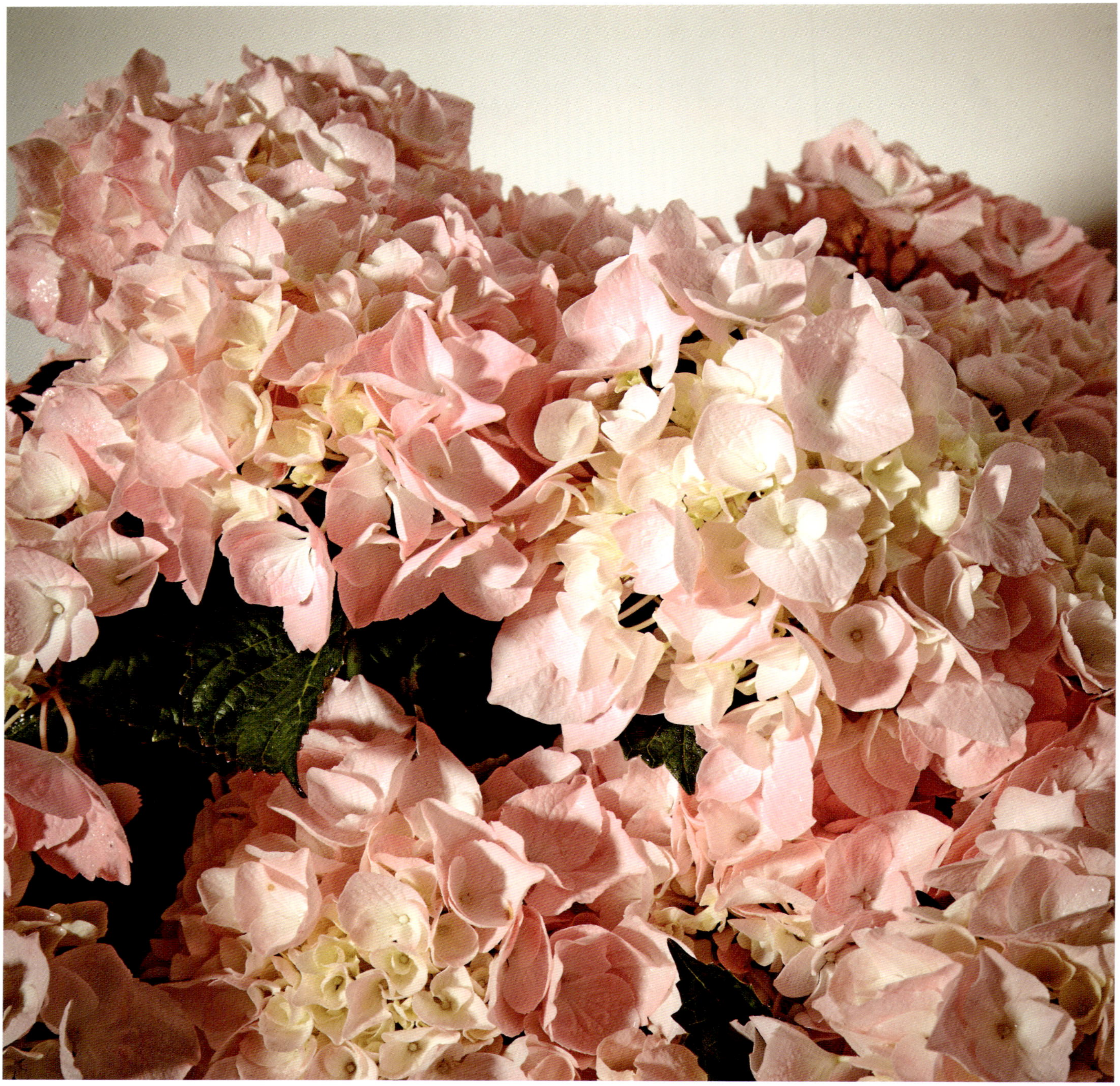

the elemental spectacle of the bloom. All that is needed is for one to have an envisioned shape for the arrangement – which will be dependent on the vessel being used to hold the flowers.

Working toward the overall shape of the composition, it's important to pick up each bloom and inspect it for weak, browned or broken petals and florets that can then be hand-picked from the flower. The same can be done with its leaves. Next, look at how beautiful the bloom is, turn it in your hand and inspect its angles and characteristics, then consciously decide upon its position in the vase or vessel. Holding an individual bloom in one's hand, it's possible to see umpteen 'good' angles that might be exploited. This should be the overriding intention in massing flowers: in one floral composition the viewer should be able to take in the countless, beautiful aspects of any one type of flower.

It is my take on floral arranging that there is not nearly enough observation and appreciation of flowers. When beginning, it takes time to absorb the features of individual blooms and to decipher their optimal position in combination with other flowers. Massing is a very good way to practise ... one becomes deft with repetition. In my work every single flower that leaves the studio has been observed and regarded by my eye.

THE WHITE LILAC, BROWNING
—
MY PEOPLE OF ANTIQUITY.

In the years of our primary schooling my sister and I would take fresh pieces of paper to my paternal grandmother for ageing treatment. She would boil the kettle and make a strong pot of billy-tea that we would then pour over the paper. When the piece dried it would appear mottled and stained, developing a texture that spoke of its fictitious 'journey' – in a matter of minutes a crisp white sheet of paper would be transformed into a thing with a history. A lengthy steeping, given the willingness of the paper to absorb pigment, gave a result that could infer a journey of many decades. It could imply that the document had in fact travelled with the First Fleet, the shiploads of European settlers to Australia, and had somehow found its way into the hands of my seven-year-old self. If we decided to go 'all the way' and carefully burn the edges of the page, its appearance had the potential to convince even the most learned teacher that before its turn as a school project on his or her desk, it had possibly spent time in the defensive pocket of a merciless pirate.

When a thing is aged this seems to improve its clout. I have spent many days in the Mitchell Library within the State Library of New South Wales – the oldest library in Australia – researching this and that plant or flower, artworks and botanical illustrations, and poring over rare books and documents on these and other subjects. The Mitchell Library Reading Room opened in 1910 and houses a treasure trove of books, maps, newspapers and magazines, documents, manuscripts, photographs and ephemera – including the original journals of Abel Tasman, James Cook and Matthew Flinders.

The stately reading room itself possesses a palpable sense of history and is a rare place in the middle of a city: it allows for quiet, uninterrupted thought and research. The grand room is lined with thousands and thousands of books as well as holding untold rare and important artworks and manuscripts. There are private and communal desks where people from all walks of life engage in all manner of 'research', from checking in on their social media sites to preparing matters for post-graduate theses that might change the world. But my favourite area consists of a few communal tables at the very back of the room that have been roped off from the rabble. The carved, heavy timber 'station' is usually manned by a stern individual – who, if presented with the right information on the appropriate slip of paper, will hand over the rarest and most precious materials available. One might be asked to use gloves to turn the ancient pages, and it goes without saying that one must not 'bend the spine'. This is my favourite part of the library, not just because of the incredible things I have seen and read there, but because I always have the feeling of being a serious contender in this atmosphere of restriction and consequence.

In contrast to the aura I like to believe I borrow from the setting of a hundred-year-old reading room, is the impression I must surely leave at the Sydney Flower Market when I am unable to disguise my wonder and enthusiasm for a mass of white lilac, whose inner flowers are already turning brown – an appearance that those more accomplished in the field of floristry would certainly pass over. What is more I would include it in a book entitled THE FLOWERS! This proclivity puts me I think in a middle ground between those wonderful florists who work essentially as sculptors, choosing only the thirstiest and gnarliest elements available – that is where they see poetry – and those florists who will only consider those flowers that are in the tightest of bud, furled, closed and crisp. For this latter group, longevity is where the value of a flower lies.

‡

The Celts considered the fragrance of the lilac tree to be enchanted, believing that the perfume had the power to transport humans to supernatural states and mystical worlds. The fragrance of the lilac – and many other flowers, including the gardenia – actually deepens and intensifies as the bloom begins to expire. I have wondered if this is the flower's last attempt at inviting pollination before its final expiration or if in fact it is pure sorcery. The fragrance is indescribable ... I often think to myself, 'Who were these

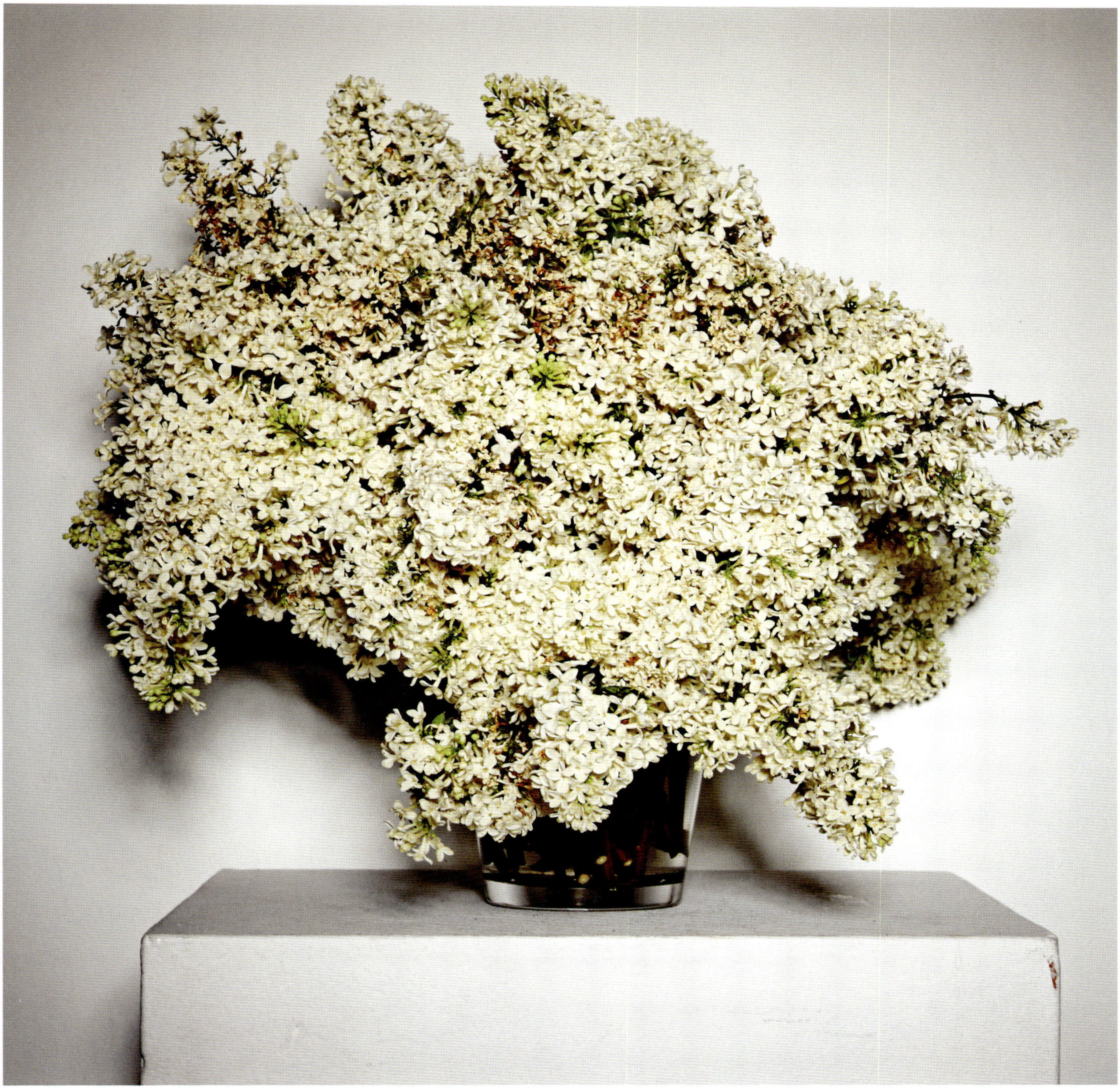

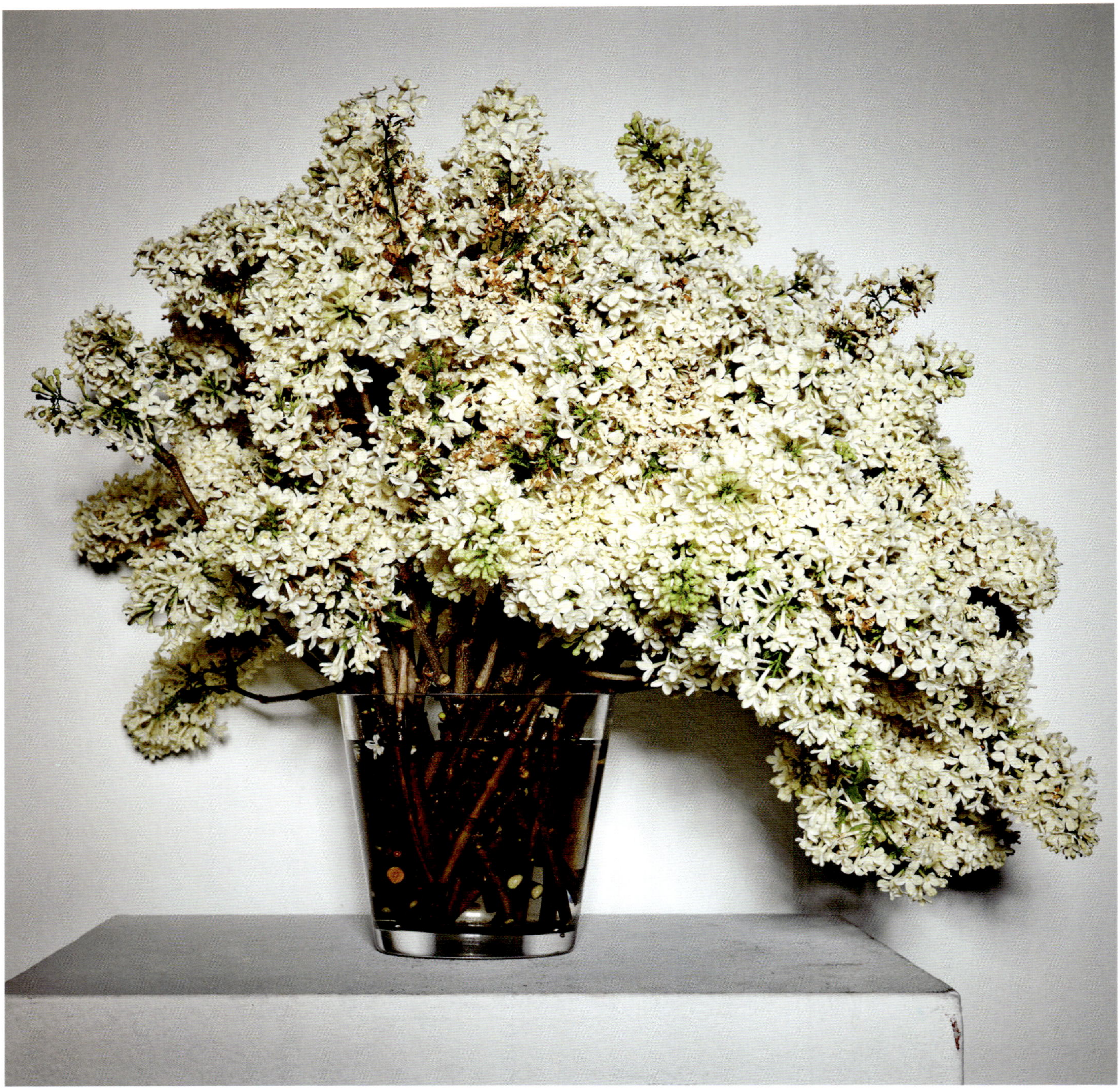

people, who first said, "That bloody lilac, that's enchanted, it has got to be … ?"' I am convinced that they were the early creatives – my people of antiquity. If I had been born in the earliest years of the formation of any human culture, I absolutely would have been a member of The Committee for Hypothesising the Mystical Attributes of Flowers. For people in some other fields of work, with less enchanted frames of mind, the notion of a fragrance being capable of transporting a human to a supernatural state might be thought of as preposterous. For me it makes complete sense. I can personally attest that in the presence of a mass of lily-of-the-valley, I have had firsthand experience of being 'transported' from a winter's day in Sydney, Australia, to Paris on the first day of spring. In a stupor of exhaustion I have been lifted by the fragrance of lilac to a state of absolute verve.

Then again, I have seen an ordinary sheet of white paper develop two hundred years of authority and consequence in an afternoon.

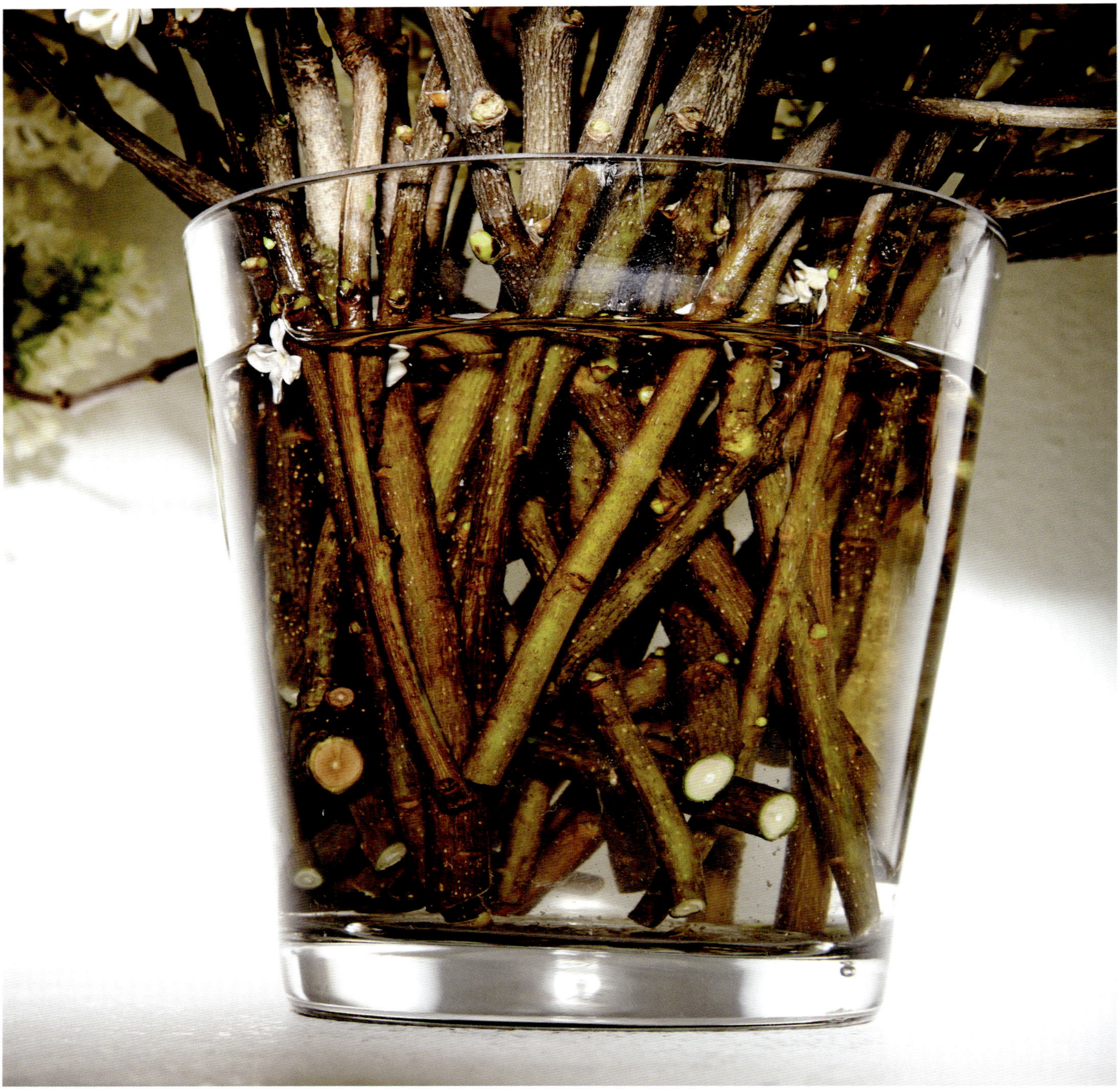

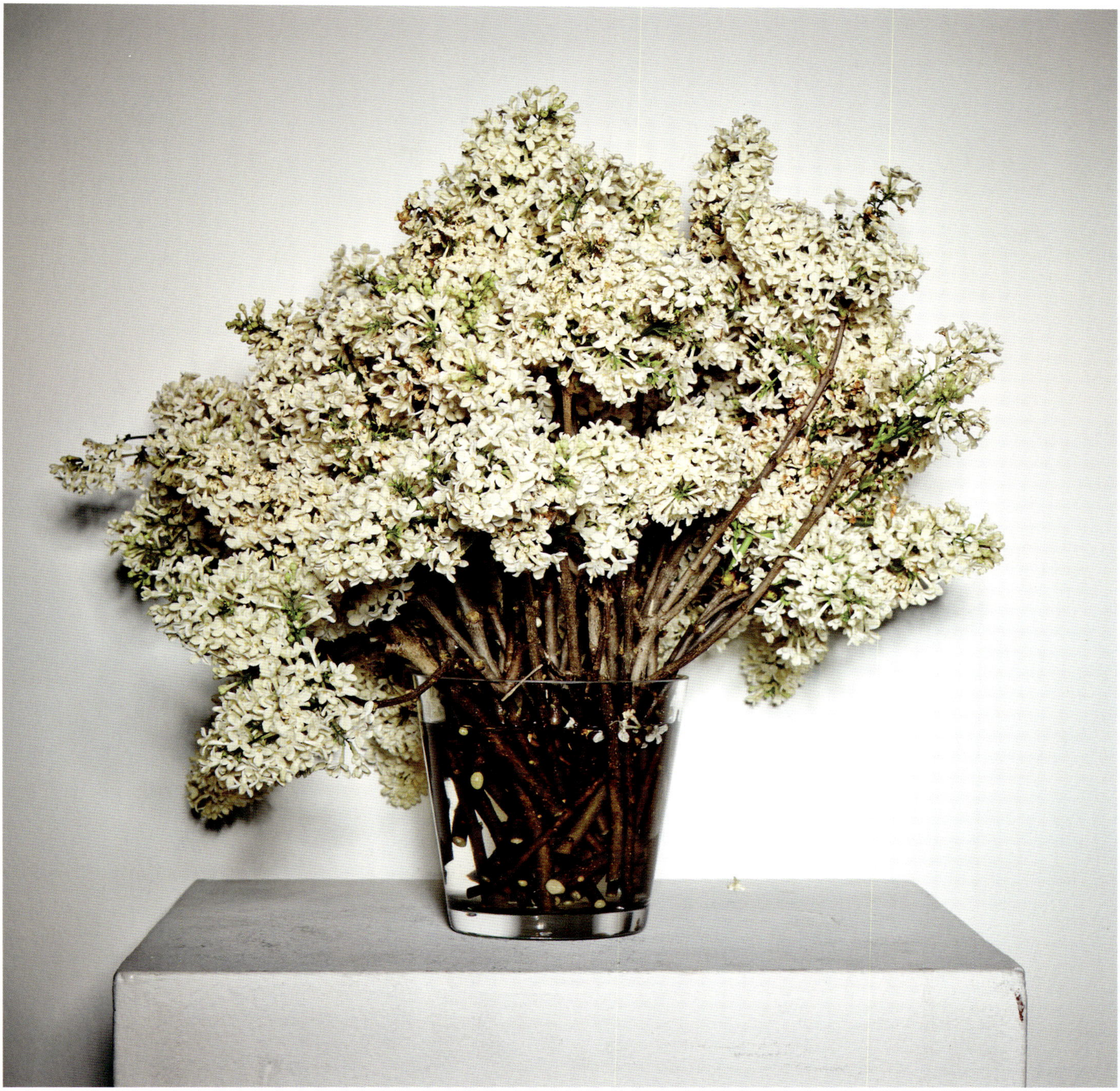

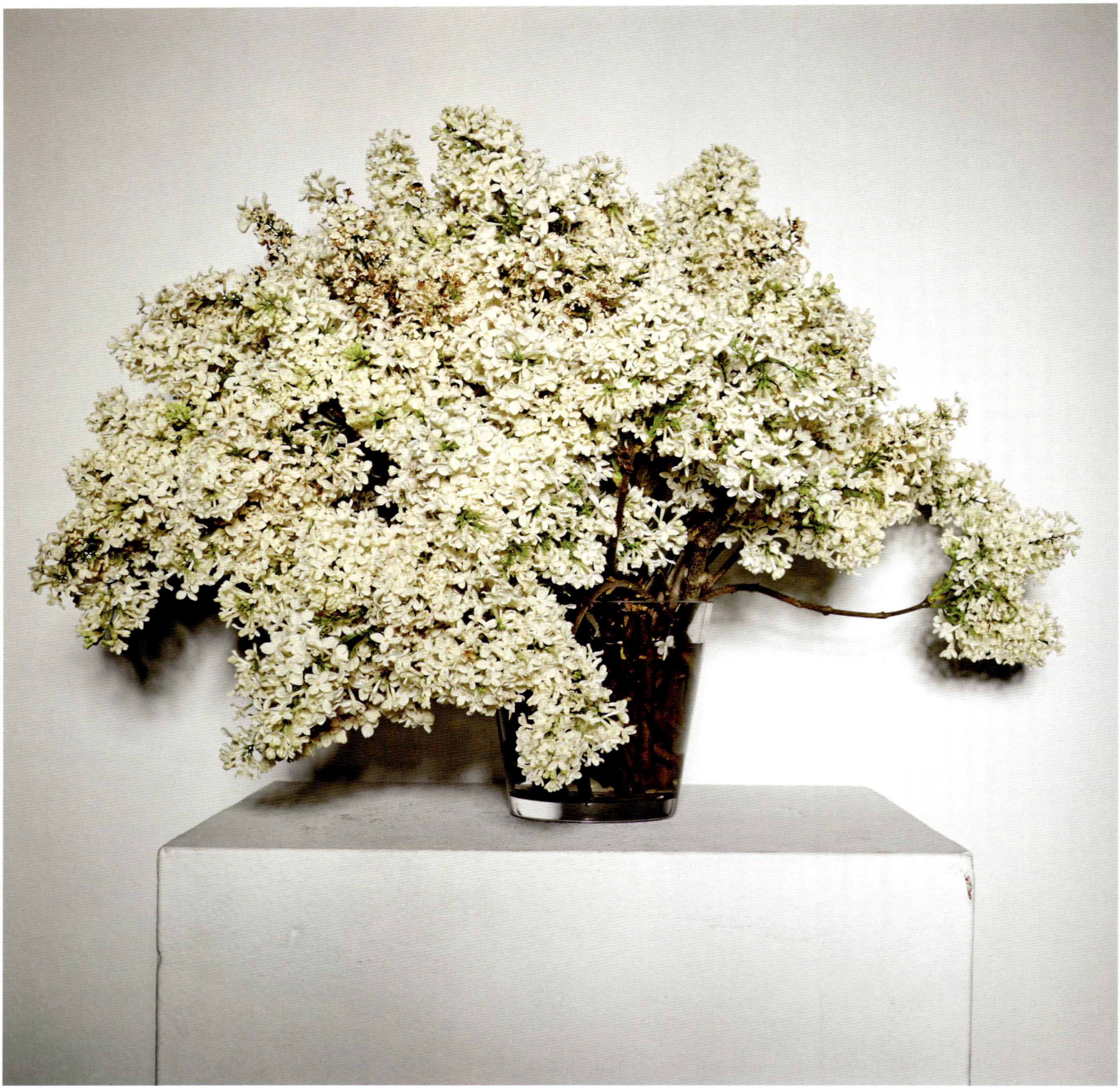

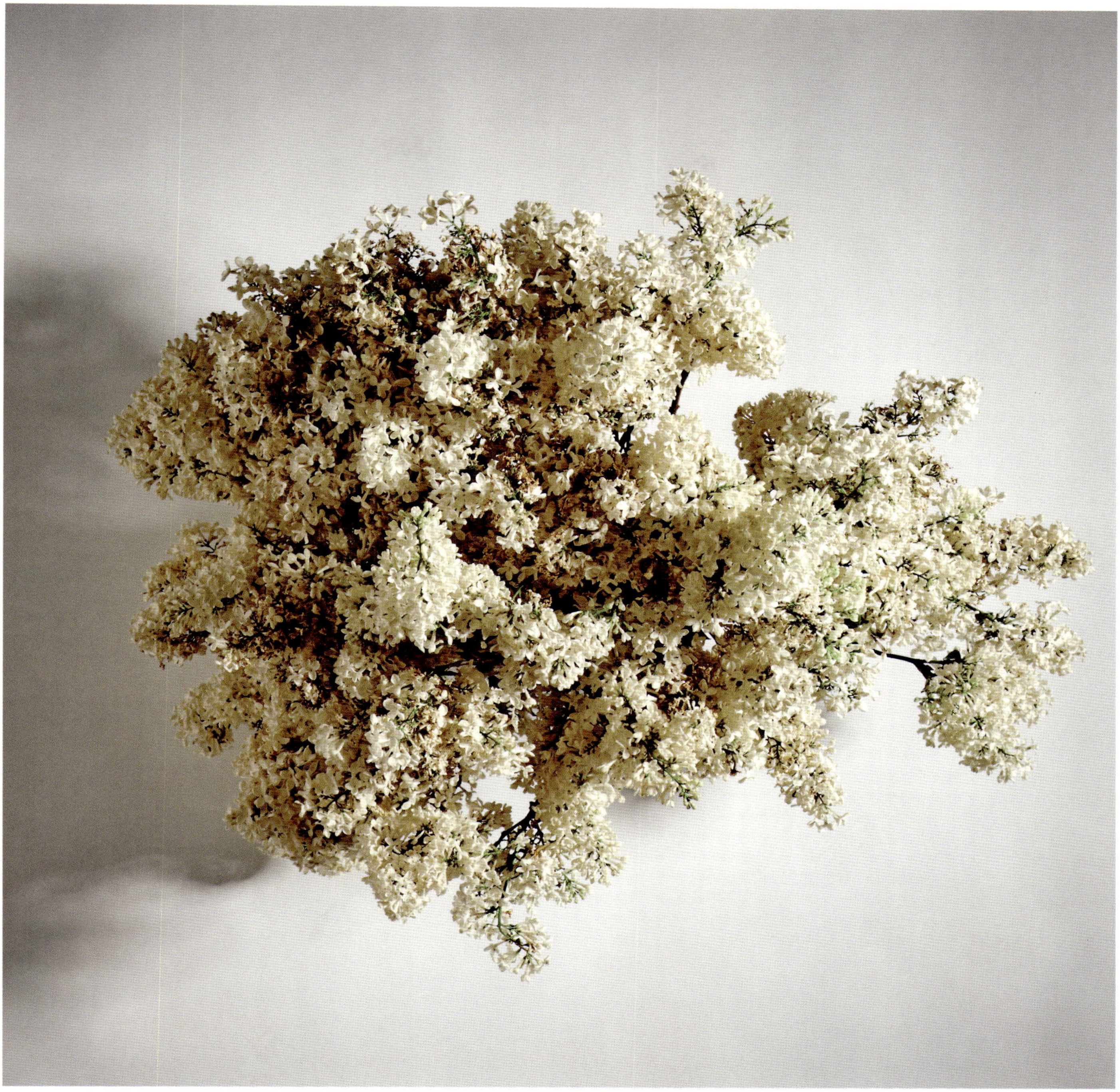

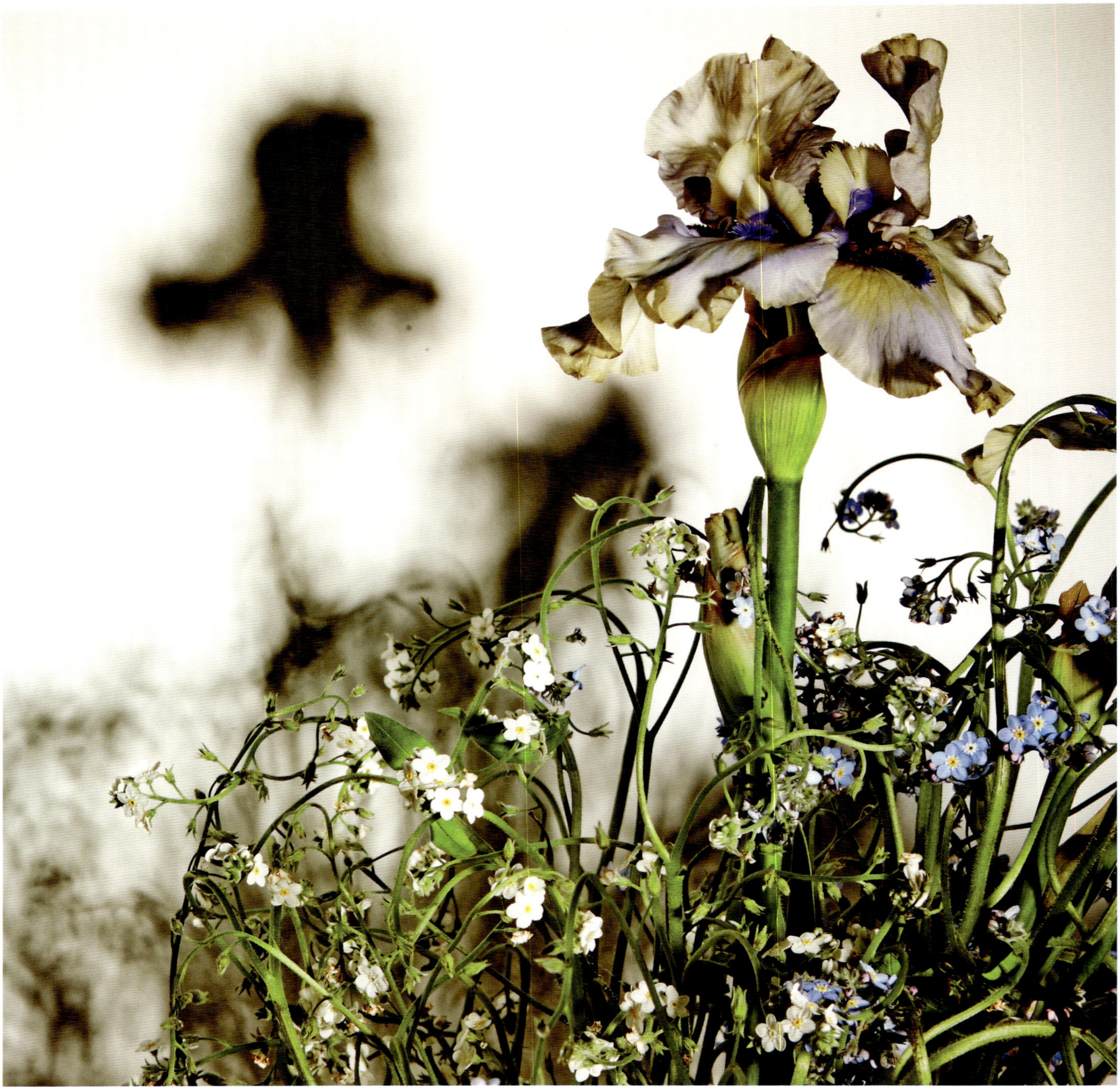

THE FORGET-ME-NOTS AND CORSAGING

—

DRAWN TOWARDS MEMORY.

For such a diminutive flower, the forget-me-not has monumental powers of evocation. Most who behold this little flower will have a memory or emotion attached to its presence. Even in the act of this writing, I am charged with sentimentality. The sight of the forget-me-not draws me toward the memory of Frank, who helped me to remember and became a man who I would not forget.

In the years that followed my father's passing I turned from a child into an adult, a transition that occurred in the shadow of grief; to say it was a difficult time is insufficient – it was the end of the world. Around three years in I found myself in the home-office of a hypnotherapist named Frank, who had put his retirement aside for an hour at the request of my family GP, who knew of Frank's immense ability. I remember sitting across from him awaiting the pendulum that might lull me and cause me inexplicably to begin acting in the manner of a chicken or a rooster despite my will and at this man's whim. He was the second oldest man I'd ever seen, second only to my great-grandfather James Garrad. His manner was gentle and he possessed a scholarly air … and his face was kind beyond description. Frank asked me a few questions and then he said, 'Do you think I can hypnotise you?' to which I replied, 'I don't know'; and then he quizzed, 'What could I do to prove it to you?' and I challenged him, 'I want to see my father again.'

Around this time I had realised that I could no longer remember my father properly. The years that had passed since I had seen him had somehow obscured the clarity of my memory of his physical presence. The days, weeks and years seemed to continually add layers that made it impossible for me to truly recall, for example, what his eyebrows looked like. That I was forgetting him was for me the deepest water in the ocean of grief.

Frank never produced a pendulum … rather, he asked me to look into his black eyes and listen to his words. With his verbal prompting I was quickly seated next to my father on the sand looking up at clouds floating in a clear blue sky and listening to the waves crashing against the shore – a repetitive scene from my childhood that Frank had asked me to choose. He had brought a memory of my father so completely to the front of my mind that it bordered on being tangible – I could see every individual hair that formed his eyebrows, I could see blood flowing through the visible veins in his forearms and I could see him smile. When finally I opened my eyes at my guide's prompting I cried deeply and struggled to express inexpressible gratitude.

Frank used his incredible skill over the following year to augment my courage, resilience and strength until the day came – as he had said it would – when I wouldn't need to see him anymore … an idea that had previously seemed inconceivable to me. During our last session he used his vast skill in hypnosis to embed a flame in my heart, telling me that for the rest of my life in times of challenge I could call upon the flame to burn more brightly.

I will forget him not.

‡

Forget-me-nots are, like most things, not created equal. The flowers in the images that accompany these memories of Frank were an early morning revelation at the flower market. It is common to see the blue variety bundled in short, dense bunches of seemingly uniform stem length, 'hedging' other flowers, suggesting that they must grow in nature like a thick, ground-covering grass. To find them as I did this day in bundles of both blue and radiant white, at differing lengths, with long stems bending and undulant, was truly wonderful.

In previous chapters I have identified the exercise of massing one type of flower as a starting point for those interested in learning to work with flowers. I have said that in the practice of grouping one type of flower the enthusiast is able to learn – through a focus on shape, balance and repetition – the importance of intention in the creation of floral compositions. The arrangement that encapsulates the story of Frank epitomises what I would recommend as a subsequent exercise – through a method I call 'corsaging', whereby a second variety of bloom is used in order to juxtapose the predominant flower. Having mastered one-tone and one-flower combinations, the introduction of a second floral element and colour to the palette – placing one bloom in proximity to another – emphasises the visual dynamism of the arrangement. In corsaging, one bloom in relation to a bulk of another type of flower is a way of harmonising the composition: it can be achieved either through a tonal or textural similarity between the two, or by exploiting the juxtaposition to focus attention on the uniqueness of a very complex or intricate flower within the whole.

The blue and white forget-me-nots that are pictured here constitute a textural dominance within the arrangement and draw the eye to the astonishing beauty of the pale-blue bearded iris. The irises seemingly rise up from within the bulk of forget-me-nots as if 'growing' above the little flowers, as they would do in nature. The iris itself possesses a complex palette that harmonises with and provides a tonal link between the blue and white forget-me-nots. The ruffled corsage of pale-blue irises emerging asymmetrically from the bed of forget-me-nots are further enhanced by a third, single, bearded iris that appears in another part of the composition. While being in tonal harmony with the other bearded irises, the outer petals of this lone bloom are edged in deep crimson and its inner ruffle is a blushed, salmon-pink colour. The placement of this aberrant iris draws attention to its complex hypnotic beauty and the variety within the species itself ... the juxtaposition illustrating the creative possibilities of 'corsaging'.

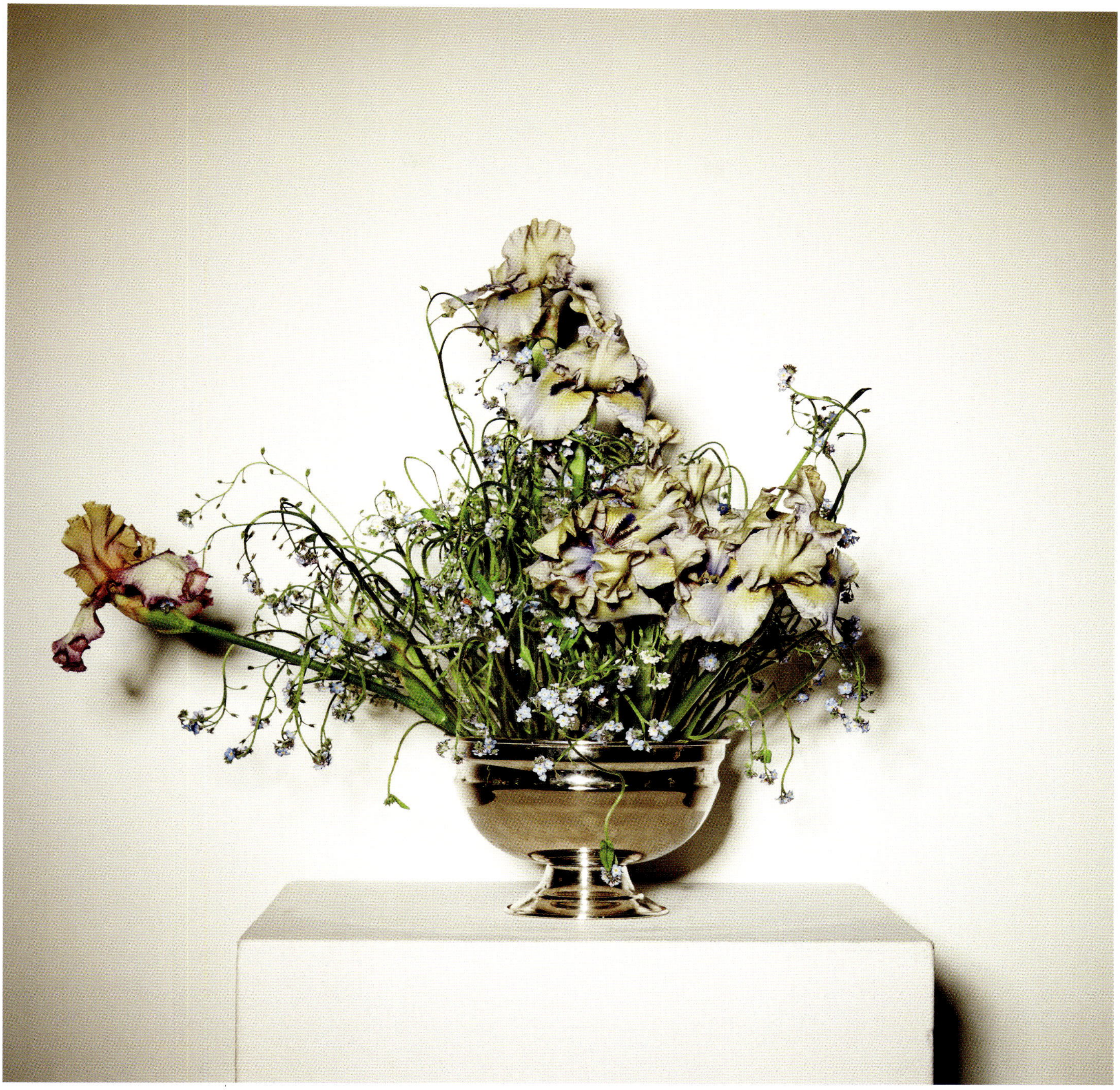

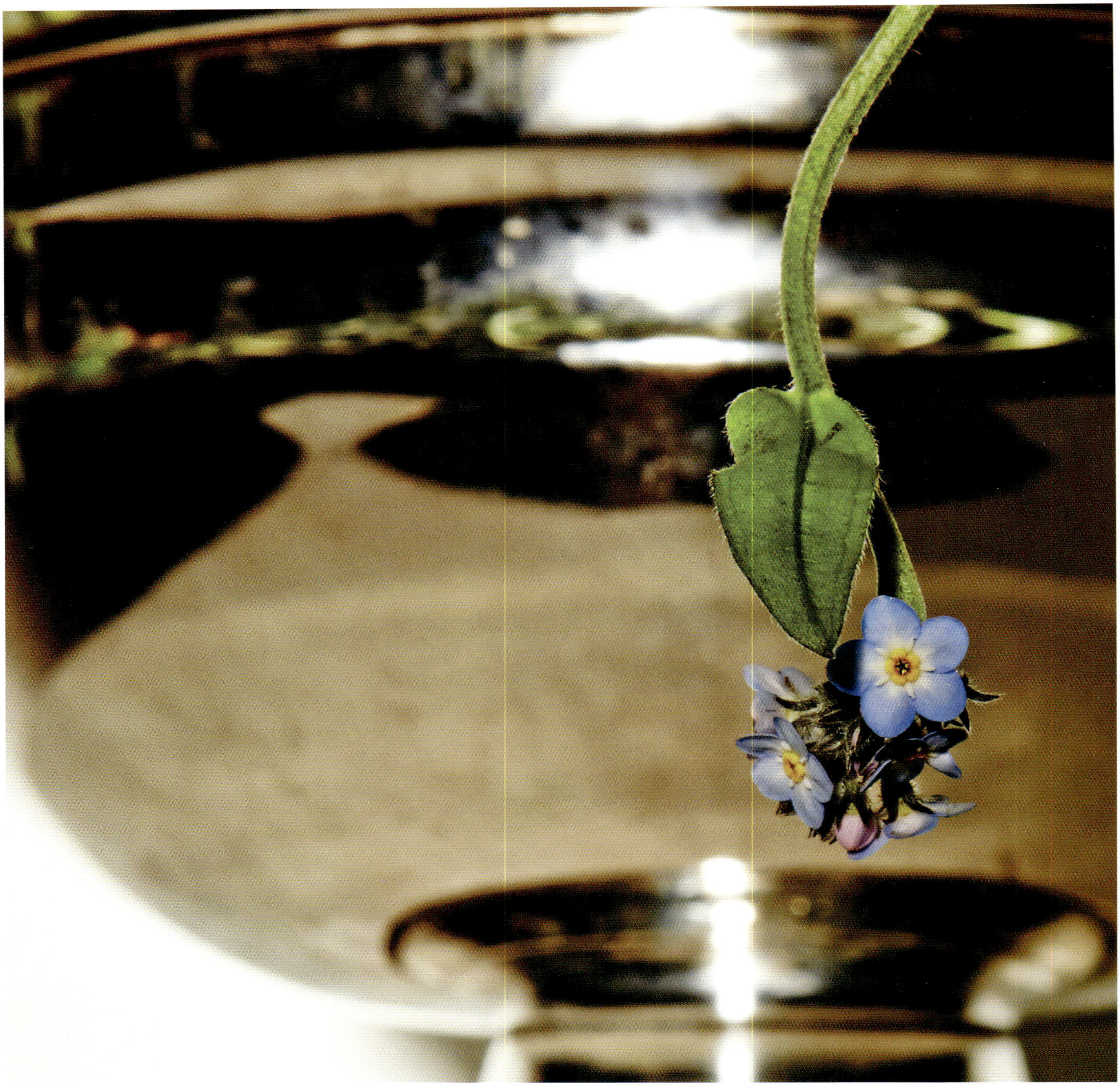

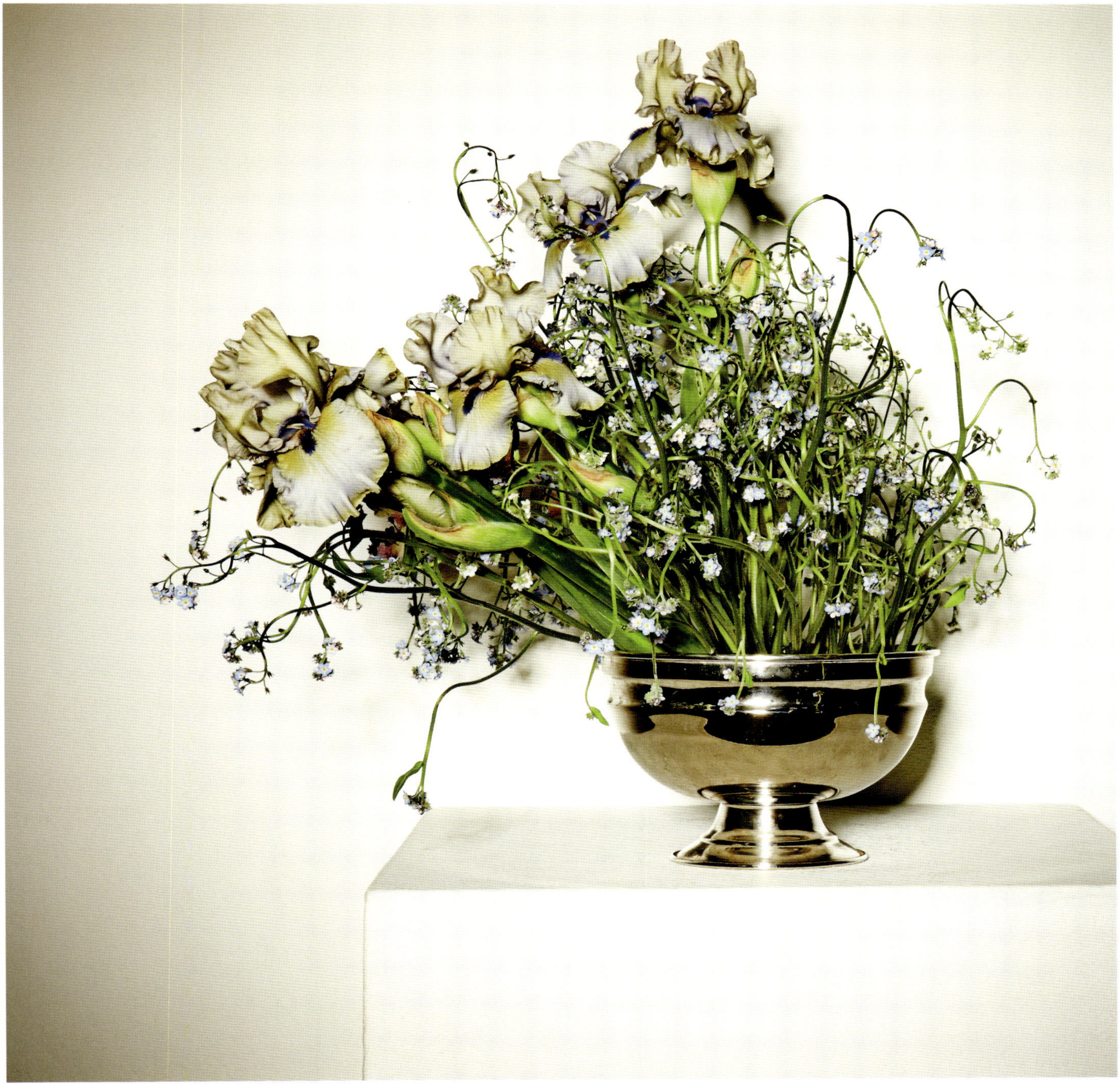

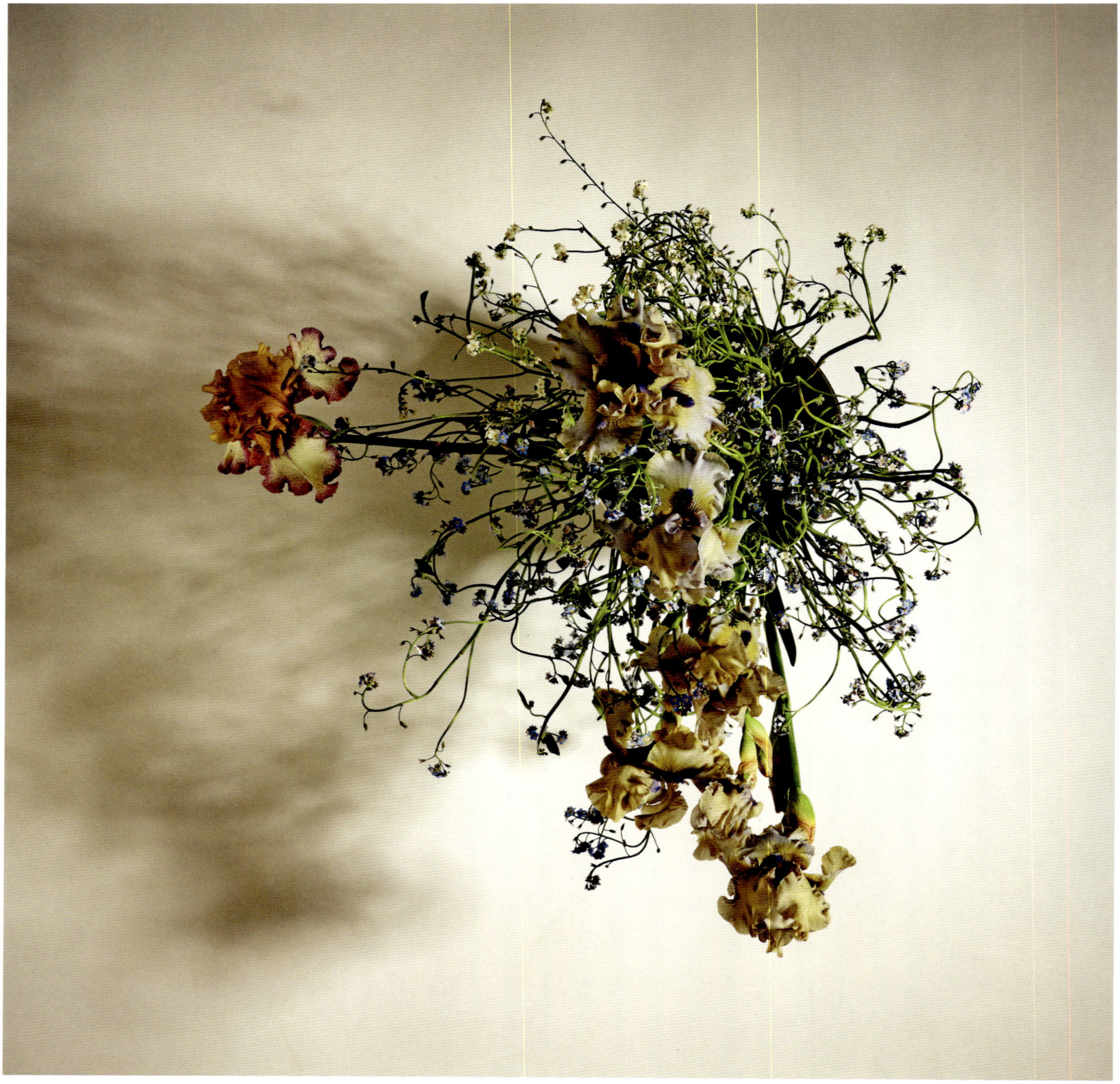

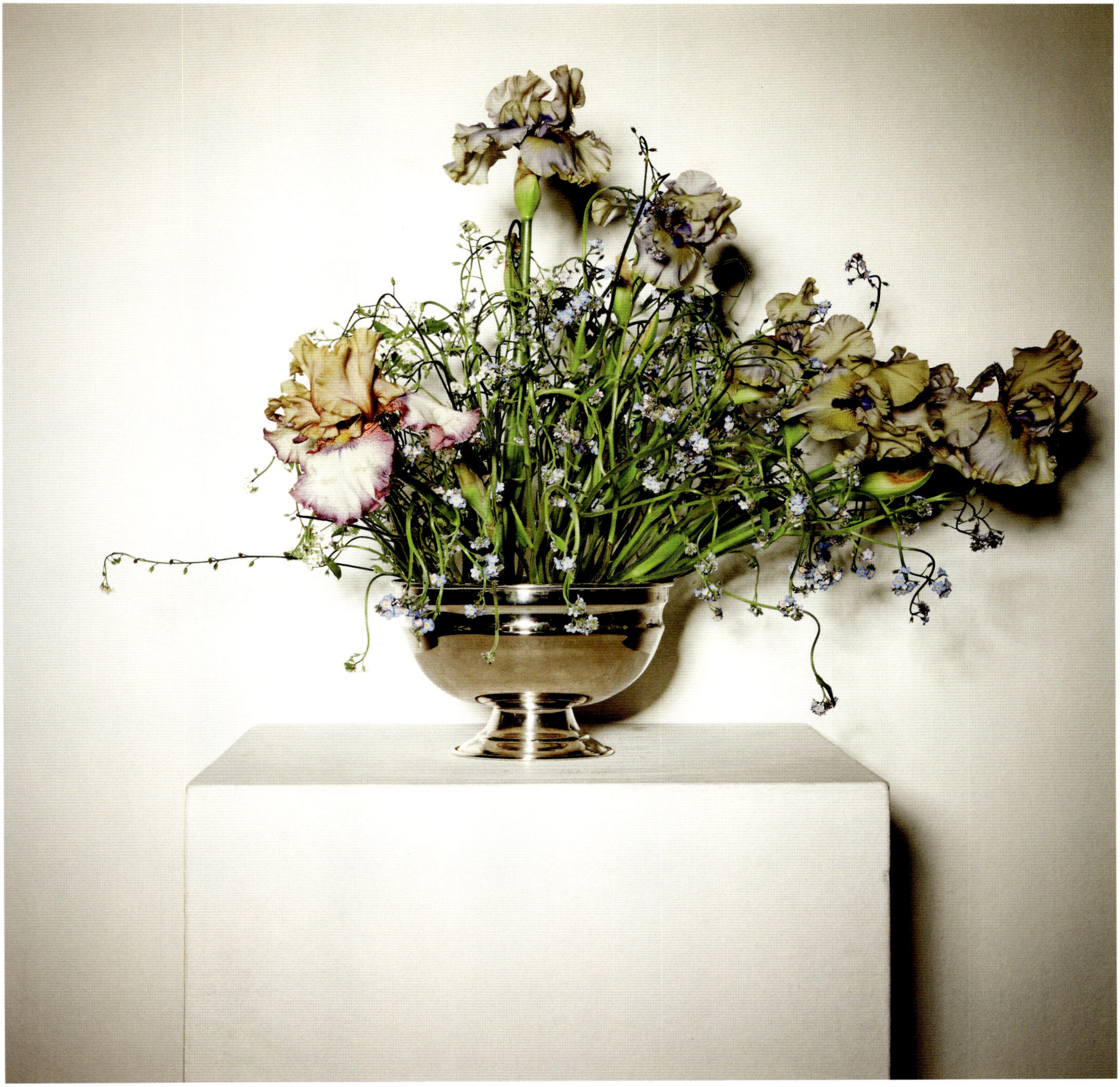

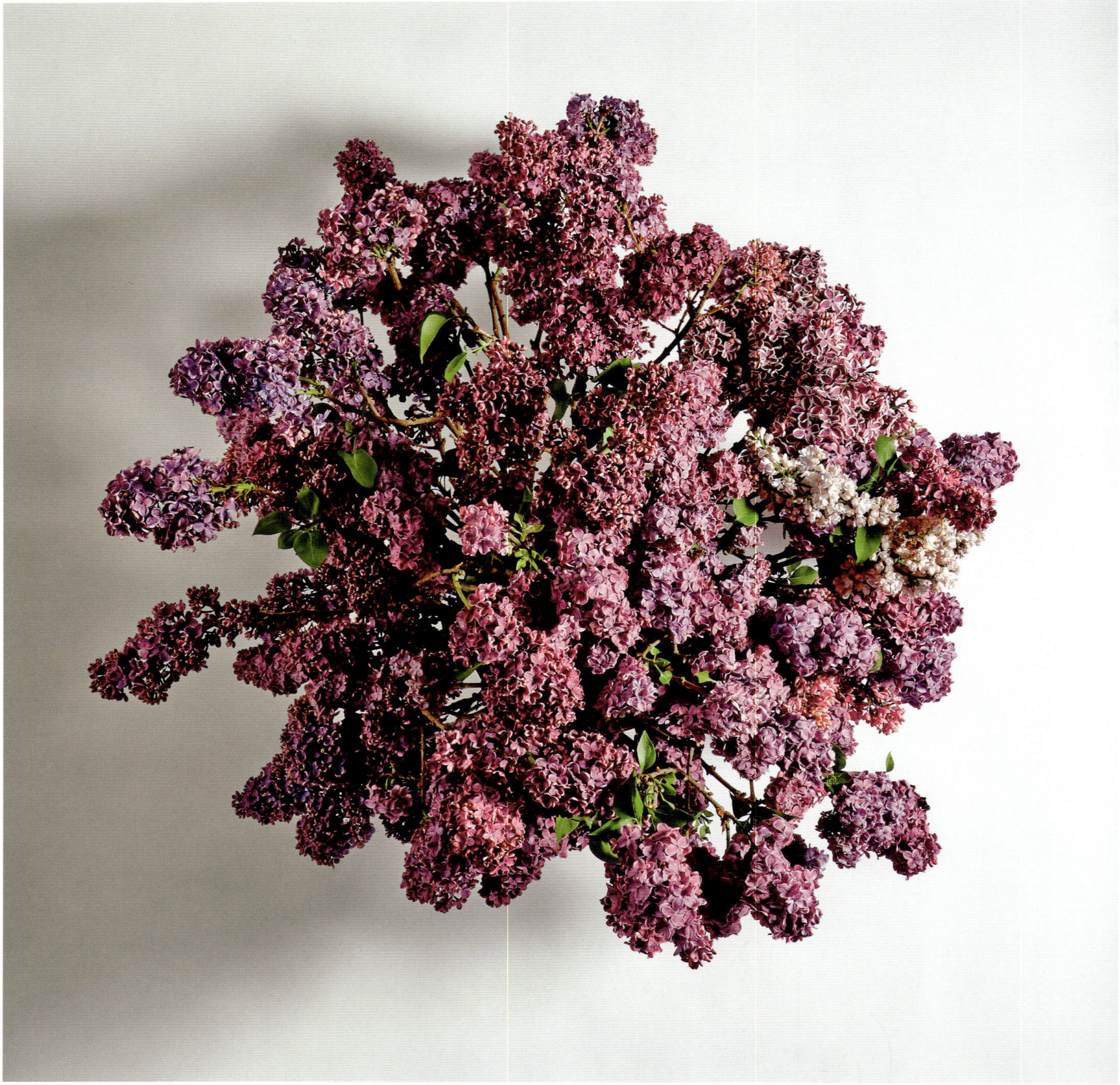

JEKYLL AND LILAC

—

IN A GARDEN ARRANGEMENT, AS IN ALL OTHER KINDS OF DECORATIVE WORK, ONE HAS NOT ONLY TO ACQUIRE A KNOWLEDGE OF WHAT TO DO, BUT ALSO TO GAIN SOME WISDOM IN PERCEIVING WHAT IT IS WELL TO LET ALONE.
— GERTRUDE JEKYLL

At a glamorous private party I attended a little while ago, I was taken on a tour of a highly discerning art collection, regaled with lively conversation and given a very generous compliment that led to a loan of two beautiful books and the discovery of an important and inspiring figure in gardening and flowers. The books were titled *Garden Ornament* and *Gardens for Small Country Houses*.

I was likened to Gertrude Jekyll …

‡

Gertrude Jekyll (1843–1932) was a British-born horticulturalist, garden designer, artist and writer. At the age of eighteen she enrolled at the South Kensington School of Art and later the Royal College of Art, both in London, in the discipline of painting; but she also studied botany, anatomy, optics and the science of colour. At the conclusion of her study she travelled, researching and practising other art forms that she observed on her travels – including singing, painting, carving, embroidery, gilding, metal work and photography – and began collecting plants. Upon her return to London, she exhibited her paintings and enjoyed a considerable reputation as an artist and craftsperson, receiving many commissions. In 1868 her mother, recently widowed, bought a home in Berkshire, 40 miles west of London, and Jekyll was given her first opportunity to design a garden. This initial 'painterly' design was much celebrated and would become the first of over 400 gardens she would design in her life, in Britain, Europe and the United States. In time she met the English architect Sir Edwin Lutyens (1869–1944), for whose projects she created numerous landscapes, and together they became one of the most influential and iconic partnerships of the Arts and Crafts movement.

Jekyll is celebrated for her creative approach to garden design, which, at the time, was an innovative departure from the traditional gardens of the day. Her work is distinguished by its use of luminous colour and the brush-like strokes of her plantings; she was deeply influenced by the painter J. M. W. Turner and the Impressionists, as well as by the work of William Morris and John Ruskin. These influences are reflected in her approach to landscaping, whereby she grouped plants according to a harmony of colour, texture and shape. She was also a prolific writer who authored more than a dozen books and at least a thousand articles for magazines and journals in her lifetime.

Due to her famously exacting standards, Jekyll was also concerned with the placement of cut flowers from the garden in the home. Unable to find glassware she deemed appropriate, she commissioned the Munstead line of flower glasses. The simple, practical vases were named after her home and plant nursery in Munstead Wood, Surrey – the place where she wrote *Flower Decoration in the House*. The glasses first produced in the 1880s were hand-blown by the Whitefriars Glass factory and sold by James Green & Nephew. Jekyll also advocated the use of salad bowls, soup tureens, glass finger bowls and ginger jars as vessels to hold cut flowers – a wildly outrageous concept at the time, but common in the work of florists today.

I have of course pored over the books that I borrowed that evening … that I've had on loan for far too long. It is the front cover of *Gardens for Small Country Houses* that I am having trouble relinquishing – it is a photograph by Michael Warren that shows a part of Vita Sackville-West's garden at Sissinghurst in the county of Kent, England. The image shows a section of the garden that is planted out in purple tones: in the foreground is an impossibly large and abundant daphne bush and in the mid-ground is the most monumental, deeply coloured lilac bush at what must be its peak bloom. I cannot seem to stop 'stepping into' that garden.

‡

The flower arrangement that accompanies this text justifies the comparison of Gertrude Jekyll with me – if but only in a minor way. She was one of the first flower authorities to contradict the high Victorian standard of complicated flower arranging that included every bloom to be found in the garden as well as fruit and foliage.

Jekyll promoted a new method of flower arranging that was less formal, less ornate and less complicated. She favoured arrangements of single varieties of flowers which, while appearing modern and sophisticated for the day, revealed the benefits for home owners with space in their gardens for beds dedicated to growing flowers for picking. This contrasted with the limited opportunities available to those without a 'cutting garden', who could only arrange fewer, and differing, blooms, lest their gardens appear bare.

The arrangement reproduced here includes four different-coloured lilac – a pale pink, a mauve, a deep purple, and a purple variegated variety. They are incredibly strong specimens, picked at the peak of the season, and of course their fragrance is legendary. While cut lilacs rarely last more than five days, their fragrance will fill the room, if not the whole house. The flowers are extraordinarily beautiful to behold ... not just for the complexity of the bloom, but also for the vivid intensity of their colours.

In order to keep them in a vase for as long as possible, it is important to use good secateurs to cut sharp angles in the stem – it is then necessary to cut and split the stems 5 centimetres up the centre. After removing most of the leaves, place the lilac blooms up to their necks in a deep bucket of cool water and let them soak for several hours or overnight. When arranging them, use a vessel that can hold plenty of cold tap water: and even though cut lilac is short-lived, the stems need to be re-cut each day and the water changed.

‡

During her years of study, Gertrude Jekyll attended the lectures of John Ruskin (1819–1900), the foremost Victorian art critic and proponent of the Arts and Crafts movement. Ruskin said a great many things that deeply influenced her work, but one statement in particular seemed to pierce her soul: 'There is material enough in a single flower for the ornament of a score of cathedrals.'

In the studio, the lilac blooms up to their necks in cool water capture the essence of Ruskin's description of a single flower. I imagine I am Gertrude Jekyll seated in the room, entranced not by words, but by the colour and complexity of every flower head ... overpowered by their deep purple fragrance. For me their presence, this moment of reflection, is as intoxicating as any glamorous party.

And, again, I find myself stepping into Vita's garden.

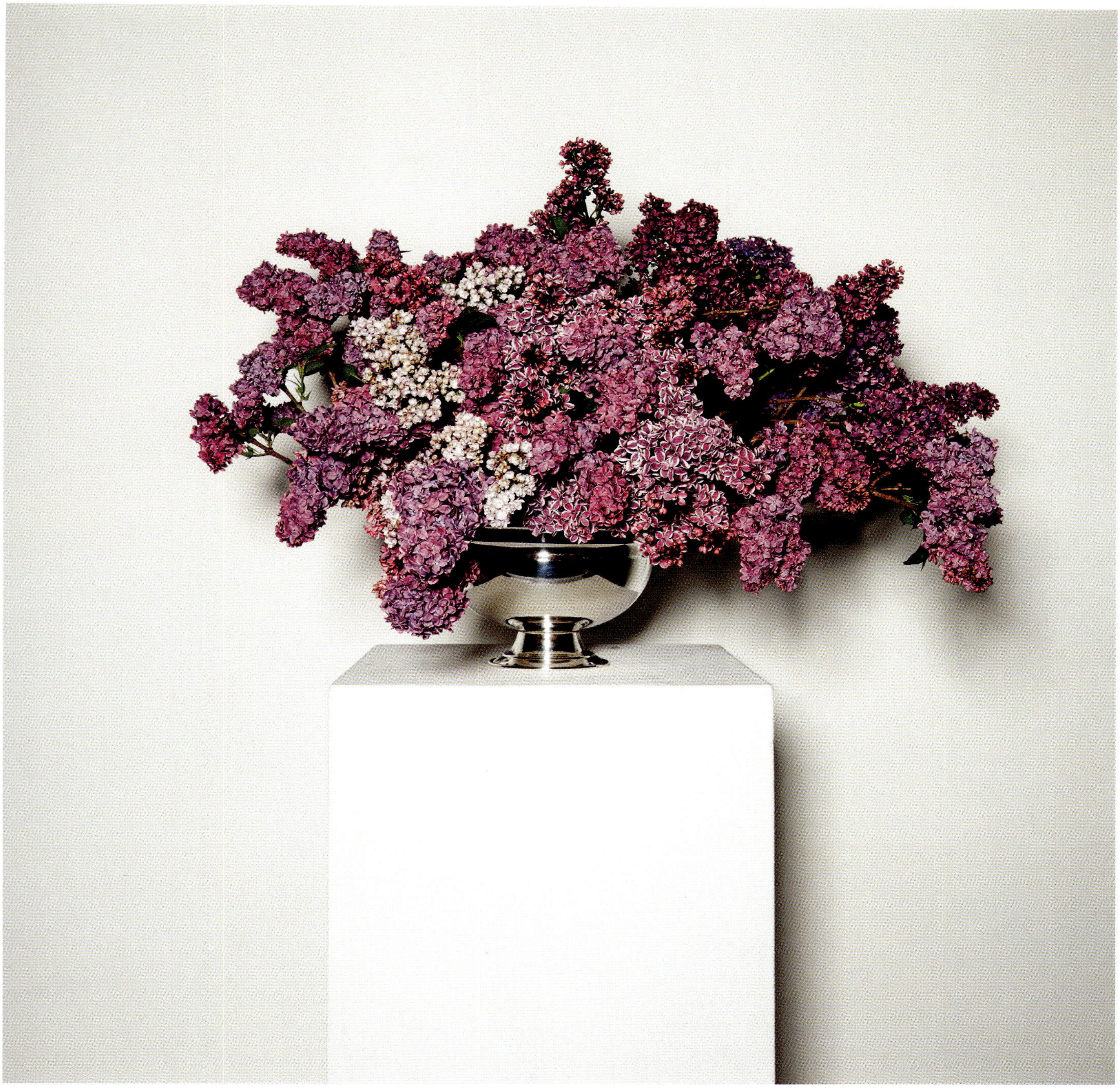

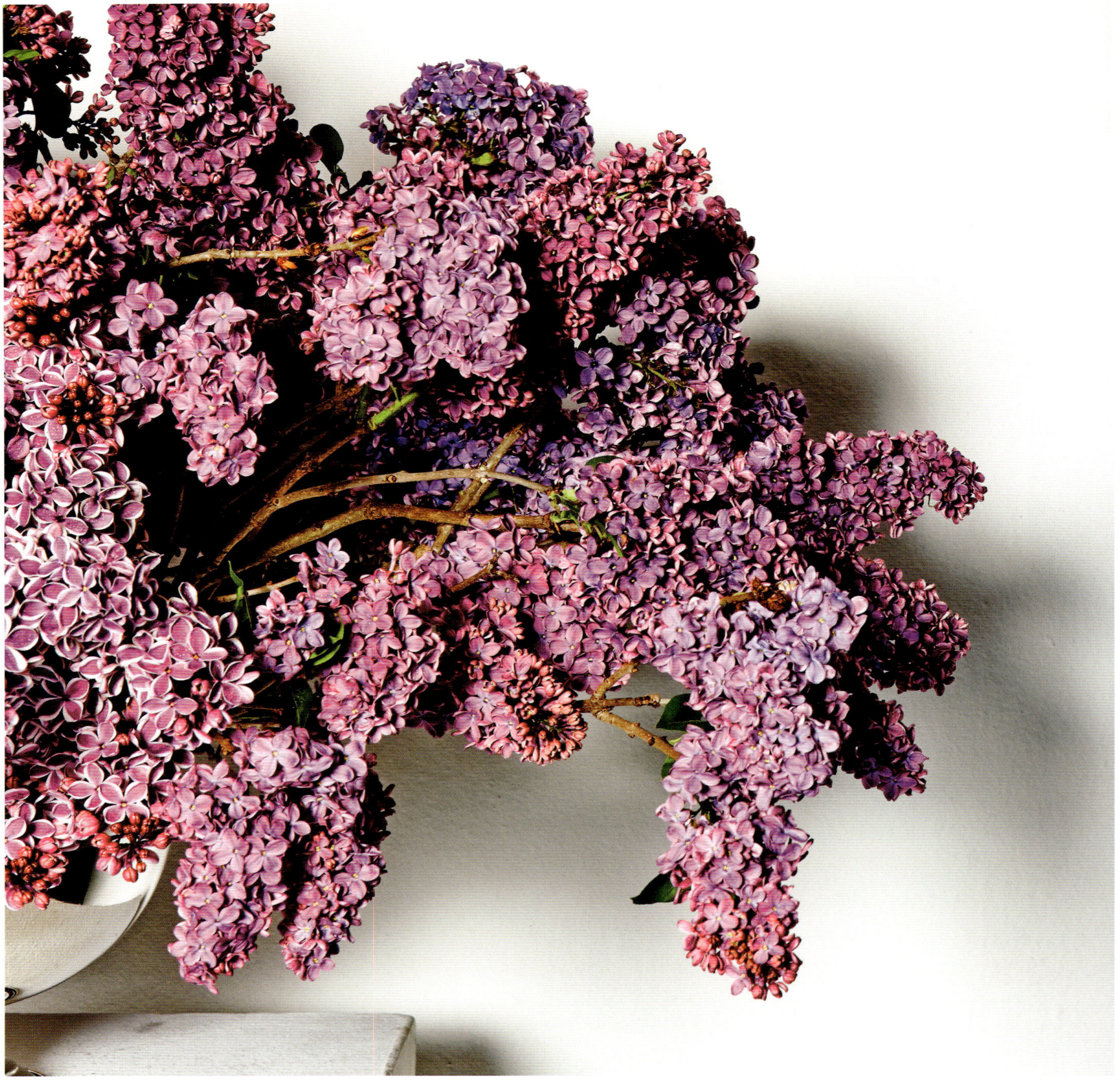

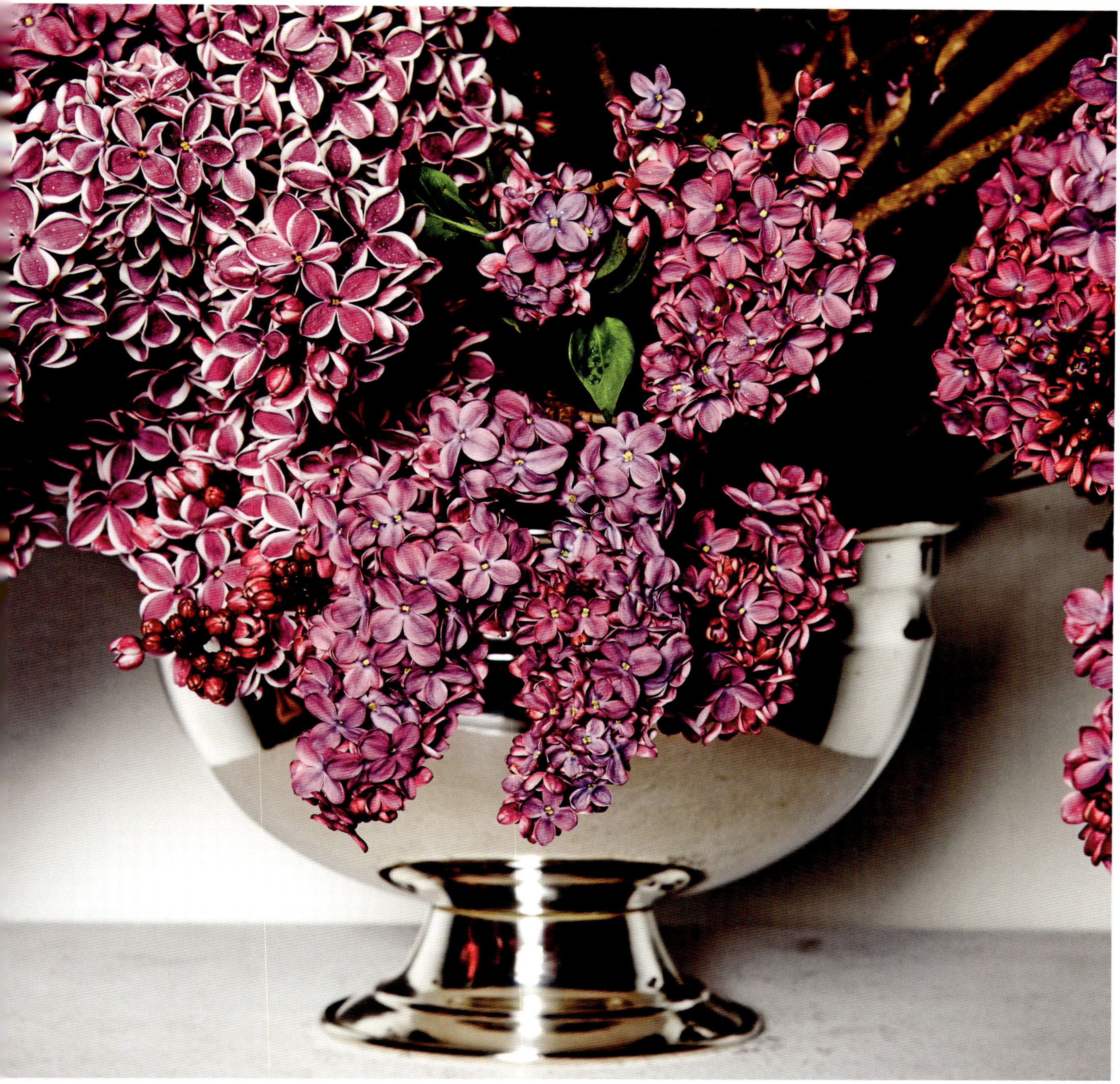

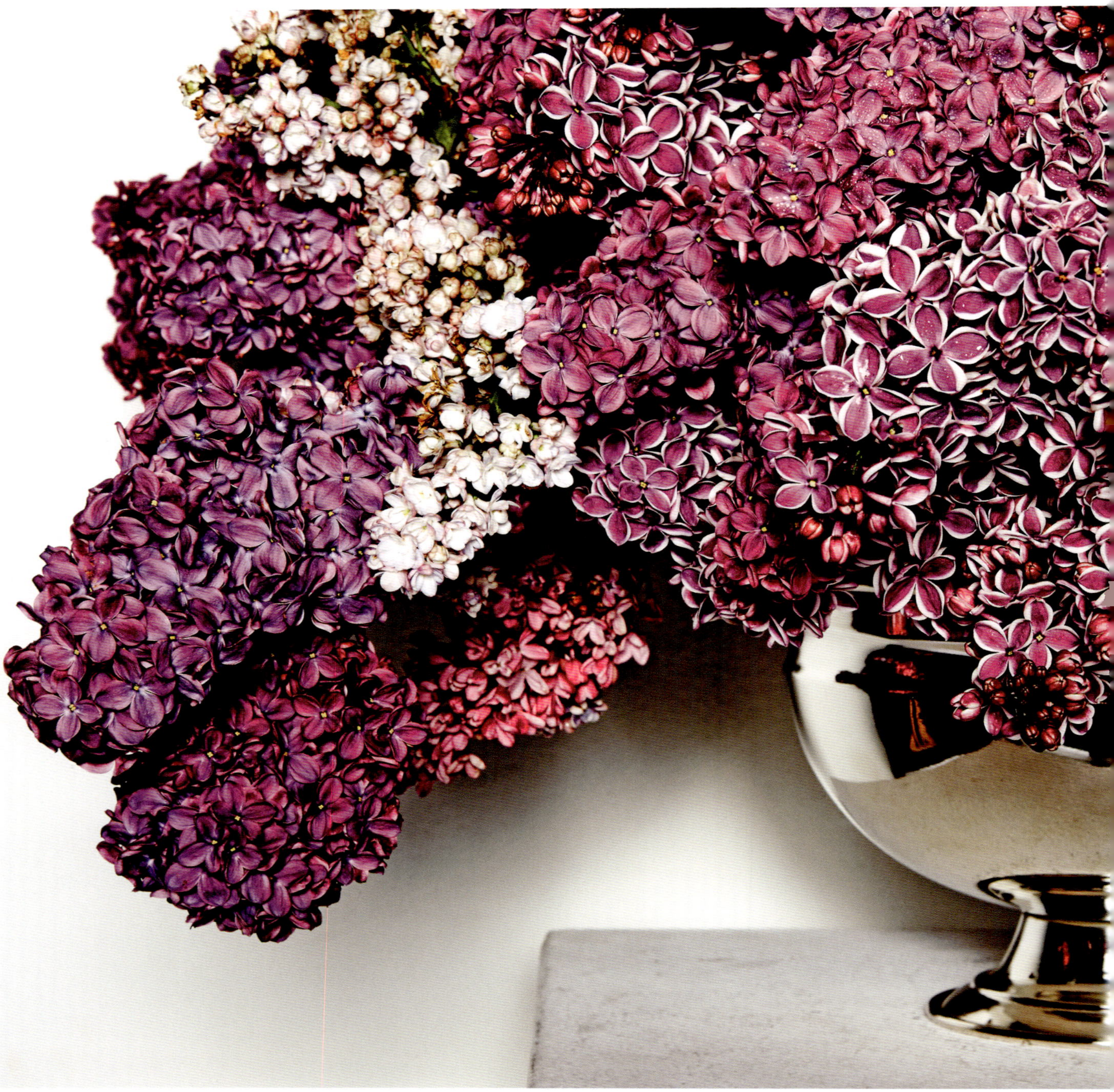

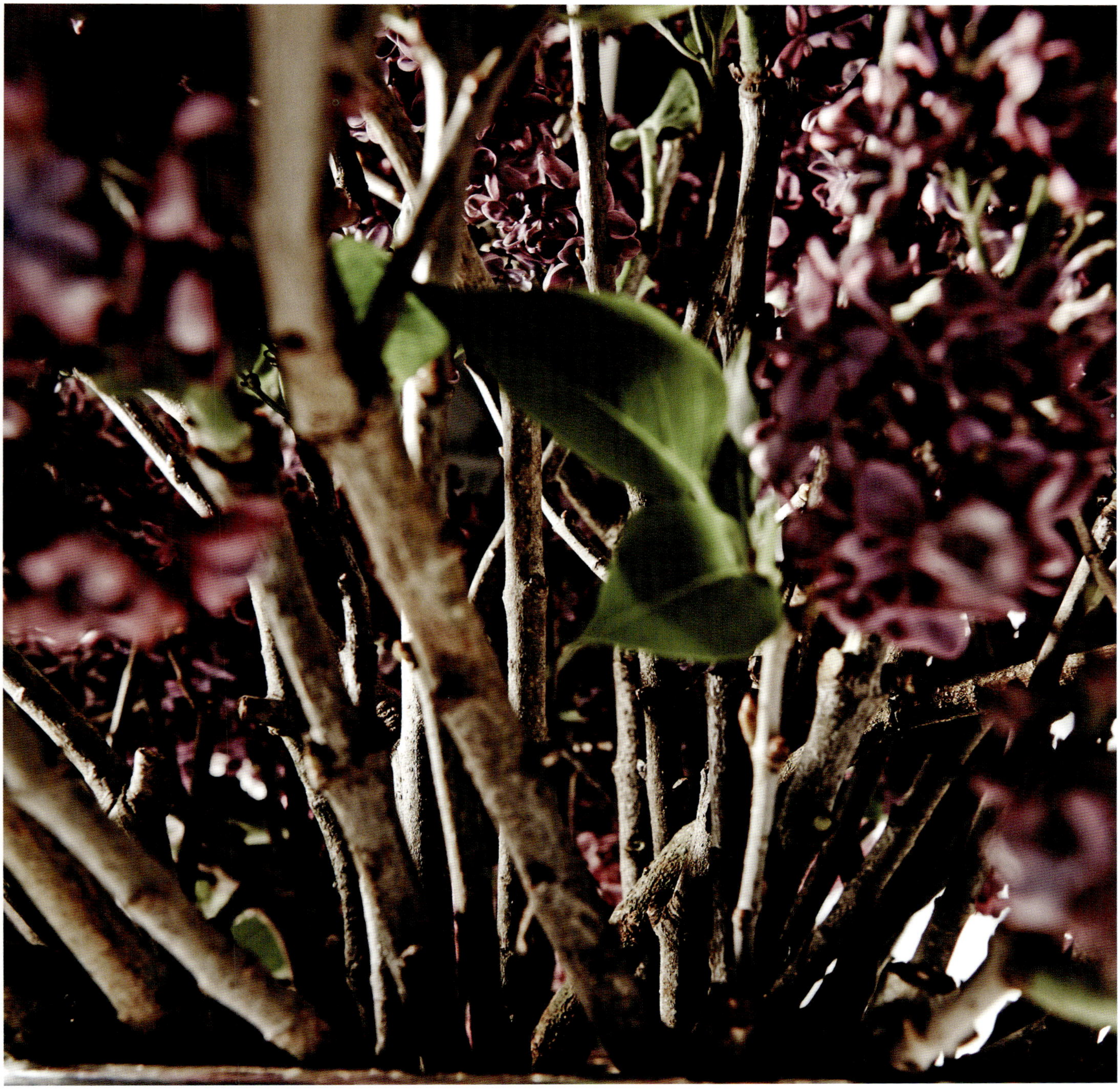

THE BEARDED IRIS

—

ANCESTORS OF THE SUPREMELY COMPLEX AND INTRICATE BLOOM CLUNG IN PAINT TO CANVASES.

On a recent trip to France I had the good fortune to visit Claude Monet's garden. After leaving my accommodation in Honfleur I spoke very little to my chauffeur, Bob, who deftly handled our hired fire-engine-red Fiat on what seemed to me – a driver from the other side of the world – the 'wrong side of the road'. The hour-and-a-half drive was relentlessly picturesque, and I spent the whole trip trying to take it all in and lock it away – committing to memory the incredible natural beauty that surrounded us. For miles and miles, enormous silver birch seemed to chaperone us through winding lanes – an army of them standing to attention on either side of the long road. At other turns in the journey a bend in the path would lead to fields of monumental green and copper beech. As if my heart could take it, we passed dozens and dozens of apple orchards the likes of which surely inspired the myths that would become the fairytales of all of our childhoods.

Since the eleventh century the apple orchards of Normandy have been deeply connected to the fortunes and thirsts of the Normans. It has been said that at the turn of the last century there was barely a field in Normandy that didn't grow apples – for producing cider. The enormous, protracted, apple-laden branches start high up the elegant trunk of the tree and grow undulant, bowing under the weight of the copious fruit each branch produces. To dislodge the ripened fruit, a 'striker' uses a long pole to shake the tree and loosen the apples, which fall onto soft green grass, to be easily collected. The fact that the branches of the trees are high on the trunk means the land can simultaneously be used for pasturing cows – the area producing some of the most delicious milk, cheese and butter in the world.

I am a bit overcome by the time we reach the village of Giverny on the right bank of the River Seine; I take in the hollyhocks growing like mad up and down Rue Claude Monet – the street (surely then by another name) where Claude Monet lived from 1883 until his death in 1926. Such extraordinary beauty, and I hadn't even seen the iconic garden yet. The grounds were enchanting, as promised, despite my being obliged to share the experience of seeing the celebrated and significant estate in early autumn with innumerable other visitors. There were no bearded irises – but there was both the memory and the promise of them in the air.

Ancestors of the supremely complex and intricate bloom clung in paint to canvases realised by Monet, a giant of Impressionism. At the time of our visit, with the summer past – summer being the season when the rhizome and leaves take in the sun's energy and light and store them as sugars – the bearded iris were silently initiating the creation of a new bloom.

‡

The different varieties of bearded iris in the arrangement that accompanies these words represent the foundations of a new obsession for the grower, Andrew. At a Rare Plant Fair some months before the time of writing he had made contact with a farmer from Orange, a city in the Central West region of New South Wales, who had propagated hundreds of varieties. The interest and complexity of the flower spurred Andrew to buy a small quantity of the rhizomes that carry the flower and see how they would grow on his land – a test patch if you like. The tall bearded iris ranges in colour from white to cream, apricot, salmon and pink, to orange, copper and tan; from icy, pale blue to lilac; from flax to royal blue and very nearly a proper black. There are primrose-yellows, golds, mulberry-purple, violet, deep crimson and browns … and the most incredible combinations of these tones, as well as varieties that are dotted, stippled and stitched with a deeper colour in intricate patterning. Their texture also has much variance, from silk and taffeta to velvet; and their falls may be ruffled or flared.

The bearded iris is a supremely beautiful cut flower that, as a consequence of its vast 'rainbow' of colours (the Greek origins of its name), is very useful when composing many different flowers together within one arrangement. The complexity of the palette and patterning of each flower means that

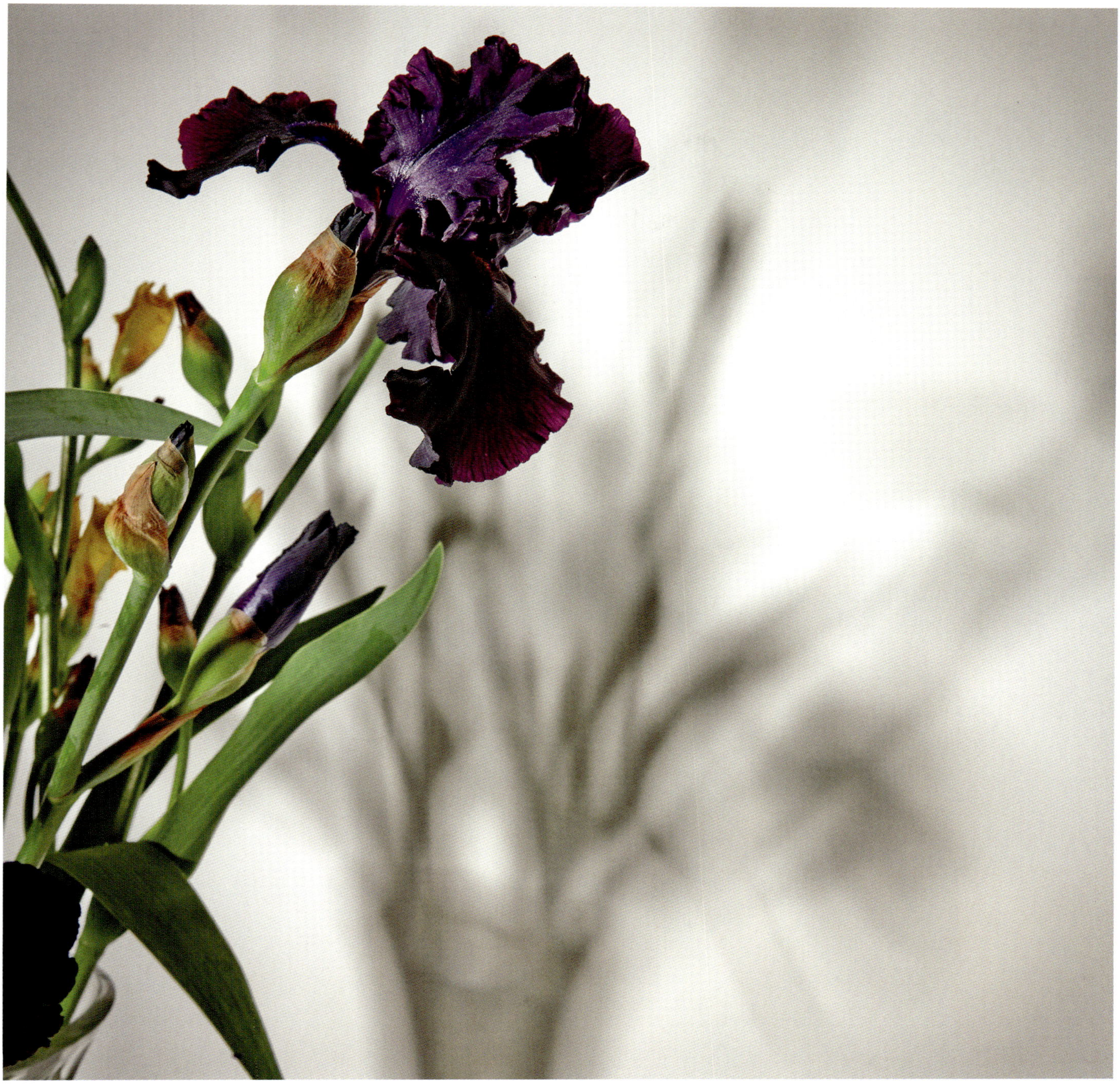

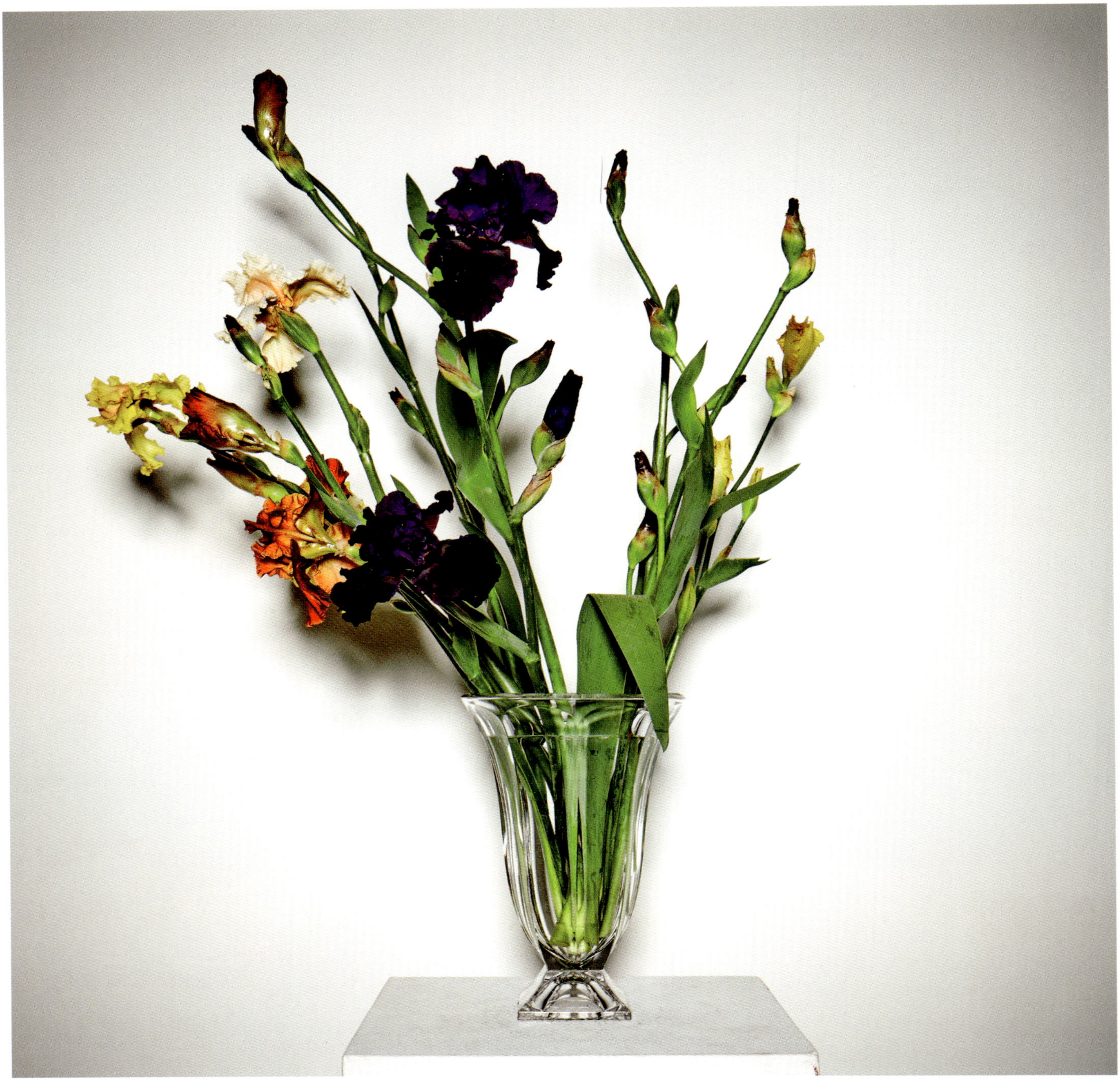

a stem of its blooms might pleasingly and surprisingly cooperate with an arrangement that is based upon a harmony within the tonal palette; and, at other times, the vibrancy of the flower's colouring, patterning and texture might contrast another palette of blooms to great effect. But, for my compositions, the staggered phases of the opening bloom that coexist on the one tall stem make it a flower that I love to cut and have at its fullest length in a clear glass vase, so that I can watch the riveting process of the flower's evolution from bud to open flower. Watching this flower unfurl is truly astonishing. Some will pick off the dying buds and watch as the others reveal their magnificent flowers, but for me the process of the flower's swift breakdown is as beautiful ... the colour and texture deepening as the bloom closes once more. But then, I am subversive that way.

‡

With a northwest aspect that allows for the warmest sun and light at a point during the day across all of the seasons, Andrew has erected a 3.3-hectare shadehouse to the southwest of his farmhouse. Under the massive shade-cloth, hydrangea, hellebore, guelder rose and Russell lupin flourish among other varieties throughout the seasons. But this past spring, in one small corner of a 60-acre property off a dirt road in Oakdale, New South Wales, a few dozen of the most beguiling flowers known to man rose high above their fanning, spear-like leaves. They were then brought to the Sydney Flower Market, where they took my breath away.

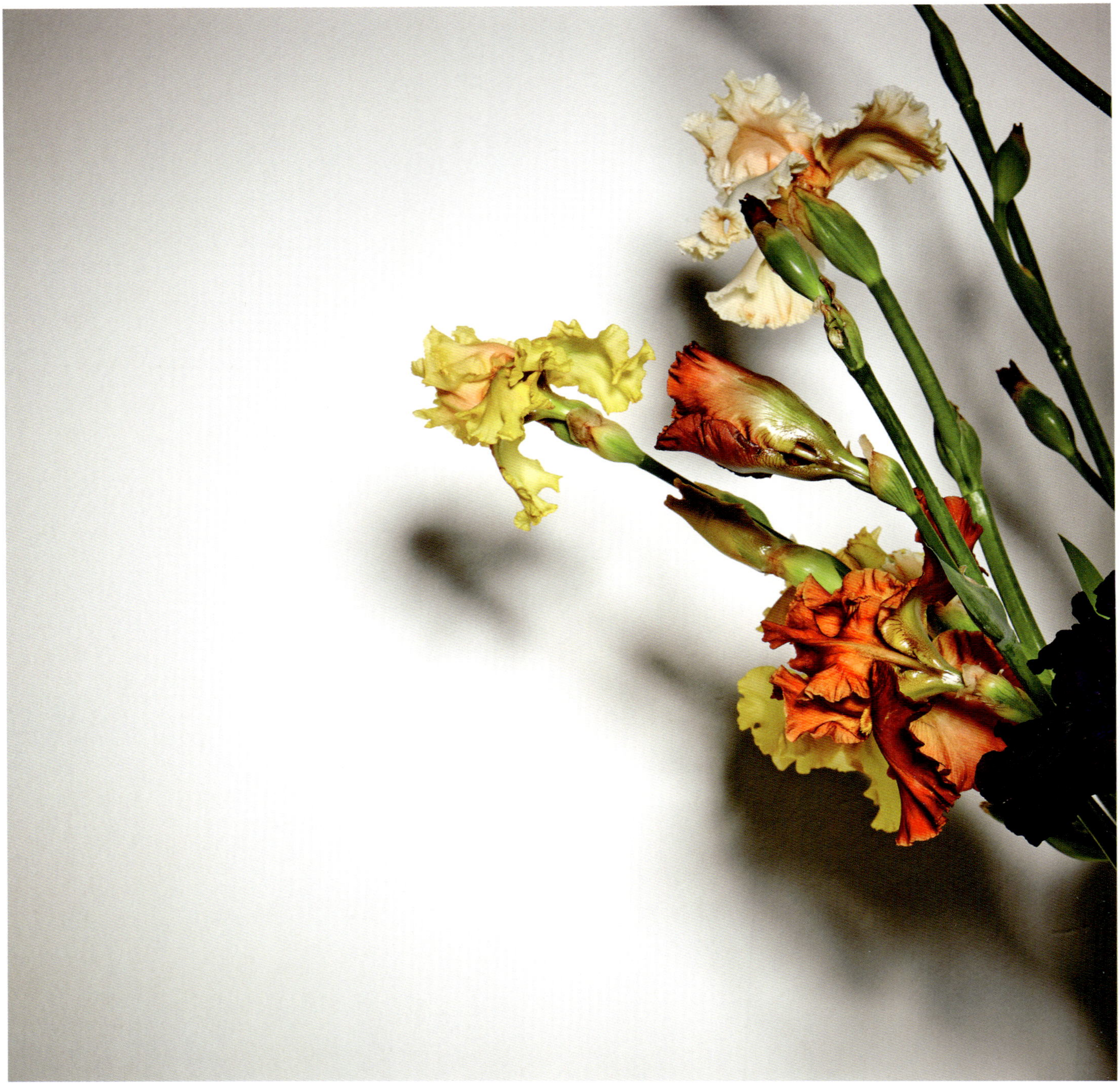

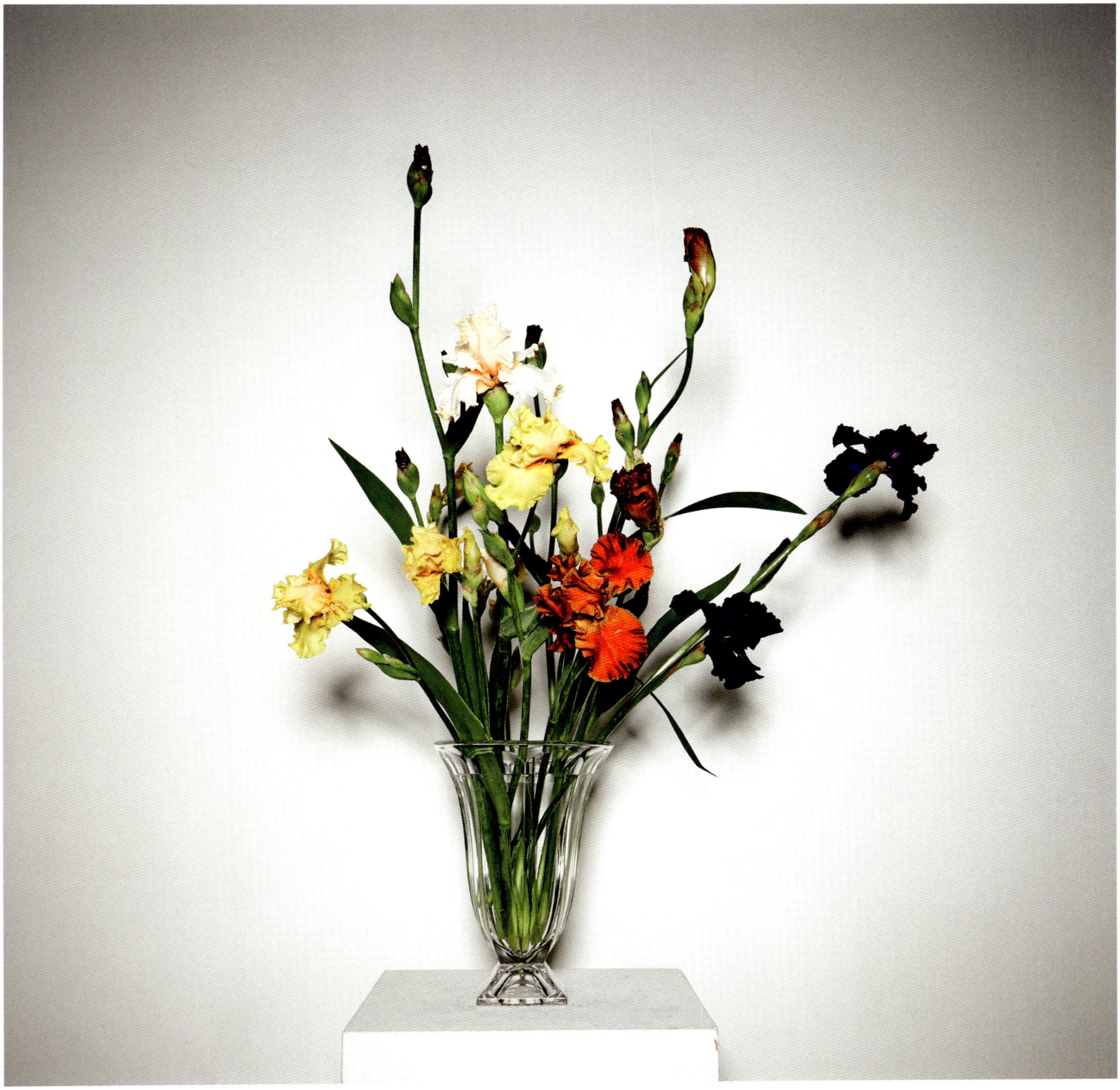

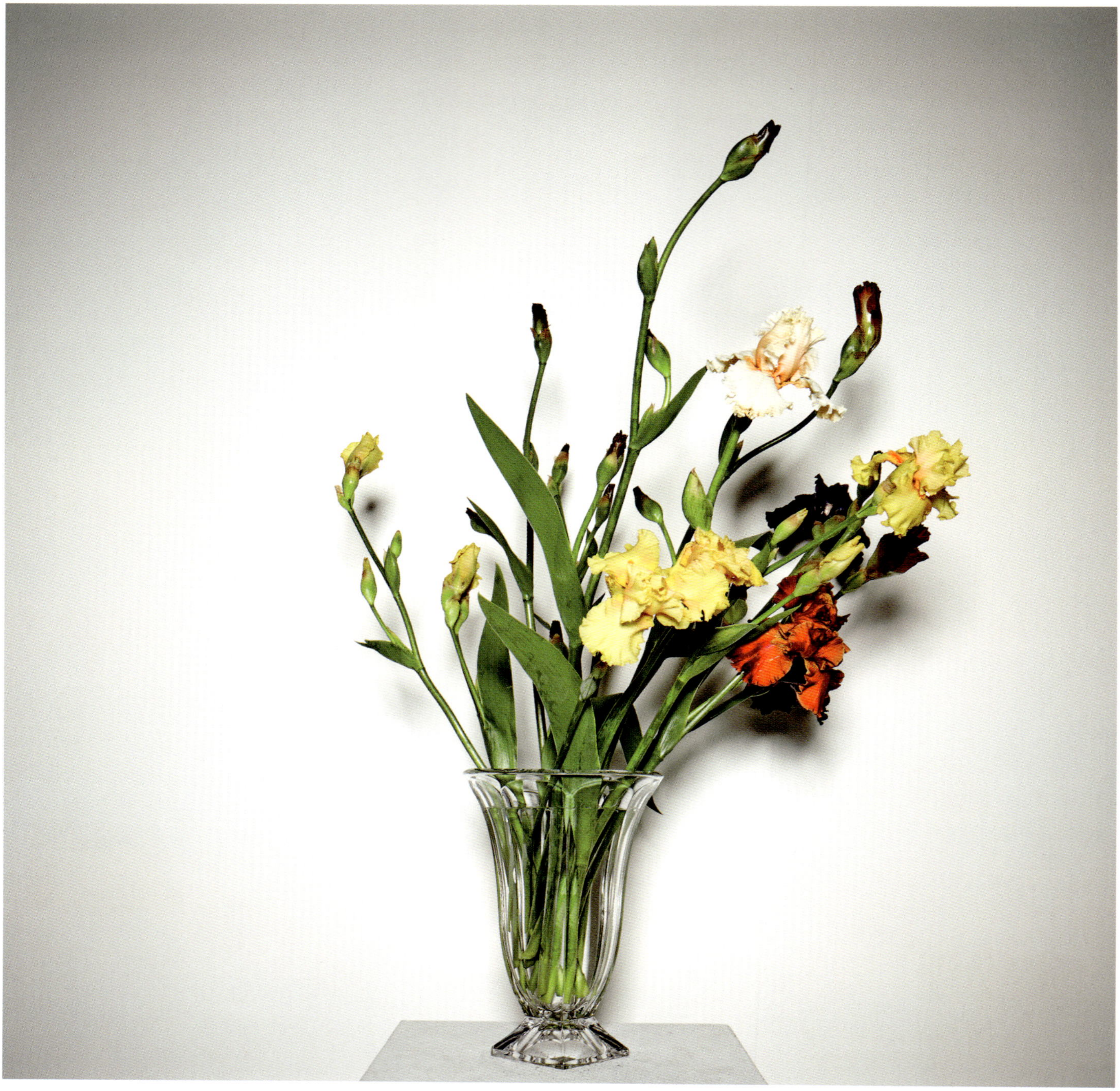

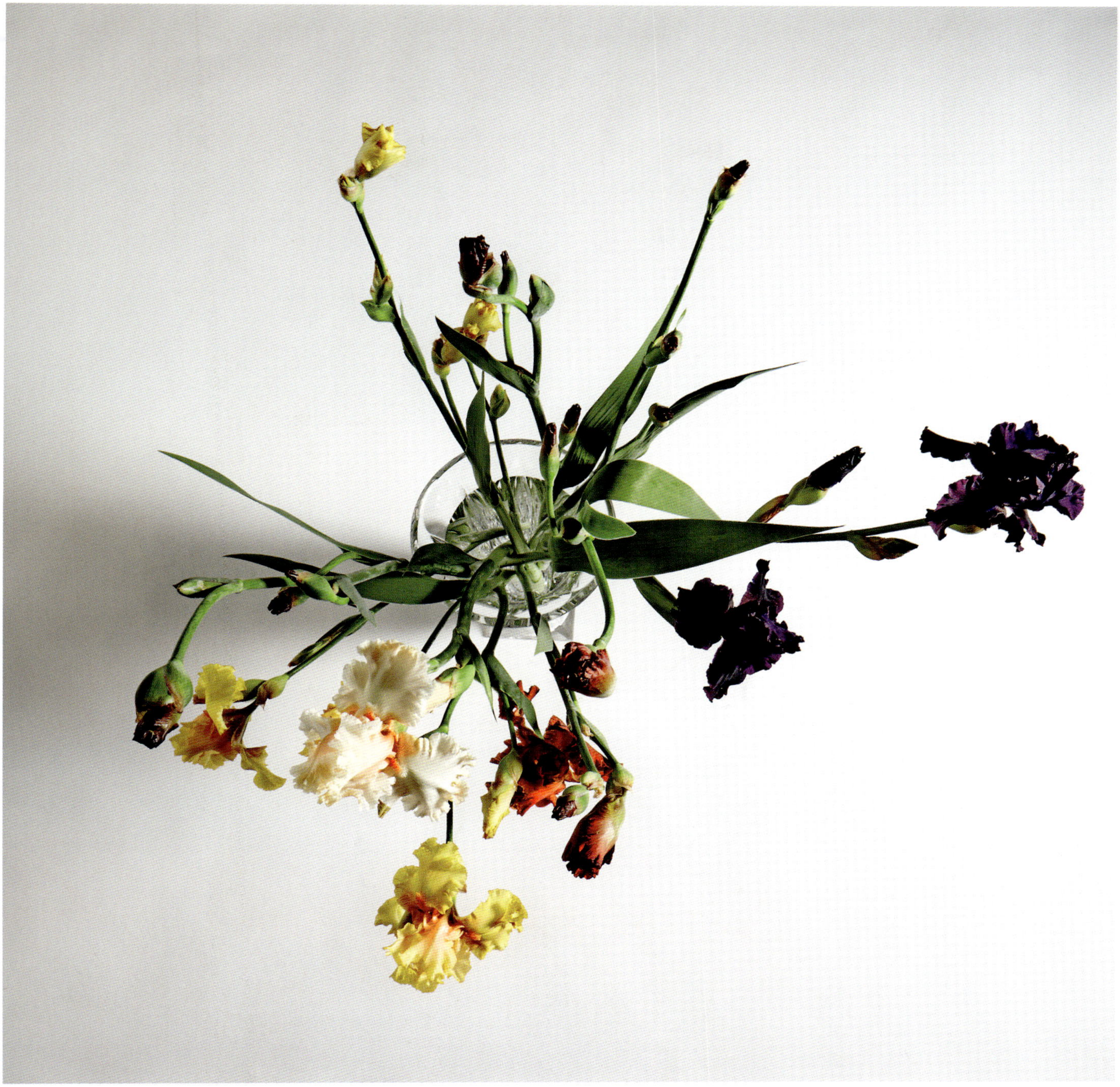

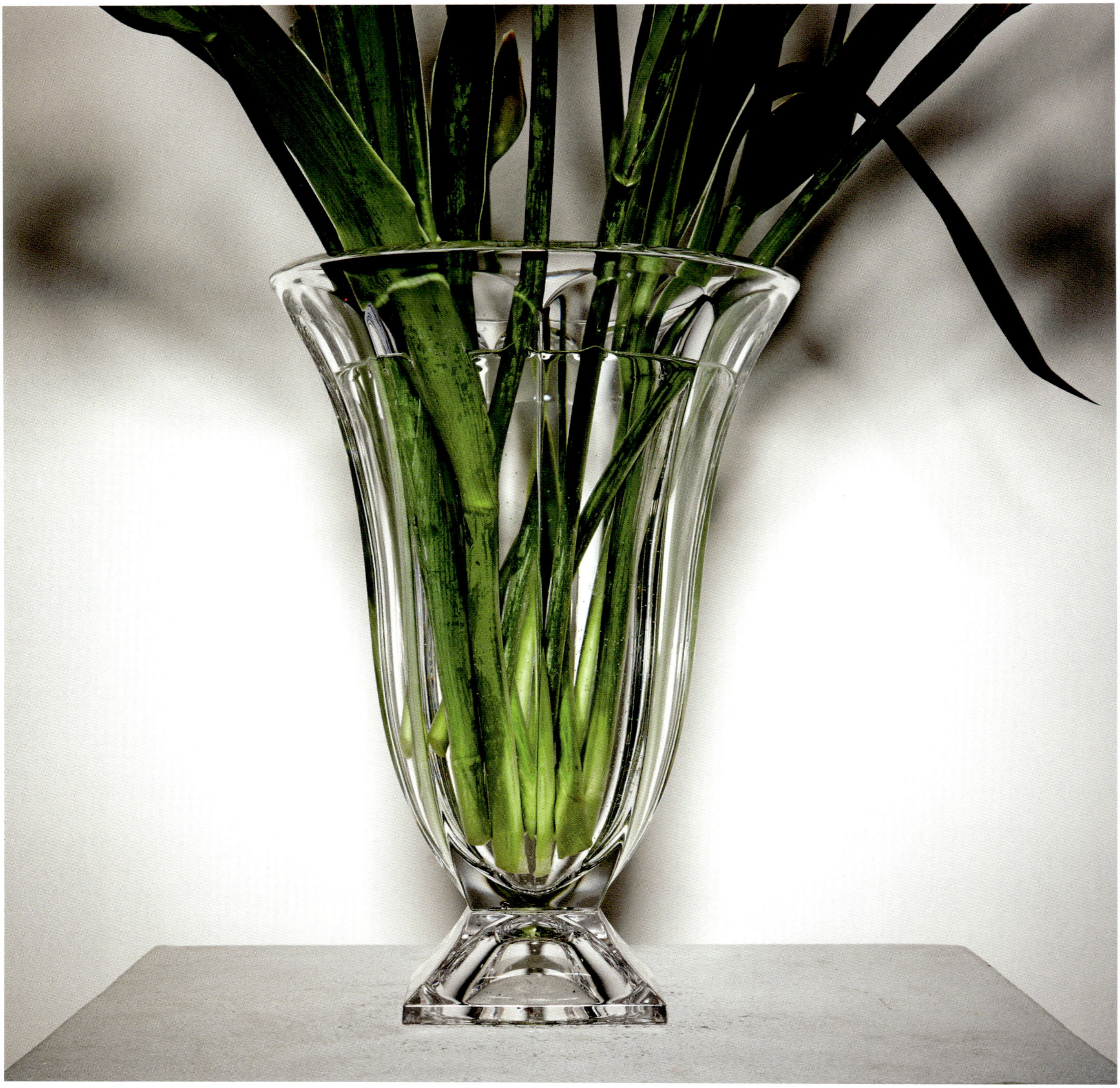

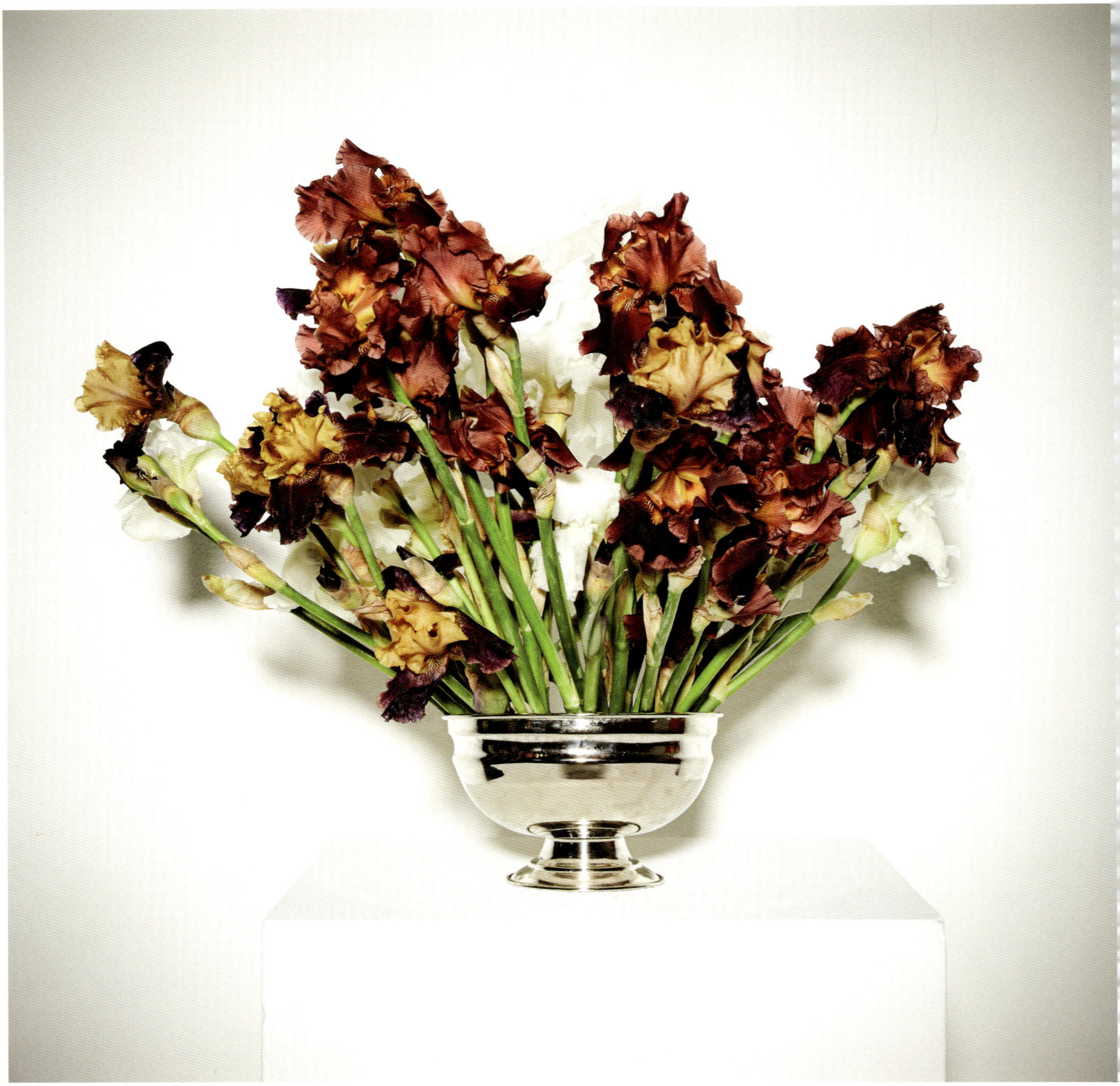

TURNER AND THE BEARDED IRIS
—

YELLOW IS A LIGHT WHICH HAS BEEN DAMPENED BY DARKNESS; BLUE IS A DARKNESS WEAKENED BY LIGHT. — JOHANN WOLFGANG VON GOETHE

Each of the seasons is, of course, marked by the emergence of certain blooms. In the winter the appearance of flowers such as hellebore, grape hyacinth and violet remind me of winters past, and of the winters my ancestors knew. I feel linked to them by the experience of bearing witness to these emergent flowers, which are at once ethereal and material – I am stirred and find myself reflecting upon the recurrent seasons that they knew. The arrival of camellia, David Austin roses, tuberose, freesia and crunchy leaves underfoot, for me, prefigure knitwear and endless cups of tea in autumn. While garden roses, field roses, spray roses and rambling roses, like people, seem to emerge in the summer vibrant and ambitious.

Perhaps because it follows the sparseness of winter and heralds the heat of summer, spring is the stuff of lore – of poetry and paint. The season of spring appears to erupt: vast fields become blankets of colour – flower shops (and studios) heave. The first flush of the roses are the best that you will see all year, the rhododendrons draw homebodies out to faraway gardens to awe. The blossoms madden with charm, there are lupins, *Eucalyptus macrocarpa*, tulips, gladioli, poppies, ranunculi, sweet peas, hyacinths, iris, blushing brides, flannel flowers, wattle, jonquils, calendula, carnations, delphiniums and forget-me-nots ... and this list constitutes merely the tip of the proverbial iceberg.

Spring is most certainly the time to buy cut flowers for the love of flowers rather than for their longevity. In this season a bunch of lily-of-the-valley that will sit in a vase for mere days may sustain the soul for years.

The best money you will ever spend on flowers is the money you spend on flowers that you are enchanted by. This past spring, very early one morning at the flower market on an otherwise unremarkable day, I became enchanted by the bearded iris that illustrate these words. I wonder if the growers know (and sometimes I sense that they do) that in cases such as this, when a flower intoxicates me, as the bearded iris did this particular morning, there is no expense that would keep me from them. I don't remember how much money it took to acquire them, as currency and frugality seemed to evaporate in their presence. The combination of their tones appeared to me to span light and darkness, and it was for this reason the bearded iris were and remain a revelation to my sensibilities.

‡

In the arrangement that accompanies these words I have used three different types of bearded iris: a pure white; a variety with both yellowy-mustard and deep crimson petals; and another that has dark mustard, almost brown, central petals and deep purple lower petals. The radiant white bearded iris is mottled nearer the stem than the flower by a papery, pale yellow-brown spathe – a part of the plant that covers the bud until it is ready to bloom. The quality of the texture of the bearded iris flower and the staggered manner in which the flowers on each stem bloom, bring to this combination a rare textural intensity. Each flower, by virtue of its many folds, layers and coexistent opacity and density, seems to me analogous to masterful brushstrokes – to the emotive potential of the skilled application of paint on canvas. The tone that this combination of flowers possesses reminds me of a painting that I have always loved for its representation of nature's obedience to force ...

Shade and Darkness – The Evening of the Deluge, was first exhibited with its companion painting, *Light and Colour (Goethe's Theory) – the Morning after the Deluge – Moses Writing the Book of Genesis*, at the Royal Academy in London, in 1843. They are the work of English painter Joseph Mallord William Turner (1775–1851). The oil painting *Shade and Darkness – The Evening of the Deluge* depicts atmospheric effects of light and weather through marks made on canvas, marks that reflect Turner's concept of vision: that the human eye will re-create nature in its perception of a blurred image. Turner believed that a viewer taking in a painting made up of light and darkness will perceive more of nature than they would in a realist depiction – in Turner's work, light and colour take the place of form.

Shade and Darkness – The Evening of the Deluge is composed of opaque and dense brushstrokes on canvas; the image is constructed in a restricted palette that spans near white to near black. Within the pictorial scope of the painting, aspects of the scene appear shrouded in degrees of darkness – the deepest, darkest paint constituting absolute 'darkness'. In this darkness, details of the scene are entirely veiled, while in other areas of the composition the scene is both constructed of, as well as diffused and obscured by, this varying depth of colour. These dark, foreboding marks are sharply contrasted in the upper centre of the painting by a sphere of light that develops out of the surrounding darkness, assuming an increasing density of white at its centre.

The white bearded iris to which this text refers is very near in colour and texture to the luminous 'centre' of Turner's painting – a mass of light which has for me always made the darkness that surrounds it appear more ominous. However, the light at the centre of the circling darkness also seems to suggest a point in time before the storm – evoking a sense of optimism – and that the scene may be a transient one. The deeper toned bearded iris are evocative of the colours and tones of the circling deluge in Turner's palette, which seems to build from white to yellowy-mustard, brown, deep purple to darkest crimson and beyond, developing ultimately to a colour close to black.

The tonal and textural comparisons between the beautiful bearded iris I happened upon at the Sydney Flower Market and Turner's *Shade and Darkness – The Evening of the Deluge* speak to the dynamic relationship between art and nature – that quintessential connection spanning human history. The flower enthusiast has a great deal to learn from even a cursory enquiry into the way that colour and texture are utilised in the creation of artworks. The work of painters, sculptors, and installation and performance artists is a limitless source of inspiration when it comes to selecting and arranging flowers. A painting about a storm could be encapsulated in a single bloom … and a composition of blooms might pay homage to the deep mysteries of nature.

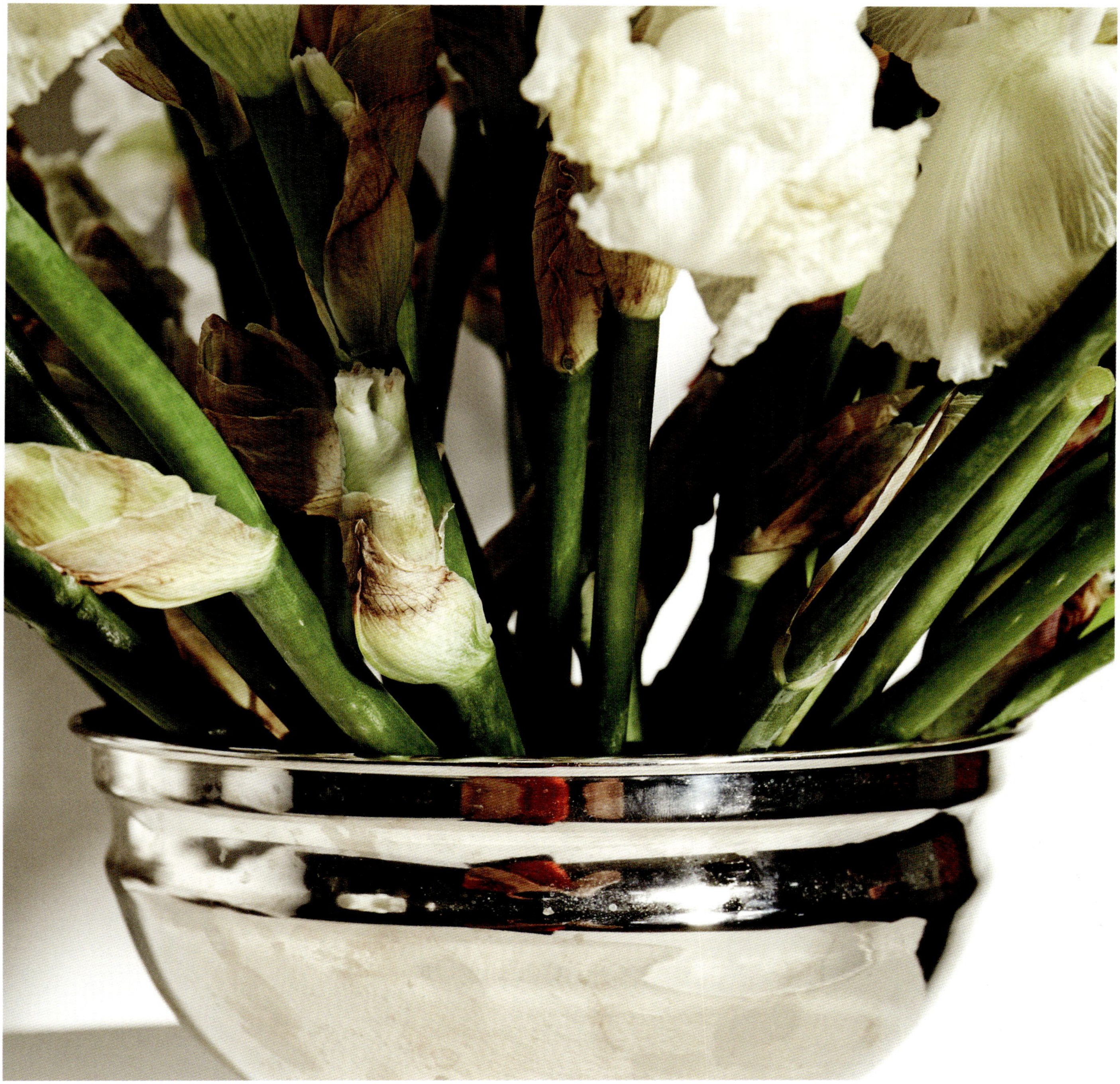

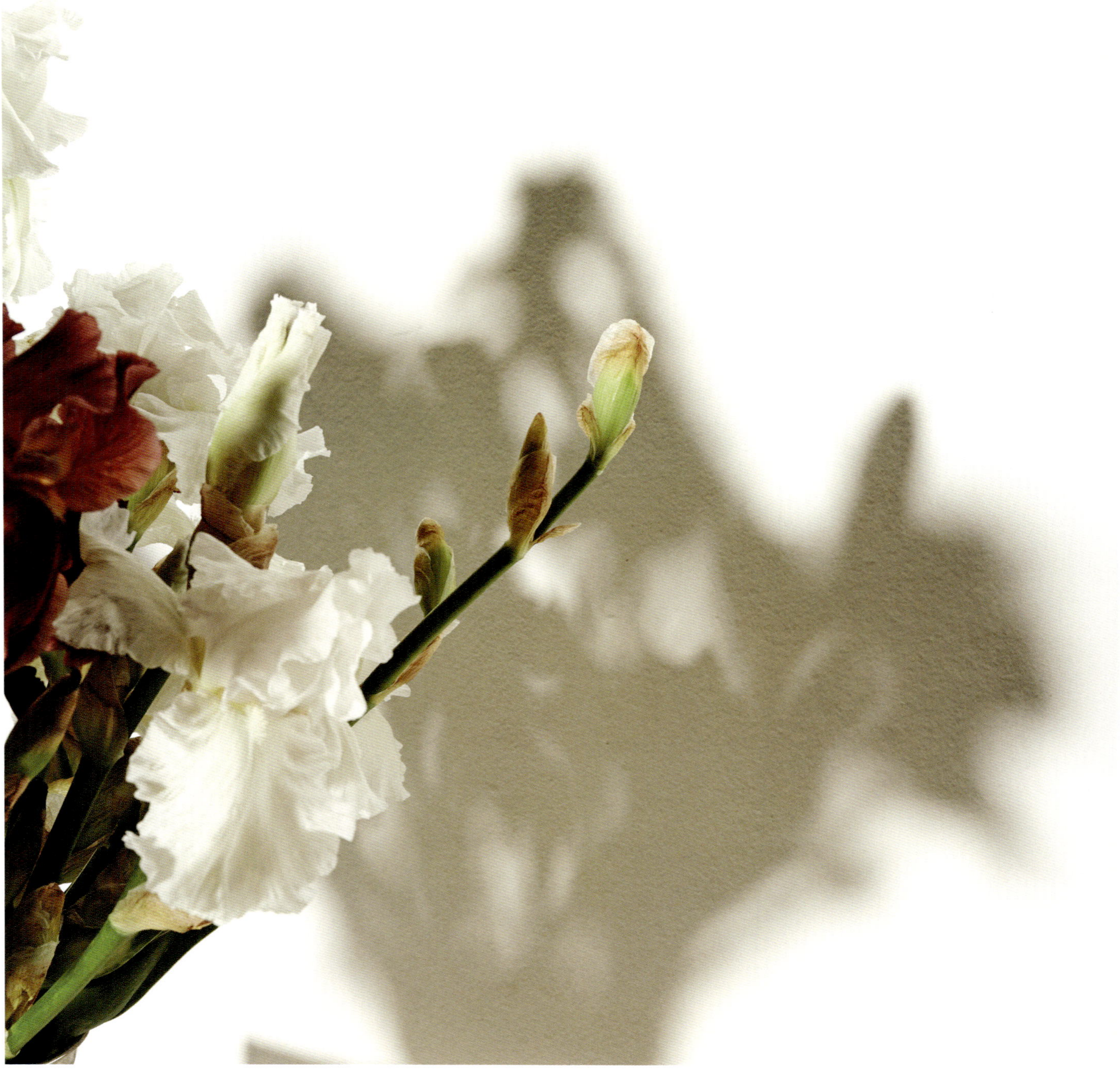

179

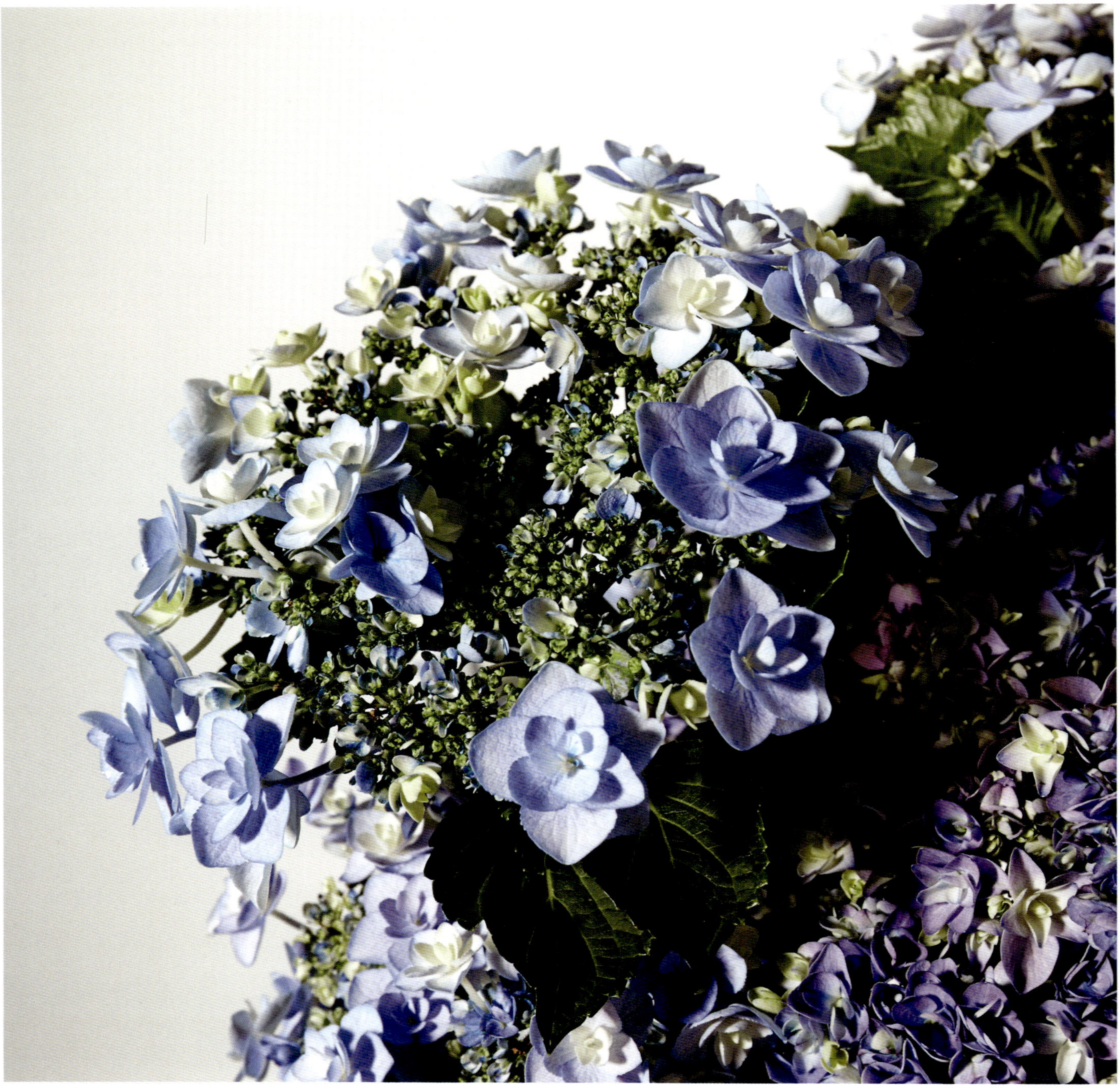

BLUE HYDRANGEA AND '1642'
—
THE TRANSIENCE OF FLOWERS AND THE SCENT I CANNOT NAME.

In October 2014, Elise Pioch Balzac – the esteemed candle maker who creates works under the label 'Maison Balzac' – and I launched our candle '1642'. The fragrance was based on an oil painting by celebrated Flemish Baroque still-life painter Adriaen van Utrecht (1599–1652), titled *Vanitas: Still Life with Bouquet and Skull*, completed in the year 1642.

The painting expresses the transience of living things. It is a deeply symbolic work composed of objects that pertain to a life and its accomplishments, but within the context of the certainty of death. In Latin, *vanitas* refers to 'emptiness' as it relates to meaninglessness, transience and vanity – a contemplation and expression of the dynamic tension between life and death. However, the futility expressed in the composition has the didactic effect of expressing a sense of reverence for the experience of living.

Ironically, the idea to create a candle after this painting was made in conversations with my life-partner of nearly a decade. It was the last tangible thing our union would produce before our decision to part in order to transition beyond what our connection would allow – before the death of 'us'. We spoke for hours about the notion of a scent born of an image created 372 years earlier and about how my work with the flowers, an extension of my art practice, was deeply connected to the transience of flowers. In our conceiving, the idea of the ephemerality of fragrance, produced by fire, oxygen and vapour in the ancient technique of candle making, seemed profoundly linked to the transitory medium of flowers. I was struck, too, by the correlation between the early use of candles as a method of measuring time (by marking along the wax) and the essential concept of time that is dominant in the vanitas genre.

Some time later, I printed a poster of the painting, which I attached to my studio wall, and elaborated and obscured the painted flowers in the image with flowers from the year 2014 – the most beautiful I could find – and 'we' photographed the result. One of the images we created that day was masterfully formed by Elise and her designer, Jim Parry, into the packaging for '1642': a beguiling box that has been picked up by consumers where the candle is sold, all around the world – Lucky.

‡

The initial idea for '1642' was developed and perfected by my enormously talented collaborator Elise. I recall in our first conversations her enthusing about 'synaesthesia' – a fascinating concept made all the more enchanting by her heavily French-accented English tongue. Synaesthesia is a (debated) neurological occurrence in which stimulus of one sensory or cognitive pathway leads to automatic, involuntary experiences in a second sensory or cognitive pathway – a kind of union of the senses. For example, a subject reading the word 'rose' in pink type on a white page might inexplicably experience the fragrance of a rose, or they might sense the taste of a rose macaron on their palate.

By the conclusion of these conversations it was decided that our ambition for the candle would be, through synaesthetic expression, to endeavour to translate a painting (*Vanitas: Still Life with Bouquet and Skull*) into a fragrance effected by the lighting of a wick.

In the months that followed, Elise worked on the fragrance and together we critiqued and assessed many different versions and combinations of scents, one of which was the 'fragrance' of silver – a testament to her courage. In time the perfume was added to wax, and versions were burnt to see how the scent would be changed when produced in this manner. Elements were added, excluded, diluted and intensified as we drew closer to achieving our goal, which had become a bond.

One day in the winter of 2014 we sat in Elise's beautiful atelier and burnt a candle that would become the original '1642' candle. We both became emotional, and I think I said: 'It bloody well smells like the painting.' I have long thought that which is born of love has wings; '1642' has sold like the proverbial clappers.

‡

The arrangement of three varieties of blue hydrangea I have used to illustrate these words exemplifies the notion of flower composition undertaken to effect textural complexity – like the olfactory intricacy of the arrangement of scents in '1642'. Each magnificent hydrangea head is made up of dozens and dozens of florets – a combination that gives the impression of hundreds of small flowers grouped together. The overall effect of this elaborate grouping gives the arrangement both density and a depth of colour that intrigues the eye … the combination appearing multi-faceted because of the thousands of component shapes included in the mass of flowers. Similarly, the countless tones contained within each flower head create a complex mass of the deepest, most tactile blue.

‡

Synaesthesia is one of those slippery terms, difficult to quantify with absolute accuracy. Across the fields of science, medicine and artistic enquiry the word is indicative of differing concepts. For Elise and I, synaesthetic expression is connected to a duality of the senses – a notion that is deeply linked to the way humankind experiences and relates to flowers. It seems that our formative experiences with the sight, scent and texture of flowers become embedded in our memories of people and places – embedded to the point of becoming fused. Like most children, my earliest observations of the flower kingdom constituted a kind of micro view. On walks in gardens or untamed natural environments my focus was exclusively on the tiny blooms that emerged very near to the earth – 'flowers' that adults seemed to consider weeds.

However, as my view of the natural world expanded, hydrangeas were most definitely the first flower I took to heart. Perhaps it was because it was the first season of spring I am able to remember … I recall holding Nanna Cooper's hand and inspecting a monumental wall of hydrangeas that flanked my grandparents' home – I could barely fathom their scale, volume or beauty. The sight of the elaborate blooms that we took in that day, many springs ago, is for me inextricably linked in my memory to the scent that Nanna wore. Though somewhat faded, that scent that I cannot name is somehow present in every hydrangea I see.

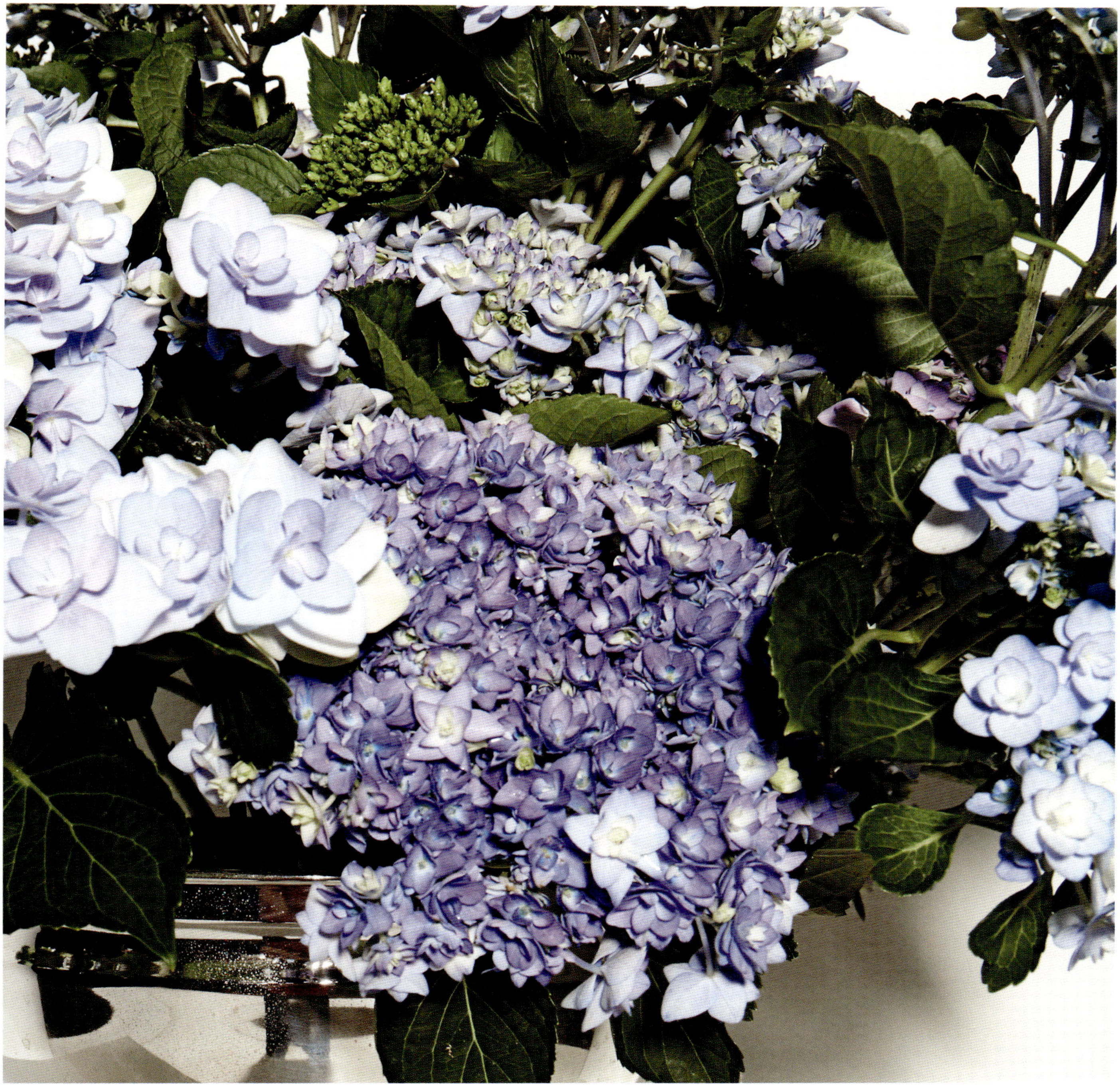

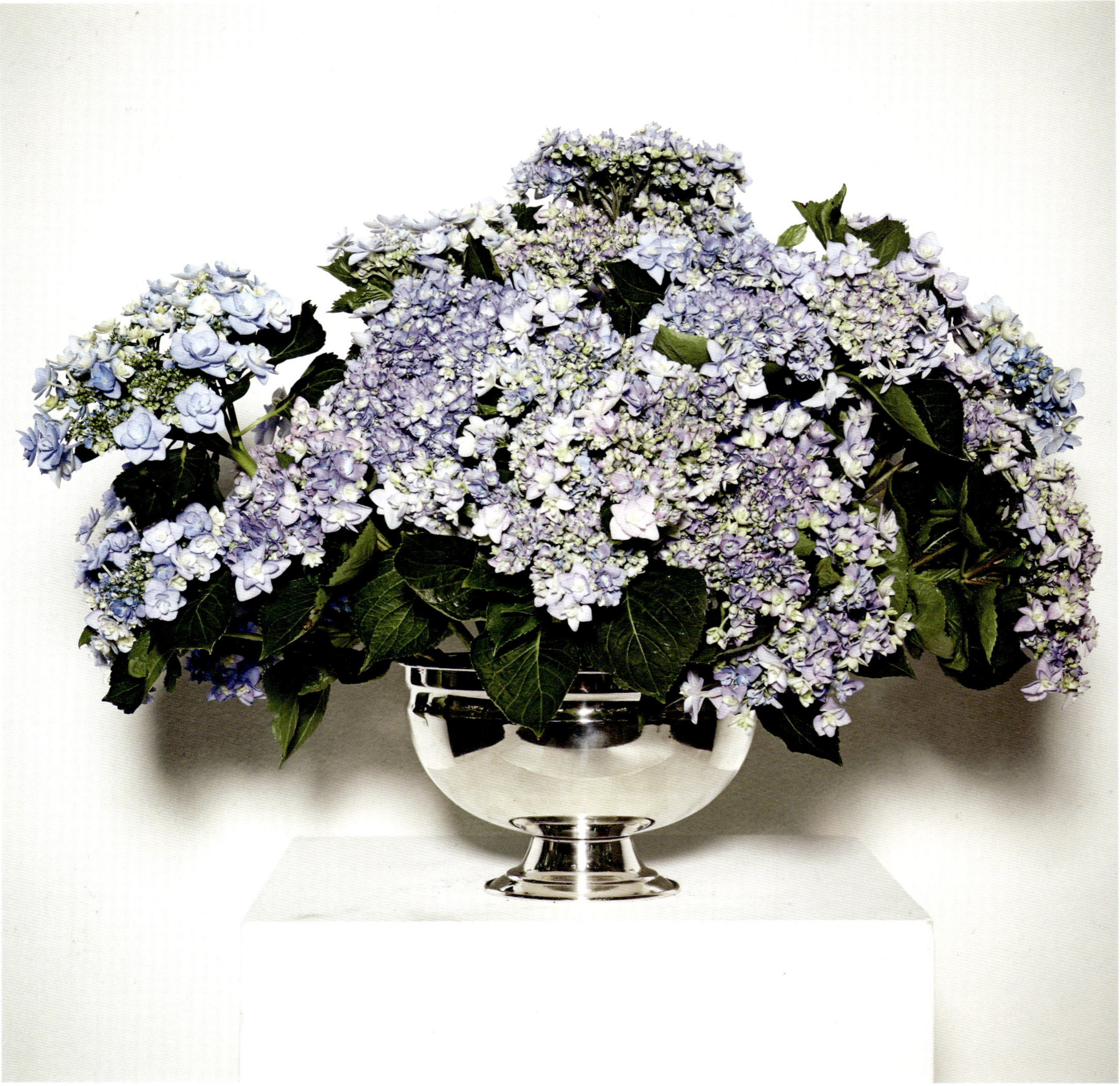

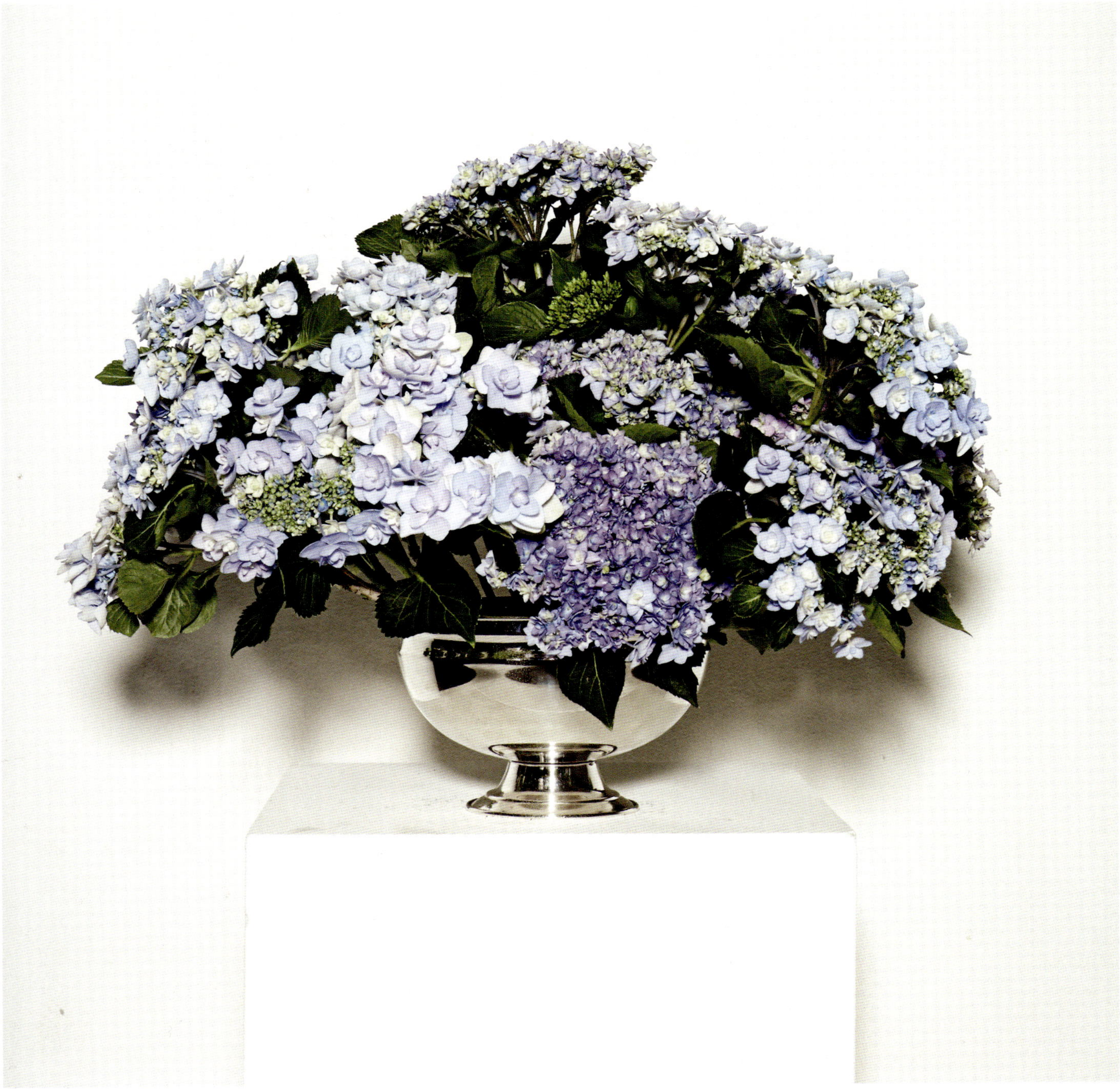

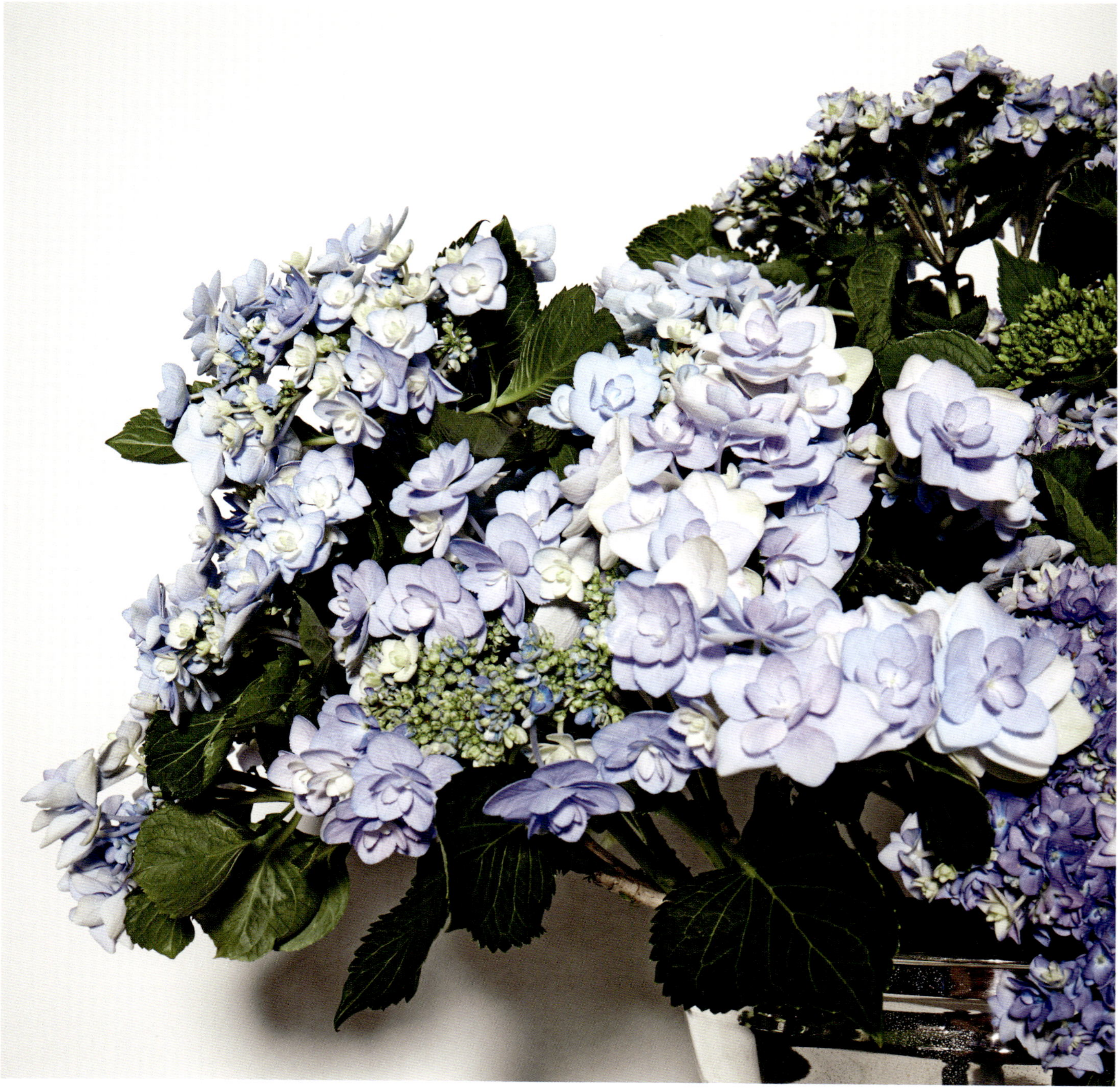

ROSES. AFTER CONSTANCE SPRY
—

THERE IS NOTHING TO ME MORE EXCITING THAN TO BE ALLOWED TO DECORATE WITH FLOWERS. — CONSTANCE SPRY

I adore everything about the books that Constance Spry authored. They are modest and slender in scale – the kind of book that can be slipped into a handbag – a book published in an era when bigger was not necessarily better. They were produced in hardback and in most cases with an idiosyncratic 'Spry' arrangement of flowers in bold 'Technicolor' on each cover. Within their pages are reproduced images of her arrangements in both colour and black-and-white print, and accompanying them are short chapters that richly recount her reasoning for the individual flower arrangements and specific events she was employed to design. Her 'voice' is authoritative and firm, and her instruction and expertise on the subjects of plants, flowers, form, palette, texture, composition and context in the discipline of floristry endure, despite the decades that have passed since the publication of her last book on the subject.

Constance Spry (1886–1960) was a prominent British educator, florist and author. In 1929 she opened her first flower shop 'Flower Decoration', in London. Spry rose to prominence in the same year when she created a winter window display for Atkinson's perfumery in Mayfair, using hops, lichen, copper beech leaves and green orchids. The display attracted admirers of such a volume that police had to be called to control the crowd. For another window display she famously used green kale leaves – considered highly unusual in flower arrangements in the 1920s – and vivid red roses; again, crowds clamoured to view her work. Spry's distinction was her pioneering approach: she utilised curious and rare objects as vessels to hold her flower arrangements and drew inspiration from seventeenth and eighteenth century Dutch flower painters. But her most important contribution to floristry – still in evidence today – was her promotion of the use of unusual plant materials ... pussy willow, weeds, grasses and ornamental kale in combination with flowers.

In 1934, Spry moved to a larger shop in Mayfair. In the same year she published her first book, *Flower Decoration*, and established the 'Constance Spry Flower School', where she employed a staff of more than 70 people. In 1936, she created the flower arrangements for the royal wedding of the Duke of Gloucester and again in June 1937, for the wedding of the Duke and Duchess (Mrs Wallis Simpson) of Windsor.

Before opening her first shop, Spry had been employed as the headmistress of an innovative school in the East End of London, where she instructed in cookery, dressmaking and flower arranging. When the Second World War began in 1939, Spry resumed her teaching career and lectured to women all over Britain.

In 1945 Spry bought into 'Le Petit Cordon Bleu Culinary School' – which had been opened in 1933 by the celebrated cook Rosemary Hume, and chef and the first female graduate of Le Cordon Bleu, Dione Lucas; when it re-opened it was re-named the 'Constance Spry Cordon Bleu School of Cookery'. But the jewel in Spry's crown was being engaged to manage the flower arrangements at Westminster Abbey and along the processional route for Queen Elizabeth II's coronation on 2 June 1953. That same year Constance Spry was appointed to the Order of the British Empire.

I could re-read the chapter, 'Coronation luncheon', in Spry's book *Party Flowers*, published in 1955, over and again ... and I have, many times. In it Spry gives such vivid, evocative detail of her work for the luncheon on Coronation Day. She describes how anxious she was about being able to acquire a sufficient quantity of flowers in tones of red to produce the effect that she wanted for a luncheon of this scale – some 350 guests. However, her concern turned to relief when she was advised that a gift of flowers would be given to the queen. A sample was sent of what might be expected in the delivery and in the week before the event she opened a box of red roses, red carnations, gladioli and strelitzias ... and so it came to pass that the tables for the luncheon were resplendent with tones of scarlet red.

Because Hume and the Cordon Bleu School had been employed to undertake the catering for the event, Spry was able to decide on the colours of the table cloths,

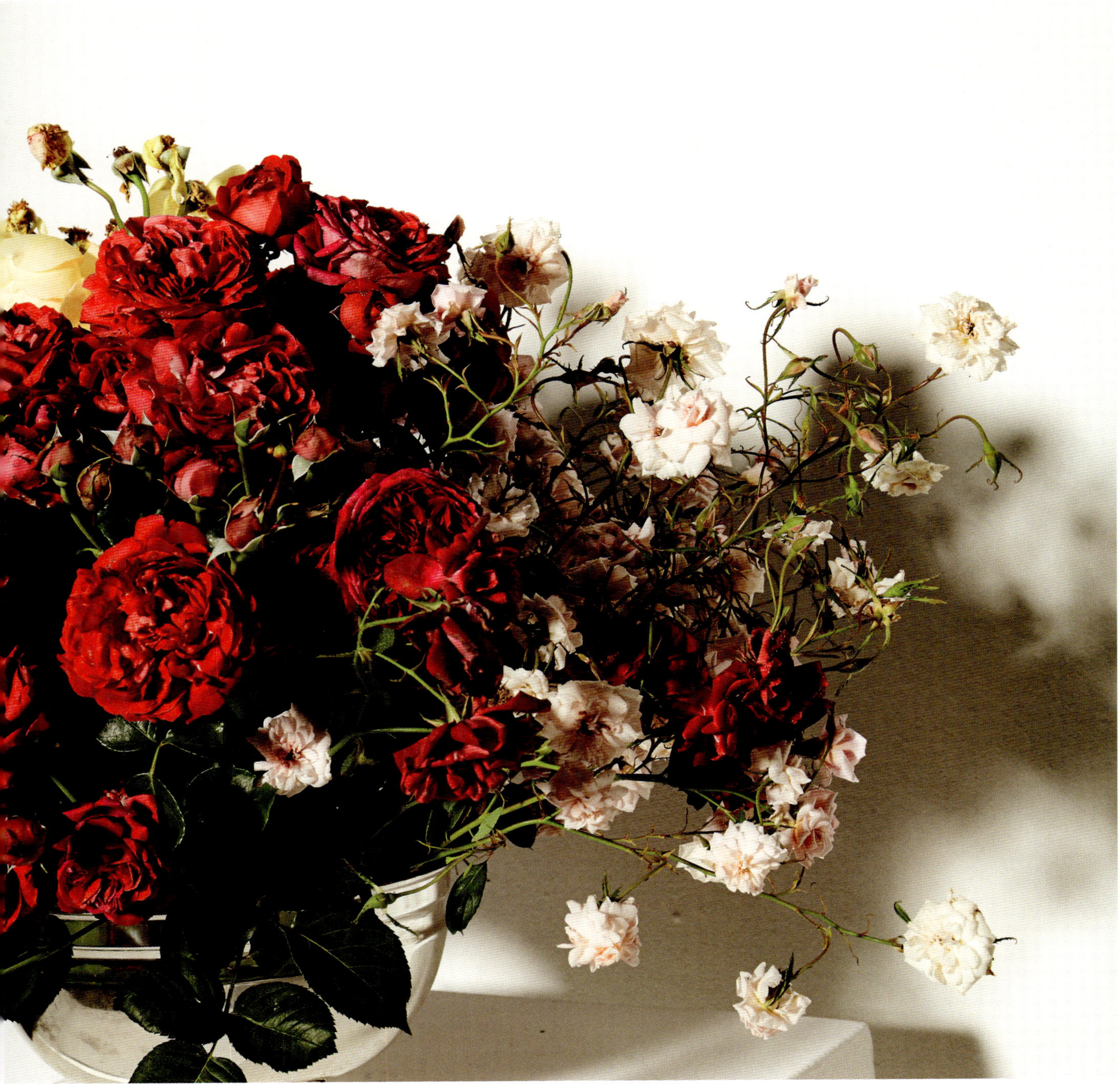

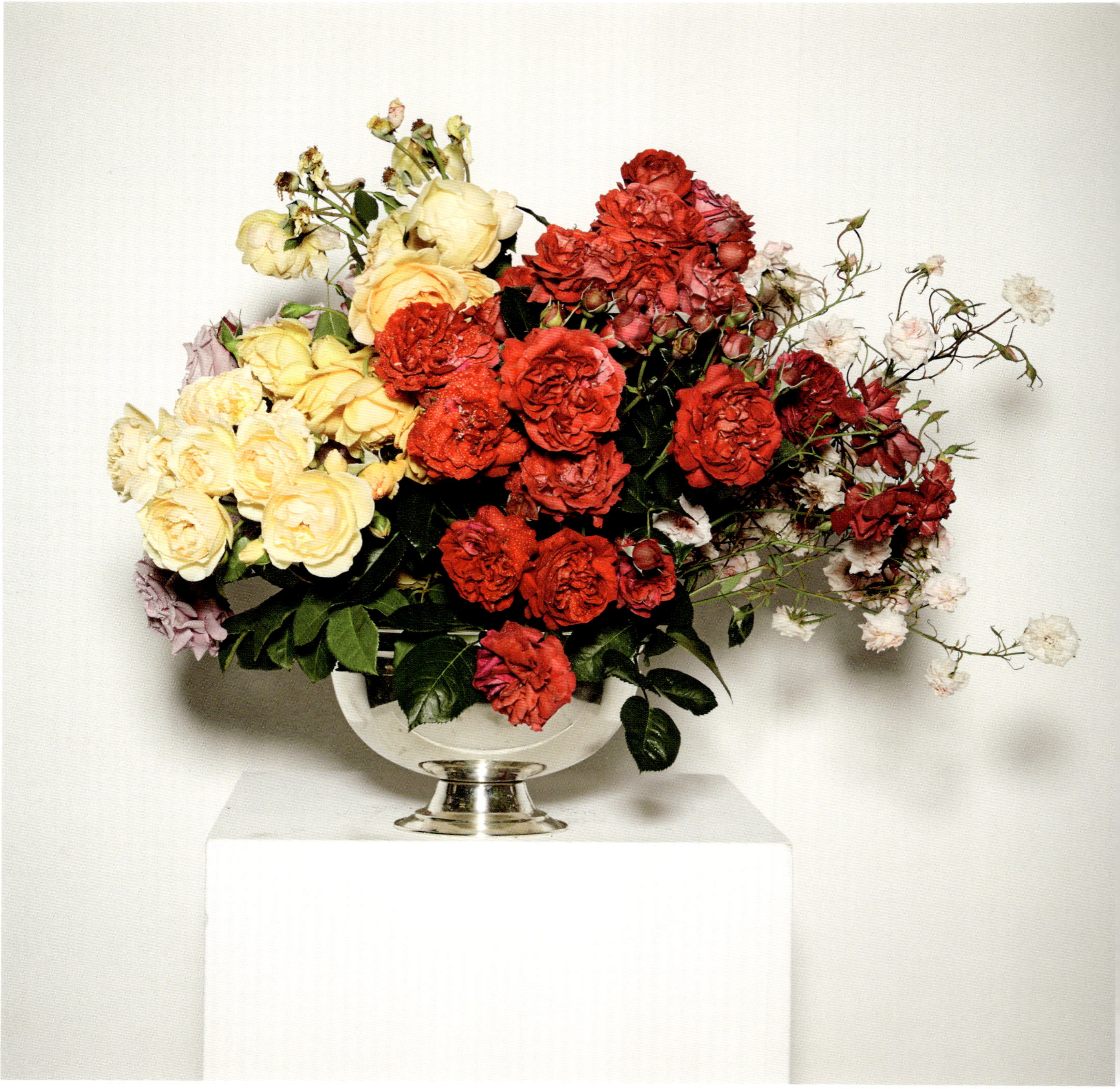

and she describes how the long serving tables that ran down both sides of the hall were draped in gleaming gold, while the table cloths were an opulent, mid-blue that contrasted with the 'glowing scarlet' arrangements. The chapter is also rich in detail about the flower preparation and Spry's rationale for every aspect of the job, including sending the flowers to hospitals on the following Tuesday.

‡

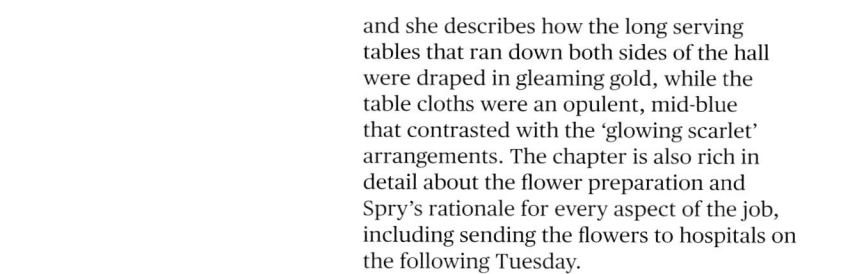

The arrangement I have chosen to accompany this text summons something of Spry's enthusiasm and extraordinary passion for flowers, and goes some way to communicating her approach. After Spry, I have endeavoured in this composition to retain the rambling nature of fragrant roses as they might grow in the garden. The combination of 'Cécile Brünner' (a rambling rose), David Austin and hybrid tea roses are arranged loosely and in block colours, rather than distributed throughout, and yet the contrasting tones intermingle as they might in the garden. It is my intention by this method to give the beholder an impression or sense of the field of garden roses that bore these wild blooms, while the fragrance of each also combine to recall a garden of roses.

Constance Spry demanded to be included in this book because of the impact of her thought and practice upon my own work. The following is a list of flower books that she wrote – I have read and re-read each of them in order to be guided in my own work by her authoritative and impassioned voice: *Flower Decoration* (1934), *Flowers in House and Garden* (1937), *Garden Notebook* (1940), *Summer and Autumn Flowers* (1951), *Winter and Spring Flowers* (1951), *How to Do the Flowers* (1952), *A Constance Spry Anthology* (1953), *Party Flowers* (1955), *Simple Flowers: 'A millionaire for a few pence'* (1957) and *Favourite Flowers* (1959).

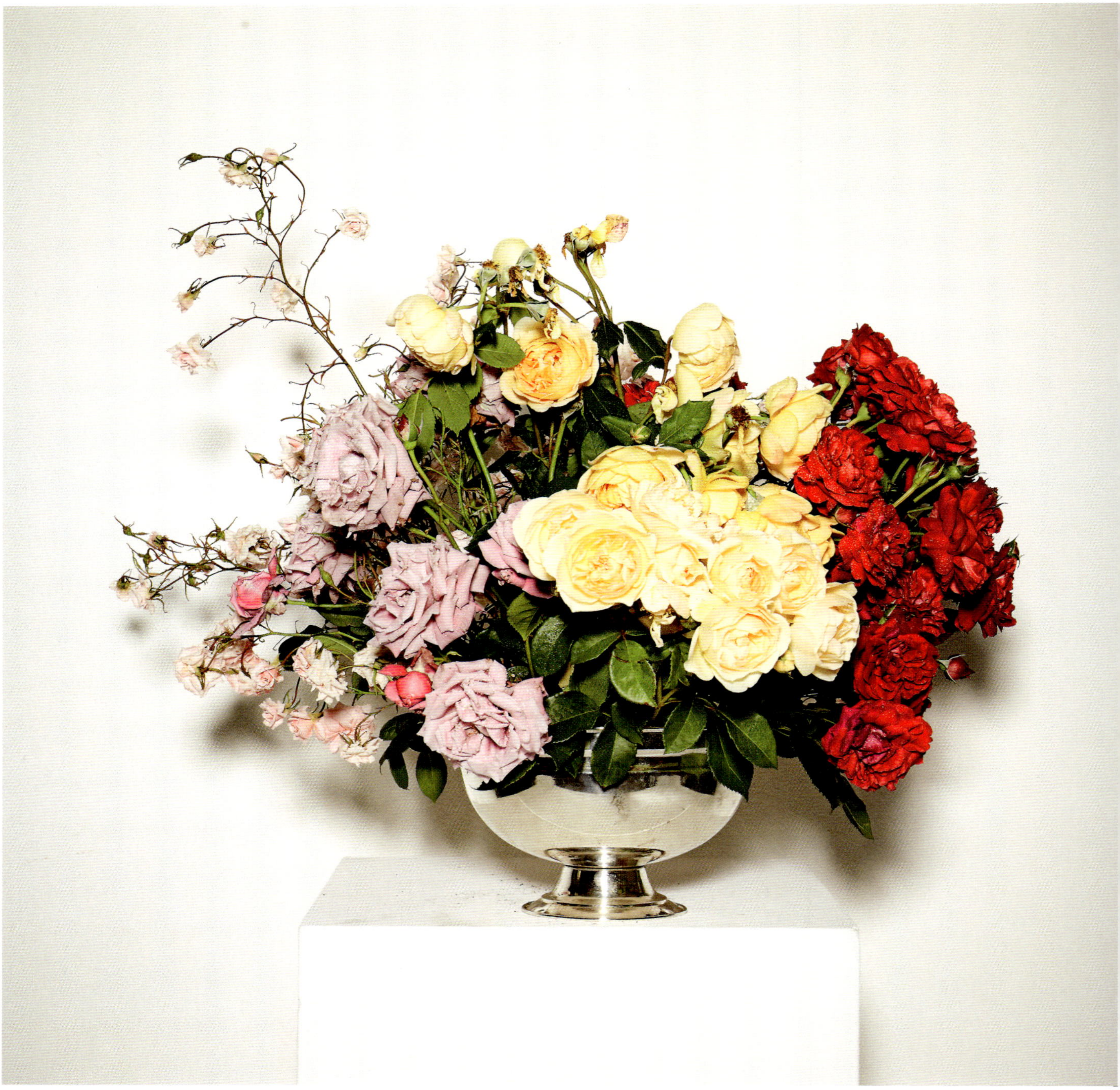

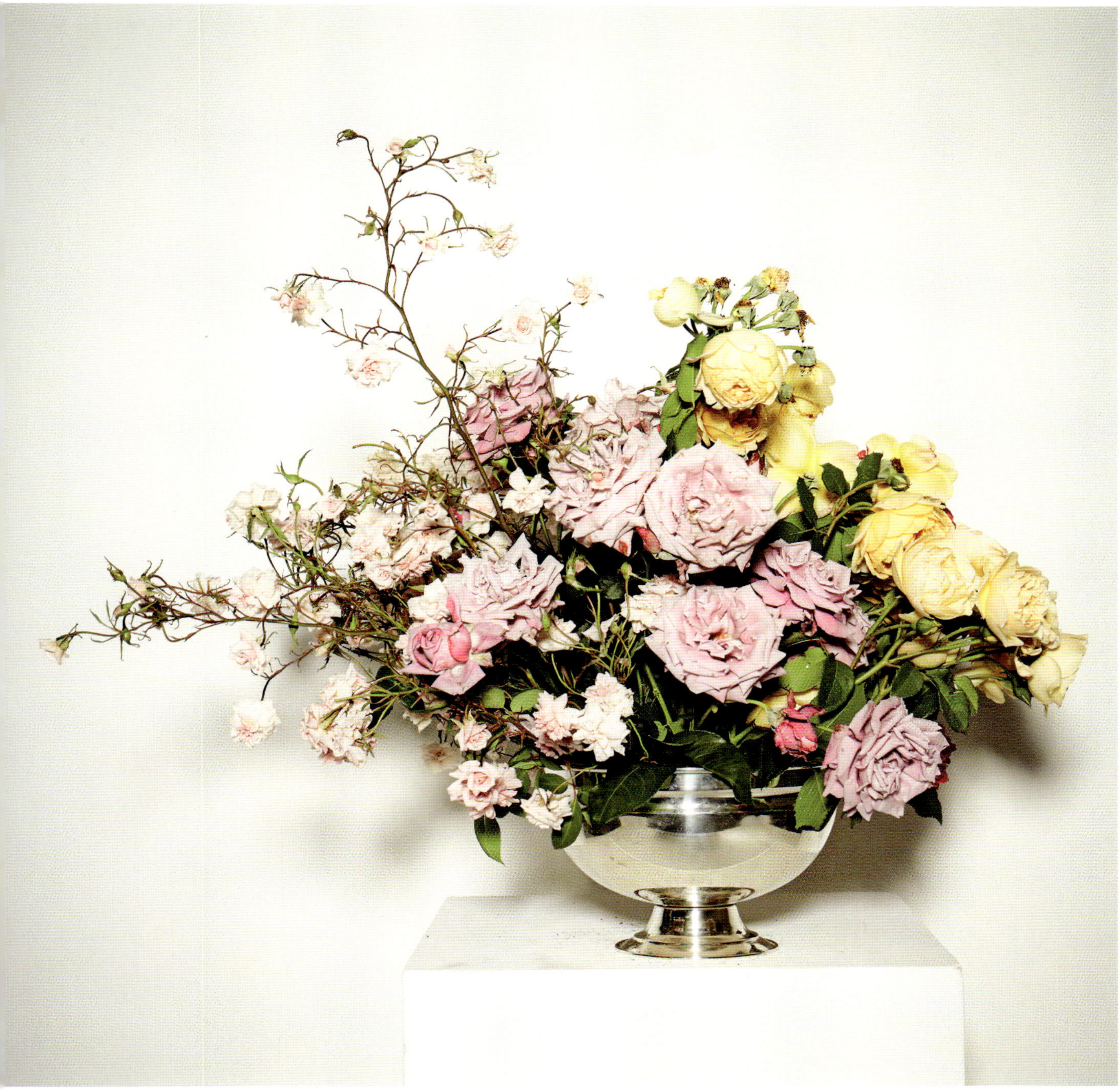

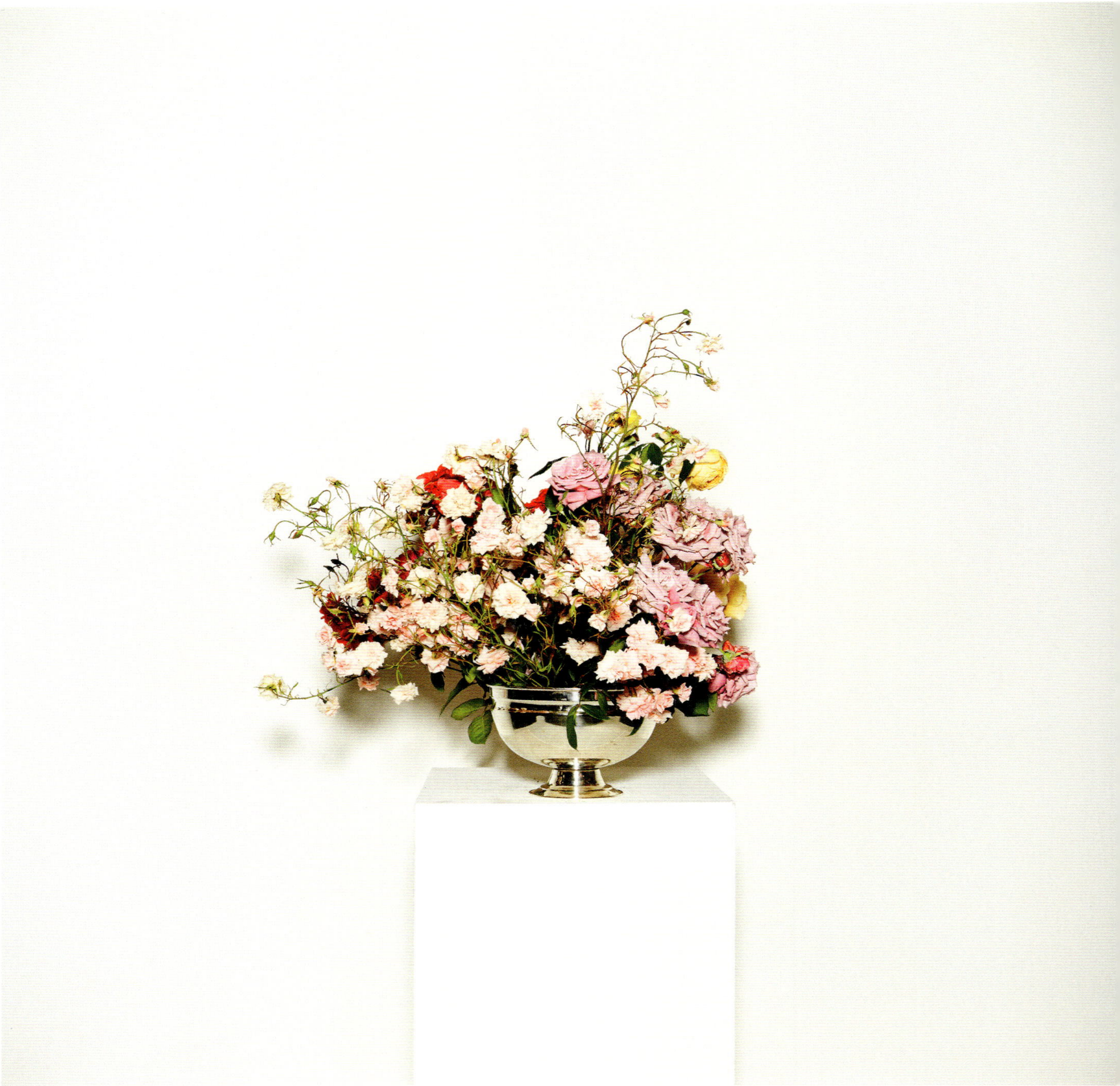

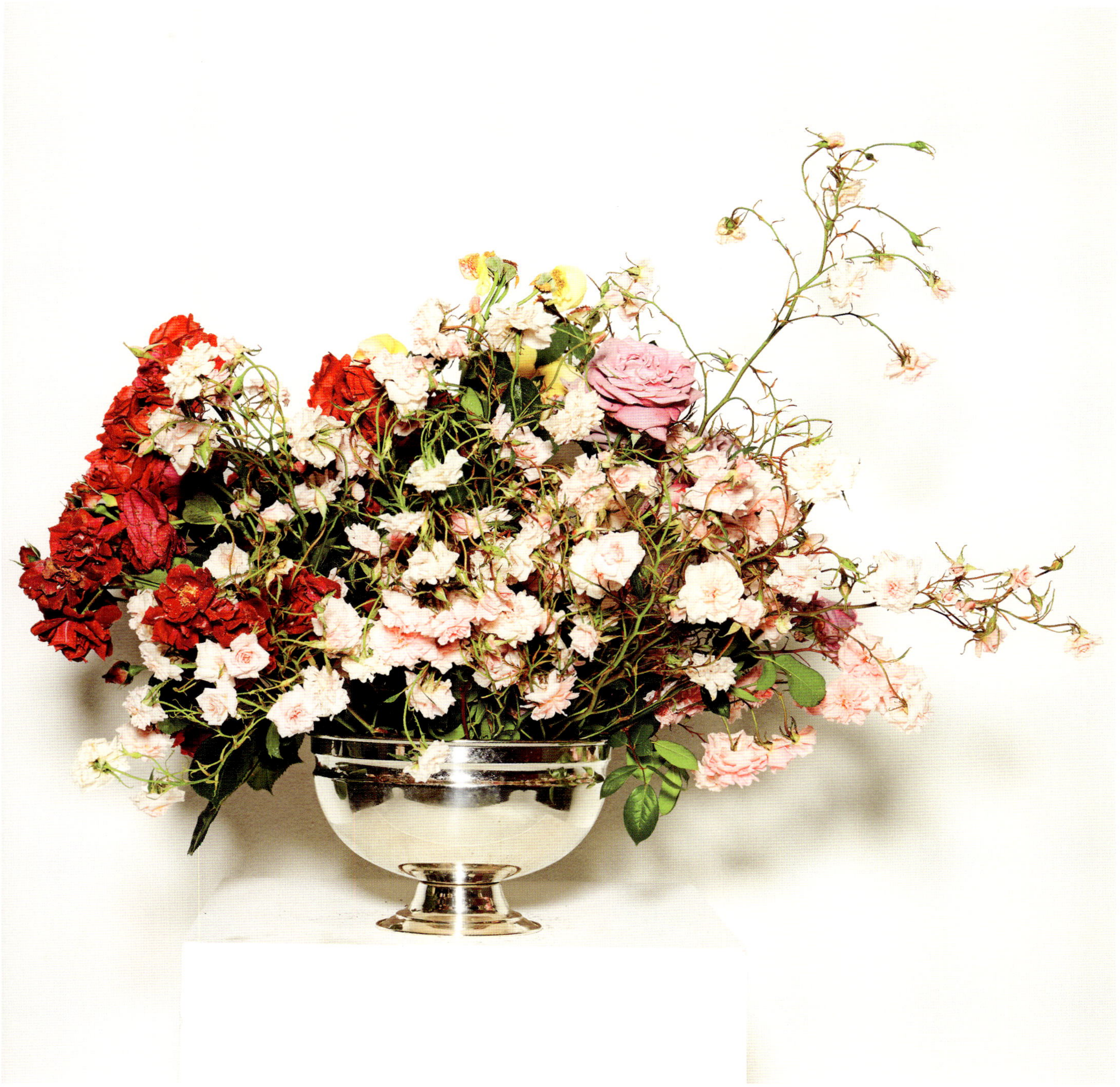

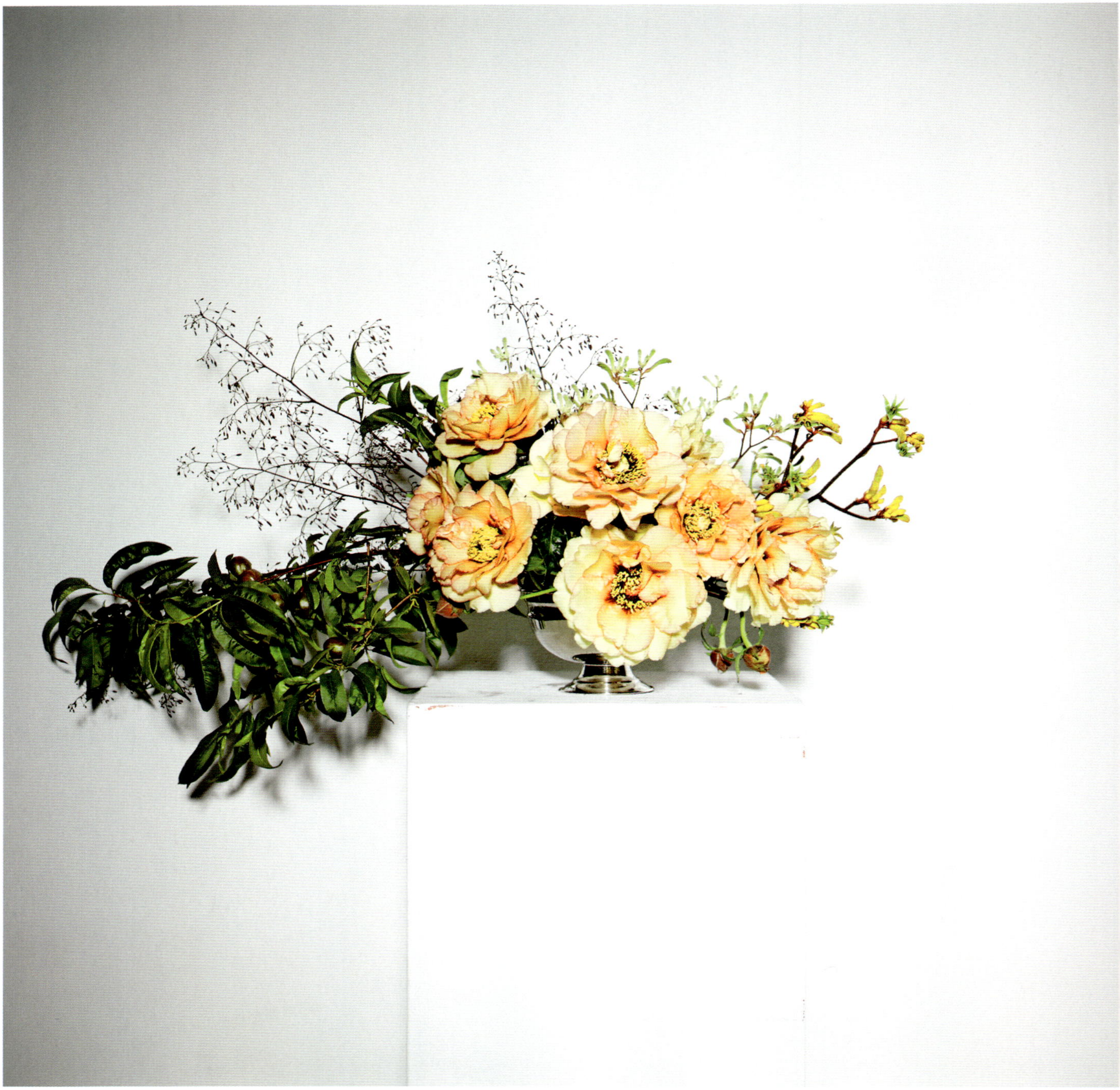

THE TREE PEONIES IN A SILVER BOWL

—

THE YEAR OF CROWNS AND THE AGE OF GOLD.

Mid 2008 I began meeting with celebrated Australian theatre director Benedict Andrews, and acclaimed theatre designer Alice Babidge, about the possibility that I might create the kings' crowns for what would be their much-celebrated production of The War of the Roses for the Sydney Theatre Company. I created three crowns, which through the course of the production had the appearance of being one.

Tom Wright and Benedict Andrews' script for The War of the Roses was a conflation of eight separate Shakespearean plays: Richard II, Henry IV parts 1 and 2, Henry V, Henry VI parts 1, 2 and 3, and Richard III – a production that ran for eight hours, in two parts.

I will never forget assembling in the massive Sydney Theatre with around 900 other souls at the play's opening in January 2009, watching Part 1, Act One – as a vast, unending fall of glittering gold confetti fell on the cast that stood almost motionless and to attention as gold foil blanketed the immense stage. At the centre of this breathtaking vision was the actress Cate Blanchett in the role of Richard II. Wearing my gold crown.

The instant the enormous heavy curtains of the massive stage drew back, the object that I knew so intimately – that I had painstakingly dragged from concept to material – was no longer mine. In this rarefied environment and now, within the shared vision of Benedict Andrews and Alice Babidge, it had become a Crown of Kings and an esteemed object in Sydney's distinguished theatre lexicon. It is rare that a thing created can become so significantly and completely re-contextualised.

In 2008, the year the crowns were commissioned, I was a deeply immersed doctoral candidate on a full-time scholarship and was supplementing my academic research with part-time work in a flower shop. My artistic practice of sculpting botanical compositions in brass and finishing them in triple-plated precious metals had gained some attention under the working title: THE BUTCHER'S DAUGHTER. I had made work in the scale of the crowns, but not often, because of the entailed labour and the cost of production. But now with the opportunity to 'stand on the shoulders of giants' I was able to fully explore the bounds of this method of work. I see this period of making the crowns as an important phase in my evolution from artist to florist.

It was a strong proclivity for composition and conceptual reasoning that led me to train first as an artist and then as a florist. But the STC commission had the effect of a revelation on me. I read the script and had long conversations with my collaborators about the significance of the crowns to their wearers and the imperatives and encumbrances such objects drag with them … from relic, to being realised as a theatrical prop for the company's 2009 production.

A crown is an entirely metaphorical object. Over the course of human existence, crowns of precious metal, laurel, oak, flowers, rare jewels, thorns and countless other materials have come to symbolise legitimacy, power, honour, glory, righteousness and resurrection, among other virtues. But the crown most effectively communicates man's proximity to the gods. It is an object that links its wearer either directly with god (in the case of monarchy), or with godlike qualities (in the case of the ancient Olympians). By this logic, I came to design the crowns for the STC production around the four cardinal directions: north, south, east and west – each a high point with a 'star' at four equal intervals of the ring. For me, this represented man and earth. Within the four 'pinnacles' that these points formed, I incorporated flora and fauna to indicate the four seasons – autumn, winter, spring and summer – a way of representing the cycle of nature, god and heaven. The spring and summer divisions were heavily embellished with roses in reference of course to the play's title and premise. The sculptural/floral compositions (the three crowns) were then triple-plated with 24-carat gold – the metal of kings.

By the time I had delivered the commission I felt like I had explored and exhausted my interest in this way of working. And once I had released the crowns to their purpose I had decided that the highest material in which to make my work was no longer gold, but rather flowers.

‡

The tree peony, 'Age of Gold', dominates the arrangement that accompanies this text: it encapsulates all that I have written. In its native China, the tree peony (*mudan*) has been grown and revered by herbalists, gardeners, artists and nobility for more than 1500 years. It is a medium-sized, spreading, shrub with fern-like leaves and incredibly large scented flowers.

For this ancient culture the peony is 'King of the Flower Kingdom' and 'Flower of Riches and Honour'. It is not hard to fathom how a flower of such majesty has inspired profound cultural symbolism and obsession.

Along with the 'hero' tree peonies, the arrangement in the silver bowl includes a good limb of juvenile nectarine. European Renaissance painters are thought to have included the fruit and leaves of nectarine in their still-life paintings – wormholes and discoloration embraced – in order to engender realism, decay and death. A corsage of 'golden' kangaroo paw – a gold flower native to Australia and embedded within Indigenous culture – and a spray of native flax, *Dianella prunina*, harmonise and balance all of the elements within this arrangement.

I cannot recall another bloom that causes a stir at the flower market like the first tree peonies of the season.

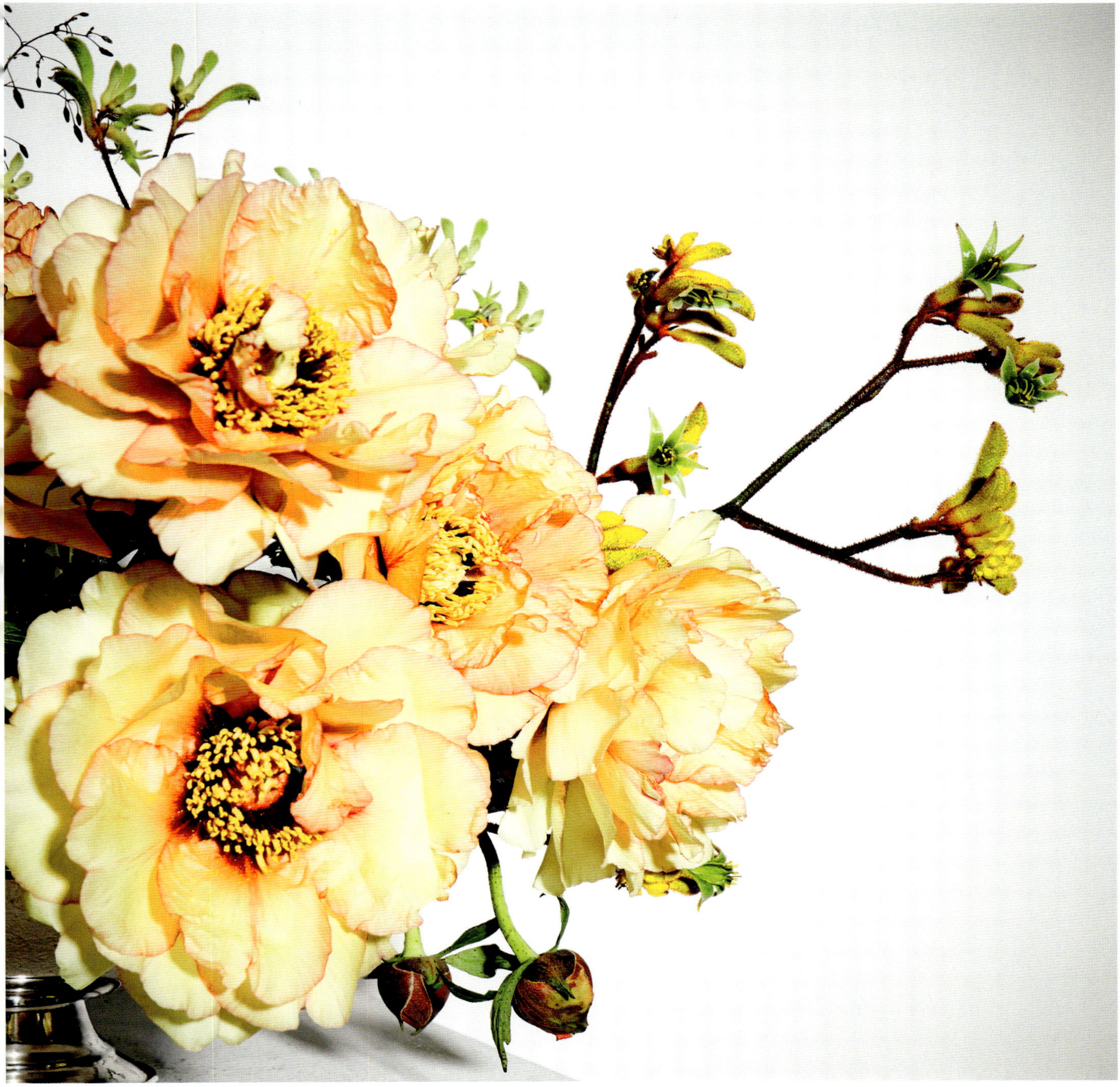

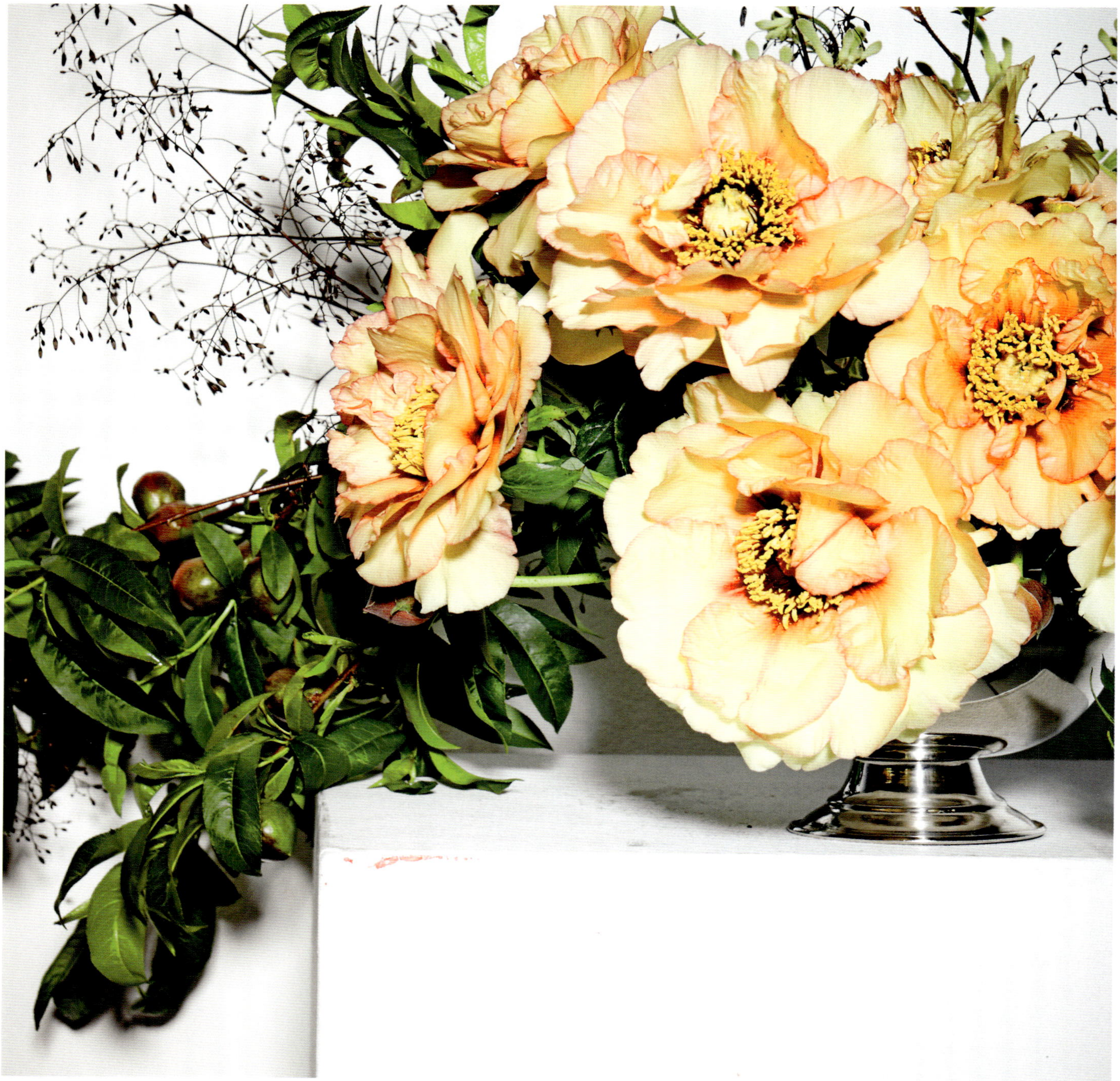

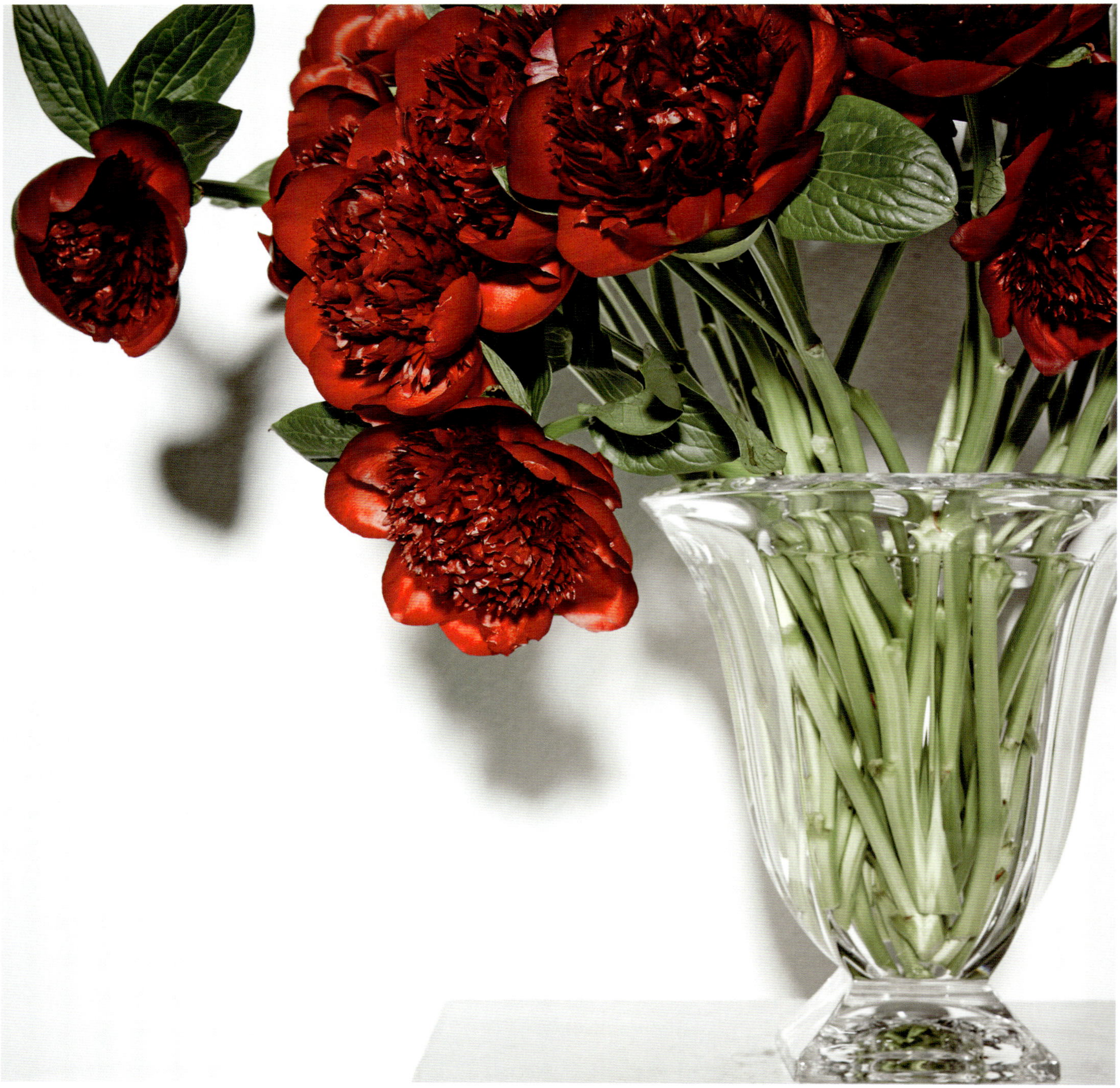

THE PEONIES AND THE HEART

BEAUTY CAPTIVATES THE FLESH IN ORDER TO OBTAIN PERMISSION TO PASS RIGHT TO THE SOUL. — SIMONE WEIL

The very first time I laid eyes on Damien I knew that I would marry him; I didn't know that we would grow apart. With distance I recognise that he was the wise, elegant tree whose shade I needed in order to grow into the oak that I have become. The colour, form, texture and majesty of the mass of deep crimson peonies I have chosen to accompany these words embody my affection for him. I was twenty when our paths crossed in a Sydney hotel called 'The Three Weeds' – perched on a street corner, a stone's throw from the art school I would attend in the ensuing years ...

For the decade that followed we were inseparable. In the course of these years I came to develop my own intellect and artistic practice in proximity to his. A bibliophile, an academic and a fierce creative (and artist in his own right), he seemed to have been created for the specific purpose of guiding my ever- (in this period) maturing sense of marvel and bewilderment at the world. Since a child I have had an intensely philosophic temperament, a disposition that has seen me interact with the world with both complete awe and degrees of confusion. Damien seemed to have a profound awareness and comprehension of every subject or concept my mind would come to rest upon. He was able to elucidate historical and cultural concepts that had previously, through ordinary language, spoken by ordinary people, evaded me. In a universe of books, he was able to select 'the book' that would broaden and cultivate my initial enquiry into this or that subject. In the years of my undergraduate study and during my Honours year he identified artists across disciplines and the course of history whose work had similar concerns to mine, and in so doing brought me to artists who have influenced my work and enriched my life.

Damien was the tree whose shade I needed in order to grow, and the dappled shadow his strong, solid form cast was love. Though it may indulge now and again, the oak has no need to ponder the shade and light in which it grows; that shade and light are embedded in its form – in its solid trunk and in every leaf on its strong branches. Every miraculous leaf that forms on the giant oak is a result of the shade and sunlight in which it initially grew. In the years that followed our separation I proved to myself, by writing my thesis and acquiring my doctorate, that I could stand alone – although something of the Damien tree exists on every page.

‡

I submitted my doctoral thesis in 2009. Titled *METAXU: A Metaphysics of the Annihilation of Self in Video-Portraiture (Imaging Mediations Between the Human and Divine)*, it is a formal exegesis – a critical elucidation of my art practice, a body of text and its representation in visual form. The thesis investigated my art practice via the model of prayer – a paradigm I developed in order to harness the threads of thought that inform and motivate my work. The notion of prayer provided a framework for the overarching focus of the research: that an artwork can be considered a communion/mediation between the artist, the content and its form, and an audience. This model was linked to the theoretical and philosophical writings of Antonin Artaud (1896–1948) and Simone Weil (1909–1943).

The philosophical thought of Antonin Artaud and Simone Weil are two of my favourite subjects (which I can talk about indefinitely) – for both Artaud and Weil there was nothing unremarkable about the experience of living, and the way they apprehended their own personal experience is extraordinary.

The subject of their work is for me like the 'Microbee' was for my Year 4 school teacher, who would seem to forget entirely about our lesson if a student could get him onto the matter of the Microbee computer, an Australian-designed computer that was distributed in limited numbers to public schools in the early 1980s by the New South Wales Department of Education. The Microbee had fully captured the heart and mind of this man, who could not seem to get off topic.

However, my diatribe here on the subject of Antonin Artaud and Simone Weil will be very limited due to the nature of this book

... so all I will say is that in both cases their books, *Le Théâtre et son Double – The Theatre and its Double*, Artaud (1938) and *Attente de Dieu – Waiting on God*, Weil (1951) are texts that I understood first with my heart and then with my intellect. Despite the fact that both writers heavily influenced my art practice and thesis, the correlative aspects of their respective thought and my work are non-academic: there is something both intangible yet absolutely vital about the impact of their thought upon me. For me, like them, there is nothing unremarkable about the experience of living.

‡

The images of deep crimson peonies that illustrate these words exemplify the life cycle. In their evolution as a cut flower they appear to demonstrate the experience of living. There is vitality in the extraordinary depth of colour of their velvety red petals; their tightly closed buds open over time to reveal a complex, many-layered flower that seems inexplicable in its magnificence and scale. Over time the slivered central petals begin to loosen and fall, echoing the fragility of all life forms.

The peony is, for many, the flower that most epitomises beauty and romantic love: which reasons why – although peonies are only in season for a few short months of the year – they are requested by flower enthusiasts all year long. If I had a dollar for every time I've heard, 'Peonies are my favourite flower, do you have peonies?' ...

In Australia, around October–November of each year, I too am intoxicated by the thought of their blooming, and become obsessed about their imminent arrival. And each year as I watch them bloom and perish I think of my decade in the shade of the Damien tree.

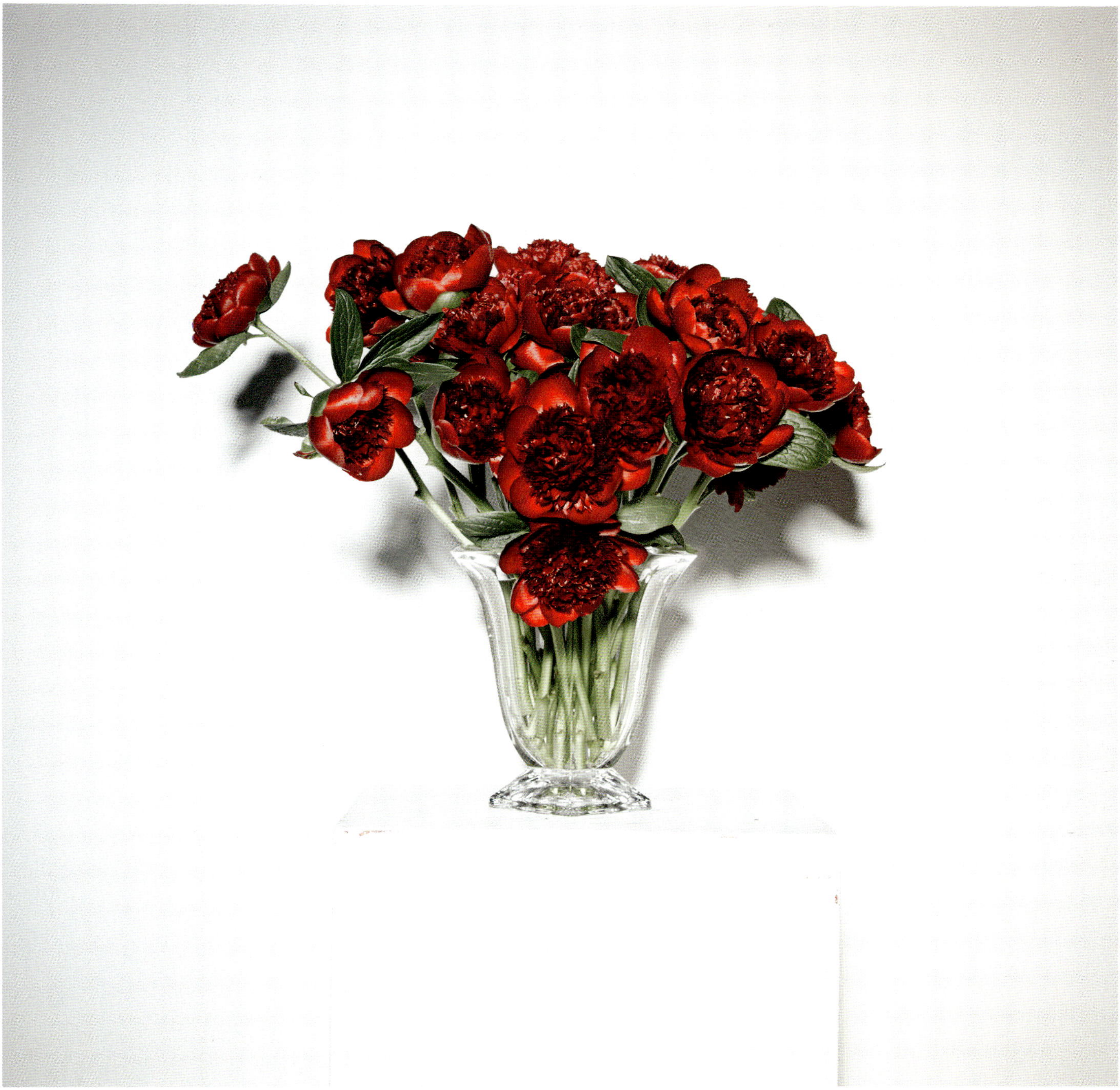

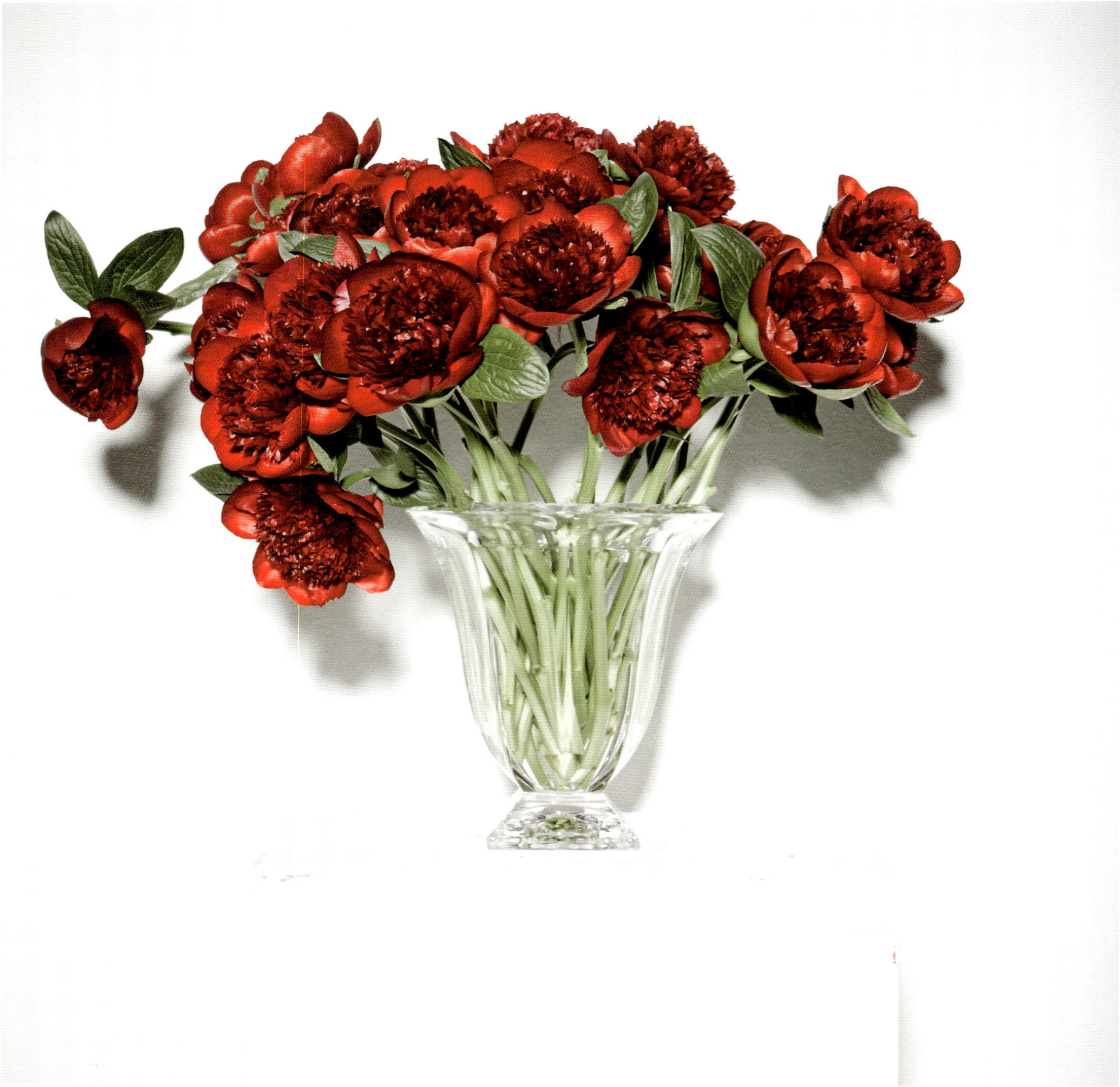

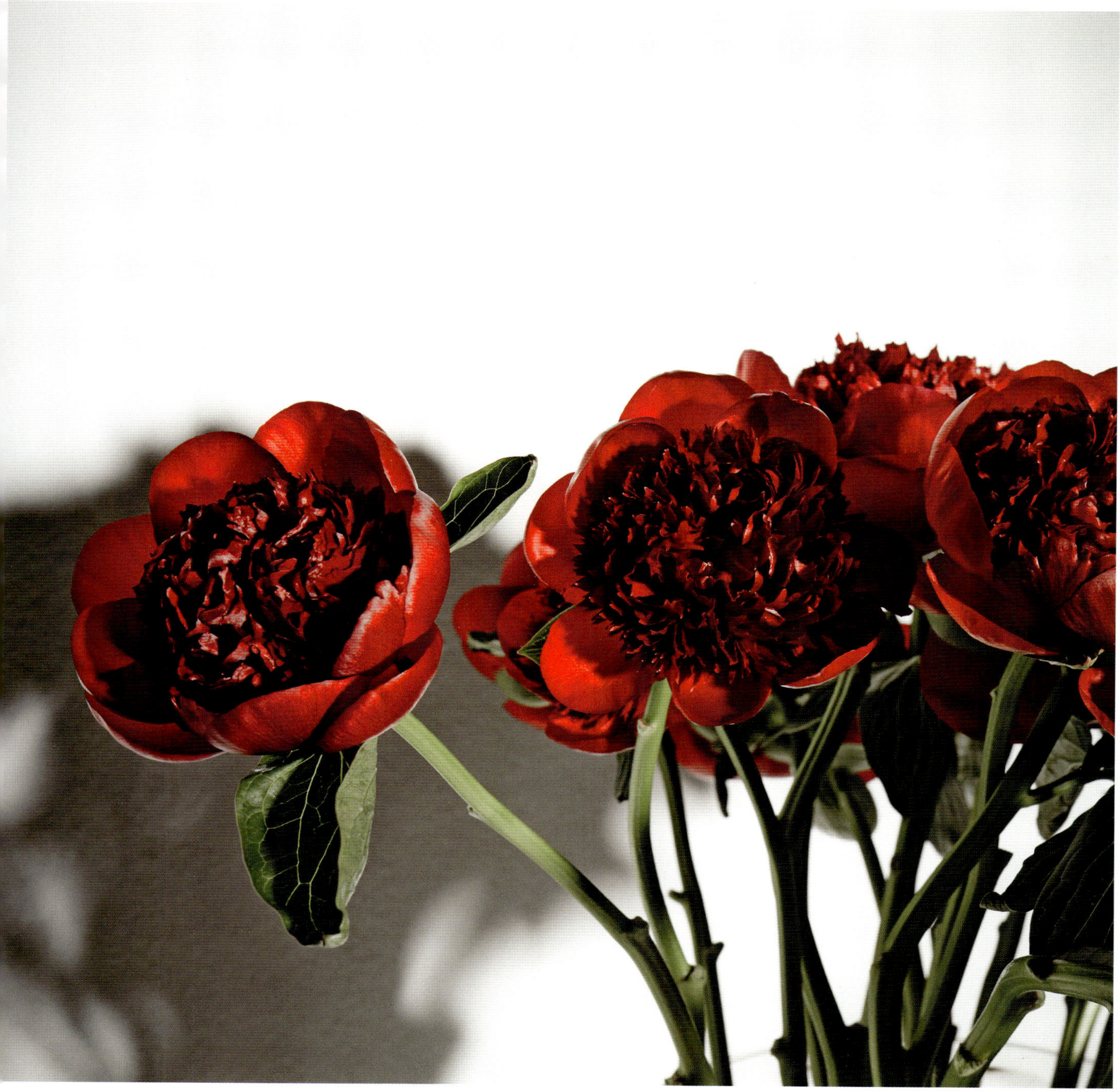

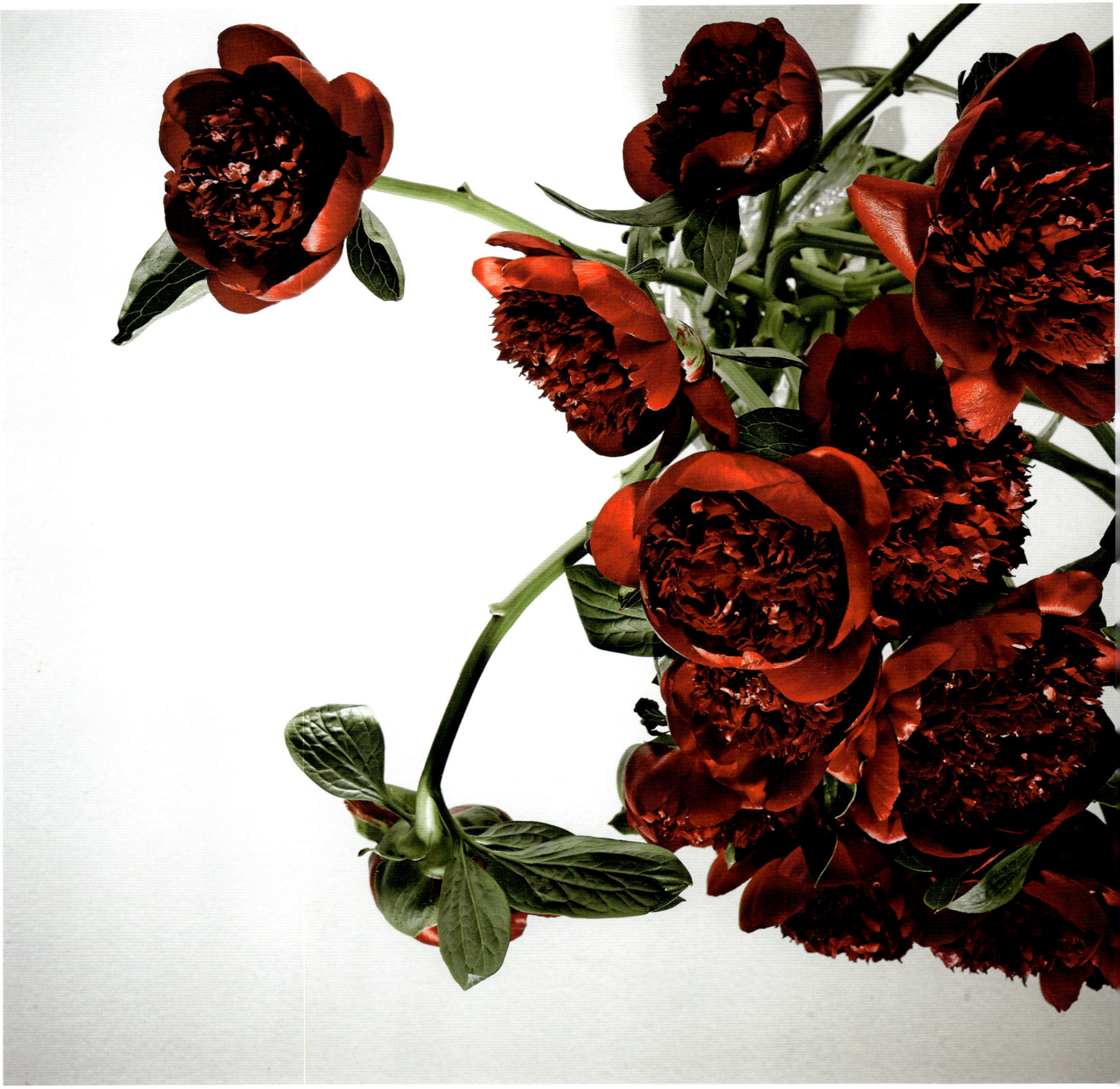

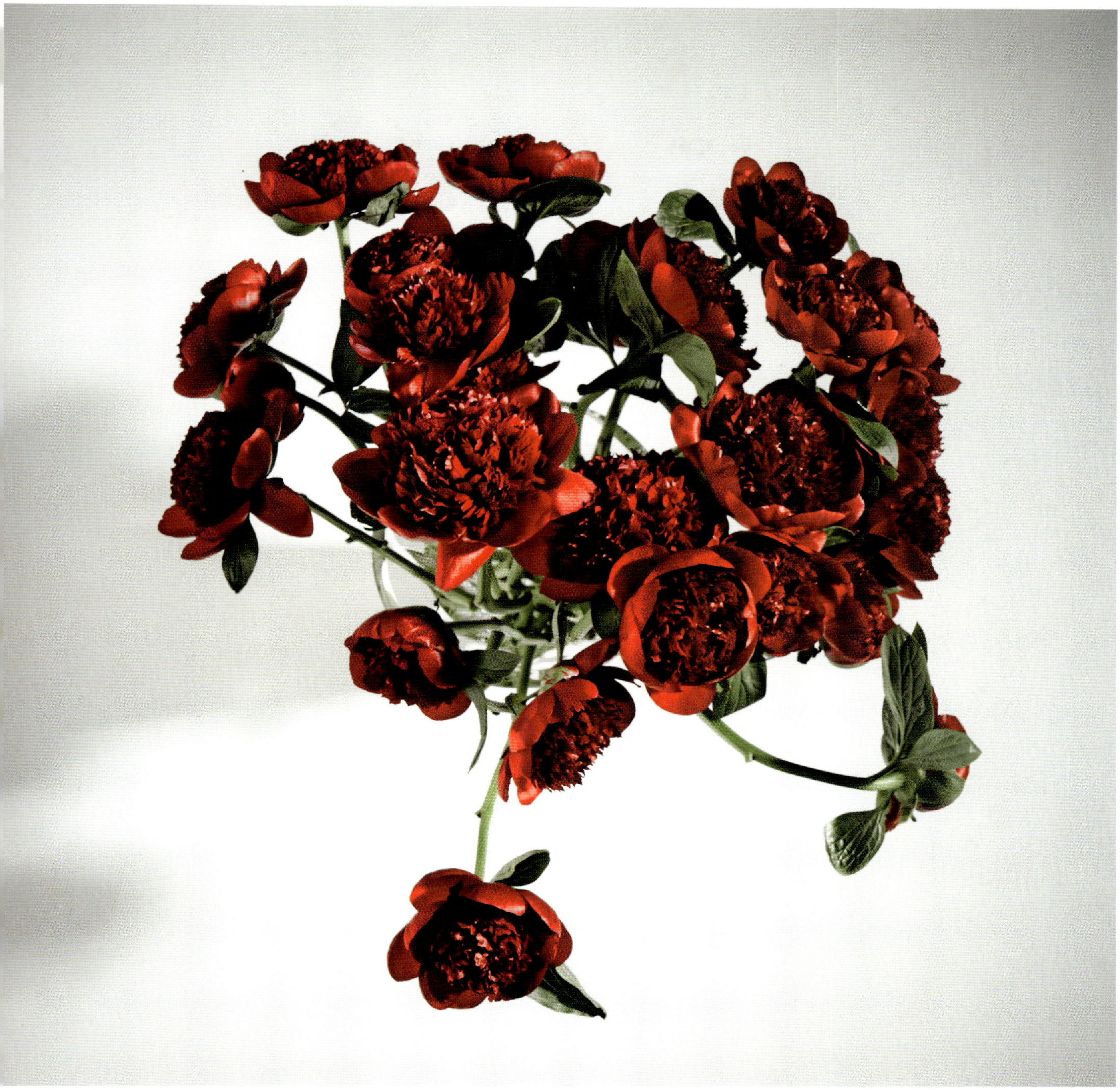

FLOWERS. THE FLOWERS
—
SOON IT WILL BE MINE.

No self-respecting book titled THE FLOWERS would be complete without fair mention of Irving Penn (1917–2009), the New York-based American photographer whose prolific and influential work spanned fashion photography, still life and portraiture. Penn's brilliance lay in his skill for capturing his subjects with compositional clarity and economy: the formality of his photographs give the impression of something fixed and set … his gaze precisely encapsulating the subject in complete and absolute detail, and in isolation from the rest of the world.

The influential magazine *Harper's Bazaar* published several of Penn's drawings while he was still a student at the Philadelphia Museum School of Industrial Arts, and in 1940 he became art director at the department store Saks Fifth Avenue. However, his professional trajectory was assured when three years later he went to work at American *Vogue* – first, as an associate in the magazine's art department but before too long, at the urging of the magazine's visionary art director Alexander Liberman, as a photographer. Penn's first cover for *Vogue* – a colour still-life photograph of a glove, a pocketbook and other accessories – was published in October 1943. It would be the first of more than 150 *Vogue* covers to be published over the following fifty years. Penn's photographic style remained remarkably consistent over his long career at *Vogue* despite the countless deviations in fashion across the decades. In a sense, Penn's rigid photographic style seemed to defy fashion; yet, ironically, it was his aesthetic that became the standard for fashion photography in the 1940s, 1950s and beyond.

Although Penn is most famous for photographing fashion models and cultural figures, his subjects were somehow democratised and equalised through the eye of his lens; compositions of objects, items of food, the underprivileged, the cultural elite, the working class and flowers, all appear to have been studied and documented with equal restraint and reverence. His technique of separating his subjects from their typical environment and positioning them in neutral settings had a sharpening, illuminating effect.

Penn's genius is exemplified in a series he began in 1948 when he took portraits of notable subjects and cultural icons – including Salvador Dali, Marcel Duchamp, Georgia O'Keeffe, Truman Capote, Marlene Dietrich, Spencer Tracy and Joe Louis – in a confined corner space made up of two well-used studio 'flats', or moveable walls, pushed together, and the floor covered with a piece of old carpet. In this series, restricting the subjects' movements (thereby limiting their gesticulation) and standardising the environment in which they were photographed had the effect of defusing the conspicuousness of the subject while simultaneously emphasising the intricacies of their unique physical presence. This stood in stark contrast with the ambitions of most fashion photographers of the day, who sought to conceal imperfections in their subjects – Penn, on the other hand, seemed to pursue imperfection by documenting his subjects in austere environments and producing images of such technical exactness that there is nothing to distract the viewer from 'flaws' in the beauty he captured.

‡

Penn began photographing flowers for the 1967 Christmas edition of *Vogue* and continued to explore the genre for over four decades. For seven years, from 1967 to 1973, he dedicated himself to photographing one particular flower: Tulips (1967); Poppies (1968); Peonies (1969); Orchids (1970); Roses (1971); Lilies (1972); and Begonias (1973). These extraordinary images were printed each year for *Vogue*'s Christmas edition, and in 1980 the photographs were collectively published as a book, simply titled *Flowers*.

I have been obsessed with this rare and expensive book for years, and whenever I go to the library I have it on the desk with me along with books on whatever other subject matter I am immersed in that day. I have photocopied its pages and studied the duplicates many times, trying to grasp and reason the beauty of its content. It is easily one of my favourite books, if not my favourite. As I write this, I am anticipating the arrival of a first edition copy of Penn's *Flowers* from a

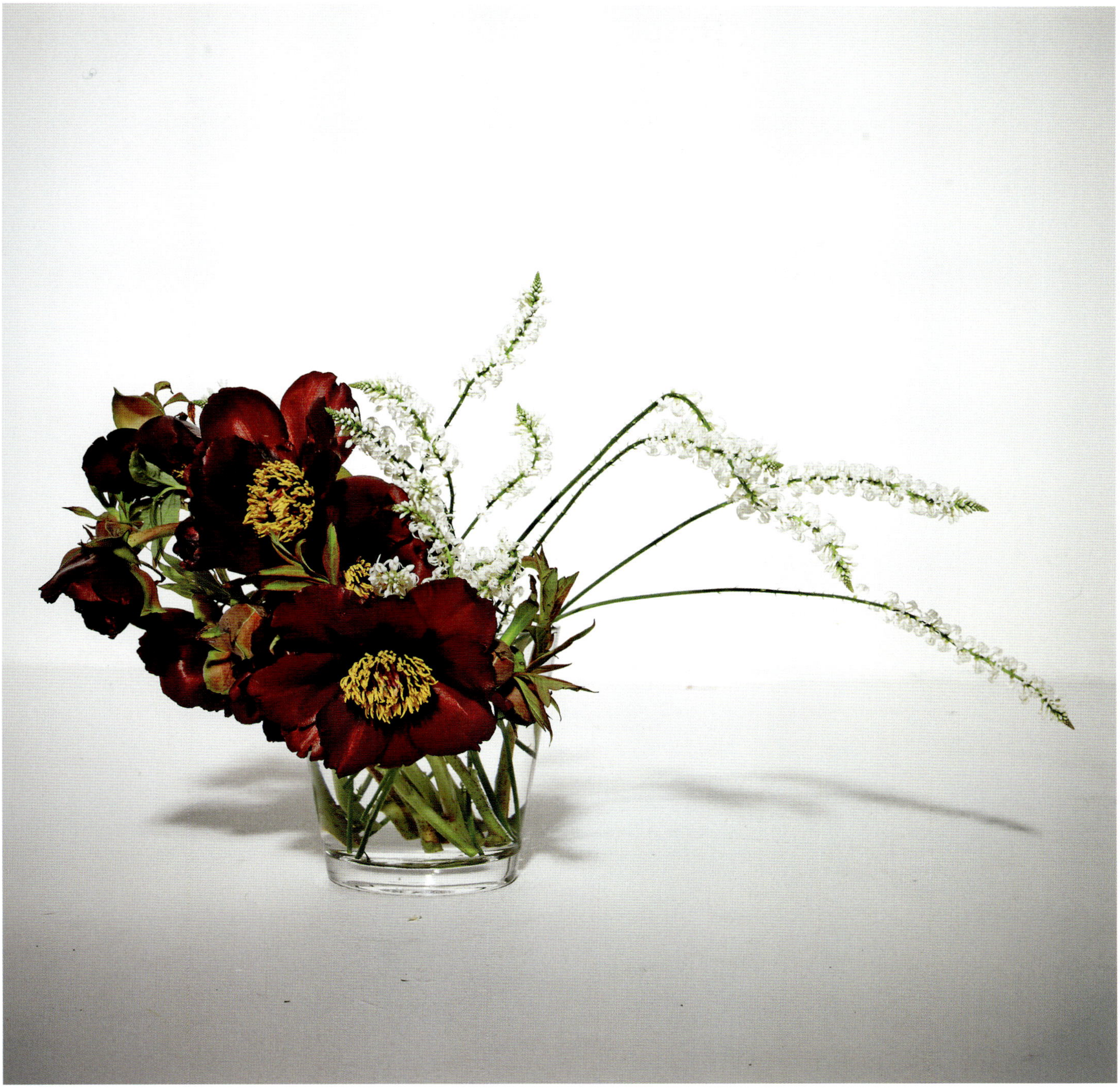

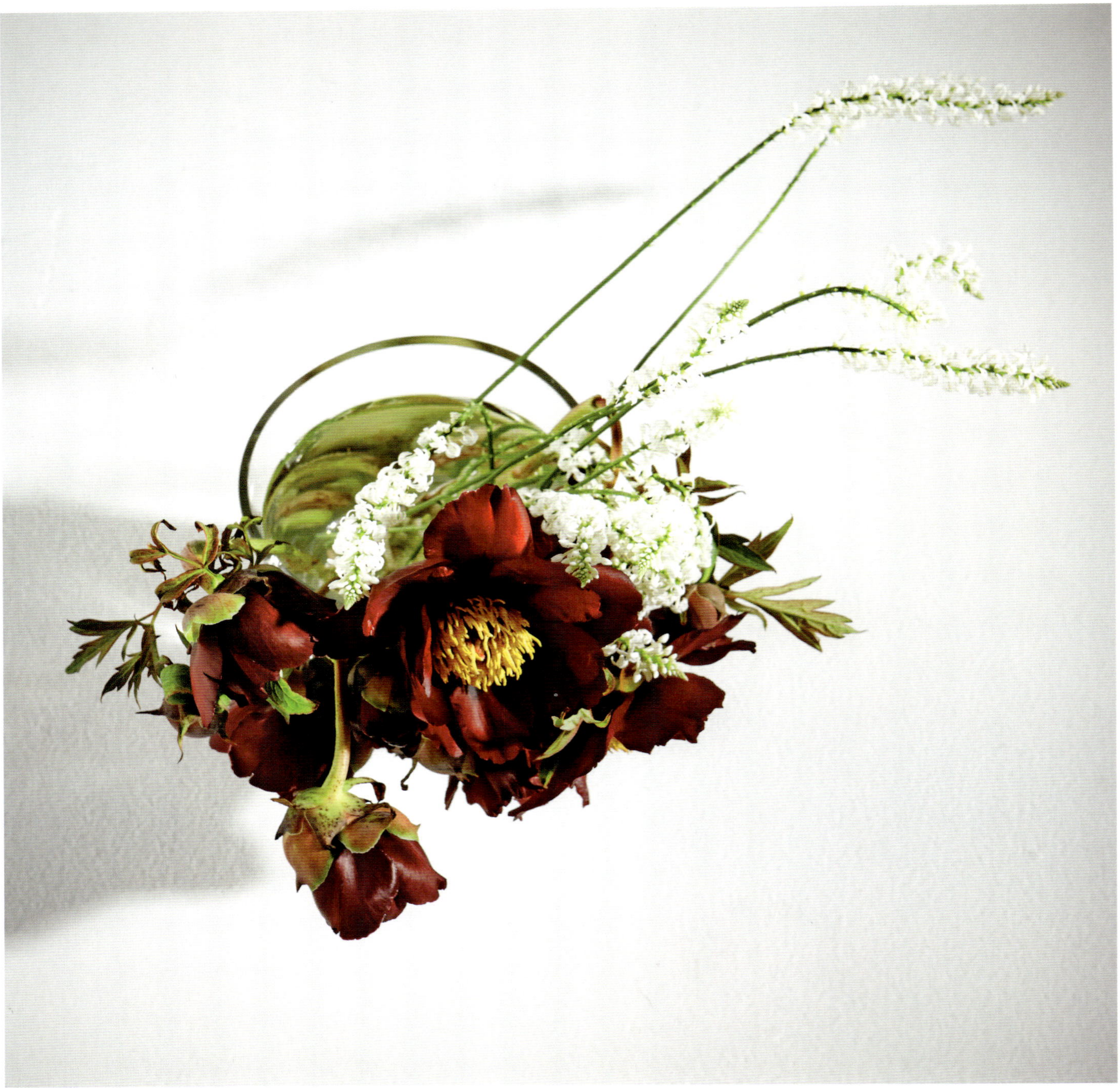

bookshop in New York. Soon it will be mine. It will be one of my most treasured possessions.

It is obvious (as you will have realised) that I have a long-held personal conviction about the importance of carefully observing individual blooms in the process of working with flowers. I do not believe it is possible to create floral compositions (or work in any other medium) without a reverence for, and intimate knowledge of, one's chosen material. Often, when I am working in my studio arranging flowers for events and as bouquets, I will pick up a single bloom and inspect it: less for its imperfections, more to take in the exquisite detail of its form and colour. Turning the flower in my hand in order to discover the angle that's most pleasing – particularly in the case of tree peonies and herbaceous peonies – my ritual recalls the haunting images of peonies in Penn's book. For instance, the image that accompanies this text is a glass vase of 'Corsair' tree peonies – a single, heavy, thick-petalled flower that has deep dark black-red blooms with darker flares and substantial yellow stamens – coupled with 'Creamy Stackhousia', an Australian native of uncommon lightness and fineness when compared with other species in the spectrum of Australian flowers. The juxtaposition of these elegantly spiked, tiny creamy-white blooms with the remarkable and majestic peony not only emphasises the extraordinary depth of colour of the 'Corsair' blooms, it also renders the stackhousia even more ethereal and whimsical.

Penn's sharp and precise portraits of individual flowers in varying stages of decay or development – each bloom depicted neither with context nor with a sense of physical scale – suggest a correspondence between beauty and transience. The way he focuses on a flower's deepening of colour or its fragile translucency or the complex folding and pleating of its petals, reveals the photographer's intent. He 'monumentalises' his subject in order to evoke allegorical and metaphorical associations.

I like to think that the way Irving Penn used his camera to explore all sides of beauty is akin to the way I now turn each bloom to find its most meaningful angle. I am indebted to his book *Flowers* …

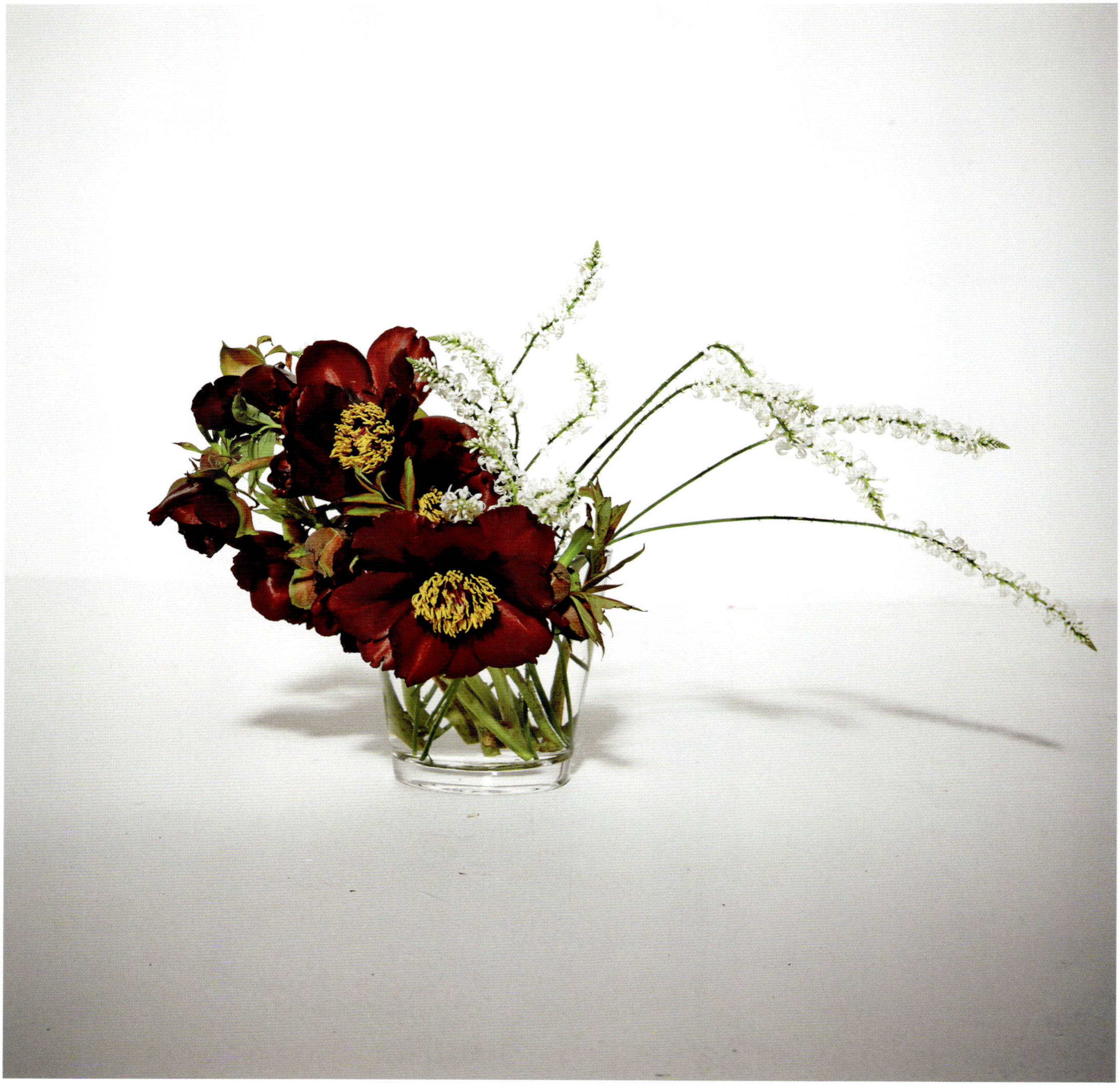

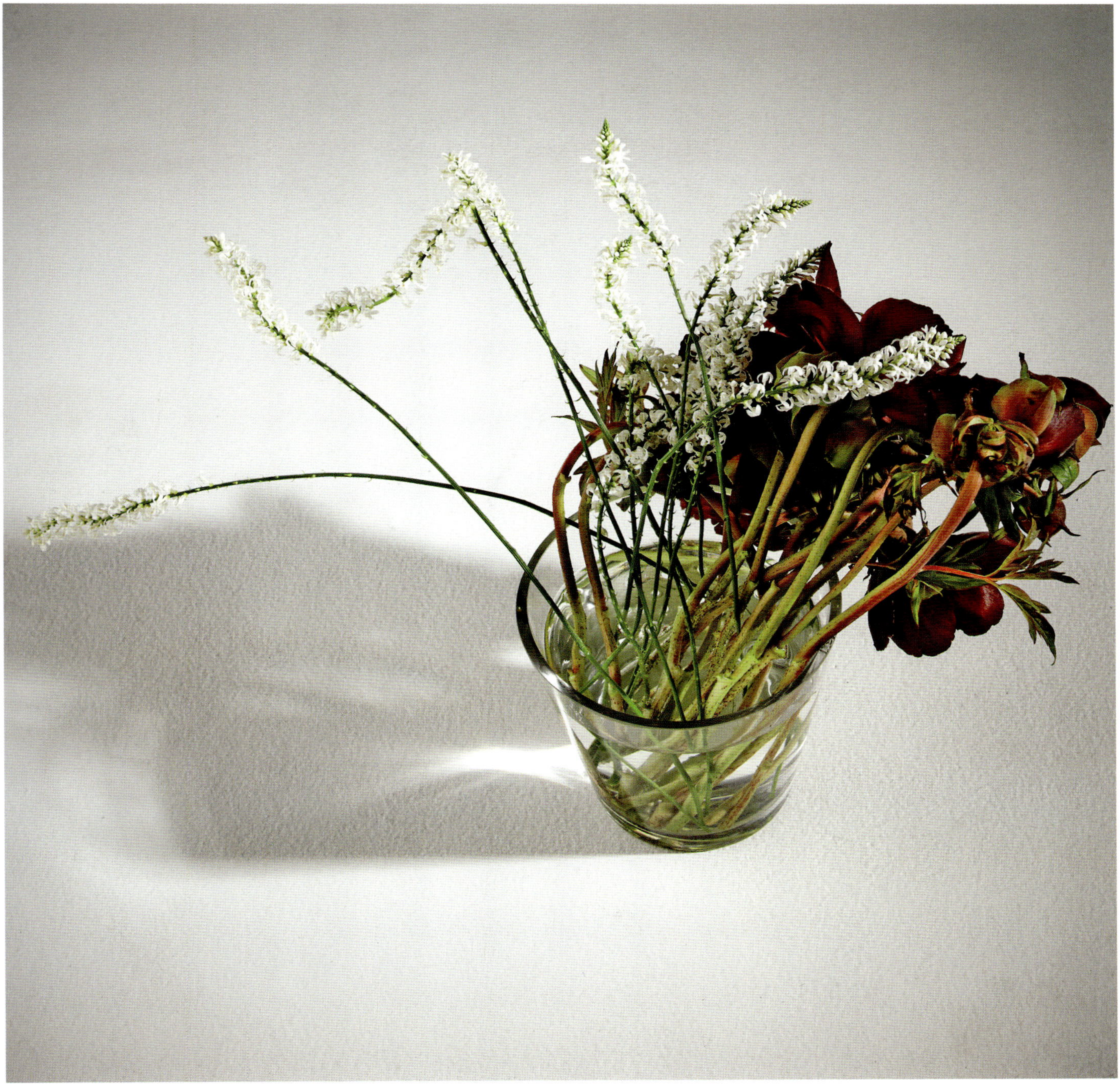

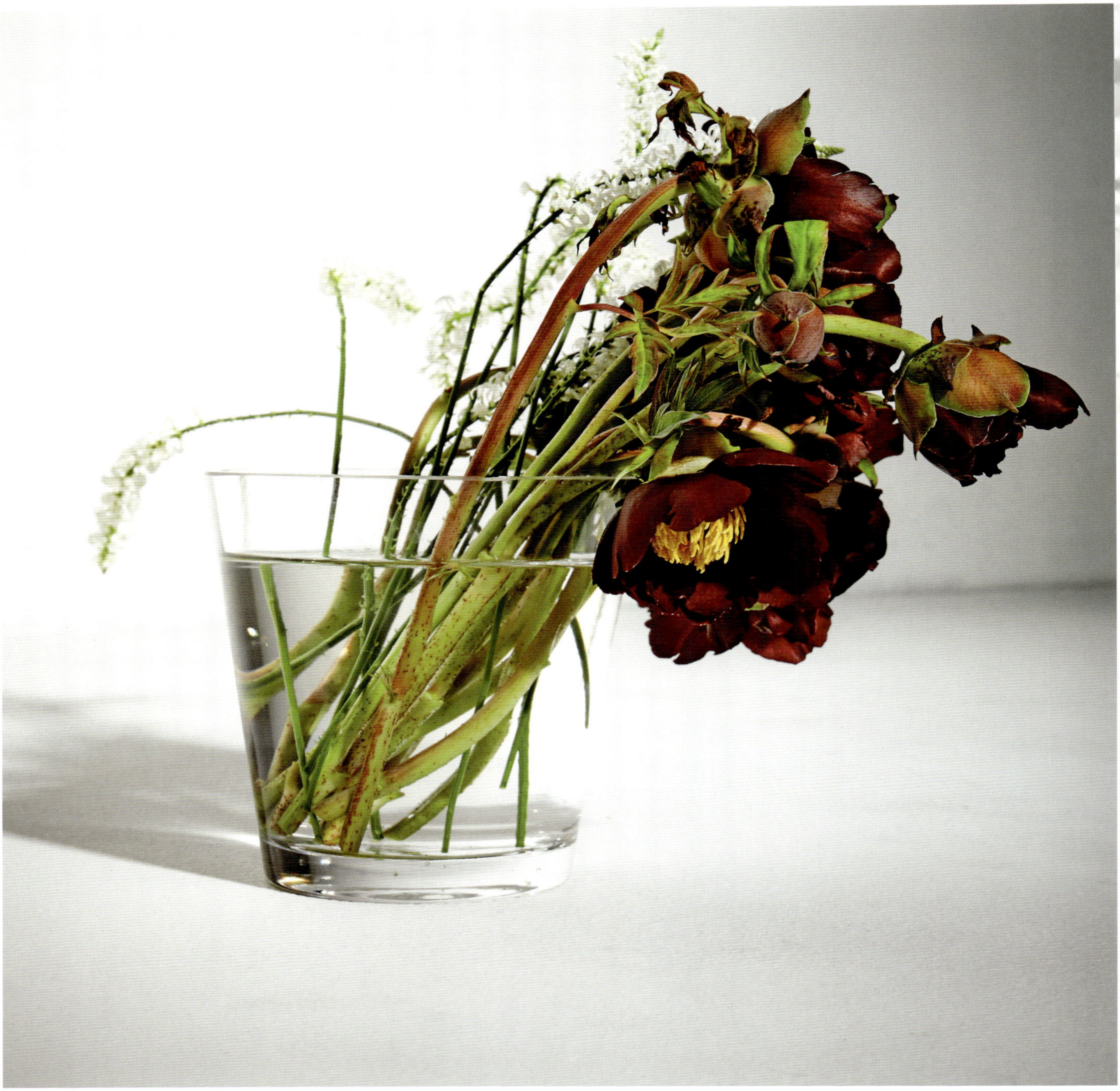

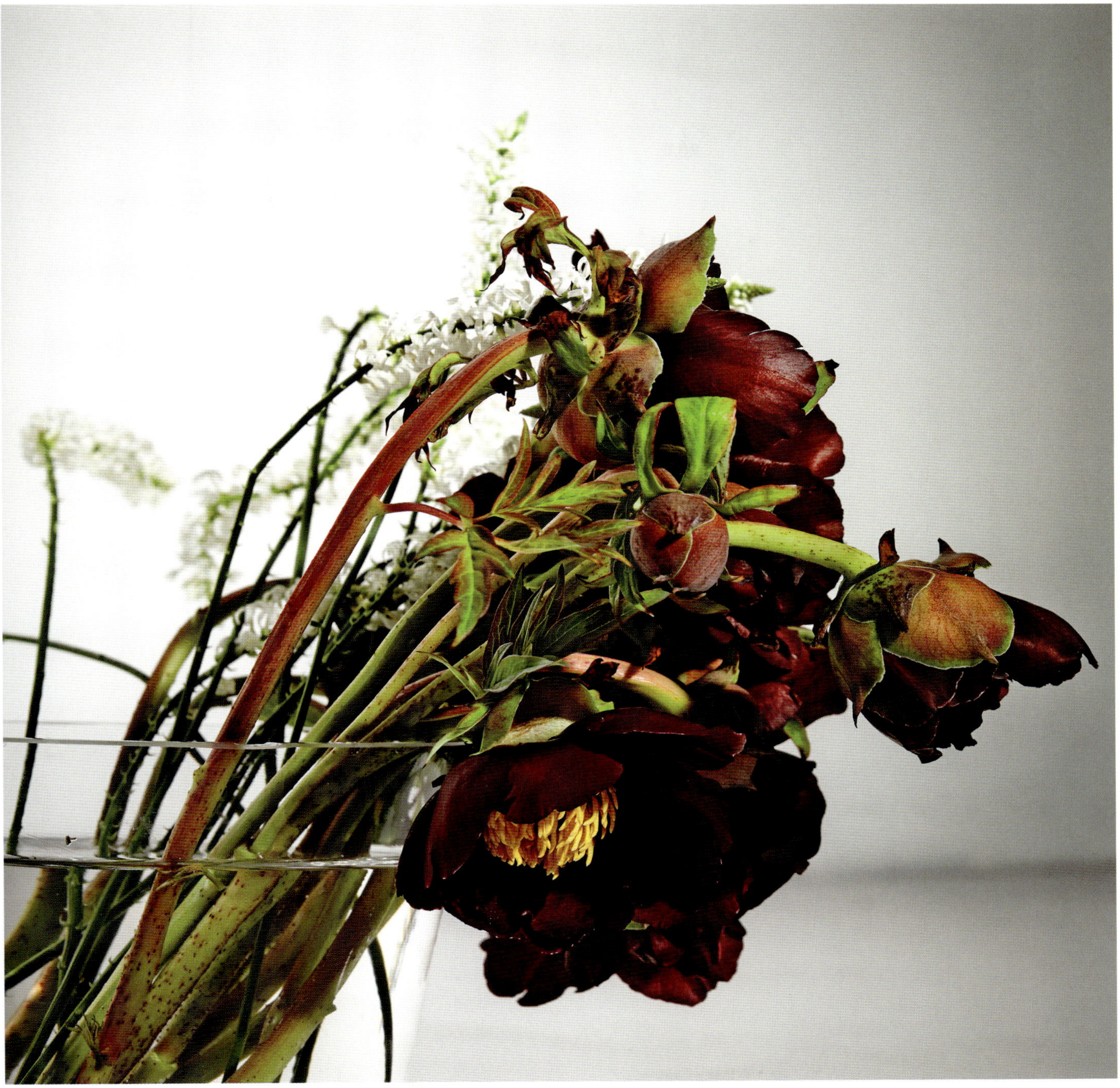

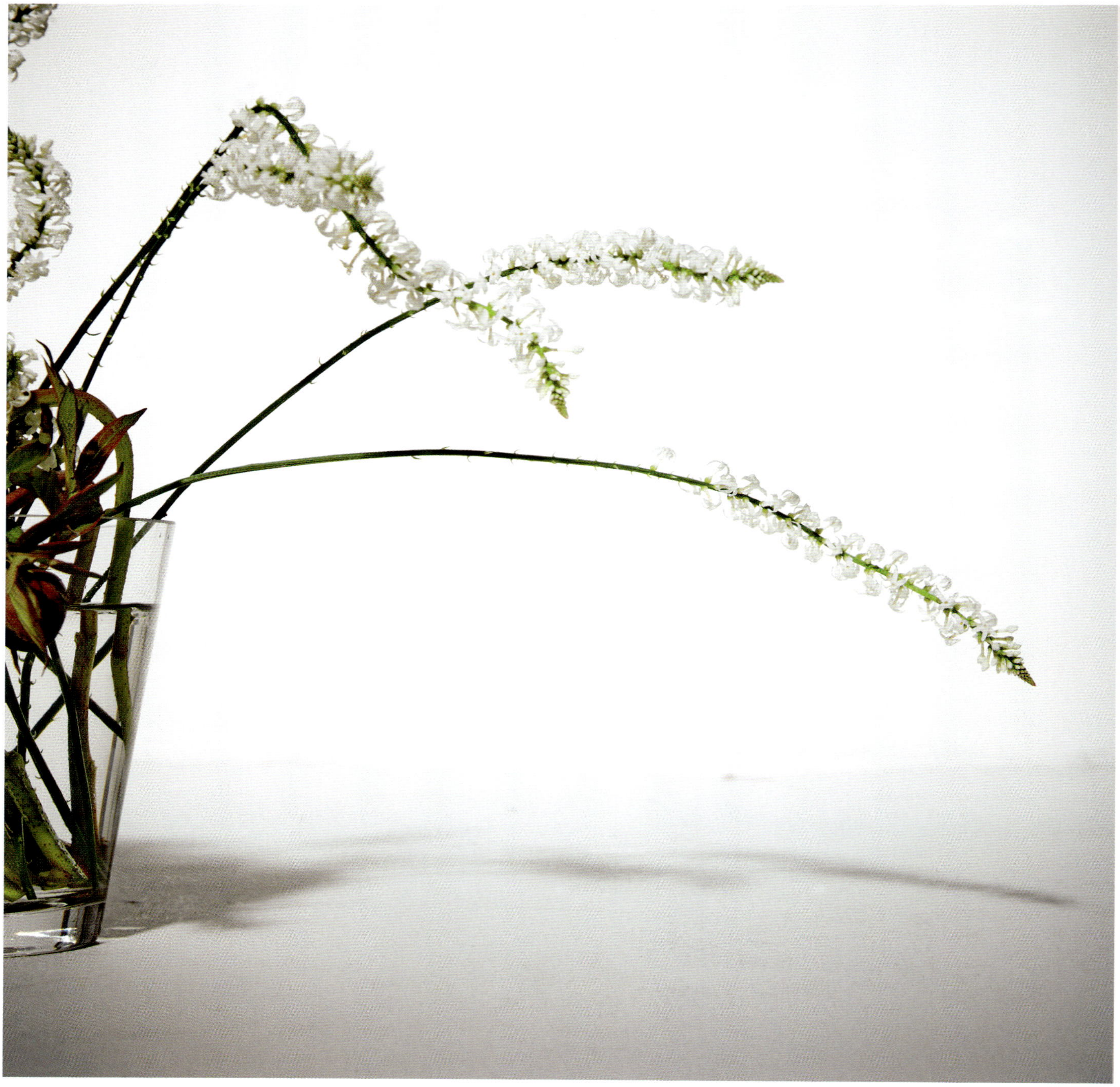

MARKS AND SCARS AND THE PASSIONFLOWER
—
THE SYMBOLIC RENDERING OF LOVE.

Until he passed away, when I was about seven years old, the oldest man I had ever known was 'Old Dad Garrad' or 'Old Dad from Gosford'. He lived in Gosford on the Central Coast of New South Wales, and the location reference differentiated him from my other grandfathers. Because of paternal links to Ireland, we referred to our grandfathers and great-grandfather as 'Old Dad' – a variation on a common Irish term for grandfather, 'Old Father'.

James Garrad lived on a hill, in a house that was even older than him. I remember visiting him at his home and feeling sure that he must have exchanged contracts with a bushranger in his purchase of the dwelling.

In the very early years of British settlement in Australia, 'bushranger' referred to escaped convicts, men distinguished by the survival skills that allowed them to use the Australian landscape as a refuge from the authorities. The term later broadened to refer to men who abandoned society and lived a life of crime, using the bush as their base. In public schools in the 1980s there was a great deal of talk about the most infamous bushranger of them all, Edward 'Ned' Kelly (1854–1880), a handsome, lawless Australian of Irish convict descent who had become, by then, a cultural icon. To my juvenile mind, it was wholly within the realms of possibility that 'Old Dad Garrad' had not only known Ned Kelly but was, perhaps, living in Kelly's old house. The 'out house' – the toilet that was a crude 'seat' over a pit – seemed truly archaic to me, and added great weight to my supposition.

Old Dad Garrad's wizened physicality was in stark contrast to his character, which radiated vitality. He had remarkably kind eyes and seemed to me to be at a degree of peace with the world. I supposed that this was connected to the years he had spent in practice on the earth; there was a perceivable harmony in his disposition. At the conclusion of every visit he had this baffling way of passing a banknote into my palm – and also my sister's – while our parents looked on, none the wiser. My sister and I would taste a kind of independence ... the gesture a short-lived gift of self-sufficiency.

A short time before he passed away – and became the first person I knew in heaven – we went to Gosford again to visit him. My recollection of the visit is vivid: I can see with clarity his arm around me as I sat on his lap. I felt his thin, strong arm through his equally thin, tanned skin as I focused on a faded anchor tattoo he had on his forearm. I asked him why he had the tattoo ... he answered: 'So you'll know me in heaven.'

‡

In 2012, I was given a singular opportunity by Nicky Andrews, Director of NAC Media Group in Sydney, and Tiffany & Co., New York, to create a suite of sculptures to celebrate the launch of the new Tiffany & Co. store in Bondi Junction, in the eastern suburbs of Sydney. I became the first non-American among a few distinguished artists to be commissioned to make work for the renowned Tiffany & Co. windows. The sculptures – titled 'The Mysteries' – were launched on 13 February 2013, the day before Saint Valentine's Day.

During the planning stages of the work, I had many conversations with the 'Creatives' at Tiffany & Co. in New York ... about the project's critical conceptual associations, the historical juggernaut that is Tiffany & Co., and the shop's geographical and cultural position in Sydney and in Australia. In the course of my research I was struck by the bold symbolism inherent in the production of Tiffany & Co.'s jewellery: historically, there has been an iconic association with symbols of love and passion. These include the love heart, the arrow, the infinity symbol, the ring, the lock and key, the sun, the moon, the Cross and the anchor, among countless others. While immersed in these symbolic representations of love, my mind returned to that day with Old Dad Garrad and his remark about heaven ... and how, over the years, his words had become a piercing, poetical justification for my own flower 'marks' or tattoos. For me, above all, each flower etched into my skin is a symbol of love.

My research for the Tiffany & Co. commission started with Australia's earliest colonial days and the arrival in January 1788

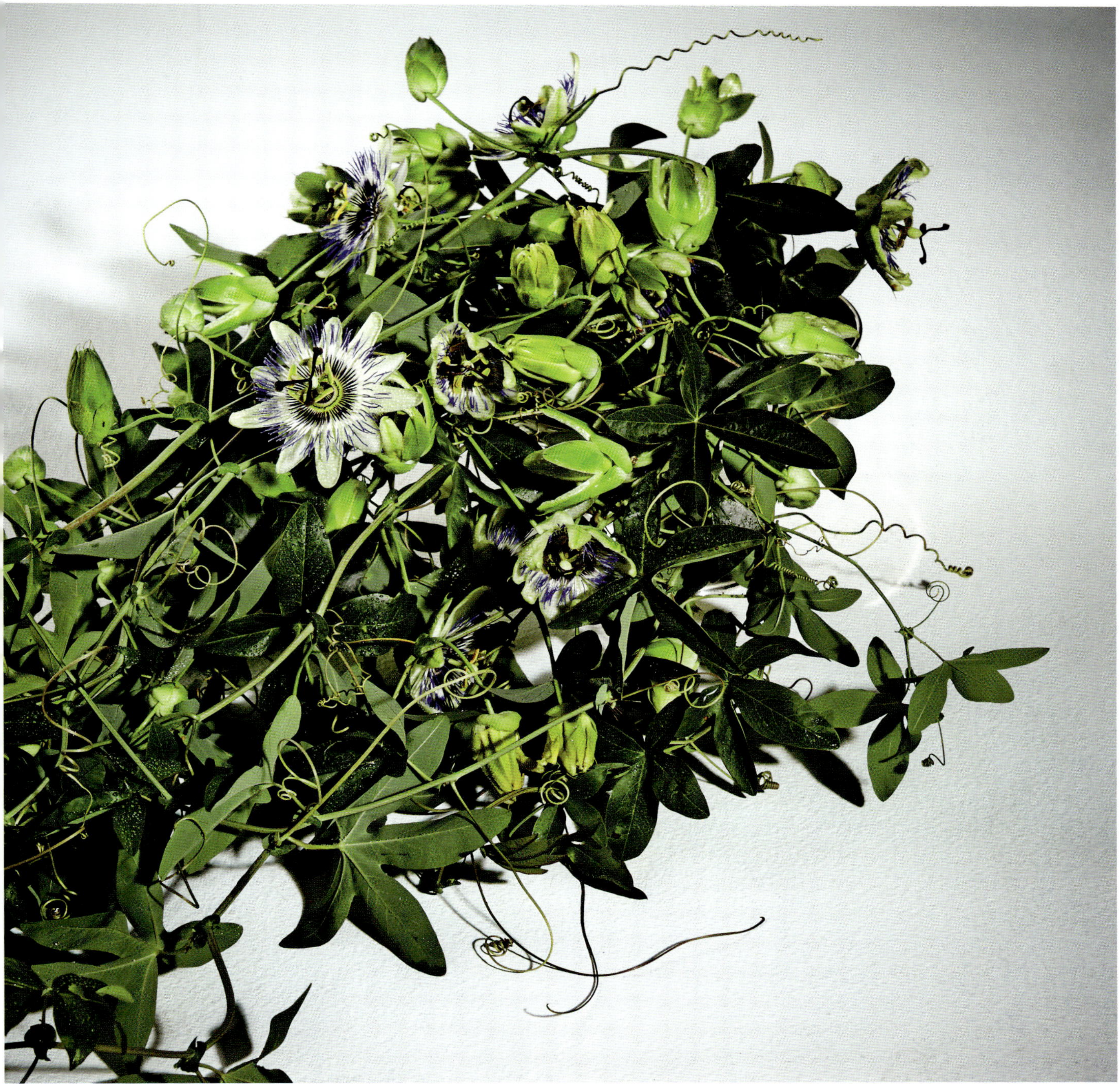

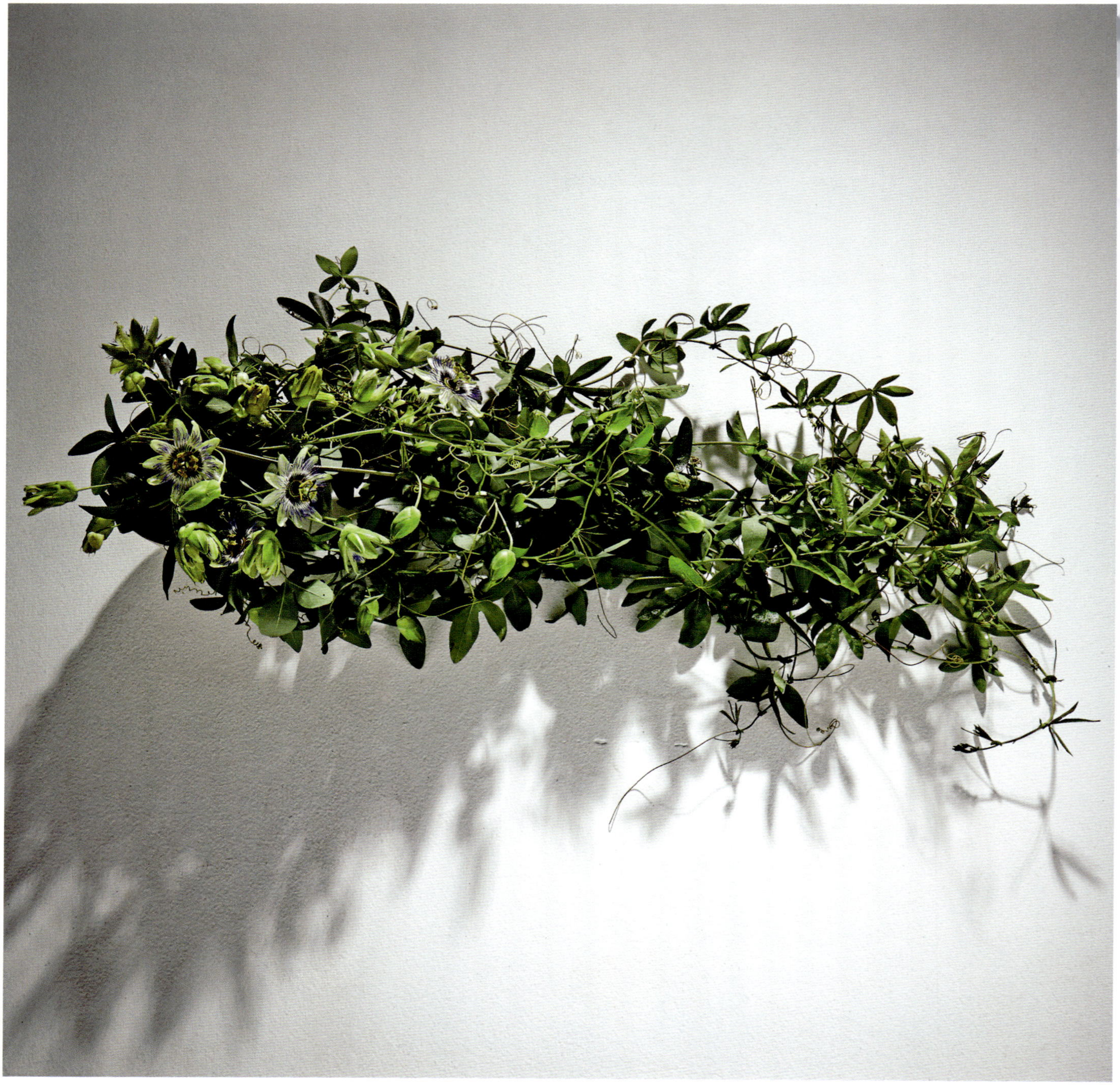

of the First Fleet – the name given to the eleven ships that left Great Britain on 13 May 1787 to establish a penal colony in Australia. Here I believed I would find versions of these symbolic references to love. In the State Library of New South Wales I gained access to convict indents on microfiche, handwritten documents that listed the details of each person who survived the journey from Great Britain to Australia. One of the heading titles in the document was 'Marks and Scars', under which a textual description of obvious marks and scars for each convict is noted. For the majority of men and women, the list includes a description of tattoos, and these tattoos read like a list of symbols used by Tiffany & Co. in the creation of objects to symbolise and make manifest emotions such as love and passion.

I have chosen the passionflower to illustrate these words for its relationship to the commission I have described here. The foundational concerns of the project were developed through a focus on love and the expression of passion and emotion. Both Charles Lewis Tiffany (1812–1902), the founder of Tiffany & Co., and those 'marked' in the First Fleet, had symbolically rendered love and passion and customised these symbols to the body. A mass of passionflower arranged as it is here, undulant and rambling and flowing or surging from the vessel that holds it, for me, epitomises passion.

For Tiffany & Co. I created four 24-carat gold-plated sculptures, each an abstracted ring-shaped form (an archetypal symbol of love) constructed in brass eucalyptus leaves – an ancient tree profoundly connected to the passions and deeply loved by the Indigenous people of Australia. In the manner of the fluid, ascending passionflower, my great-grandfather's response to my enquiry about his faded anchor tattoo – 'So you'll know me in heaven' – became the foundational poetic impetus for a suite of sculptures concerned with a concept of love spanning hundreds of thousands of years.

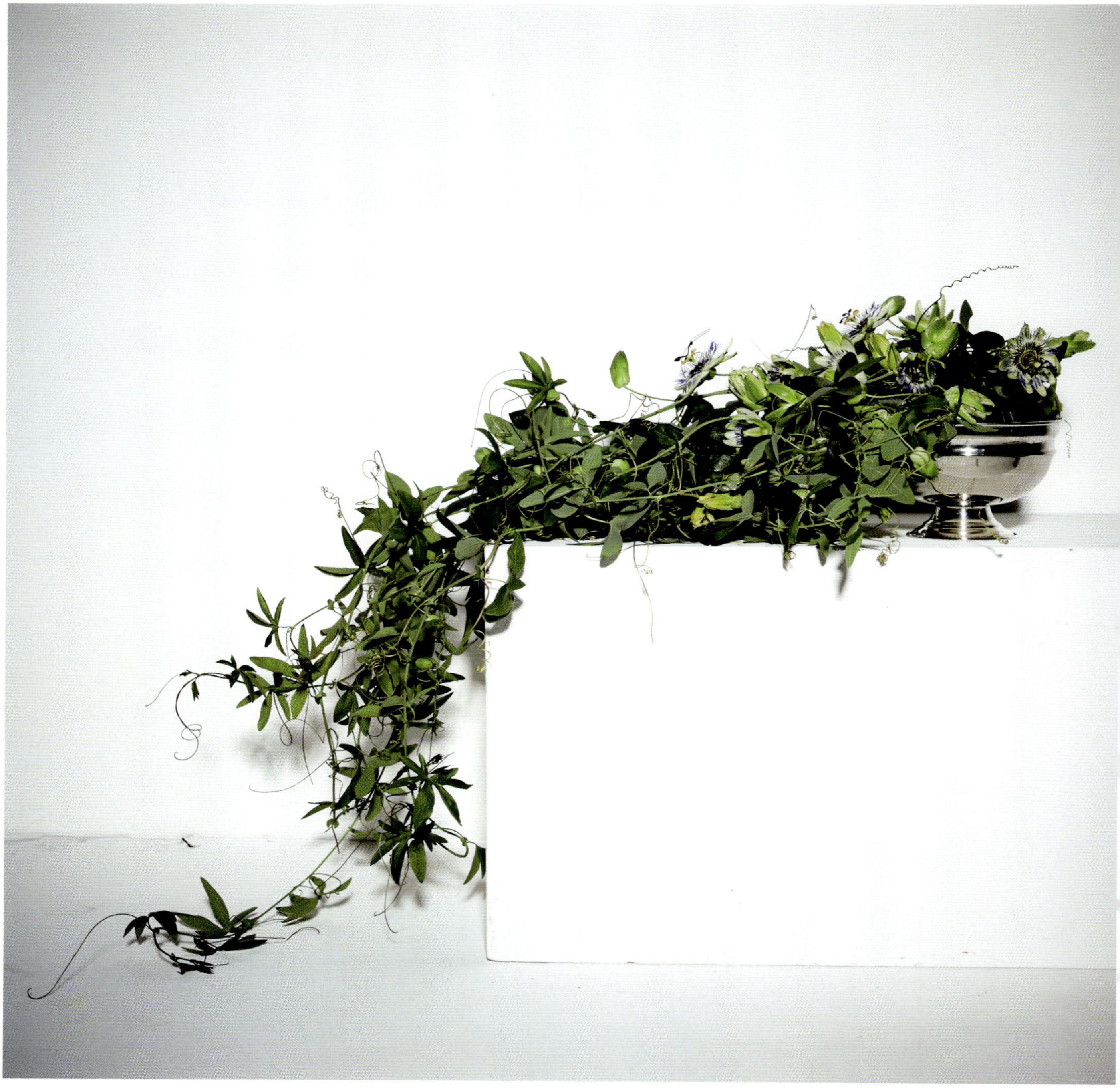

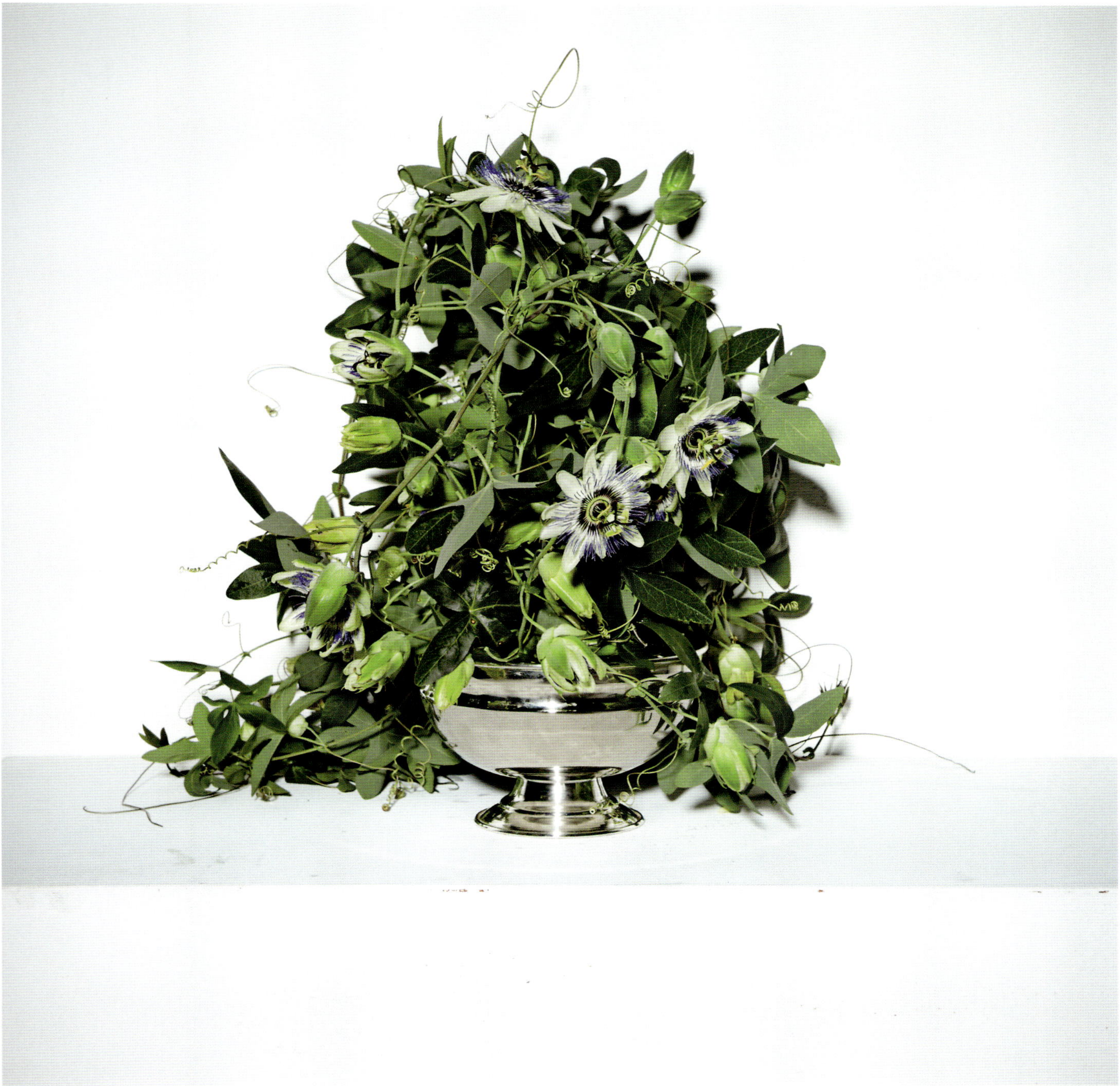

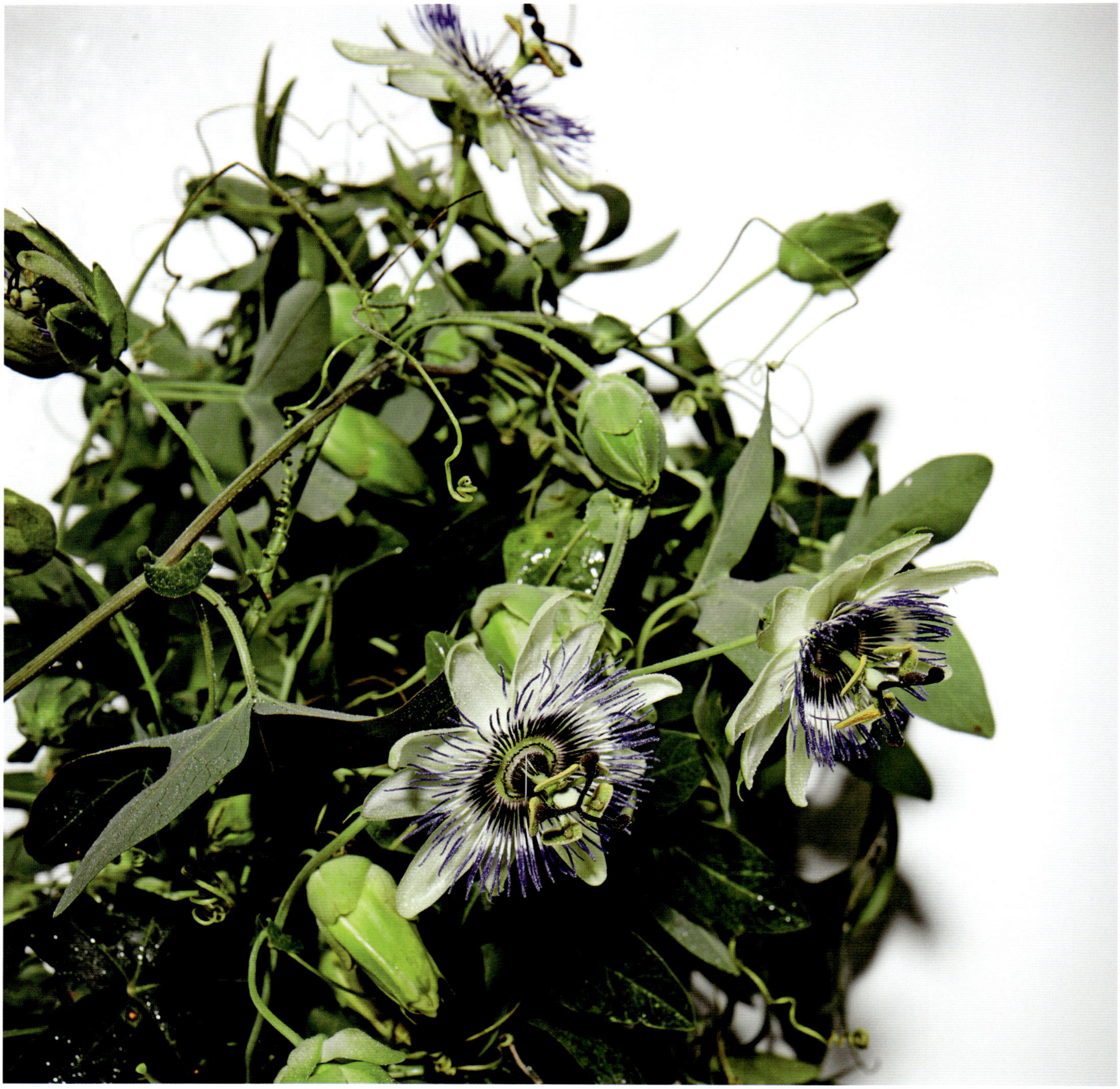

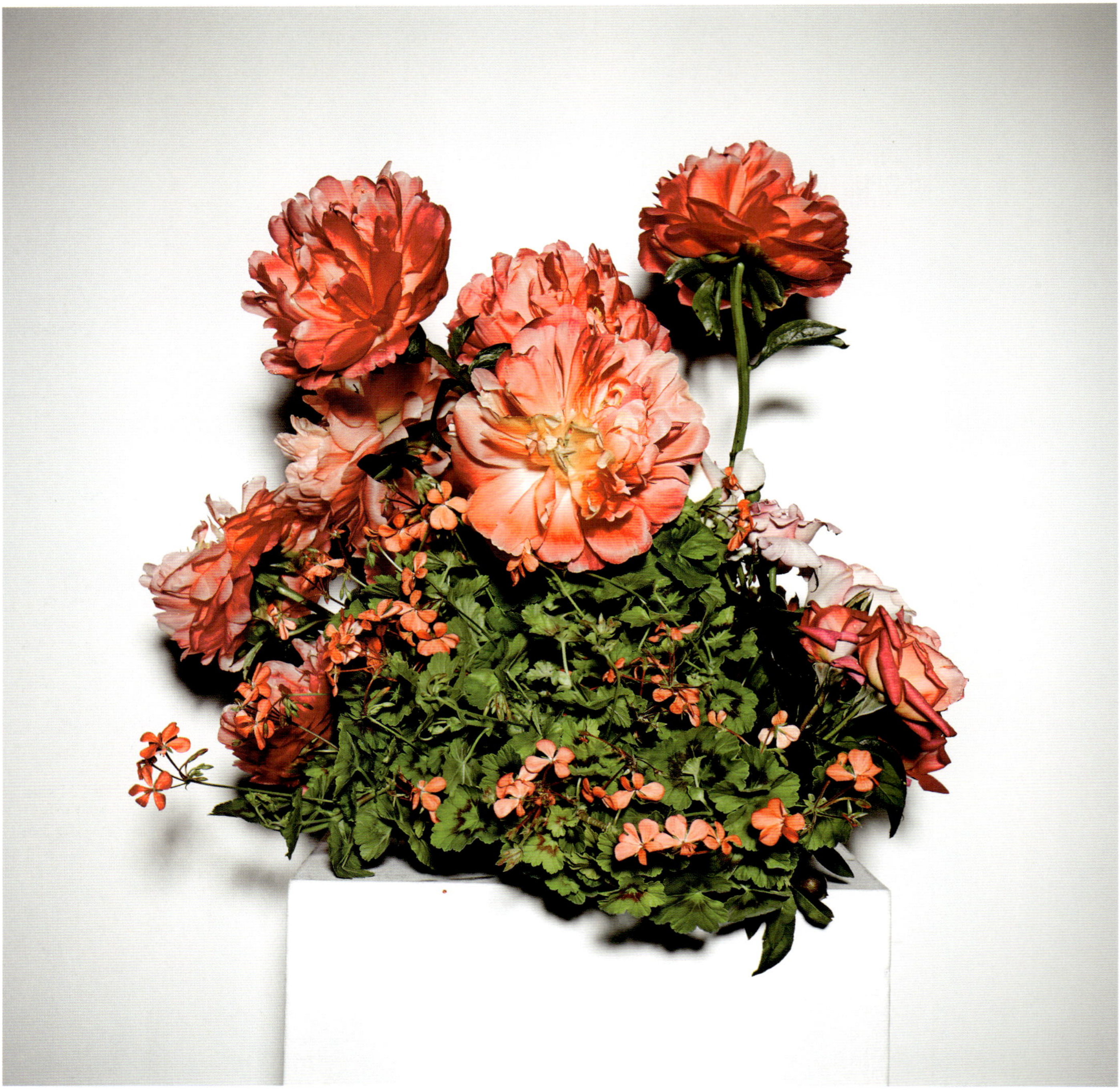

THE PRINCESS AND THE PEONIES
—

AN OBSESSIVE GATHERING OF IMAGES AND AN ANARCHIC ARRANGEMENT.

A few years after my paternal grandmother passed away, my grandfather gifted me her art supplies and her art books. It was a generous bequest and I was honoured to have these items that had been so precious to her. I open her pencil boxes now and then and am flooded with recollections of watching her sketch and paint … birds, flowers, ships, religious icons and romanticised women in idealised scenes. In her later years her creativity seemed to ramble and undulate toward a developing eccentricity; yet, as a younger woman, she had been regarded for the intricate, microcosmic terrariums she created, which the women of her local community commissioned for their homes. And there were always a number of beautiful terrariums in my grandparents' home. However, as the years rolled on, the terrariums 'evolved', and in the final years of my grandmother's life, figurines would be moved from their staunch positions in the glass cabinet to new and increasingly tropical locations. Trapped within a glass sphere, beautiful 'geisha girls', for instance, would unexpectedly find themselves encircled by delicate ferns and damp moss – an environment my grandmother would assure me was more pleasing to them.

For as long as I can remember a large reproduction oil painting had hung above my grandparents' lounge suite. It was a classic Australian bush scene: surrounded by enormous eucalyptus trees, simply dressed Europeans were depicted gathered around a fire. The painting was decorative; it was visually bland. Despite its scale, its thick ornate frame and its prominent position in my grandparents' home, the painting 'ruffled no feathers' … it just faded into the background, except perhaps for those infrequent visitors to whom it whispered of my grandmother's artistic bent. For frequent visitors such as myself, the absence of the painting, its sudden removal, would have conjured far more interest than the painting itself – until one particular day. On this visit, the small, nonchalant fire that the subjects in the painting had seemingly arranged in order to boil the 'billy' for tea, suddenly seemed to burn more brightly … in fact, it had become a roaring blaze. So too a number of trees in the background of the image: they seemed to have miraculously fallen into a ray of sunlight that ignited a previously unobserved vibrant green in their dusty leaves. It turned out that my grandmother, after decades of compliancy and frustration, had finally decided that with her own oil paints and artistic skill she could further develop and enhance the painting – enliven a canvas whose dullness she had endured for too many years.

I found my grandmother's increasing artistic anarchy inspiring. I recognised that with age she had become somewhat liberated from the social order, and this liberty was reflected not only in her creative output but also in her attitudes as well as in the opinions she voiced during our long conversations. She had always told me stories about the people and the time in her life before I was born, but in this later period, the stories – like the painting – developed greater, more vibrant detail …

‡

On the day that my grandfather gifted me my grandmother's art supplies and books, I took them home and began to pore over the wealth of objects and associated memories. When I came to leafing through the books, a slip of paper hit the floor, and then another. As I looked down to inspect them, Lady Diana, Princess of Wales, smiled demurely back at me, tiara on her head and in duplicate. As I continued through the pages of the thick art book, meticulously cut-out pictures of Lady Diana's head (and only her head) seemed to multiply; there were many dozens of head-shaped pieces of magazine-quality paper, all with a reproduced likeness of the Princess of Wales on them. For some, this find might have been shocking or even perhaps a little disturbing, but I knew of my grandmother's affection for Lady Diana, Princess of Wales … she had deeply empathised with the beautiful royal for many years and, given the princess's poise and grace, had taken great exception to the prince's treatment of her.

Of course, I quickly inspected the remaining books for further cut-outs and obsessions, and found hundreds of flowers carefully cut out of books and magazines – every conceivable flower variety and colour was represented. I asked my grandfather for his thoughts on my find and he said: 'She just thought they were beautiful.' Amassing beautiful things in order to compose and arrange them is, for me, like it was for my grandmother, a way of life.

‡

Thinking about my grandmother's predilection for beauty, I decided in the pages of this book to observe her obsessive gathering of images in an arrangement composed of three elements: coral peonies, geranium and garden roses – distinct blooms of varying textural layers that would capture the necessary complexity within the composition. This trilogy of blooms embraces a spectrum of pinks … from coral, rose, watermelon, blush and hot pink, to salmon and strawberry. There is something of my own eccentricity in this combination: there is a lack of formality that some would see as anarchic, but drawing on the spirit of my grandmother, there is an idiosyncratic logic in the coupling of the 'King of the Flower Kingdom' – the peony in full magnificent bloom – with a 'corsage' of various fragrant pink garden roses chosen for their scent rather than their flawless appearance. Adding the richly textured, ornately patterned geranium leaf and its vibrant pink flower does little to soften the composition – for 'purists' the inclusion would be jarring – but for me, it simply enforces the 'anarchic' energy discovered by my grandmother once she had abandoned the constraints of politeness; a discovery that will always serve as a source of inspiration in my work with the flowers.

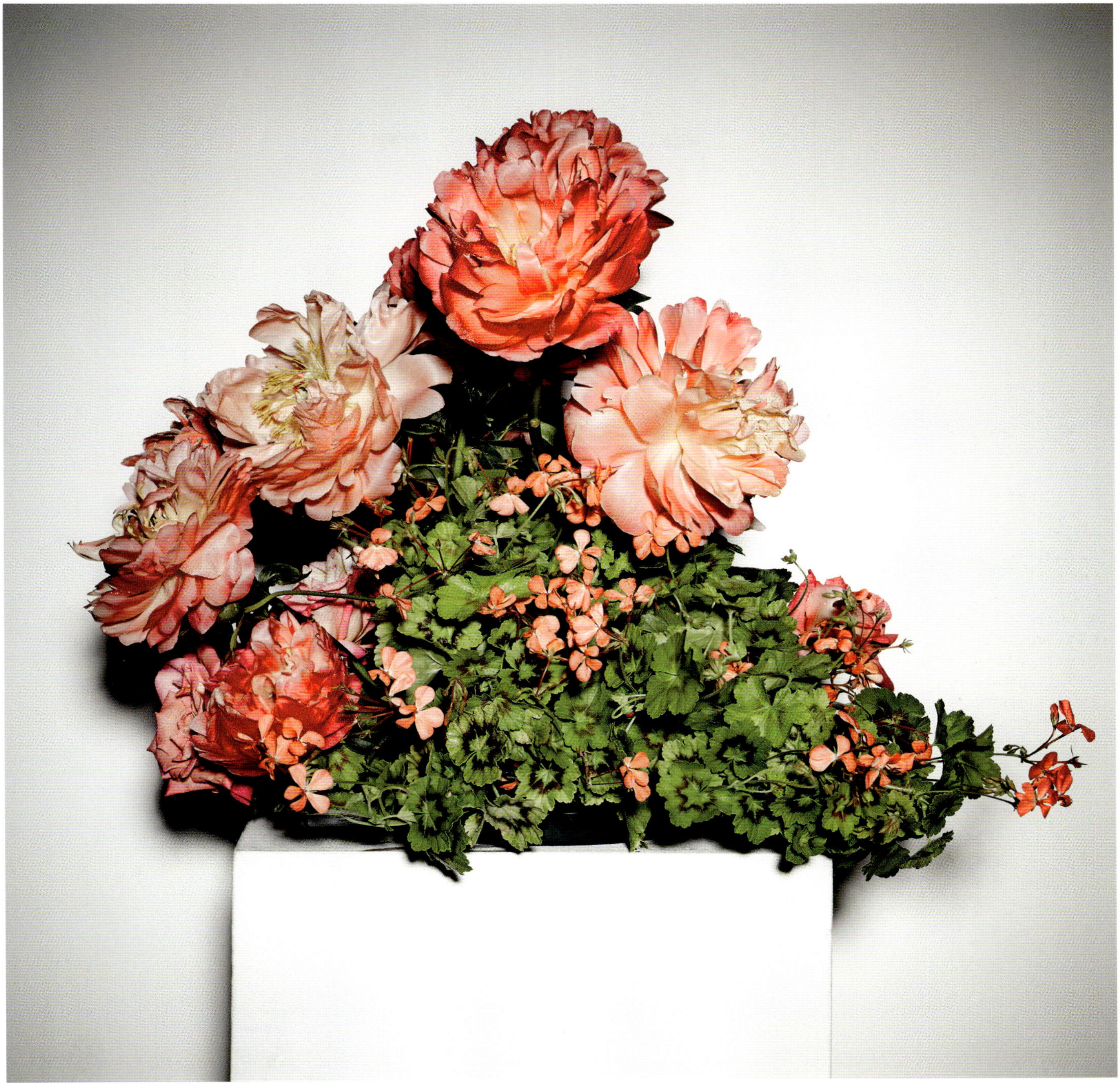

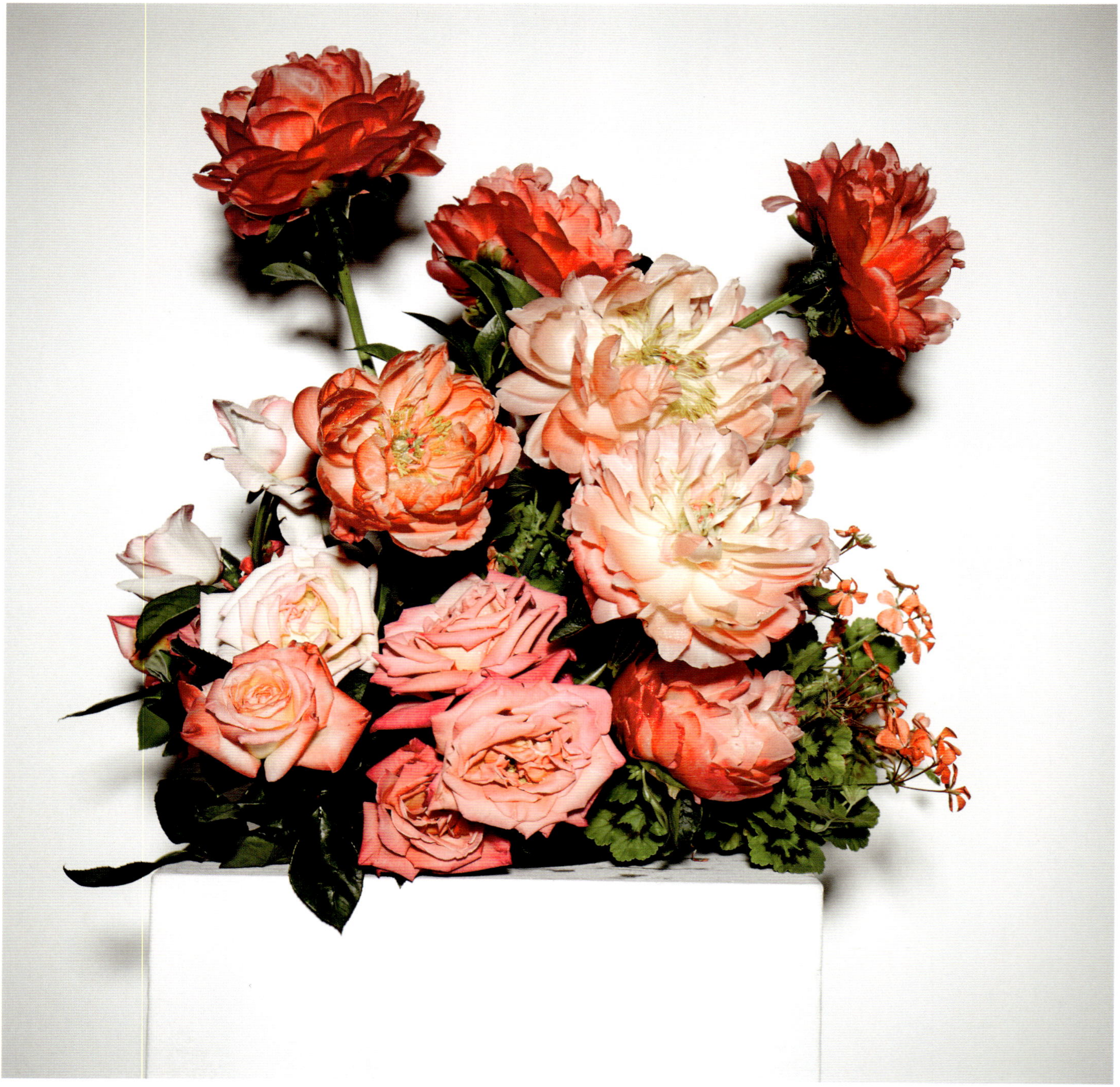

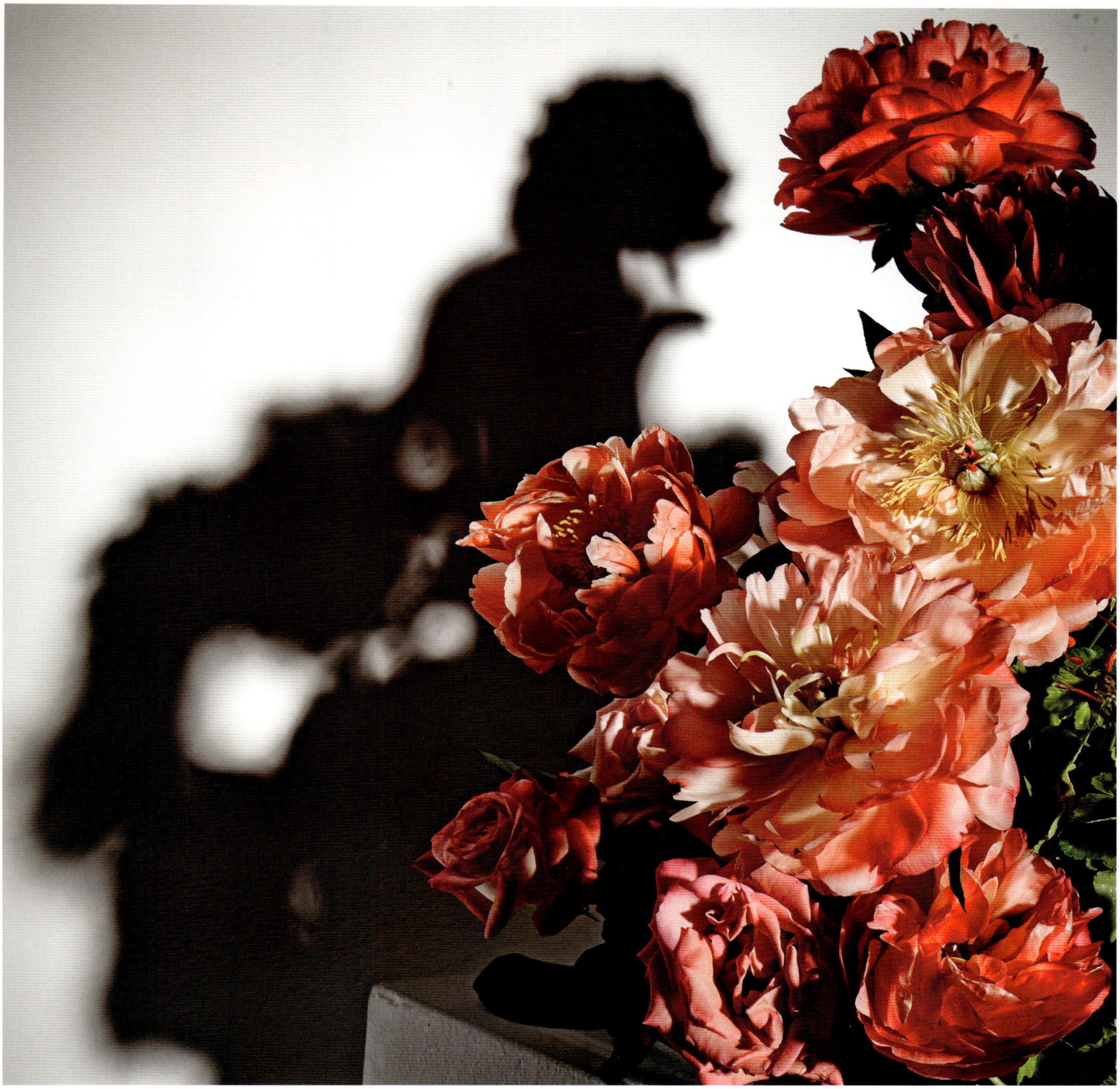

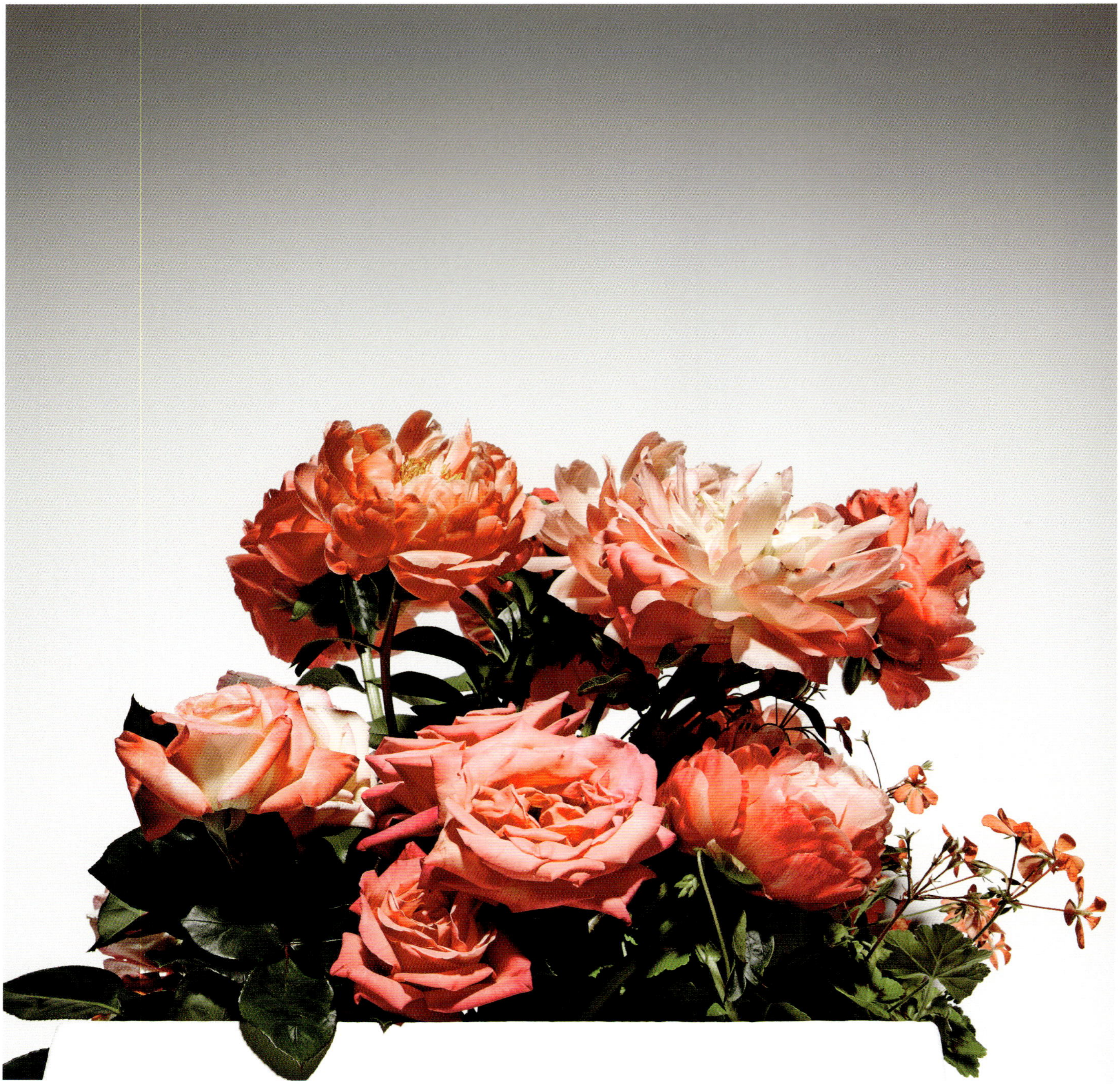

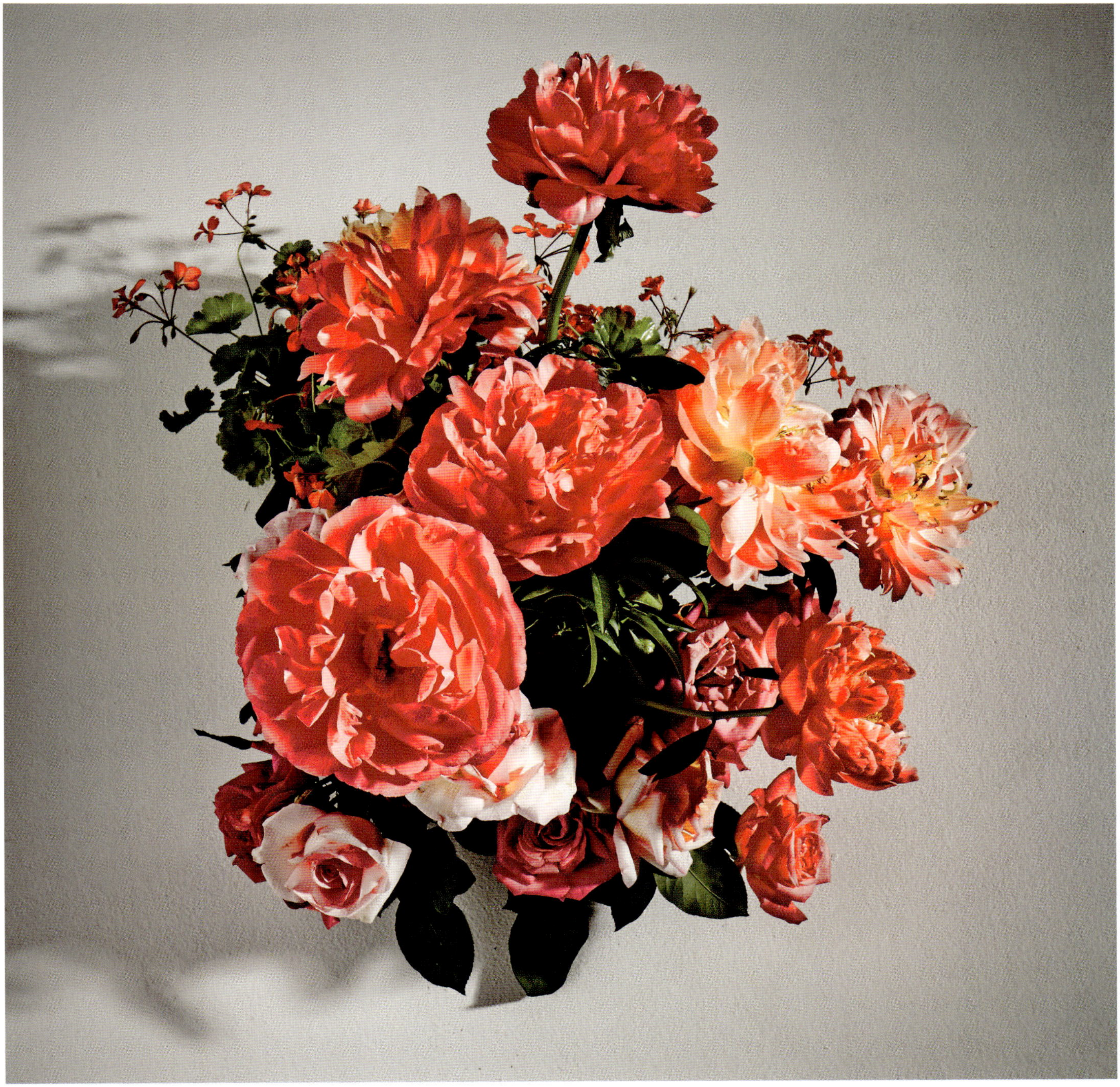

METAXU, UNTIL THE NEXT BLUE MOON
—
STILL THE DOCTOR WORKS BETWEEN.

METAXU: A Metaphysics of the Annihilation of Self in Video-Portraiture (Imaging Mediations Between the Human and Divine) was the title of my doctoral thesis. The term 'metaxu', explained below in a passage taken from the introduction of my thesis, also applies to my work as described in THE FLOWERS.

Metaxu is a Platonic term that refers to numbers, which stand 'between' forms or ideas and the sense world. Simone Weil (1909–1943) vastly extends the use of the word to cover all mediators 'between' the divine and human. My work is reducible to this single term: Metaxu – describing intermediaries – 'bridges' between the conceptual and the material. In my practice ineffable human experience is projected … Metaxu – refers to the space between the concrete and the abstract world and by analogical extension is equivalent to the space between the divine and human. It is the tensions, transitions and exchanges between the modalities of these inner and outer worlds that define the space in which my work operates.

In previous chapters I have referred to my approach to working with flowers as being principally concerned with 'the expression of human emotion'. In the years of my prior artistic practice I explored this expression of human emotion through mediums such as paint, gold, plaster, video technology, installation and projection. These methods of making, for me, became redundant in light of the flowers, and as a result, flowers became my primary medium – there is no higher medium for the expression of human emotion than flowers.

However, the work I do today with flowers is still deeply connected to my training and work as an artist, not just philosophically, but experientially – the years I spent grinding pigment into paint and negotiating the compositional complications in layering brushstrokes on canvas constitute my formative training. Likewise, my work with video technology, digital manipulation, installation and projection (which was for many years my primary medium) is immeasurable. Through an emphasis on 'portrayal' and 'projection', I worked for many years examining the notion of an 'inner-portrait'.

Projection is at its core a form of geometry modelled on properties of light that allow for a correspondence between a two-dimensional picture plan and three-dimensional space – a means of rationalising vision and space. The projected image both is and is not there; it is at once material and non-material – it is pure motion, colour and light.

Flowers, through their innate capacity to 'project' emotion such as love, concern and joy are, like the projected image, at once material and non-material. The technology of projection brings about an immersive environment that enables a metaphorical collapse between interior and exterior worlds. So, too, do the flowers – flowers given in love are received both by both the recipient's hands (the exterior) and their heart (the interior).

‡

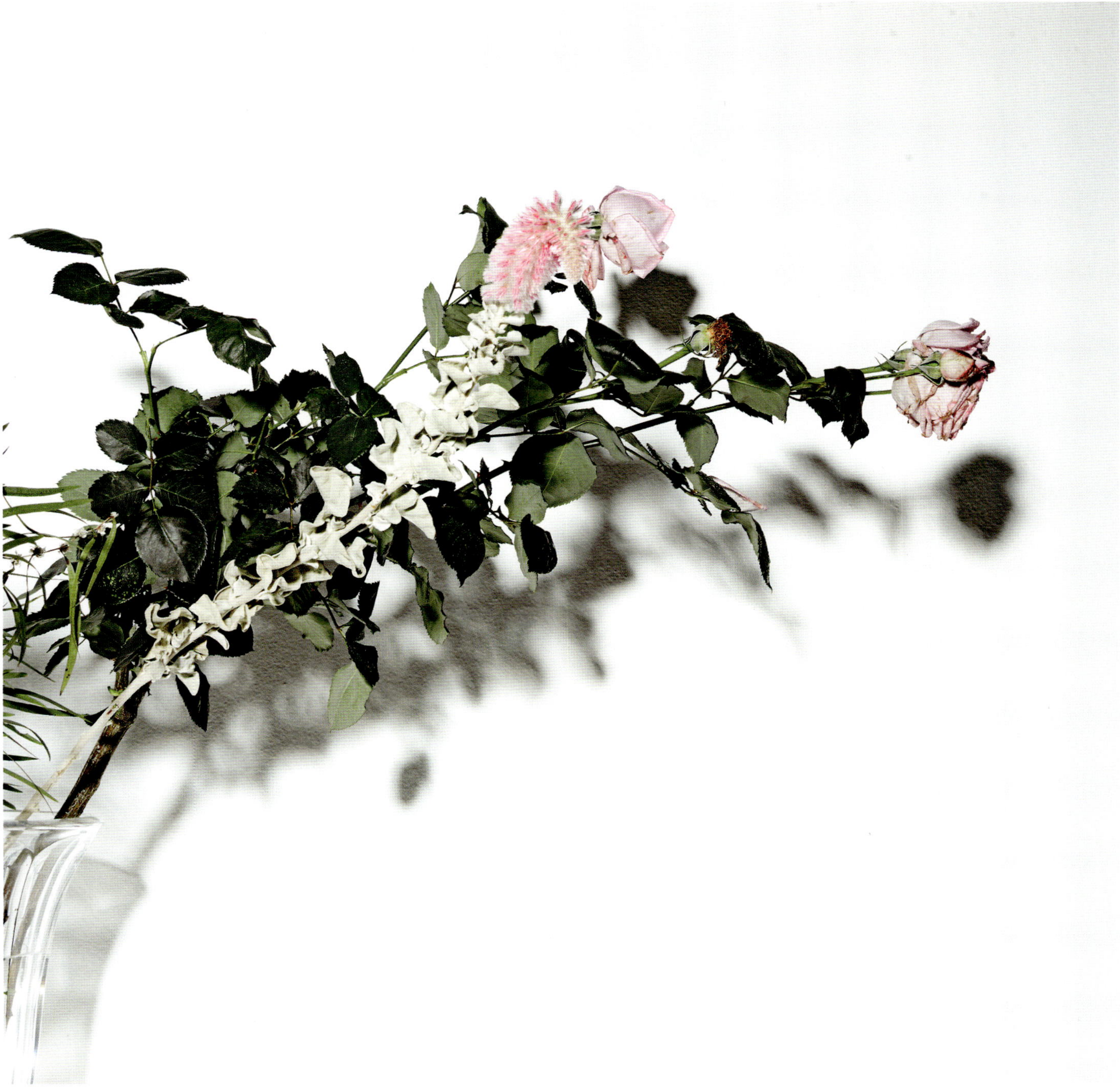

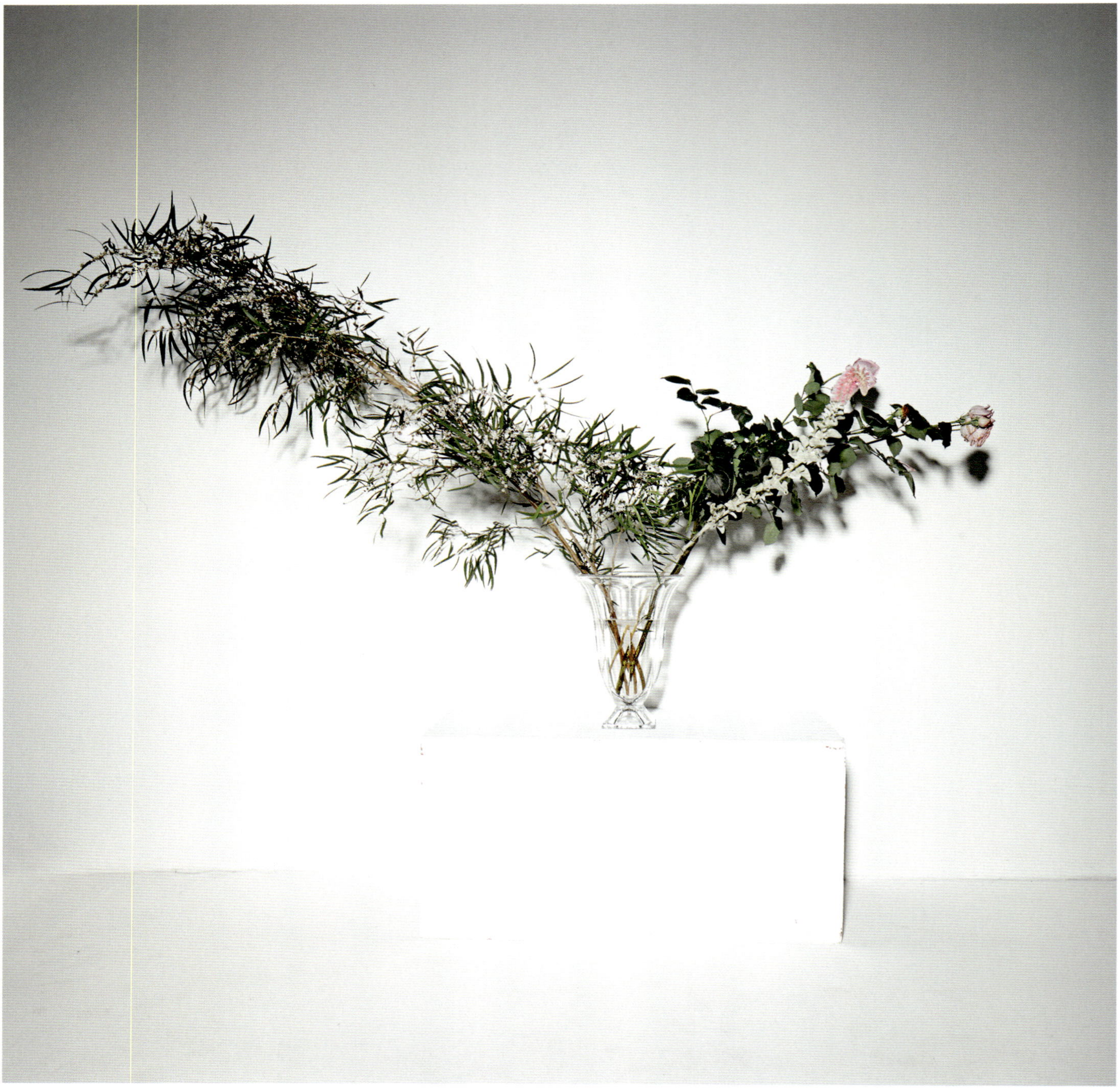

I chose the title of this book, THE FLOWERS, in order to summon for the potential reader the subject matter – the reproductive structure of flowering plants, those blooms and blossoms that emerge astonishingly all across the surface of the earth. The flowers that have, across the span of human history, been revered for their intrinsic beauty and profound interconnectedness to human ritual, religion, medicine, desire and nourishment.

However, the title THE FLOWERS also refers to 'the flowers' – the people who I have known in this 'garden' of life – whose influence upon my own personal growth and work is indicated in the preceding pages. This book, of course, does not constitute an exhaustive survey of the many people who have influenced and inspired me – the recollections conveyed in these pages are plucked from a vast field of 'flowers'. This book constitutes only a bouquet.

The pictorial bouquet of flowers that accompanies these thoughts exemplifies the collection of memories expressed in this book. The trailing 'Blue Moon' rose was a gift from the rose grower's private garden. It was an exception to the rule of the hundreds of other roses on the massive property – permitted to ramble across the exterior of the enormous packing shed. It was given to me because the rose grower understands my proclivity for the exceptional. Likewise, the native flower grower gifted me the extraordinary single royal mulla mulla – the curved, feathery, pink flower with the powdery-leafed stem – a specimen that had inexplicably grown to a remarkable scale in contrast to a field of uniform-height, obedient mulla mulla. The spray of willow myrtle that reaches outward, away from the centre of the arrangement, was chosen for the compositional interest I observed in its singularly beautiful branch. The combination of these blooms is at once disparate and harmonious ...

‡

It is pre-dawn and I am driving to the Sydney Flower Markets; I am sure I am one of the first to see the full moon, bright in the sky. I think of how the rose grower told me that when there is a full moon the roses 'flush' in extraordinary numbers, and at the farm it is a monumental task to harvest the great quantity of roses that 'come off' all at once. I think of the 'Montague' who was my first love – and of the first roses I ever received in a gesture of romantic love. I recall the roses that flooded our family home when my father died and their embodiment of the cycle of life and death. Of the 'Blue Moon' roses that my grandfather grew, whose stems were bound in foil for my school teacher in a gesture of gratitude, and I reflect upon the image of Saint Thérèse of Lisieux and her armful of blood-red roses that has hung above my bed in an oval frame all of my life. And I know that the flowers that I will buy today and compose into bouquets will pass from hands to hearts – where they will remain.

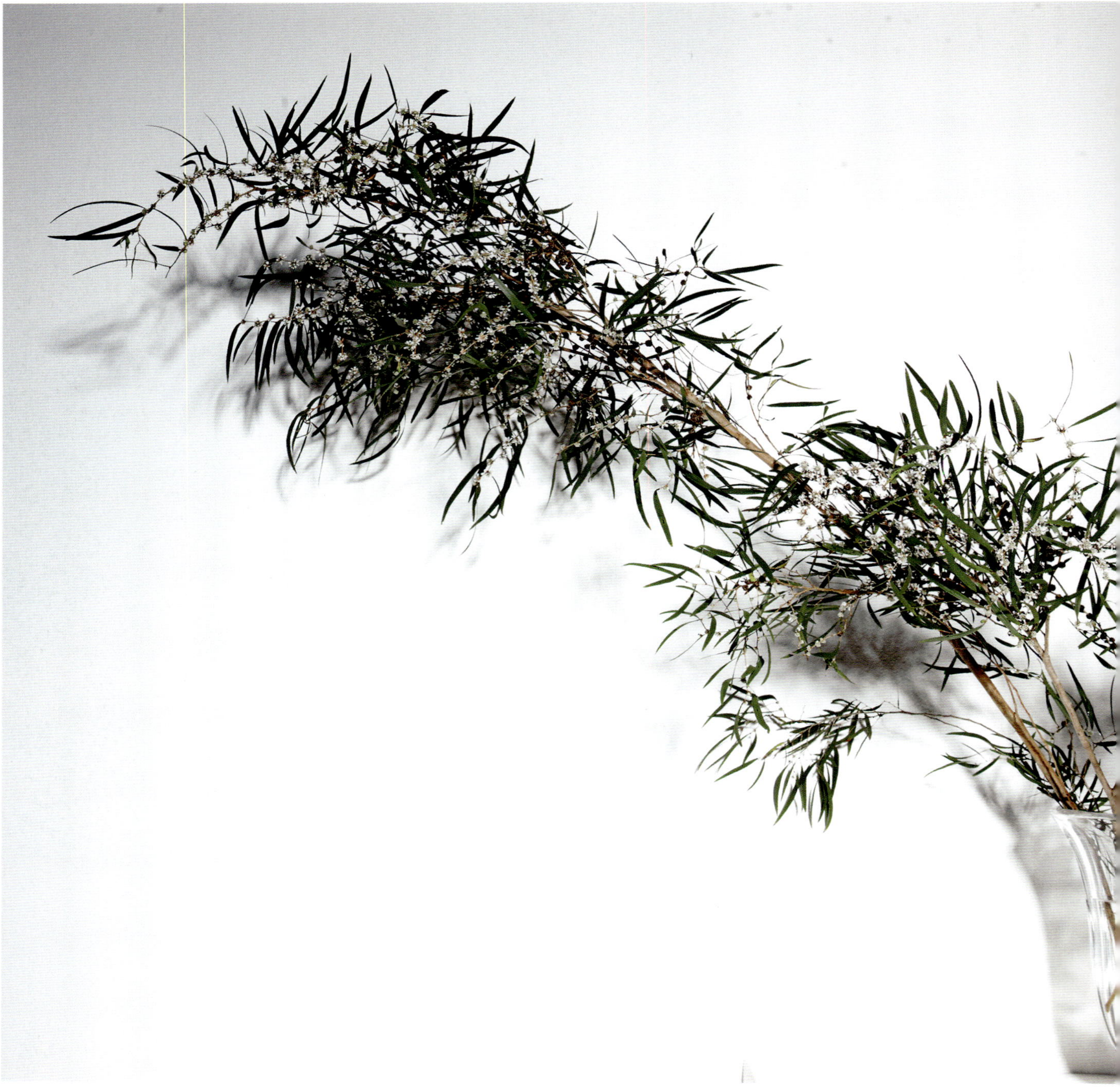

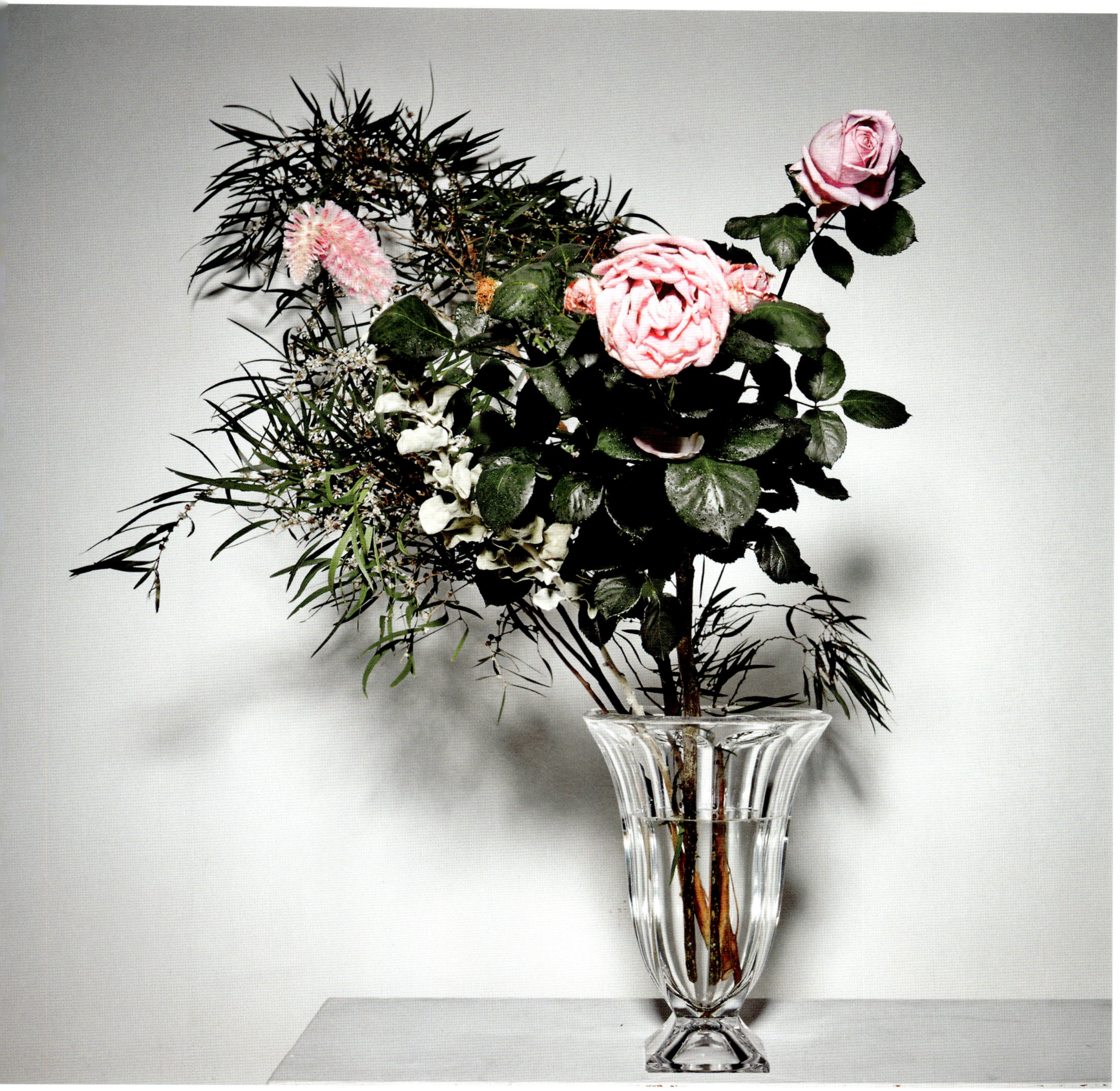

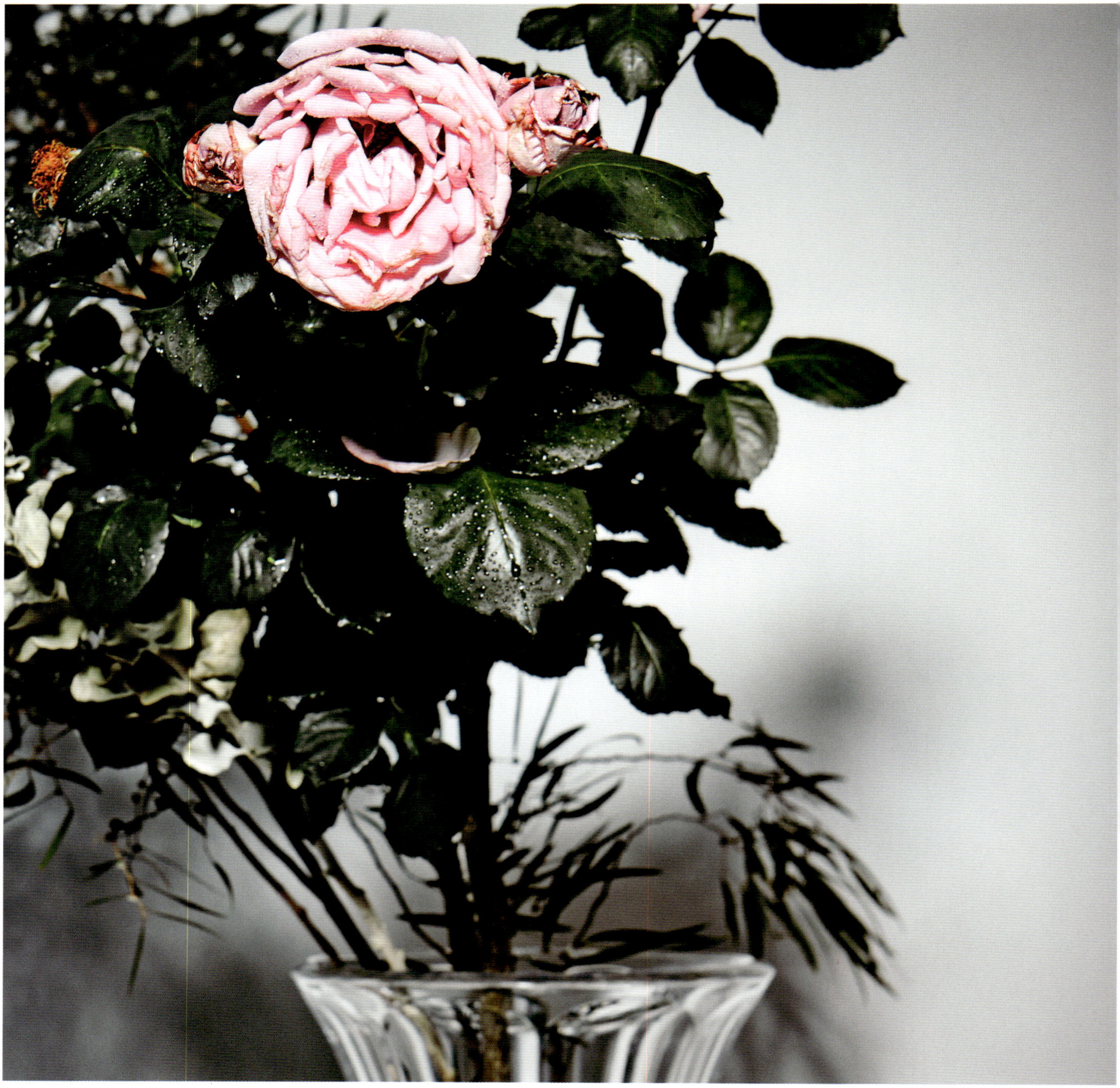

IT IS OBVIOUS (AS YOU WILL HAVE REALISED) THAT I HAVE A LONG-HELD PERSONAL CONVICTION ABOUT THE IMPORTANCE OF CAREFULLY OBSERVING INDIVIDUAL BLOOMS IN THE PROCESS OF WORKING WITH FLOWERS. I DO NOT BELIEVE IT IS POSSIBLE TO CREATE FLORAL COMPOSITIONS (OR WORK IN ANY OTHER MEDIUM) WITHOUT A REVERENCE FOR, AND INTIMATE KNOWLEDGE OF, ONE'S CHOSEN MATERIAL.

THE FOLK

'G'. THE COURIER.

HAROLD DAVID. THE PHOTOGRAPHER.

ME.

ABOUT THE AUTHOR
—

DR LISA COOPER

Artist and florist Dr Lisa Cooper holds a Doctorate of Philosophy in Fine Art from the College of Fine Arts, University of New South Wales. DOCTOR COOPER STUDIO is her commercial flower business, spanning major floral installations to hand-delivered flower gestures. Cooper's work has been featured in many Australian and international books, magazines and journals. Her distinctive floral works have been commissioned by such influential clients in the business and arts world as the National Gallery of Australia; the Museum of Contemporary Art, Sydney; Club 21; Westfield; Toni Maticevski; Tiffany & Co.; Deutsche Bank; the Australian Ballet; Romance Was Born; and the Sydney Theatre Company.

**MY OAK TREE RING WITH HERBS
(WHILE I LIVE I'LL GROW).**

ACKNOWLEDGEMENTS

✣

DIANA HILL
FOR BEING MY PUBLISHER AND EDITOR AND SEEING THE FLOWERS I SAW.

HAROLD DAVID
FOR YOUR ENORMOUS TALENT.

EWEN MCDONALD
FOR SPEAKING THE LANGUAGE OF ARTISTS AND BEING MY GUIDE IN ARTICULATING MY HEART.

MARCUS PIPER
FOR YOUR GREAT SKILL AND RESTRAINT.

TAM (BOB) HORAN
FOR DRIVING WHEN IT WAS PITCH BLACK AND I COULDN'T SEE THE WAY.

KAREN MCCARTNEY
FOR BEING THE FIRST TO KNOW THAT THIS SHOULD BE A BOOK AND ALERTING ME.

PHILIPPA CARNEMOLLA
FOR YOUR EAR, YOUR HEART AND YOUR INTELLECT.

MELISSA LABIZA
FOR BEING MY SISTER.

PAUL ALLAM AND DAVID MCGUINNESS
WHO BOUGHT ME THE DESK I WROTE MY THESIS ON AND THE REST.

THE GROWERS
INCLUDING THE ONES WHO ARE NOT INCLUDED IN THIS BOOK, FOR YOUR TOIL AND HEART.

THE FLOWERS
FOR GIVING CONTEXT TO MY PECULIARITY AND PURPOSE TO MY LIFE.

SAINT THÉRÈSE OF LISIEUX
FOR BRINGING ME TO THE FLOWERS.

ST T. BY ADRIANA PICKER

PUBLISHED IN 2015 BY MURDOCH BOOKS, AN IMPRINT OF ALLEN & UNWIN

Murdoch Books Australia
83 Alexander Street
Crows Nest NSW 2065
Phone: +61 (0)2 8425 0100
Fax: +61 (0)2 9906 2218
murdochbooks.com.au
info@murdochbooks.com.au

Murdoch Books UK
Erico House, 6th Floor
93-99 Upper Richmond Road
Putney, London SW15 2TG
Phone: +44 (0) 20 8785 5995
murdochbooks.co.uk
info@murdochbooks.co.uk

For Corporate Orders & Custom Publishing contact Noel Hammond,
National Business Development Manager, Murdoch Books Australia

Publisher Diana Hill
Editorial Manager Emma Hutchinson
Design Manager Hugh Ford
Designer Marcus Piper (marcuspiper.com)
Photographer Harold David
Production Manager Mary Bjelobrk

Text © Lisa Cooper 2015
The moral right of the author has been asserted.
Design © Murdoch Books 2015
Photography © Harold David 2015

Every reasonable effort has been made to trace the owners of copyright materials in this book, but in some instances this has proven impossible. The author(s) and publisher will be glad to receive information leading to more complete acknowledgements in subsequent printings of the book and in the meantime extend their apologies for any omissions.

All rights reserved. No part of this publication may be reproduced, stored in a retrieval system or transmitted in any form or by any means, electronic, mechanical, photocopying, recording or otherwise, without the prior written permission of the publisher.

A cataloguing-in-publication entry is available from the catalogue of the National Library of Australia at nla.gov.au.

ISBN 978 1 74336 321 8 Australia
ISBN 978 1 74336 338 6 UK

A catalogue record for this book is available from the British Library.

Colour reproduction by Splitting Image Colour Studio Pty Ltd, Clayton, Victoria
Printed by 1010 Printing International Limited, China